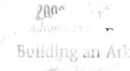

200~
Advance Pra~

Building an Ark

As E. F. Schumacher said, "the real problems facing the planet are not economic or technical, they are philosophical". The heart must lead the mind. There is no question that this would be a better planet for all life including humans if we moved toward the philosophy outlined in this book. It shows the way to a better place, philosophically and practically.

— Robert Bateman, Artist and Naturalist

Finally, a practical and engaging book of solutions for animals! You don't have to worry that this is one of those books about animal suffering that's too sad to bear. Just the opposite — *Building an Ark* is full of so many hopeful, positive ideas that enable each of us to become enthusiastic partners in creating a more compassionate world.

— Zoe Weil, President, Institute for Humane Education, and author of *Above All, Be Kind; The Power and Promise of Humane Education*; and *So, You Love Animals: An Action-Packed, Fun-Filled Book to Help Kids Help Animals*

Building an Ark is a most welcomed and needed book. Every individual can make a positive difference to heal our wounded world, and this easy to read book tells us how to do it and how to keep our dreams alive. Read it carefully and share it widely. I sure will.

— Marc Bekoff, University of Colorado; author of *The Emotional Lives of Animals* and *Animals Matter*

On every page of *Building an Ark*, you will hear the animals calling to you, and urging you to turn compassion into action for the animals. Whether you have been working for animal rights for over twenty years, or just starting on your path, this is the book you will want to read and re-read for information, resources, inspiration, and hope.

— Lorri Bauston, President of Animal Acres, L.A. Farmed Animal Sanctuary and Co-founder of Farm Sanctuary

BUILDING AN ARK

101 SOLUTIONS TO ANIMAL SUFFERING

ETHAN SMITH with GUY DAUNCEY

Foreword by JANE GOODALL, Ph.D., DBE

NEW SOCIETY PUBLISHERS

Cataloging in Publication Data:
A catalog record for this publication is available from the National Library of Canada.

Cover design by Diane McIntosh.
Images: iStock

Printed in Canada.
First printing October 2007.

New Society Publishers acknowledges the support of the Government of Canada through the Book Publishing Industry Development Program (BPIDP) for our publishing activities.

Paperback ISBN: 978-0-86571-566-0

Inquiries regarding requests to reprint all or part of *Building an Ark* should be addressed to New Society Publishers at the address below.

To order directly from the publishers, please call toll-free (North America) 1-800-567-6772, or order online at www.newsociety.com

Any other inquiries can be directed by mail to:

New Society Publishers
P.O. Box 189, Gabriola Island, BC V0R 1X0, Canada
(250) 247-9737

New Society Publishers' mission is to publish books that contribute in fundamental ways to building an ecologically sustainable and just society, and to do so with the least possible impact on the environment, in a manner that models this vision. We are committed to doing this not just through education, but through action. We are acting on our commitment to the world's remaining ancient forests by phasing out our paper supply from ancient forests worldwide. This book is one step toward ending global deforestation and climate change. It is printed on acid-free paper that is **100% old growth forest-free** (100% post-consumer recycled), processed chlorine free, and printed with vegetable-based, low-VOC inks. For further information, or to browse our full list of books and purchase securely, visit our website at: www.newsociety.com

NEW SOCIETY PUBLISHERS   www.newsociety.com

Contents

Author's Preface

by Ethan Smith

My childhood was spent in the embrace of nature, in a thickly forested valley in southern British Columbia, surrounded by wildlife and wonder. Our parents taught us respect for life, farming the land with a gentle touch, unencumbered and unaided by the luxuries of modern life. There was no electricity, no television and few distractions from the natural world. It was hard work, tending to our gardens, orchards, pastures and hayfields. We had to pay close attention to the beautiful, wild world around us to take care of our animals and the land that sustained us. On our farm and in the forest around us, I was part of the birth of spring, the warm blossoming of summer, the musty decay of autumn and the snowy slumber of winter. As the seasons became years, in a forest teeming with thousands of species of life, nature climbed deeply into my soul and never left.

For years after leaving the valley and leaping into the charge of civilization, I was stunned at society's disconnection from nature. I didn't do much about it for a while, though. I would either fly into a rant about the need for more respect for life, or I'd flee into the woods and find solace in the embrace of a mossy stump. On one hand, humans were beautiful, intelligent beings capable of staggering feats of innovation and compassion. On the other hand, we were a species unto ourselves — speeding away from our inherent connection to all other species on Earth, on a reckless path to a very uncertain future. I discovered the great suffering of animals on factory farms, saw pets abused and

neglected by their owners, forests scalped by careless logging, and wildlife robbed of its habitat. I learned of lab animals having toxic chemicals tested on them, gagged when I saw calves being throttled by ropes in the name of sport and nearly cried when I heard of the thousands of species of animal and plant life going extinct every year. How could this be? How was it that I was so alone in a society that seemingly just didn't care?

In 2001 I adopted a vegan lifestyle, avoiding animal products as much as possible, and began to learn everything I could about our connection to animals, the environment and each other. My wife and I brought armfuls of books home from the library, did Internet searches, sought out vegan and organic products to buy and found that we were very much not alone. We traveled around North America, seeking "green" places and gathering heaps of information along the way. When we returned home, I wrote letters to many of the people who had inspired us in one way or another on our journey and compiled an anthology called *Softly on This Earth: Joining Those Who Are Healing Our Planet*. The book contained essays by 30 courageous souls from around the States and Canada, tied together by my own story. The self-published work enjoyed modest sales around North America, but its real success was in earning me an invitation to take on a much larger project — one that would become *Building an Ark: 101 Solutions to Animal Suffering*.

When I began *Building an Ark*, I created a database of like-minded organizations that were dedicated to animals and the environment. To my delight and surprise, I found over 200 well-established organizations around the world, and that was just scratching the surface. I learned of hundreds of groups working to raise awareness, thousands of people making a difference in the lives of animals and millions taking steps to lesson their impact on the natural world. I began searching for inspiring examples and discovered something very exciting. From urban farms to tropical forests, a movement is underway. From testing labs to supermarkets, animal awareness is spreading. Schools, businesses, cities and national governments are joining animal advocates and action groups in cultivating compassion. The growth of consciousness is traveling toward a critical mass — a point at which a new global attitude will be accepted as being self-evident. A time when we remember our connection to all life on Earth. But we must reach that critical mass as soon as possible, because the planet is losing 50,000 species of life every year. We have already lost 95% of the large fish from our oceans, and 80% of the world's old-growth forests.

Building an Ark begins with an overview of our relationship with animals — 25 specific topics and the pressing issues surrounding them — followed by 101 solutions based on inspiring examples from around the world. Within these pages there are over 500 websites and reading resources to learn more about every solution. These solutions are about helping animals, and they're about much more — they're about regaining balance for life on Earth.

Find your solution within these pages or create your own. Hug it to you proudly, and make it yours. This world needs your compassionate embrace.

— Ethan Smith
Spring, 2007
www.earthfuture.com/ark

Author's Preface

by Guy Dauncey

I have never met a chimpanzee, except in a zoo. But I see them in my mind, and I know we share a close ancestry. After listening to Jane Goodall speak, I know how they greet each other with a soft "whoo - whoo - whoo".

We have similar eyes, lungs and hearts. We have the same ten fingers, the same four arms and legs. And I would wager we share many of the same feelings, including love, fear and joy.

We share almost 99% of our DNA with the chimps: they are our closest living relatives in the animal kingdom. And yet in parts of Africa, they are killed, sold and eaten. Due to humans taking over their habitat, there are only 120,000 to 150,000 chimps in Africa today, where there were once two million. After tens of millions of years, they have lost 93% of their population in just 45 years.

Albert Schweitzer once wrote: *Until we extend the circle of compassion to all living things, we will not find peace.*

It was not so long ago that people thought it normal to lock away the mentally ill in lunatic asylums and take a Sunday outing to stare at them. Today we have learnt that mental illness can happen to any of us, and we strive to include those who suffer in our circle of compassion. The same goes for people we used to capture and abuse as slaves, and to the children we used to send down the coal mines.

This book is for all who believe that we must strive to include the animals we share this beautiful world with in our circle of compassion. We have written it so that you may use your skills and influence to achieve greater success.

The book is Ethan Smith's, not mine — I only wrote the climate change solutions. My role was to invite Ethan to write the book as part of The Solutions Project and then to encourage, support and advise him as he crafted it into the finished pages you now hold.

The Solutions Project is a wider initiative, encouraged by New Society Publishers, designed to address each of the world's major problems and to demonstrate that, if there is creativity and a will to succeed, there are solutions to all of them.

I believe that there are only two real problems on Earth. The first is the sum of all our social, economic, environmental, political and behavioral problems. The second is the belief that we cannot solve them.

It is all in our minds. You can never win a game of soccer or an Olympic medal if you believe it's impossible. Today, in the early years of the 21st century, we face environmental problems on our planet Earth that are vast and that can seem overwhelming.

But it is not so, even for the greatest of our problems. We have it within us to be bold, creative and determined and to embrace intelligent solutions for all our problems.

Why should we believe otherwise? We have the capacity to achieve extraordinary things. We have the capacity for incredible kindness and forgiveness. We have the capacity to reject institutions and traditions that no longer serve us, and to create the world we want, serving the needs of humans and animals alike. We have the capacity to protect all the world's ecosystems and still enjoy deep happiness.

How indeed could there be lasting happiness if we did not extend our kindness to the whole world? Happiness is a bird that sits on your shoulder when your heart is engaged in a life of kindness and service to this incredible Creation.

So listen up! Our future beckons us, inviting us to visualize and create a world in which all creatures and peoples live together in friendship.

It invites us to create a world in which all people and nations work together as we explore the potential we have been gifted with.

So take your courage in your hands. Link up with others. Choose one of the many challenges outlined in these pages and be joyful and bold. Extend the circle of compassion until it embraces all living beings.

Back in the jungle, the chimps do not have the capacity to protect themselves against the bulldozers that are destroying their habitat. The whales do not have the capacity to protect themselves against the harpoons of whaling nations. The puppies born into cruel puppy mills do not have the capacity to write the legislation that would ban such practices for ever.

But we do. And deep within their hearts, they are cheering us on.

On behalf of the world's animals, the chimps call "Whoo! Whoo! Whoo! We greet you. We need you. We reach out to you."

And we, we can respond.

— Guy Dauncey
Spring, 2007

WSPA

Acknowledgments

First and foremost, thank you to Guy Dauncey for handing me his idea and asking me to run with it. You were right, Guy — it has been a triathlon, and it has also been tremendously rewarding. Guy's experience and tireless attention to the details kept me on track time and time again throughout the project.

Thank you also to Chris and Judith Plant, as well as Ingrid Witvoet and the editorial team at New Society Publishers, for producing the Solutions Project, and bringing *Building an Ark* to life. NSP's books are inspiring readers to recreate their world — one in which I very much want to live. I'm delighted and humbled to have joined the very accomplished list of New Society authors.

Thank you to editor extraordinaire Judith Brand who crafted the manuscript into its finished form, and to Sue Custance and her design team for creating our wonderful cover.

Thank you to my advisory team who gave me much-needed ideas, edits and answers over the past two years: Dr. Neal Barnard, Lorri Bauston, Dr. Marc Bekoff, Nancy Callan, Sinikka Crosland, Jennifer Fearing, Caryn Hartglass, Dr. Elliot Katz, Tricia Ritterbusch, Diana Saakian-Bokhari, Kim Stallwood, Vivienne Verdon-Roe and Zoe Weil. Their expertise, patience and enthusiasm for this project have been greatly appreciated.

Thank you to Jane Goodall who wrote the wonderful foreword to the *Ark*. Her presence with the project has helped immeasurably, and it has been an honor to meet her and have her grace our book with her support.

A big thank you to Dan Piraro, whose generous contribution of his great cartoons to the introductory pages of the book brings humor to sometimes disheartening subjects.

Thank you to all the people who contributed photos to the project. It was a huge job gathering all the wonderful images for these pages, and many people made it possible. The search for great images was aided immensely by the generous donation of multiple photos by several exceptional photographers: Ian McAllister, Shel Neufeld, Jim Robertson and Bob Walsh all contributed a great selection of their amazing work — I only wish I had space for all of their photos. A big thank you to Trisha Ritterbusch and Farm Sanctuary for sending me so many wonderful photos (many of which were taken by photographer Derek Goodwin). Thank you also to Franmarie Gregg and the Jane Goodall Institute for their great photos, as well as Heather Locke and WSPA who came through with several wonderful photos that helped me finish off the project. Each photo has been credited, but many people have helped behind the scenes. Thanks so much to Shelby Temple, Kyle Cornforth, Helen van de Bund, Diana Saakian-Bokhari, Sinikka Crosland, Joan Walsh (my Mom), Jeremy Schumacher, Sara Chenoweth, Alyson Powers, Jeanne Schieffer, Gary Nafis, Corinne McAuley and Tracey McIntire who went out of their way to ensure I had multiple photos to choose from. Many more people were instrumental in bringing these photos together, and a big hug goes out to all of them.

A special thank you to Andrea Morton for reviewing my fish farming information and advising me on such an important issue.

Thank you to my partner, my love and my best friend, Tania Honan, whose patience and support during this project, while we were caring for our new daughter, Sitka, and building a house at the same time, were tremendously appreciated.

Thank you to my family, friends and everyone else who has added support and ideas to this project. Together, we have created something extraordinary.

foreword

by Dr. Jane Goodall

Building an Ark is a book after my own heart: it is all about taking action to make the world a better place. When I look at my three grandchildren and think how we have damaged the world since I was their age, I feel a deep pain — and anger.

The natural world is in deep trouble. Forests have been destroyed, chemicals have been used mindlessly and millions of people have no access to clean drinking water. As we burn fossil fuels, the climate around the globe is changing. Ice caps and glaciers are melting. Millions of people living in abject poverty are destroying the environment around them in order to survive. Others enjoy unsustainable lifestyles, demanding far more than their fair share. We are destroying our only planet and the future of our children.

It is not only humans who are suffering. Chimpanzees, our closest living relatives, the species I have been studying for more than 40 years, numbered at least one million across Africa when I began my work in 1960. There are thought to be no more than 150,000 today. Many other species are equally endangered.

It seems there has been a disconnect between the clever human brain and the compassionate human heart. We are moving ever further from the belief of most indigenous people: that the natural world and everything in it is sacred.

Deep in the heart of the forest of Gombe is a spectacular waterfall that cascades from a rocky ledge 80 feet above the stream bed. When the water drops, it displaces the air, and there is always a breeze that makes the vines and ferns sway. Sometimes, when chimpanzees approach this place and hear the thundering of the water, their hair starts to bristle with excitement. They start a rhythmic display, standing upright in the stream bed, swaying from foot to foot, picking up and throwing large rocks, stamping and slapping in the shallow, fast-running water. Sometimes they climb the slender vines that hang beside the waterfall and push out into the spray. Then they may sit and watch the falling water, following it with their eyes. If the chimpanzees had a language to discuss the emotions that trigger these displays, might this not lead to some kind of primitive religion; an animistic worship of the mysterious forces of the natural world?

It is clear that there is no sharp line between us and chimpanzees, between us and the rest of the animal kingdom. The more we learn, the more blurry the line becomes. We are not the only beings on the planet with personalities and minds capable of rational thought and feelings. Often I lie sleepless at night thinking of all the ways in which we exploit so many other animal beings. The animals in research laboratories. The billions tortured in intensive farms. The harsh, often cruel, training of animals for circuses and other entertainment. The abuse of pets. Wild animals losing their habitat, being trapped, hunted and captured for the live animal trade. The list goes on and on.

The question I am asked most often is whether I really have hope for the future. The answer is yes, but can we do so in time? We do not, I fear, have long. We are fast approaching a time when the environment will be unable to recover from our abuses, when life on Earth as we know it will end. We must take action now, before it is too late. That is why Ethan Smith and Guy Dauncey have written this book.

My first reason for hope is the human brain. Through millions of years, our species has survived by using our problem-solving abilities. Now that we have begun to understand and face up to the problems that threaten us, we are coming up with all kinds of ways to live in greater harmony with nature. We must reestablish that vital link between brain and heart, and join hands to find more ways to heal our planet.

My second reason for hope lies in the resilience of nature. I have visited Nagasaki, site of the second atomic bomb that ended World War II. Scientists predicted that nothing could grow there for at least 30 years. But, amazingly, plant life returned much more quickly. One sapling actually managed to survive through that ghastly bombing, and today it is a large tree. There are great cracks and fissures in the trunk, all black inside, but every spring this tree produces leaves. I carry one of those leaves with me as a powerful symbol of hope.

My third reason for hope lies in the indomitable human spirit. History is filled with the stories of individuals whose vision has led them to tackle seemingly impossible missions, and to succeed against all odds. Such leaders have the courage of their convictions to stand up against authority or corporate power. While these people stand out in history, the indomitable human spirit is illustrated by countless ordinary people who do extraordinary things.

My fourth reason for hope lies in the increasing involvement of children in determining their future. My involvement with youth began when I realized how many high-school and university students seemed to have lost hope. They all told me more or less the same thing: that we had compromised their future, and there was nothing they could do about it. Their future has been compromised ... but it is not true that they can do nothing about it.

I started the Jane Goodall Institute's Roots & Shoots (www.RootsAndShoots.org) program for the very reason that Ethan and Guy have written *Building an Ark*: because we want, most desperately, to share our conviction that we can create the change that will save our planet.

Each Roots & Shoots group works on three kinds of projects: to improve things for humans, for the environment and for animals. We have more than 8,000 active groups in over 90 countries, and programs from preschool through university. As they work on their projects, the young people become empowered, realizing that they are creating change.

Building an Ark will give our groups so many new ideas. It will help us realize the importance of small actions we can take each day. When billions routinely make these little changes, we shall see big changes.

We must remember that we have this power, and we must start using it now, because we do not have much time. We all have to roll up our sleeves and do our bit. *Building an Ark* will help all who read it to understand how each of us can create change, help animals and make the world a better place for all.

— Jane Goodall, PhD, DBE
Founder, The Jane Goodall Institute and
UN Messenger of Peace www.janegoodall.org

To Sitka,
may your generation be the first to never lose
their reverence for Life,
and to Tania,
for reminding me of mine.

PART I

HEATHER SMITH

Introduction: A Path Beyond Suffering

A Call to Compassionate Arms

I would like to propose something a little different: that a sensible and coherent theory of animal rights should focus on just one right for animals. That is the right not to be treated as the property of humans.

— Gary Francione, professor of law, Rutgers University School of Law, New Jersey[1]

This world doesn't belong to us, nor do its 1.5 million animal species. We are newcomers here, just another species in the 4.5 billion year history of this spectacular Earth. In fact, 99% of all organisms that ever lived on Earth were extinct before we ever arrived. If we spin up our planet's illustrious history into a 24-hour day, the first multicellular organisms would appear at around 8 PM, and humans wouldn't check in until less than a minute before midnight.[2]

Had the early humans brought with them a little Sold sign, tapping it into the earth with a blunt stone, they might have been promptly stampeded by a herd of irate rhinos. Yet somehow over the millennia, our fleshy, relatively defenseless species has done most of the stampeding. With a hunger for "progress," we have altered the landscape immensely, causing loss of life at an unprecedented rate. In less than 100 years — a mere blip on history's radar — we have caused the pollution of our atmosphere, contamination of our oceans, wasting of our grasslands, destruction of our forests and the extinction of animal and plant life at 137 species per day.[3]

Give Your Head a Shake

It's like staring into the sun. How could you and I be contributing to the loss of 137 species a

GLORIA CURRIE

day? How can we lose 50,000 species every year and still survive? Actually, we can't. We won't be able to. We've created an imbalance of colossal proportions, but we've been smart enough to figure out everything so far, so we must be smart enough to find solutions for this. So take a deep breath and stay loose. This is important work we're up to.

Out of Compassion

We are capable of vast love and empathy, able to move mountains with the strength of our compassionate arms. Yet along the way, something happened. Animals became our "property." We dominated their lives and applied designations. Some wild animals became our pets. Some became laboratory animals. Pigs became pork, cows became beef and elk became game. From zoos and aquariums to circuses and rodeos, every animal fell into some category for human use. Taken from the wild, becoming our expendable "resources," animals have been stripped of their autonomy. Around the world every day, animals are subjected to suffering in ways that are insensitive at best and horrific at worst.

Have we run out of compassion? We think not. Nor do the people who helped bring this book together, or the 200 partner organizations and individuals whose dedication to animal welfare have contributed to the project.

The First Few Steps

The choices we make as consumers, parents, community leaders, elected representatives, farmers, fishers, teachers and students all affect the world around us. It doesn't matter if we can't see the results of our choices — they happen anyway. They're creating our future right now.

The vast majority of animal suffering results from a lack of understanding on the part of humans who are simply going about their daily lives. Most of us would never choose to cause suffering to an animal if we really understood.

So, how do we create compassion and respect in an apparent void? The first step may be motivation. With greater understanding, an individual or a community may realize that if they treat life around them with compassion and respect, their world will thrive instead of suffering. That's pretty good motivation, and we want people to act out of love, not fear.

We're appealing for animal messengers because the voiceless among us can't be heard. Swallows, sheep, geckos and guinea pigs can't speak our languages. Their inability to speak English or French or Swahili makes them no less worthy of our respect and compassion. They are living beings on this planet, sharing the same air, breathing the same cool wind and basking in the same warm sun. They thrive on life the same way we do.

This is a call to compassionate arms. A call for each of us to reach inside our hearts and find the love and compassion that pulses to the beat of universal life. That same pulse is felt by every animal on Earth. Now is the time to work together for a compassionate, sustainable future.

Paws to Reflect

> Our intelligence, cooperation, and many other features we have as modern humans, developed from our attempts to out-smart the predator.
>
> — Dr. Robert W. Sussman, Washington University, St. Louis

We have walked this Earth for at least 6 million years, and our complex co-evolution with other species has seen dramatic change. Here, in a nutshell, is the history of humans and animals:[1]

- 6 million to 3 million years ago — Our earliest ancestors ate a vegetable diet, feeding on a relatively abundant supply of vegetation in East Africa.

- 2.8 million years ago — Woodlands in Africa began to shrivel away, leaving open terrain and depleted food sources. Our ancestors were forced to start eating roots, termites and anything else they could get their hands on, including the animal kills of other predators. We became excellent scavengers.

- 2 million years ago — We developed tools and began using them to cut into large animals that had been scavenged from predators. This changed the way we lived and would eventually lead to our expansion beyond Africa.

- 800,000 years ago — We began using fire, enabling us to cook and eat larger quantities of meat.

Recommended Reading
- *Man the Hunted: Primates, Predators and Human Evolution*, by Donna Hart and Robert Sussman, Westview Press, 2005
- *Hunters, Herders and Hamburgers: the Past and Future of Human-Animal Relationships*, by Richard Bulliet, Columbia University Press, 2005

- 100,000 years ago — We journeyed beyond Africa to Asia, Europe and Australia.

- 50,000 years ago — We began hunting horses and other large animals.

- 10,000 years ago — Agriculture began with widespread food crop farming.

- 10,000 years ago — Animals that had been hunted began being captured and farmed, with selective breeding beginning. Farmers realized that they could breed animals to produce offspring with the size, color and general appearance they desired. This is how all domestic animals developed.

- 4,000 BC — Evidence of horseback riding has been found for this period in the Ukrainian steppes, although significant riding didn't develop elsewhere for thousands of years.

- 2,000 BC — Horses began being used as a draft animal in Eurasia.

- Middle Ages through the 18th century — A strange time in our history, when animals in Europe were frequently brought up on charges, and were executed for "committing heinous crimes."

- 1500 – 1600 AD — Animals in Europe began being used in experimentation.

- 1800 — Animal experimentation was now mainstream.

- 1824 — The RSPCA was founded in England.

- 1850s — Our human population passed 1 billion.

- 1866 — The US SPCA was founded in New York.

- 1869 — The Canadian SPCA was founded in Montreal.
- 1890 — A movement toward protection of animals from experimentation began, and several laws were presented to the US Congress.
- 1914 — Artificial refrigeration became widespread in the US by commercial meat-packing houses, enabling meat to be mass-produced, transported and preserved.
- 1920s — Cattle farming grew dramatically in North America and replaced the buffalo that used to roam freely across the Great Plains.
- 1950s — Farm production increased quickly as we consumed more and more meat. Between 1950 and 2000, America's per capita meat consumption would double.
- 1951 — The Animal Welfare Institute was founded to devote attention to animal research.
- 1954 — The Humane Society of the United States was founded.
- 1960s — Our human population passed 2.5 billion.
- 1966 — The Laboratory Animal Welfare Act was passed by the US Congress. It would be amended in 1970, and renamed the Animal Welfare Act. However, birds, rats and mice were excluded from the act, and remain excluded today.
- Today our population has passed 6 billion.
- 76% of the world's fisheries are depleted or in steep decline, due to overfishing and pollution, having already lost 90% of tuna, marlins, swordfish, cod and sharks.

- In the United States alone:
  - Nearly 10 billion mammals and birds are killed for food every year. This number doesn't include fish.[2]
  - Vegetarianism is on the increase, with 10% of Americans aged 18-34, and 6% overall, avoiding meat.[3]
  - 860 million animals die through over-crowding, disease and transportation before they ever reach the slaughter-house.
  - Some supermarkets have begun calling for humane treatment of animals by their suppliers, including farming, transport and slaughter.
  - 135 million animals are killed for sport, 25 million are used in biomedical research and testing and 10 million unwanted animals are euthanized in pounds.
  - Animal welfare has become the focus of local, national and international action groups, conferences and groundbreaking legislation.
- 2050 — At our current rate of extinction, if we don't change our way of living, we will have lost over one-quarter of all land-based animals and plants currently living on Earth.

Sentience and Sensibility

We are living through an ethical revolution when it comes to animals — shifting from seeing them as objects, commodities and resources, to seeing them as beings in their own right.

— Andrew Linzey, animal rights theologian, Oxford University

In North America, Europe and most of the industrialized world, humans have their moral rights protected by law, however imperfect, giving legal support for us, but until very recently, absolutely nothing for every other species on Earth. Locked in the traditions of our forefathers, we have passed along the beliefs of those like Rashi, the medieval Jewish scholar who taught that, "Since animals exist for the sake of man, their survival without man would be pointless."

We've clung to our perception of animals as a commodity for a long time, much the same as we hung on to slavery, and how men didn't allow women to vote until less than a century ago.

And How Would We Know?

Animals think, feel and experience life, defining them, and us, as sentient beings. Some exhibit feelings similar to ours, and some are markedly different, yet all are worthy of our respect and dignity.

It's easy to see why most people are in the dark about animal sentience. Over 70% of us live in cities.[1] For many North Americans, their primary contact with most animals is shrink-wrapped in a grocery store. No wonder we don't question animal sentience.

Sentience Among Species

- Chimpanzees share 99% of our DNA.[2] They communicate, solve complex problems, live in a diverse community, count and demonstrate emotions very similar to our own.

- Elephants have a deep social bond among their herd. They communicate using over 70 distinct vocalizations and can recognize the individual voices of a hundred other elephants.

- Dogs thrive on social contact, fitting easily into human families, and their nurturing nature is very strong. In 2005 a stray dog in Nairobi "adopted" a two-day-old abandoned human baby, caring for her along with her own puppies until discovered by children.

- Foxes will feign death, laying on their backs with their eyes closed and tongues hanging out. As a bird swoops down on their "corpse," the fox will spring to life and grab them.

- Humpback whales sing complex songs of musical notes that sweep up and down in an ordered sequence. The songs can last up to 35 minutes, and each whale has songs that are unique to it.

- Lions understand strength in numbers. When approaching a competing pride, they will advance if their numbers are greater and retreat if they are less.

- Cats learn from and adapt to their environment very quickly, figuring out how to open

- Animal Legal Defense Fund: www.aldf.org
- Animal Sentience: www.animalsentience.com
- Center for the Expansion of Fundamental Rights: www.cefr.org
- Rutgers Animal Rights Law Project: www.animal-law.org
- Society for Animal Protective Legislation: www.saplonline.org

door handles, unwrap packages and find their way home from miles away.

- Mongooses disguise themselves as flowers to catch prey. They climb into bunches of red flowers, turn their red bums up to the sky and wait for unsuspecting insects to land before spinning around and catching them.

- Ostriches divert predators from their nests by pretending to be hurt and limping badly. As the predator heads toward them, they bolt off into the distance to completely distract the other animal from their nest.

- Prairie dogs are very social, living in complex underground cities that can cover 160 acres of land. They have specific "friends" whom they greet each day, touching noses, grooming and sunbathing together. They make specific warning cries for each type of advancing predator.

- Ravens are very playful birds who love to do balancing games on thin branches. They role-play while wrestling, taking turns being the winner and the loser.

- Sea otters are masters at using tools. When encountering tough shellfish to crack, they dive to the bottom of the ocean, scoop up an appropriate flat stone, return to the surface, float on their backs and pound open the shellfish with the stone.

- Woodpecker finches peck open a hole in wood to discover grubs. Then they search out a sharp stick or cactus spine and return to the hole, using the tool to impale grubs that are too far inside to reach with their beaks.

- Zebras are very social and tend to stand next to each other head to tail. This enables both zebras to be on the lookout for danger, while flicking flies away from their friend's face with their tail.[3]

Drawing the Line: Science and the case for animal rights, by Steven M. Wise. A comprehensive and inspiring comparison of the autonomy of different species.

Suffering on Our Plates

> Mindful eating brings compassion into our hearts.
>
> — Thich Nhat Hanh

Over the past 50 years, our appetites have grown dramatically, with confined animal feed operations (CAFOs) making meat far more accessible than it was, leading to a five-fold increase in meat consumption in North America since the 1950s.[1] This vast increase, combined with the mass exodus of traditional farming families to urban centers, has led to a sorrowful disassociation with our meals. Our global community eats 45 billion animals a year.[2] The United States, with just under 5% of the world's human population, accounts for nearly a quarter of all animals killed for food in the world.[3]

Way Back When

At the beginning of the 20th century, 90% of North Americans lived on farms. The crops our families grew, and the animals they raised, were of vital importance. Slaughtering a steer for the winter's worth of meat, or hunting for food to sustain a family through a season without produce, meant something very significant: they were interacting with nature, sustaining themselves off the land while taking just what they needed. Back then, entire families would live off the meat of one or two cows per year.

Today, the average North American eats 256 pounds of meat[4] and is responsible for the deaths of over 30 land animals annually for meat consumption alone.

Requiem for Respect

On the small family farm in British Columbia where I was raised, we worked hard for, and with, the animals that shared our land. They were deeply connected to the Earth just like we were and were dependent on the same fertile soil, warm sun and cool rain. We raised dairy cows, and

50 million turkeys wind up on North American dinner tables every Thanksgiving.

- American Grassfed Association: www.americangrassfed.org
- American Pastured Poultry Producers Association: www.apppa.org
- Compassionate Consumers: www.compassionateconsumers.org
- Eat Wild: www.eatwild.com/animals.html
- Food Routes: www.foodroutes.org
- Organic Consumers Association: www.organicconsumers.org

A Word on Waste

Before it ever reaches consumers, 40% to 50% of the United States' edible food is wasted. Some of the loss is due to inefficient agricultural practices, processing and transportation, but most is lost at the retail level. Convenience stores throw away 26% of all the food they purchase, followed by fast-food restaurants (10%), full service restaurants (3%) and supermarkets (1%). Between these four retail sectors, 36 million pounds of meat is thrown away every day.[8]

their male calves became our yearly supply of beef. Slaughtering the steers was always difficult, because we had fostered a relationship with them. It was also heavy, smelly and rather disgusting work that we did anyway, and we did it with respect because this living being had given its life for our family's dinner table. Once on the table, our meal was treated with no less respect, remembering the animal it came from, and the work that was involved in providing the meal for us.

Respect is no longer synonymous with meat consumption. But it could be, if each person sitting down to a meat-based meal were to consider the life that went into its creation.

- What was its life like? Was it raised on a family farm and treated with respect, or was it the product of a CAFO, living in mass crowding and fear?
- Was it slaughtered humanely by people who respected the life they were taking, or was it killed on an assembly line?
- Was it forced to endure overcrowded mass-transport systems, or was it allowed to roam freely on pastures?
- Did it get a chance to enjoy life?

Compassionate Eating

The first action on the path to ending animal suffering is the practice of compassionate eating. What we eat is of great importance, not only for our own well-being, but also for that of every creature and the future of the planet. Our meat consumption is inexorably connected to our environment.

Half of the water used for all purposes in the United States goes into meat production.[5] A single hamburger uses 1,300 gallons of water and enough fuel to drive 20 miles, while causing the loss of five times its weight in topsoil.[6]

Ironically, meat consumption is very much connected to our own hunger in another way. An acre of farmland dedicated to legumes (beans, peas and lentils) produces ten times more protein than the same acre dedicated to beef production.[7] Even a slight reduction in the amount of meat we eat would free up enough land to significantly reduce world hunger.

For animals, for the environment and for each other, it's time to return to a reverence for our meals, respecting what went into them, and being truly grateful for the life energy they provide.

Fury over Factories

Animals raised for food in this country, especially those in industrial or factory farms — over nine billion a year — are forced to endure the most unimaginable kind of suffering.

— Amy Trakinski, animal law attorney

It took an entrepreneurial truck driver to change the face of agriculture forever. In 1936 John Tyson picked up a load of 500 chickens, and instead of taking them to a local slaughterhouse, he hauled them 600 miles to Chicago where he could get a better price. In doing so, Tyson broke the bond between farmers and local slaughterhouses, showing that higher profits were available through mass production and transportation. Not content to rest on his groundbreaking laurels, Tyson went on to buy up hatcheries, feed plants, slaughterhouses and production contracts until Tyson Foods was able to own and manage their chicken production from start to finish. Thus, factory farming was born.

A Whole New Landscape

Confined animal feeding operations (CAFOs), or factory farms, have grown dramatically since John Tyson's first chicken delivery. They accounted for 30% of the world's meat production in 1990, 40% in 2000 and are spreading rapidly.[1] Globalized trade, lower meat prices and mass urbanization are driving the spread of industrialized meat production to all areas of the planet. Factory farms are now seeing their fastest growth in Asia, Africa and Latin America. These gigantic production machines can be found close to nearly any large urban center. Livestock inhabits two-thirds of the planet's agricultural land. China is home to over half the world's pig population of 950 million. Poultry production worldwide has quadrupled in the past 50 years, with a global fowl population of 4.2 billion in 1961 ballooning to 17.8 billion today.[2]

Factory farms make great short-term business sense. By confining animals in one location and controlling everything about their environment, a farmer can maximize the productivity of meat, eggs or dairy products. Pasture land is limited, so controlling animals' diets allows farmers to feed them large amounts of food to maximize production. Factory farms make it easier and cheaper to gather, slaughter and bring animals to market, while antibiotics are readily available to combat the spread of illness caused by confining large numbers of animals together.

Yet factory farming isn't for everyone. The entire industry is run by a select group of very powerful corporations. In the United States, 81% of all beef is processed by just four companies (Tyson, ConAgra, Cargill and Farmland Nation).[3]

For animals, factory farms have created an intolerable level of suffering, with overcrowding, heavy antibiotic use, disease, transport and slaughter transforming sentient beings into production units, forcing them into a life of confinement and continued suffering.

- Ask Farmer Brown: www.askfarmerbrown.com
- Canadian Coalition for Farm Animals: www.humanefood.ca
- Compassion in World Farming Trust: www.ciwf.org.uk
- Farm Animal Reform Movement: www.farmusa.org
- Farm Sanctuary: www.farmsanctuary.org
- Food Animal Concerns Trust: www.fact.cc

For employees, factory farms have created a dangerous, underpaid, morale-crushing environment. Workers are required to work as quickly as possible to sustain the never-ending demand for meat. Working around terrified animals and a lot of machinery includes an inherent risk of injury and a wide range of diseases transmitted from infected animals, often under unsanitary conditions.

For the environment, factory farms create a dangerous situation, using large amounts of water and resources, leaving contaminated water, soil and air everywhere they exist. They are consuming natural resources far faster than nature can replenish them.

For people, factory farms are creating widespread health problems. Since the inception of industrialized farming a half-century ago, the incidences of cancer, diabetes, heart disease and obesity have skyrocketed in North America. Diets this high in animal products are making us sick.[4]

Forward from Factories

We need to foster a new awareness beyond factory farming. CAFOs must practice more humane ways of handling animals, and consumers must become more educated about the benefits of eating organic, grass-fed meat and switching to a plant-based diet that is inherently healthier for humans, for the environment and for animals everywhere.

Global Meat Production in 2004[5]

Source	Quantity in million tons	Percentage of world total
Pork	100.9	38
Poultry	77.2	30
Beef	62.2	25
Other (sheep, goats, yak ...)	12.6	7

In chicken heaven, I hope Colonel Sanders' nuggets are on permanent display.

© DAN PIRARO. REPRINTED WITH PERMISSION OF KING FEATURES SYNDICATE.

Deceptions of Dairy

There is overwhelming evidence that milk and milk products are harmful to many people, both adults and infants. Milk is a contributing factor in constipation, chronic fatigue, arthritis, headaches, muscle cramps, obesity, allergies and heart problems.

— Dr. William Ellis, an osteopathic physician who has researched the effects of dairy products for 42 years

My family raised dairy cows on our small farm in southern British Columbia. Twice a day, we would make our way up to the barn to milk our Jersey cows. They were great, gentle creatures with large, fuzzy bellies that kept us warm on even the coldest winter mornings. I also attended many of our cows' births. The bond between each mother and her calf was unforgettable. She would lick them affectionately and tirelessly, often getting caught up in the moment and licking us, too.

Our cows were wonderful mothers and demonstrated a deep connection to their calves, though their lives were not entirely idyllic. We did take their calves away from them to ensure they got just the amount of milk they needed while we got the rest. This separation was very difficult for the new mothers, who would bawl sorrowfully for days afterward. And their male calves, after a relatively happy year and a half of roaming about our pastures, wound up as our winter supply of beef. No mother likes to see that happen.

- Dairy Truth: www.dairytruth.com
- Inside Dairy Production: www.insidedairyproduction.com
- Mercy for Animals — dairy and veal: www.mercyforanimals.org/dairy_and_veal.asp
- Milk Imperative: www.milkimperative.com
- No Veal.org: www.noveal.org
- Not Milk.com: www.notmilk.com

Years later, as I became more aware of the plight of animals everywhere, my heart ached for the commercial dairy cows and calves I learned of that were stripped of their autonomy and subjected to great suffering. It all seems so far away from the little farm I knew.

A Common Misconception

People frequently defend their dairy consumption, saying they could never live without milk and cheese and arguing that nothing has to die or suffer in its production.

Nothing has to die? Cows die. Dairy cows make up over 40% of the United States' hamburger consumption. In New York State, that figure is over 75%.[1] After 4 or 5 years, once dairy cows aren't producing a peak quantity of milk, they are slaughtered. Under natural circumstances, they could have lived to be 25.[2]

And calves die. Virtually all male dairy calves become veal, the production of which involves, arguably, the most suffering of any commercial farming practice. Within days of birth, they are tethered to a tiny stall where they can't walk or lie down, while being fed iron-deficient meals so that their muscles won't develop[3] and their meat will become pale and soft.

In order to produce milk, dairy cows must be kept continuously pregnant. In this competitive industry, a cow must produce. When not able to produce, she is slaughtered. Along the way, cows are subjected to overcrowding, distended udders, injuries and illness.

But everywhere, on milk cartons, billboards, delivery trucks and buses, advertisers show us pictures of happy cows and frolicking calves. People continue to believe what they are told about their milk and cheese: that it comes from a blissful utopia. It doesn't. Even on an organic family farm, the cows must be kept pregnant to produce milk, and you still have the male calves to contend with.

More Importantly

It's time to look beyond our shock to a place in our hearts where we can create a new coexistence with these gentle creatures. Not eating them and not drinking their milk might be a good start.

A rescued dairy cow at Farm Sanctuary.

DEREK GOODWIN FOR FARM SANCTUARY

Milk Facts

- No other species on Earth, besides humans and their domesticated animals, drink milk beyond infancy. Nor do any drink the milk of another species.

- The American Gastroenterological Association cites cow's milk as being the number one cause of food allergies among infants and children.[4]

- 30-50 million Americans suffer from lactose intolerance (painful bloating, indigestion and asthma caused by cows' milk), including up to 90% of all Asian-Americans and 75% of all Native and African-Americans. A 2005 Cornell University study found that 60% of the world's population is lactose intolerant.[5]

- Autism and schizophrenia in children have been linked to the body's inability to digest the milk protein casein. Two 1999 studies at the University of Florida observed that symptoms of both diseases diminished or disappeared in 80% of children who switched to dairy-free diets.[6]

Weird Science

> The evidence we see over and over again, from the Netherlands in 2003, Japan in 2004 and Egypt in 2006, is that lethal bird flu breaks out in large-scale industrial chicken farms and then spreads.
>
> — Devlin Kuyek, GRAIN

What happens when you take a plant-eating animal such as a cow and feed it animal parts, including those of its own species? What if you add a heavy dose of antibiotics, and other antimicrobials? We're finding out the answer right now.

Fishy Ingredients

- Both Canada and the United States feed billions of pounds of animal by-products to their livestock annually to boost meat production.[1]
- Calves are routinely weaned on cattle blood to achieve the same goal.[2]

SCRO-o-o-o-o-OGE! Change your ways before it's too late!

THE GHOST OF CHRISTMAS DINNER

- By-products from cows are routinely fed to pigs and chicken, which are in turn fed back to cattle.[3]
- Despite the global fisheries crisis, a third of the global fish catch goes to the production of fishmeal, two-thirds of which is fed to cows, chickens and pigs to boost production.[4]
- Commercially raised meat, including fish, contains significant levels of persistent organic pollutants (POPs), polychlorinated biphenyls (PCBs), arsenic, hormones and other chemicals.[5]
- The majority of North American livestock is fed genetically modified (GM) food crops to enhance production.[6]
- 91% percent of all GM crops grown worldwide in the year 2001 came from one company: Monsanto.[7]

Consequences of Tampering with Nature

- **Mad Cow Disease** (bovine spongiform encephalopathy or BSE) is a neurological disease that causes great suffering to cattle and is always fatal. It is also contractible by humans as Creutzfeldt-Jacob Disease (CJD). Despite the fact that feeding cattle to cattle is the primary means of spreading BSE, the practice remains legal in North America. It takes the consumption of just one milligram of material contaminated with BSE to contract the brain-wasting disease.[8]
- **Avian Flu** (H5N1), or bird flu, is a virus that exists naturally in the intestines of wild birds, although they rarely get sick from it. Avian

flu is very contagious and having lots of birds in a crowded space (as most farmed birds are) is the perfect incubator for the virus. Avian flu spreads easily through an infected flock of poultry, causing sickness and death. Although it's rarely contracted by humans, confirmed occurrences of people becoming infected with Avian Flu began in 1997 and have become a global concern today.[9]

- **Foot and Mouth Disease** (CMD) is a highly infectious virus that affects cloven-hoofed animals such as cows, sheep and pigs. Its highly contagious nature (it can be blown like pollen in the wind) makes it easily contractible among farm animals. CMD has been so infectious that, in the United Kingdom, entire herds of affected animals have been burned to stop the spread of the disease. There have been occurrences of humans contracting CMD from being in close proximity to infected animals, although there are no confirmed cases of it being passed between humans.[10]

- **Environmental contamination** is affecting communities wherever factory farms exist. Researchers are only now realizing the extent to which this is affecting animal, and human, populations. Affected communities are seeing increased rates of neurological disorders, respiratory diseases, miscarriages, bacterial infections, diarrhea, stomach ailments and permanent disability. A Scripps Howard News Service synopsis of a US Senate Agricultural Committee report stated,

"Catastrophic cases of pollution, sickness and death are occurring in areas where livestock operations are concentrated."[11] The report warned that animal waste from CAFOs is "untreated and unsanitary, bubbling with chemicals and diseased organisms. It goes onto the soil and into the water that many people will ultimately bathe in, wash their clothes with and drink."

- Factory farming diseases: www.animalconcerns.org
- Human health hazards: www.factoryfarming.com/health.htm
- Mad Cow Disease: www.harpers.org/MadCowDisease.html
- People, food and agriculture: www.peopleandplanet.net

Bacteria is Becoming Drug Resistant

In 2001 the US Food and Drug Administration randomly selected beef and poultry products from supermarkets in the Washington, DC area and tested them for antibiotic-resistant bacteria. Sixty-seven percent of the chicken, 34% of the turkey and 66% of the beef samples tested positive for Enterococcus strains, showing resistance to antibiotics commonly used in animal feed.[12] A similar study by the Centers for Disease Control and Prevention in Atlanta in 2001 tested 407 chickens, purchased from 26 groceries in 4 states, with 86% testing positive for the bacterium Enterococcus faecium,[13] a bug that can last in a human digestive system for two weeks.[14]

Meanwhile, Back at the Family Farm

> We believe a healthy soil will produce healthy food. We believe the soil is living and, as such, needs to be fed and cared for.
> — Harlan Lundberg, Lundberg Family Farms

Despite the growth of factory farming, there are holdouts. Dotting the landscape through farming country, there are successful, sustainable family farms that have no intention of bowing to the pressure from industry to sell and move on. They live in harmony with their animals and the land, understanding the connection between soil, air, water and life. To them, humane animal husbandry not only feels ethically right, it is the only sustainable option along their path. These are family farm values.

A Farming Family

If you were to pay a visit to Lundberg Family Farms in Richdale, California, you might see one of the Lundbergs out in their fields, carefully placing stakes in the fertile soil. The Lundbergs know that ducks and pheasants build nests in their fields, and the stakes mark the nests so that they can work around them with their equipment. As well as helping the birds, they're helping themselves because the birds fertilize their soil. The Lundbergs have been using organic farming practices and family farm values for many decades, ever since their parents brought them to California in the 1930s. They understand how vital their connection to the land is, and their dedication to its preservation is key to their continued success. They use no pesticides on their fields, relying on natural pest control by birds, snakes and ladybugs. They preserve their environment for all the species that step foot on their soil. They've been farming this way for so long, they know how to coexist with their land, and they aren't about to change.

Benefits of the Family Farm for:

- **Farm animals** — family farms are small enough in scale, with more people per animal, that they can practice humane animal husbandry, paying attention to the needs of the animals and ensuring their wellbeing.
- **Wildlife** — 60% of farms in the US are smaller than 180 acres, making them key to biodiversity, with small farms leaving 17% of their area to woodlands (on average), compared to 5% on big farms.[1]
- **Resource use** — small farms have to be more committed to the preservation of water, soil

FARM SANCTUARY

- Community Alliance with Family Farmers: www.caff.org
- Family Farm Defenders: www.familyfarmdefenders.org
- Family Farmer: www.familyfarmer.org
- Local Harvest: www.localharvest.org
- Lundberg Family Farms: www.lundberg.com
- National Farm Coalition: www.nffc.net
- Family farming: www.sustainusa.org/familyfarmed

and air than large farms are, benefiting farm animals, wildlife, families and the environment.

- **Productivity** — small, integrated farms can produce more ($/acre) than large monoculture farms can, with the smallest farms (under 27 acres) sometimes earning ten times more per acre.[2] This is due to small farmers specializing in higher-value crops like vegetables (instead of monocultured corn or soy) and devoting more attention to their land.

- **Community** — decentralized land ownership means farmers rely more on local businesses, boosting the economy of rural areas, taking more accountability for their actions and having a stake in the well-being of the community.

- **Family** — with family ownership, farms can be passed on through the generations, cultivating values of stewardship and sustainability.

Agriculture and Agribusiness

With all these benefits, why are family farms in crisis, with 4 million American farms going bankrupt in the past 50 years?[3] Because farmland is being taken over by corporations like Monsanto and Cargill, replacing people with machines and mixed crops with monocrops, while introducing chemical pesticides and fertilizers, and genetically modified plants. The farming giants have forced the price of input costs (energy and fertilizer) up, while forcing the price of products down, driving family farmers into debt, or off their land.

Farming Families Wanted[4]

Average age of American farmers	55
Percentage of farmers under the age of 36	6%
Number of days primary farmers work off the farm each year	200
Percentage of family farms that support themselves solely from their land	7%
Number of family farms in operation in the United States	565,000
Percentage of North Americans who trust family farms to produce safe food	85%

A Very Fishy Tale

> Fish are not swimming vegetables. They feel pain just like other animals; like we do. It's only a matter of time before we look upon cruelty to fish in the exact same way we look upon cruelty to dogs and cats.
>
> — Karin Robertson, Fish Empathy Project

Many people choose to eat fish rather than land animals because they've been told that fish don't suffer. Certainly those who do a lot of fishing would like to believe that. Quite the opposite, however. Fish are vertebrate creatures with a brain, nervous system and pain receptors throughout their bodies, much like us.[1] Beyond that biological evidence, research by marine scientists is repeatedly proving that fish feel not only pain but also stress and fear.[2] And the methods employed by commercial fishers and fish farmers virtually guarantee suffering.

Animal suffering runs deep under the surface of our waters, with so much suffering in commercial fishing that most people choose not to think about it. Although protective legislation for other animals is weak in most areas of the world, its existence does indicate a general awareness. Nothing of the kind exists for fish, and it's time for that to change.

World Fishing 101

There are 20,000 species of fish in the world's waters, 9,000 of which are commonly caught through commercial and recreational fishing. Despite the diversity, global fish populations are declining rapidly because the same species continue to be fished until they're gone. Of the world's large predatory fish (tuna, sharks, cod, swordfish, halibut and marlins), 90% have disappeared in the past 50 years.[3] The common skate has already been fished to extinction in the Irish Sea, as has the blue pike in Lake Erie; both species that were once part of important commercial markets. In the Atlantic Ocean, cod, haddock and capelin populations are seriously threatened, as are some species of salmon, halibut and anchovies in the Pacific.

From 1950 to 1988, global fish production increased from 19 million to 89 million tons annually, even surpassing the increase in beef production (19 million to 54 million tons).[4] In 2001 global fisheries produced 92 million tons of fish,[5] and despite a few localized regulations governing overfishing, it continues at a vastly unsustainable pace.

In 2006 Stanford University in California announced the results of a four-year study on the global collapse of marine ecosystems,

NOAA

warning that at the current rate of depletion, all commercial fish stocks will be eliminated by 2048.[6]

Fishing Off-Target

When anything but the target species of fish is pulled from the sea, it becomes part of the unwanted bycatch, accounting for nearly a quarter of everything harvested. In some instances, such as the Gulf of Mexico's shrimp fishery, it is believed that bycatch outweighs the "profitable" catch by 10 to 1.[7] Usually maimed or dead, the undersized fish, sea birds and marine mammals are thrown overboard where they quickly becomes food for predators.

During the Catch

There are many ways for fish, and other marine life, to suffer during the catch. Trawl nets routinely crush them, they suffocate out of water and are gutted while still alive. Longline fishing routinely maims fish, birds and mammals when the line, up to 80 miles long and strung with 10,000 hooks, tears through their mouths.

A Lost Habitat

The once-spectacular ocean floor has been scraped and altered dramatically since the advent of modern fishing methods. This has resulted in the loss of habitat for tens of thousands of sea life species. Commercial fishers routinely use drift nets, bottom trawls, and purse seine nets, all of which are responsible for environmental destruction and high quantities of bycatch.

- Fish farming: www.advocatesforanimals.org.uk/resources/farmed/fish.html
- All Creatures — Fish: www.all-creatures.org/anex/fish.html
- Cruelty of fishing: www.animal-lib.org.au/lists/fish/fish.shtml
- David Suzuki Foundation: www.davidsuzuki.org/Oceans
- Fishing Hurts: www.fishinghurts.com

Messing with Mother Nature

Profitability, along with the collapse of many commercial fisheries, has led to the creation of fish farms, where fish are kept in confined spaces; reared and slaughtered under the control of humans. These factory farms of the sea have resulted in the spread of disease, sea lice, environmental contamination and suffering of the fish. Sea lice from fish farms on northern Vancouver Island have caused the decline of seven genetically distinct runs of wild salmon,[8] and British Columbia's fish farms discharge the collective raw sewage equivalent of a city of 500,000 people.[9] As well, the farmed fish escape, spreading disease and displacing wild fish. Yet fish farming is big business worldwide, with fish farms accounting for 58% of global salmon consumption. The US leads the world, consuming 228,000 tons of farmed salmon annually,[10] most of which is imported from Chile and Canada.

Hunting:
Subsistence vs. Sport

We've been hunting animals for a very long time, and until fairly recent times, every part of an animal was used to help a family, or a community, survive. In many cultures, great reverence was given to the animals who had given up their lives so that people could live. Reverence today is shown by mounting an animal's stuffed head upon a mantelpiece.

Hunting for Subsistence
In many parts of the world, people need to hunt to survive. If an Inuit person in Canada's Far North, where there is little or no growing season, decided to go vegetarian, they would have to rely on sad-looking produce that had been shipped in from thousands of miles away. To exist in that beautiful yet rugged land, people need to hunt to sustain themselves.

Even in areas where fruit and vegetables grow in abundance, some families choose to hunt wild meat over the convenience of commercially raised meat in supermarkets. For health, environmental

- Care for the Wild International: www.careforthewild.org
- Defenders of Wildlife: www.defenders.org
- Humane Society of the United States: www.hsus.org/wildlife/hunting
- National Wildlife Federation: www.careforthewild.org
- World Society for the Protection of Animals: www.wspa-international.org
- World Wildlife Fund: www.worldwildlife.org

One of the things on which [future generations] will look back in disbelief is that at the beginning of the third millennium we were still debating in this Chamber whether it was right and proper to allow people to chase an animal to exhaustion, with its killers closing in on it, causing it the most unspeakable fear before its death, and all in the name of tradition.

— Ann Widdecombe, British MP, on the tradition of fox hunting

and ethical reasons, it makes a lot of sense (if you are going to eat meat) to take the life of an animal that has lived its whole life in a natural environment. Yet something altogether different is happening around the world.

Trophy Hunting
Trophy hunting is big business. In the US, 13 million trophy hunters spend 20 billion dollars annually.[1] In Africa, home to the world's most famous trophy animals and a multi-billion-dollar hunting industry, hunters will pay large fees to the guiding organizations who take them to their kill: from $12,000 for a Cape buffalo to $30,000 for a male lion.[2] It's small wonder that governments are reluctant to place restrictions on hunting practices. For the short-term gain of a nation's economy, trophy hunting looks like a true blessing. For the legacy of the people, the wild places that these animals lived in, and the dignity of the animals themselves, it's a disaster.

Penned Hunts
Penned hunts, canned hunts, game ranches and shooting preserves are all the same thing. They are private facilities where animals, both native and exotic, are held captive until someone pays to come and shoot them. Even though they are inhumane and very unsporting to even dedicated hunters, penned hunts are an expanding industry. In the United States, there are over

1000 such facilities spread across 28 states. The right to shoot a zebra ranges from $800 to $2,000. A sable antelope kill can net a game rancher $3,000 to $8,000. The animals don't stand a chance. Taken from the wilds long ago, usually purchased from zoos, these animals are completely domesticated and tend to lack all fear of humans. Hunters are paying money to walk right up and shoot their target. This is "hunting" that requires no skill, which is why it attracts inexperienced hunters who routinely miss and maim the animals before killing them.

Internet Hunting

Society may have reached a new low with Internet hunting: online sites where you can pay to shoot animals through cyberspace. They are real animals, held captive in game ranches equipped with electronic rifles that fire real bullets with the click of a mouse from your home computer. This requires no experience or skill whatsoever and routinely involves animals being maimed by errant bullets. Opposition to Internet hunting has united animal advocates, the National Rifle Association and many hunters in calling for an end to the industry, which has already been banned in 23 states.[3]

IAN MCALLISTER/RAINCOAST.ORG

Bushmeat

Bushmeat is the illegally hunted meat of wild animals, whether taken for subsistence or income. With increasing urbanization in Africa, bushmeat has become a lucrative trade. In some developing nations, species of all kinds, including primates, are being hunted to extinction. Logging roads make for easy access to wildlife that was once inaccessible, and the loggers themselves are often involved in the trade. Commercial hunters build camps along logging roads, selling their fresh kills to the loggers, who transport the meat to market. The World Society for the Protection of Animals estimates that 800 gorillas are killed for bushmeat every year in Eastern Cameroon alone.[4]

Laboratory Labyrinth

We see this movement as the beginning of a process of turning from the widespread use of animals in product safety testing and scientific research to newer, more sophisticated tests.

— Alan Goldberg, John Hopkins University

The level of suffering endured by animals for the purpose of experimentation is extreme and unnecessary. The relevance of animal dissections in public schools, as well as experiments in colleges, industrial product testing and medical laboratories has always been questionable. With many readily available alternatives, they have now become redundant. The cruelty that exists for animals in labs is intolerable, and needs to stop.

Hey, Einstein! How about working on a cure for insensitivity to other species?

Dist. by King Features

HAPPY BIRTHDAY, ASHLEY 6·4·03

© Dan Piraro. Reprinted with permission of King Features Syndicate.

In the Name of Education

In American high schools, six million animals are killed every year in classroom dissections.[1] Dissections involve everything from rabbits, frogs and pigeons to bats, fetal (unborn) pigs and foxes. If it can be captured, or taken from a pet shelter, it is being dissected somewhere in a classroom.

In the Name of Medicine

Medical laboratories justify the testing of medications and surgeries on animals by arguing the necessity of improved treatments for humans. Yet no animal test has ever been as accurate as tests on a person for the simple reason that we are a unique species.[2] Medications and surgeries that are tested on chimpanzees or pigs have often been found to be unreliable when applied to humans, yet the practice goes on.

In the United States in a single year (2002)[3] …

312 thousand rabbits, 304 thousand guinea pigs, 96 thousand primates, 77 thousand dogs and 77 thousand cats were among the 1.5 million animals reportedly used in animal experiments — an increase of 16.3% from the previous year. Birds, mice, rats and reptiles were not recorded and are the animals most frequently used. The estimated actual total of all species used was 24 million (66 thousand a day).

In the Name of Commerce

A veil of secrecy surrounds the use of animals in industrial testing, whether for hazardous chemicals or cosmetics. Industrial labs harbor much suffering, while chemicals are tested on animals to find products that can safely be used by humans. The numbers of animals used in labs worldwide can only be guessed at, because nobody wants to share the information, nor do they want anyone to see inside the labs. However, organizations like People for the Ethical Treatment of Animals (PETA) and the World Society for the Protection of Animals (WSPA) have found ways to get inside the facilities and film what happens.

Alternatives Abound

CD-Roms that provide detailed step-by-step procedures for dissections are readily available for less than $30. Plastic 3-D models and computer simulations are available that have astounding accuracy for the purpose of education. Science has also created many non-animal, laboratory-grown cells that can are far more accurate for product testing than are live animals. For education, medicine or product testing, there is no excuse for the continued exploitation of animals.

Sensitivity to Life

Beyond the suffering endured by the animals themselves, something else needs to be looked at. Students who are made to cut open animals, and workers who test toxic products on animals stand a great risk of losing their sensitivity to life. We have an inherent will to act compassionately. That's what maintains our species. By repeatedly acting uncompassionately, especially when we feel forced to, something dies inside us. We lose our natural tendency for compassion.

Coming Together for Compassion

In May 2005 an influential committee made up of scientists, philosophers, animal welfare advocates and a lawyer released the findings of a two-year study into the ethics of animal experiments. The report by the Nuffield Council on Bioethics concluded that alternatives to animal experiments must be utilized: "A world in which the important benefits of such research could be achieved without causing pain, suffering, distress, lasting harm or death to animals involved in research must be the ultimate goal."

- American Anti-Vivisection Society: www.aavs.org/intro.html
- Ethologists for the Ethical Treatment of Animals: www.ethologicalethics.org
- European Coalition to End Animal Experiments: www.eceae.org
- John Hopkins Center for Alternatives to Animal Testing: http://caat.jhsph.edu
- Medical Research Modernization Committee: www.mrmcmed.org
- Physicians Committee for Responsible Medicine: www.pcrm.org

The Price of Entertainment

Our habit of taking wild animals from their natural environment and forcing them to live in captivity for the entertainment of people is a tragedy. Wild animals routinely die in transport before ever reaching their destination of a zoo, aquarium, circus or someone's home. If they do survive, their lives tend to be very short. It's estimated that 90% of all wildlife kept as pets are dead within the first two years of captivity.[1] If they do live a long life in captivity, it tends to

> The training of performing animals is both unnatural and callous, as wild animals are deprived of their species for normal social interaction, and their habitat where they roam free. A brutal regime of repetitive training and domination by their trainers frequently involves coercion and physical punishment.
>
> — Jan Creamer, Animal Defenders International

be a very tedious life, often full of suffering, and all that just to entertain people.

Yet people are flocking to zoos and aquariums in record numbers, perhaps unaware that the animals they're seeing are tired shadows of the wild beings they once were. People still show up in droves for rodeos; fiercely protecting the history of this Western culture, despite the cruelty that exists for the animals.

Wild Animals As Pets

Tigers, lions, monkeys, snakes, foxes, exotic birds, bears, reptiles, wolves, tropical fish and almost any other interesting animals you can think of are being used as pets around the world. Their captivity is cruel beyond simply stripping them of their freedom. The majority of exotic pets in the United States were originally obtained illegally and will live short, suffering-filled lives. Wild animals carry diseases such as rabies, salmonella, tuberculosis, hepatitis-A, scabies, Ebola and measles, all of which are contractible by humans,[2] with 93,000 cases of salmonella being attributed to contact with reptiles every year in the US.[3] Wild animals also pose a very real physical threat to their owners. In recent years, there have been hundreds of documented cases of bears, tigers and primates attacking and killing adults and children in North America.

Your brain is even bigger than ours.

Perhaps that's why we don't find imprisoning you & forcing you to do tricks "entertaining."

BIZARRO.COM

Dist. by King Features

The exotic pet trade is so out of control that there are now more tigers living in the United States than there are wild tigers in the world.[4] Millions of unwanted exotic pets from goldfish and budgies to wolves and cheetahs perish every year because of a lack of understanding by humans.

From Zoos and Aquariums to Wildlife Sanctuaries

Zoos and aquariums are not all cut from the same cloth. Many are deeply reliant on the trade of exotic animals. They use powerful advertising to convince people that their facilities exist for the purpose of species preservation and education. Some do, and some are just making it up. Some are hiding an enormous amount of animal suffering. Yet zoos and aquariums hold the solution to this enormous problem. They have the facilities and, to some extent, the knowledge to help with the huge population of captive and unwanted wildlife in North America and around the world. Zoos and aquariums could be sanctuaries where animals can spend the rest of their lives in relative peace, not for the entertainment of people, but for the preservation and better understanding of their species. Some facilities are already serving this purpose.

What's the difference between a zoo (or aquarium) and a sanctuary? True sanctuaries don't make dolphins do tricks and behave like humans, despite the argument that they're enjoying it. True sanctuaries do not hold bears on captive display for humans, allowing them, instead, adequate space to exist in privacy. True

- Born Free: www.bornfree.org.uk
- Captive Animal Protection Society: www.captiveanimals.org
- Captive Wild Animal Protection Coalition: www.cwapc.org
- Coalition for No Whales in Captivity: www.whaleprotection.org
- Performing Animal Welfare Society: www.greyhoundpets.org
- Zoo Check Canada: www.zoocheck.com

sanctuaries allow animals to exist with dignity and don't put them on a stage for us.

Performance Anxiety

Whether under the guise of zoos, aquariums, circuses or rodeos, animals should not be forced to perform for humans. For every successful performance, there were many hours of resistance during the training process, punishing the animal for its lack of cooperation and breaking its spirit. Once broken, most animals will behave as humans want them to.

Exotic Pet Ownership in the United States[5]

Great apes (chimps, bonobos, gorillas, orangutans)	3 thousand
Monkeys	12 thousand
Large cats (lions, tigers, cheetahs, etc.)	10-20 thousand
Reptiles	8.8 million
Birds	17 million
Annual value of the industry (exotic and wild animals for pets)	$15 billion

from Pets to Companions

As a society we need to step up and take responsibility for the animals in our care and in our communities. When we take a cat into our home, we are agreeing to provide food, safety, care and loving companionship for his or her lifetime.

— Lorie Chortyk, BC SPCA

They are our companion animals. Thousands of years ago, we domesticated the ancient ancestors of today's cats and dogs because they seemed to enjoy being around us. They gave us a form of unconditional love, a fierce loyalty and open gratitude for our existence. We made them our companions, breeding them to isolate the genetic traits we desired the most. Some dogs were bred for their ferocity and ability to hunt down prey. Some were bred for their cuteness and willingness to sit on our laps. Thus began a relationship between companion animals and their human guardians that has endured through thousands of years.

Of Course There's a Catch

Relatively recently, we developed a problem. Our growing population all wanted pets, and all those pets began reproducing faster than we were, resulting in a whole lot of unwanted animals. And companion animals are far too easy to get rid of. You can't just decide you don't want a human member of your family around, and ship him off to a shelter or have him put down. But it happens to animals all the time.

The birthrate for pets in North America dwarfs that of humans: 70,000 dogs and cats a day in the US, versus 10,000 humans.[1] The companion animal population in the US is estimated to be 378 million — nearly 100 million more pets than people.[2] The birthrate is highly unsustainable, since there can never be enough homes for all these animals. As a result, every year, 4 to 6 million animals are euthanized because there are no homes for them.[3]

In New Mexico alone, unwanted animals from shelters in the major centers account for over 580 tons of landfill every year. The animal shelters keep track of such things because they want a solution to be found. In the city of Albuquerque, unwanted animals from shelters account for over 230 tons of landfill a year.[4]

These numbers are not unique to New Mexico. It is happening in every city in North America and around the planet. This awful reality of overpopulation and unwanted pets is part of our society's underbelly that nobody wants to look at. But the animal rescue organizations and shelter operators have no choice.

Solutions, Please

The most obvious solution to the problem is to spay and neuter as many dogs and cats as possible. There are shelters, veterinary offices, animal welfare organizations and individuals working in nearly every area of the continent to help with this mission. They need the support of pet owners and communities to be effective.

The follow-up step is to care for all the unwanted pets that already exist. Every cat, dog, rabbit, gerbil and parrot that was born into our domesticated world deserves our respect and dignity. This means treating them humanely, providing safe havens for them to live in, feeding the hungry and, when possible, adopting them into a nurturing home.

The long-term solution is to stop calling them pets altogether, and to let go of a vision of people being "pet owners." We need to accept our role in having domesticated these living creatures, and become their guardians. They do not belong to us — they are entrusted to us. Before we accept that responsibility, we must look carefully into our lives and ensure that we are ready for the responsibility. Adopting a companion animal is not like buying a bicycle; you can't stick it in the shed once the novelty has worn off. And yet, that's exactly what happens every day.

How much do we spend on our pets each year?[5]

	Total	Per Person*
Australia	$1.7 billion	$85
Canada	$2.1 billion	$66
United Kingdom	$6.8 billion	$113
United States	$35.9 billion	$120

*Based on total population, many of whom are not pet owners, so actual cost per guardian is significantly higher.

- Animal Spirit: www.theanimalspirit.com/adopt.html
- Companion Animal Protection Society: www.caps-web.org
- Companion Animal Rescue Effort: www.carepets.org
- Humane Society for Companion Animals: www.hsca.net
- New Leash on Life: www.newleash.org
- Pets 911: www.pets911.org

A Day in the Life
of a Puppy Mill

I wish that when people saw that cute little puppy in the pet store window, they could also see that puppy's mother and father. If they could, they'd realize that these dogs are living lives of isolation, deprivation, poor health and fear.

— Bill Smith, Main Line Animal Rescue

The problem of unwanted pets is so huge that it necessitates another look at the source of the problem. With so many wonderful animals that need a good home, it seems like an obvious choice to bring one home from a shelter, rather than buying it from a store. Yet the pet trade in North America is booming. Pet stores in the United States sell upwards of 500,000 puppies a year.[1] With 5 million healthy, adoptable pets being euthanized every year in the US, why are we still breeding pets?

Exposing the Puppy Mill

Puppy and kitty mills are mass-breeding facilities that churn out hundreds of thousands of puppies and kittens every year. Although they don't sell directly to consumers, few people know they exist, yet they are the primary supplier of pets in North America. They're fueling the pet population crisis across the continent, doing so through the friendly face of pet stores, classified ads and the Internet.

Thanks to repeated investigations by groups such as the Humane Society and PETA, however, the grim reality of life inside these mills is becoming public knowledge. The breeding stock animals live in cages and are kept continuously pregnant for years without any human companionship until they are literally worn out and are killed.

A Host of Problems

Just as unfortunate as the breeding-stock animals are the puppies and kitties that are mass-produced by the mills. Transported in huge numbers to be sold all over the continent and overseas, these babies see none of the nurturing that is so essential in their infancy. Even if a family offers the little creature a happy, lifelong home, it may never recover from its initial trauma from crowding and transportation. Many new pet owners can't figure out why their dog barks nonstop or their cat lives in terror of everything that moves. Invariably, it is because they began their life in a breeding mill. The irony is that people tend to avoid bringing home shelter animals because they fear they'll be wounded or traumatized. Quite the opposite is true. Shelter animals were often born in someone's caring home and are generally far more adaptable to human companionship than a store-bought, mass-bred pet.

Where Credit Is Due

There are reputable breeders who put the well-being of their companion animals above all else,

An End to Backyard Breeding

Many pet "enthusiasts" who operate backyard breeding businesses are contributing to the population crisis. Operators have to be sneaky since people are often turned off by the idea of buying a pet from a backyard pet breeder, and it's illegal in many areas. They place their adorable babies for sale in classified ads or on bulletin boards, offering beautiful pure-bred pups for a fraction of the price at a pet store. They package the sale as though it were their first such litter, and they're sad to part with them. And they're massively successful at it. The good ones can dupe buyers out of hundreds or thousands of dollars.

ensuring that every animal is treated well and sold to a loving home. How do you know? Consult the Humane Society's "How to Find a Good Dog Breeder" checklist, talk to your veterinarian or ask local animal welfare groups. A reputable breeder will not sell their puppies and kittens through a pet store, or any other means that doesn't allow them to directly interview prospective guardians.

Despite the compassionate efforts of many credible pet breeders, the fact remains that the industry contributes to an out-of-control population crisis that can only be reduced by finding homes for stray and abandoned animals, not by breeding more.

All in a Name

While the term "puppy mill" has come to mean any commercial pet-breeding operation, there are far more than puppies and kittens being produced. Birds, guinea pigs, ferrets, reptiles and many other animals are mass-produced through pet-breeding operations and then sold through retail pet stores. More than 90% of all animals sold in pet stores are the product of mass-breeding operations.[2]

Summing It All Up

If you are considering bringing a companion animal into your life, bypass the pet store and adopt from an animal shelter.

- How to Find a Good Dog Breeder checklist: www.hsus.org/web-files/PDF/Good_breeder.pdf
- IDA — puppy mills: www.idausa.org/facts/pmfacts.html
- No Puppy Mills Canada: www.nopuppymillscanada.ca
- Pet Mills: www.imom.org
- Puppy Mill Rescue: www.puppymillrescue.com
- Stop Puppy Mills: www.stoppuppymills.org

PETSAFE.NET

Beauty Is Only Skin Deep

Fur, down, silk, wool and leather all cause suffering for animals. Why would I want to be a part of that when I can be cruelty-free, given the countless alternatives to all of these things?

— Pamela Rice,
animal issues columnist and author

The world is waking up to the cruelty and suffering that exists in the fashion industry. Yet, even with international exposure and campaigns against it, the industry is going strong. In 2003 the UK finally enacted legislation that bans the farming of animals "solely or primarily for their fur." Worldwide, however, 40 million animals are killed annually for their fur — 110,000 every day.[1]

Fur Industry 101
The majority of the fur used in the fashion industry is a product of two sources: factory farms and trapping. Fur farming involves the captivity of animals in cramped quarters, until they are ready to be gassed and pelted. The most heavily farmed fur-bearing animal in the world is the mink: a wild, solitary animal that has been raised in captivity for less than 100 years. What happens when you confine solitary animals together in cramped wire cages? Sadly, psychotic behavior; constant pacing, perpetual gnawing at the cages, self-mutilation and cannibalism.[2]

Trapping involves the capture of wild animals for their fur. The two most common traps are the leghold trap, which clamps down on any part of an animal that makes contact with it and holds them until a trapper shows up to kill them, and the conibear trap, which uses a powerful spring to clamp down and kill its target animal — theoretically.

Leghold traps have gained international recognition as being horribly inhumane. Captured animals are often in so much agony that they chew off their legs in an effort to escape. This self-mutilating escape, referred to as "wringing off" by trappers, is estimated to be done by as many as a quarter of all animals trapped.

Conibear traps are designed to be more painless, quickly killing the animal they're made for. The problem is it only works for one kind of animal and only if the animal steps into it properly.

Trapping is still widespread, even though most dedicated trappers earn less than $500 a year from it. Nor does it have anything to do with conservation, being ineffective as population control. So why does it continue? Sadly, it would appear that people are trapping and killing animals because they enjoy doing so.

THE HUMANE SOCIETY OF THE UNITED STATES

A fox's fur is his own to wear.

Native History?

Europeans introduced commercial trapping to native peoples, promoting the killing of animals for money, instead of for food, shelter and clothing. Trapping today is done, for the majority, by white North Americans. Only 3% of all fur for sale in North America comes from native trapping, and those natives who do trap only bring home about $225 per year — far below subsistence level.[3] Native/Animal Brotherhood founder Paul Hollingsworth said, "The fur industry took us away from our traditional ways. It is time we reunited with our animal brothers, to seek a world which respects Mother Earth and all beings."

One Person's Pet = Another's Fur

Across much of Asia, the greatest abundance of fur production comes not from farming or trapping, but from cats and dogs that are rounded up, often as strays, and killed for their fur. The Asian markets label domestic fur, to boost sales, as "mountain goat," "lamb" or "sobaki." The Humane Society of the United States (HSUS) has found cat and dog fur products-usually as trim for jackets-in Europe and the United States. The Burlington Coat Factory recently pulled dog and cat fur products from its production line and donated $100,000 to the HSUS, after the organization did an investigation, and tested DNA samples that identified domestic animal fur in the factory's products.

The Leathery Truth

The skins of cows, bison, elephants, boars, kangaroos, snakes, sharks, dolphins and many other animals go into luxury items, all of which can be, and are, produced with available alternatives. Beef cows, non-productive dairy cows and dairy calves lead the way in producing leather for fashion and convenience.[4]

Number of alligator skins (their bellies) that go into one handbag	2-3
Number of cows killed for each leather car interior	4-15
Number of cows who die annually to make leather footballs	35 thousand
Number of kangaroos killed annually for soccer shoes	6 million
Number of animals killed annually by the global leather industry	1 billion
Animal-free alternatives to leather	Cotton, synthetics, linen, rubber, canvas, ramie, chlorenol, hemp ...

- CAAT's animal-free clothing links: www.humanecarolina.org/clothing2.html
- Coalition to Abolish the Fur Trade: www.caft.org.uk
- Fur Free Alliance: www.infurmation.com
- Fur Free Zone: www.furfree.info
- Furisdead.com: www.furisdead.com

Wasting Their Habitat

It wasn't the Exxon Valdez captain's driving that caused the Alaskan oil spill. It was yours.

— Greenpeace advertisement,
New York Times, February 25, 1990

The connection between habitat loss and animal suffering isn't always easy to see. Entire species can disappear while we're busy with our lives, and few of us notice. Habitat loss tends to happen out in nature; a distant land far from where our urban populations live. We may feel saddened to hear that songbirds are no longer returning because we've sprayed outlying fields too heavily with pesticides. We're disheartened to learn that the plant we work at is being criticized for improperly disposing of its wastes. Yet we need our jobs.

Habitat loss is happening all the time, all around us. It is the result of what we spill, what we litter, what we disrupt and, ultimately, what we consume. We are consuming the very wildness of the planet.

Habitat Loss and Animal Suffering

Animals don't suddenly find they have nowhere to live and unanimously go extinct. There are lots of warning signs, and many animals suffer as their habitats become wasted.

- Endangered Species Coalition: www.stopextinction.org
- National Audubon Society: www.audubon.org
- Rainforest Action Network: www.ran.org
- Sierra Club: www.sierraclub.org
- Sierra Club of Canada: www.sierraclub.ca
- World Commission on Protected Areas: www.iucn.org/themes/wcpa

- The world's lakes, rivers and wetlands have lost 50% of all species since 1970, and the oceans have lost 30%.[1] In the water, where most of our contaminants end up, fish and marine mammals are being subjected to industrial effluents, raw sewage, agricultural runoff, fuel spills and human garbage. Fish have become so contaminated with mercury that the US Environmental Protection Agency issued a warning in 2004 advising pregnant women, nursing mothers and young children not to consume more than 6 ounces of fish a week (one average serving), because of potential damage to developing nervous systems.[2]

- On land, animals are having their habitat wiped out by deforestation, at a rate of 30 football fields per minute,[3] and by residential, agricultural, commercial and industrial development, while contending with pollution from all four sectors. Habitat is changing and being lost too quickly for wildlife to adapt. A quarter of all mammals are in danger of extinction within the century.[4]

- In the air, where our smoke stacks, vehicle exhaust pipes and jet trails contribute to climate change and contaminate the very air we breathe, birds and land animals are falling prey to respiratory conditions,[5] migration disruption[6] and acid rain.[7]

Animals will evolve. That's part of nature. But we're not moving at nature's speed. We're moving much too fast for animals, and ultimately ourselves, to keep up.

What's Being Done?

In 2006 the polar bear and the hippopotamus were added to the World Conservation Union's (ICUN's) Red List, which now lists 16,000 species threatened with extinction: 80% of the listed birds, mammals and amphibians are directly affected by habitat loss.[8] The IUCN warns that loss of biodiversity is increasing, despite global efforts to stop it.

There are several international bodies in place with a united goal of stopping biodiversity loss and protecting more land for wildlife, including the IUCN, the United Nations Environment Programme and the Convention on Biological Diversity, which originally called for a global effort to significantly reduce biodiversity loss by 2010. All three involve a majority of the world's governments, and the IUCN works very closely with international conservation groups such as the World Wildlife Fund.

In 2006 biodiversity scientists and policy-makers from 13 countries called for a unified scientific voice to inform government decision-making on global conservation. Experts from Canada, Chile, China, France, Germany, Ghana, India, Mexico, the Netherlands, Norway, South Africa, the US and the UK called for the establishment of an Intergovernmental Panel on Biodiversity to parallel the Intergovernmental Panel on Climate Change. The IUCN supports the creation of the global panel but stresses that it will need the committed financial support, and willingness to enforce regulations, of national governments.[9]

JIM ROBERTSON/ANIMALSINTHEWILD.COM

Protected Areas

The IUCN's World Commission on Protected Areas promotes the establishment and management of an international network of terrestrial and marine protected areas. With 1000 members in 140 countries, World Commission on Protected Areas (WCPA) works with individual governments and global conservation groups to strategically plan key conservation areas, create effective policy and find funding for conservation initiatives. When the Republic of Korea signed on as a member nation with IUCN in 2006, it became the 82nd nation to do so, giving its support to the WCPA and the increasing global conservation effort. As of 2005, 12% of the world's land surface had been designated as protected areas, while less than 1% of the marine environment was protected, despite covering 70% of the planet's surface.[10]

The Ravages of Climate Change

This is not some slow, controlled change we're talking about. It's fast, it's unpredictable and it's unprecedented during human civilization.
— Adam Markham,
World Wide Fund for Nature

When we widen our minds to take in global climate change, the thought of caring for cows, or animals who are mistreated in puppy mills, seems relatively safe, even reassuring. At least the world stays the same while we are campaigning to relieve their suffering. Global climate change is so daunting and packed with ominous warnings that it requires us to sit up sharply and pay very close attention.

The science is clear. Burning fossil fuels releases carbon from plants and trees that lived millions of years ago. The carbon mixes with oxygen to form carbon dioxide (CO_2), which traps heat in the atmosphere. CO_2 levels are rising dramatically, and so is the temperature. For a clear presentation of the science, watch Al Gore's movie, *An Inconvenient Truth*.

Here are some of the impacts we can expect if we do not get climate change under control:

- Sea levels around the world may rise by as much as 13 feet this century as the Greenland and West Antarctic ice-caps melt and warming waters expand. This will cause more than 100 million people to abandon

- *An Inconvenient Truth*: www.climatecrisis.net
- *Stormy Weather: 101 Solutions to Global Climate Change,* by Guy Dauncey with Patrick Mazza, New Society Publishers, 2001: www.earthfuture.com
- Union of Concerned Scientists: www.ucsusa.org/global_warming

their homes as areas of coastal China, India, Bangladesh, Europe and the US go under water. It will also cause the loss of countless coastal wetlands, home to a myriad species of animals and birds.[1]

- A third of the Earth's land will turn into desert, especially in Africa — and this may be an underestimate. Many million people will have to abandon their farms and villages, and millions of animals will die from hunger and thirst as the rains fail and rivers and water-holes dry up. Cows, goats, camels, elephants, hippos, tigers, lions, gazelles — they all need to drink.[2]

- Up to a quarter of all land-based animals and plants will be unable to adapt to changes caused by the rising temperature and will face extinction by 2050. That's a million species that will disappear from existence, after millions of years of evolution.[3]

- The polar bears face extinction as the floating sea ice they depend on to hunt seals melts away to nothing.

- The Amazon rainforest, home to a million species of animals, plants and insects, faces collapse due to unprecedented drought that is causing rivers to dry up and the forest to catch fire. Climate scientists feared this would happen by 2050, but it is happening now.[4]

These are very dire warnings, but they are premised on one condition: *if we do not act to reduce our greenhouse gas emissions*. It is important that we get a grasp of this, so that we can do what is necessary to move our planet to a more cooperative, peaceful, sustainable way of living.

The climate change problem has four main causes. First, it is caused by the fossil fuels (coal, oil and gas) we use to heat our homes, run our vehicles, produce our electricity and power our industries. The solution is to embrace a new energy revolution based on energy from the sun, wind, tides, biofuels and electric vehicles, combined with making every car, light bulb and appliance ten times more efficient. It involves rediscovering the pleasures of walking and cycling, investing in public transit and railways and designing our towns and cities so that it is easy to get around without a car. It involves redesigning manufacturing and industry so that everything is reused and recycled.

It also asks that we stop consuming so much. If everyone in the world lived the way people do in the West, we would need three more planets to provide the resources.

Second, it is caused by deforestation: when the trees are gone, they are no longer able to absorb carbon. The solutions are to adopt sustainable forest management practices throughout the world and plant trees in all our urban and rural areas.

Third, it is caused by farming, and cattle in particular, due to the oil that is needed to supply and feed a cow, the methane they burp from their stomachs and nitrous oxide from the use of nitrogen fertilizers.[5] The simplest solution is to eat less meat.

Fourth, it is caused by chemicals called "F" gases (HFCs, PFCs, SF6), which industry simply needs to phase out.

There are many reasons for alarm, but there are also good reasons for hope, because many of the world's nations, states, cities and businesses are working to reduce their emissions (see Solution 63 and Solution 97). If we care about the world, our children and the world's creatures, this is one we can not sit out.

R&C Buchanan

The Deep, Grey Sea

Such deep-sea habitats are among the least known areas of the oceans, and by pledging not to fish in them, these companies have taken a great step towards sustainability.

— Carl Gustaf Lundin, IUCN Global Marine Programme, on the voluntary fishing moratorium by SIODFA

Oceans cover 71% of the Earth's surface. They are vast in size, and importance, to the world. They control climate, sustain live and drive economies. Life itself began in the beautiful oceans, some 3 billion years ago. Today the oceans are home to over a million species of life, including many we've never seen.

The Toxic Tide

Every day the marine environment becomes increasingly contaminated by the direct discharge of sewage treatment plants, chemical and pharmaceutical manufacturers, and offshore oil and gas rigs. Indirectly it's contaminated by land from agricultural and urban runoff, and by air from sources such as waste incineration plants. Beluga whales in Canada's St. Lawrence Seaway are so contaminated with industrial chemicals, primarily polychlorinated biphenyls (PCBs), that their carcasses are classified as toxic waste.[1] In the Arctic, the level of a fire-retardant called polybrominated diphenylether is doubling every five years in Arctic ringed seals, and polar bears are developing intersex genitals because of exposure to endocrine-disrupting chemicals, blocking hormone transmission in their bodies.[2] Some of the common uses for these chemicals are pesticides, fungicides, insecticides and pharmaceuticals.

Overloading on Nutrients

Nutrient overloading is caused by runoff from residential, agricultural and industrial areas. Nutrients are essential to life in the ocean, but accelerated levels of nitrates and phosphates in coastal waters are causing the extreme growth of unicellular marine algae referred to as algae blooms. The algae blooms die, decomposing from bacteria that uses a large amount of oxygen, and resulting in the surrounding water becoming oxygen deficient. This process, called eutrophication, produces dead zones on the ocean floor as large as 40,000 square miles, where marine animals and plants die from suffocation.[3] Algae blooms are the cause of red tides, when the sea becomes discolored by the concentration of algae, some of which is toxic, and contaminates shellfish.

ETHAN SMITH

There are 230 cruise ships plying the world's seas, each discharging up to 30,000 gallons of sewage a day.

- Marine Conservation Alliance: www.marineconservationalliance.org
- Marine Conservation Society: www.mcsuk.org
- National Coalition for Marine Conservation: www.savethefish.org
- Ocean Conservancy: www.oceanconservancy.org
- Pew Institute for Ocean Science: www.pewmarine.org

Traffic Jam

There is a non-stop rush hour going on in our oceans. From freighters and cruise ships to fishing boats and pleasure craft, there is a constant buzz of activity. This results in a deafening level of noise pollution for marine mammals, since water magnifies sound, and causes constant collisions with sea life, leaving increasingly fewer places for marine animals to escape.

Exploring the Depths

Oceans comprise 97% of the Earth's water, with 90% of the water lying beyond the shallow continental margins, and most being deeper than 1.5 miles. There are still huge areas of the oceans' depths that humans haven't explored or recorded, yet the advance in technology is impacting marine habitat far below the surface. Fishing, mining, oil exploration and pipelines are exploiting previously undisturbed areas, with serious consequences for the slow-growing deep-sea life.

Bottom trawling is particularly harmful to the deep marine environment, involving large nets weighted with chains, rollers or rock-hopper gear being dragged along the ocean floor, scooping up as much as 15 tons of fish in a single load.[4] Trawl nets catch everything in their path, including corals and sponges that create habitat for a wide variety of marine life and take centuries to recover.[5]

The Good News

In 2006 four large fishing companies made a major announcement, the first of its kind in the world. Austral Fisheries Pty Ltd (Australia), Bel Ocean II Ltd (Mauritius), Sealord Group (New Zealand) and TransNamibia Fishing Pty Ltd (Namibia) voluntarily halted their trawling operations in 11 areas of the southern Indian Ocean. These companies, the primary trawling operators in the area, have formed the Southern Indian Ocean Deepwater Fishers' Association (SIODFA), consulting with the United Nations to set aside 190,000 square miles of ocean floor. To verify compliance with the voluntary restrictions, SIODFA will track its vessels with a satellite monitoring system.

A Day at the Beach

The Marine Conservation Society's Beachwatch program reported an 80% increase in beach litter along UK shorelines between 1995 and 2005. Worldwide, over a million birds and 100,000 marine mammals and turtles die from entanglement or ingestion of plastics each year.[6] What's found on the beach is the tip of the iceberg, because it's impossible to tell how much litter is in the ocean, drifting in the wind and ocean currents. Even colorful balloons, released into the air from events far inland, eventually fall into the ocean, where they're mistaken for food by marine life, clogging digestive tracts and killing them. Another reason not to litter.

Cetaceans: Our Elders, Our Teachers

Cetaceans, the global family that includes whales, dolphins and porpoises, share a relationship with each other that we can only guess at. They are highly intelligent, graceful beings, steeped in folklore and mystery. The larger whales dwarf any land mammal, and yet they move swiftly through the ocean as though they were weightless. From little clicking sounds to elaborate songs, cetaceans can communicate across vast bodies of water, gifted with a level of communication that we can't comprehend. Although genetically very different from humans, their social behavior is quite similar to ours. They live in tight communities, raising their young for 18 to 20 years. Cetaceans have been around for millions of years longer than us, and there's an unavoidable feeling that they know far more about life.

Dr. Louis M. Herman/NOAA

There's absolutely no reason to kill whales. Japan, for reasons that remain a mystery to the international community, continues to invoke "cultural tradition" to justify its whaling, as if any country's culture remains forever stagnant, and unaffected by research, discoveries and humane trends.

— Kitty Block, Humane Society International

An End to Whaling

Although the majority of the world now respects, and even reveres, cetaceans, this certainly hasn't always been the case. Through the 1700s, 1800s and half-way through the 1900s, whales were hunted commercially in vast numbers. There was great prestige in being able to hunt and kill the world's largest animals, and it was done with little thought to conservation. Even though the practice slowed dramatically 50 years ago, cetacean populations have yet to recover. In 1986 the International Whaling Commission (IWC) announced a moratorium on whaling, yet Japan, Norway and Iceland continue to hunt whales, using a loophole in the IWC agreement allowing "scientific research." Every year, Japan lobbies aggressively to have the moratorium lifted altogether and, in 2006, persuaded enough trading partners to support them, causing a split vote, and giving the moratorium an uncertain future (see Solution 75). Since the 1986 moratorium began, 25,000 whales have been killed.[1]

Coping with Traffic

Heavy ship traffic on the oceans also causes problems for cetaceans. Ship strikes happen often, with larger whales being unable to get out of the path of freighters and cruise ships. The constant presence of ships also causes deafening noise pollution for the cetaceans, making it impossible for them to communicate. In the

- America's Whale Alliance: www.americaswhalealliance.org
- American Cetacean Society: www.acsonline.org
- Blue Dolphin Alliance: www.bluedolphin.org
- International Whaling Commission: www.iwcoffice.org
- Seaflow: www.seaflow.org
- Seatrust: www.seatrust.org.uk
- Whale and Dolphin Conservation Society: www.wdcs.org

case of the US Navy's Low Frequency Active Sonar (LFA), the noise pollution is actually killing them. The LFA's blasts are a million times louder than our human pain threshold.[2] Commercial fishing traffic is another casualty for cetaceans; they often become entrapped and suffocate in the fishing nets.

Overfishing

Globally, commercial fisheries are stripping the food supply away from the cetaceans that depend on fish far more than we do, relying on healthy fish populations for their survival. The Yangtze River dolphin in China, for instance, has lost so much of its food supply to the burgeoning human population that scientists are calling it the world's most endangered mammal, with just 17 living individuals.[3] A conservation effort is underway for the freshwater dolphins, involving the relocation of some of them to a nearby lake, where a reserve is being established.

Overfishing is not the fishing industry's only threat to cetaceans. Accidental capture and entanglement in fishing gear is the biggest threat to whales, dolphins and porpoises, killing 300,000 animals a year.[4]

Pollution

The increasing toxicity of their marine habitat is also having a heavy impact on cetaceans. In their position at the top of the food chain, their bodies accumulate the persistent chemicals that are affecting nearly all sea life lower on the food chain. Because of their long lifespan (most whales live to age 70), the chemicals build up over many years, concentrating in the fatty tissue of whale blubber. In 2002 a dead female orca off Washington's Olympic Peninsula had levels of 1,000 parts PCBs per 1,000,000 parts blubber — one of the highest levels of toxin ever found in a marine mammal.[5] Studies have shown that female orcas transfer 90% of their contaminants, including PCBs and DDT, to their first-born calf.[6]

Cetaceans on the Endangered Species List[7]

Species	Status
Beluga whale	Vulnerable
Blue whale	Endangered
Chinese (Yangtze) River dolphin	Critical
Common (harbor) porpoise	Vulnerable
Fin whale	Endangered
Gulf of California harbor porpoise	Critical
Grey whale (Western North Pacific)	Critical
Humpback whale	Vulnerable
Indus River dolphin	Endangered
Killer whale (Orca — Southern Resident)	Endangered
Right whale (Northern Pacific)	Endangered
Sei whale	Endangered
Sperm whale	Vulnerable

Animals and Faith

> I care not much for a man's religion whose dog and cat are not the better for it.
>
> — Abraham Lincoln

Animal welfare and religion seem destined to be forever entwined. Muslims, Jews, Christians, Buddhists, Hindus and Sikhs all follow sacred texts that are based on the common premise of reverent living and loving one another. Yet translating the words of the ancient texts, and applying their doctrines to the modern world, creates ethical challenges in times of change.

In 2004 the British government rejected a campaign by the Farm Animal Welfare Council (FAWC) calling for legislation to ban the halal and kosher methods of meat production required by Muslims and Jews. The campaign stated that the process causes undue suffering to animals because their throats are cut without stunning them first. After the government's decision, the president of the Halal Food Authority said, "Jewish and Muslim methods cannot be changed, because they are in the religious books."[1]

FAWC said it appreciated that the slaughter methods have been imbedded in religions for thousands of years and that both religions are concerned with animal welfare, but added, "The method at the time the rules were written was probably the most humane way of killing an animal, but of course that has changed."

Dominion and Domination

> Let them [humans] have dominion over the fish of the sea, and over the fowl of the air, and over the cattle, and over all the earth. (Genesis 1:26)

The Bible's reference of human "dominion" has long been used to justify the domination of animals. The exploitation of the Bible's message reached an absurd level in Europe from the later Middle Ages through the 18th century, when animals were suspected of affiliation with Satan and were forced to stand trial, facing execution for their crimes.[2]

Today concerned Christians and other animal welfare advocates have suggested that dominion places the responsibility of the Earth's preservation in human hands, making us the stewards for "all creatures great and small."

A Vatican Voice for the Animals

Pope John Paul II was an animal advocate, and one of the first things he did after becoming pope was to travel to Assisi, the birthplace of St. Francis, where he spoke of the saint's love for animals. Over the years, Pope John Paul II frequently spoke of the importance of our relationship with animals, saying that they are, "as near to God as men are." In 1990 the Pope stated that, "The animals possess a soul and men must love and feel solidarity with our smaller brethren." The Pope's commitment to animals led to the mourning of his passing in 2005, not just by Catholics, but by compassionate souls everywhere.

- Animal welfare and Christianity: www.all-creatures.org
- Bhagavad-Gita and vegetarianism: www.gitamrta.org/articles/why%20vegetarianism.htm
- Christian Vegetarian Association: www.christianveg.com
- Islam and animal welfare: www.islamicconcern.org
- Jewish Veg: www.jewishveg.com
- Modern Religion: www.themodernreligion.com/an_main.htm

Inside the Sacred Texts

Buddhism

- All living things fear being put to death. Putting oneself in the place of the other, let no one kill nor cause another to kill (Dhammapada verse no.129).
- When a man has pity on all living creatures then only is he noble (Buddha Siddhartha Gautama).

Christianity

- The Lord is good to all, and his compassion is over all that he has made (Psalm 145:9).
- Not to hurt our humble brethren is our first duty to them, but to stop there is not enough. We have a higher mission — to be of service to them wherever they require it (St. Francis of Assisi).

Hinduism

- He, who injures harmless creatures from a wish to give himself pleasure, never finds happiness in this life or the next (Manu-samhita 5.45).
- One is dearest to God who has no enemies among the living beings, who is nonviolent to all creatures. (Bhagavad-Gita).

Islam

- There is not an animal on Earth, nor a bird that flies on its wings, but they are communities like you (The Koran 6:38).
- Whoever is kind to the creatures of God is kind to himself (Mohammed).

GALÁPAGOS NETWORK/ECOVENTURA S.A

Judaism

- It is forbidden, according to the law of the Torah, to inflict pain upon any living creature. On the contrary, it is our duty to relieve the pain of any creature, even if it is ownerless or belongs to a non Jew (Code of Jewish Law).
- There is no difference between the pain of humans and the pain of other living beings, since the love and tenderness of the mother for the young are not produced by reasoning, but by feeling, and this faculty exists not only in humans but in most living beings (Rabbi Moses ben Maimo).

God loved the birds and invented trees. Man loved the birds and invented cages.
— Jacques Deval, *Afin de vivre bel et bien*

Animals in the Boardroom

Clarity, a shared understanding of what we are trying to achieve and a framework to use in moving forward, are tremendous sources of hope and inspiration.

— Dr. Karl-Henrik Robért, founder of The Natural Step

In our increasingly globalized world, corporations have immense power, accounting for 51 of the world's 100 largest economies (the other 49 are countries).[1] Corporations have the wealth and influence to create positive change on a global scale, yet they must answer to their shareholders, making choices that increase profits, even if it's at the expense of animals, people and the environment.

The Path of a Giant

The multinational corporation Monsanto has a 95% share of the world's genetically engineered seeds and reported an annual profit of $5.4 billion in 2004.[2] With 15,000 employees worldwide, it produces its flagship product, Roundup, along with a wide variety of other agricultural chemicals and livestock growth hormones. In the early 1900s, Monsanto was responsible for introducing caffeine to Coca-Cola and became a leading manufacturer of

plastics, sulfuric acid, aspartame (NutraSweet) and PCBs. During World War II, Monsanto operated the laboratory that created the world's first nuclear bomb and continued its development of chemical weapons, producing Agent Orange for the US army during the Vietnam War. It wasn't until 1982 that its scientists became the first to modify a plant cell, yet, by the '90s, the company dominated global agriculture, successfully suing Canadian and US farmers for the sale of crops containing its patented genes; a result of wind carrying seeds from neighboring crops. Monsanto's industry dominance and its aggressive legal and lobbying practices have earned it international criticism and contributed to many small farmers being driven out of business by corporate agriculture. Its impact on animals is extensive, from those subjected to the cruelty of factory farms to wildlife losing its habitat.

No More Corporate Takeover

Profit-driven corporations are eroding ecosystems, economies and hope for a sustainable world, and they're getting away with it. For the trend to stop, federal governments need to set rules for how corporations operate, both at home and in foreign countries, with companies reporting emission levels, accidents, legal violations and progress on conservation programs to offset environmental impact. And individuals must be accountable for their role as consumers, avoiding companies that contribute to the exploitation of animals and supporting those committed to global sustainability.

- Forbes 500 List: www.forbes.com/lists
- IUCN's SEAPRISE: www.iucn.org/themes/ceesp/seaprise.htm
- The Natural Step Canada: www.naturalstep.ca
- The Natural Step US: www.naturalstep.org
- *The Natural Step Story: Seeding a Quiet Revolution*, by Karl-Henrik Robert and Ray Anderson, New Society, 2002
- *The No-Nonsense Guide to Globalization*, by Wayne Ellwood, Verso, 2001

The Natural Step

Founded in 1989, The Natural Step (TNS) is an international non-profit research, education and advisory organization committed to creating an ecologically, socially and economically sustainable path for the global community. With 70 people working in 12 countries, TNS provides education and coaching to companies and communities, drawing upon a network of scientists, sustainability experts, universities and companies, while being guided by this fundamental question: How do we make economic progress, giving everyone the opportunity for a fulfilling life, without continuing to damage the natural systems upon which we all depend? Hundreds of corporations and communities use the TNS Framework, including IKEA (see Solution 50), Collins Pine (see Solution 49), Home Depot, Nike and Interface.

Giving 1% Back to the Earth

In 2005 the World Conservation Union's SEAPRISE proposed a global private-sector finance initiative, the 1% Earth Profits Fund, with which participating companies would commit 1% of their after-tax profits to the conservation of the world's IUCN red-listed species. If the top 500 revenue-generating companies in the world dedicated 1% of their profits to the collective pool, it would amount to $10 billion annually — a relatively modest payback for a global ecosystem that provides services valued at $33 trillion a year.[3]

TANIA HONAN

Don't Believe Everything Your Spin Doctor Tells You

Advertising means success for corporations as they spend millions of dollars on persuasive campaigns. McDonald's, alone, spends far more in advertising in a week ($19 million) than the US National Institutes of Health spend in a year ($1 million) on the government's 5 A Day nutrition program.[4] Some advertising is obvious, and some is subtly placed in the background of movies or disguised as news. Animal welfare is deeply connected to advertising, because it influences what we eat, what we wear, where we invest and what we support. Yet corporations can also help animals in a profound way through their advertising, as Pepsi did by ending its sponsorship of bullfighting events in Mexico, and MasterCard and VISA did by pulling their support from animal circuses (see Solution 45).

The Power of Business

By donating a portion of income from my business, Competitive Edge Resumes, I can make at least a small dent in the inhumane treatment of animals.

— Carolyn Cott, on her company's commitment to the WSPA

Businesses can, and do, make an enormous contribution to animal welfare. With advertising budgets that dwarf those of action groups, and sometimes those of governments, they are able to promote causes very effectively, while influencing the corporate community to follow suit. From local cooperatives to international corporations, businesses drive economies and set cultural trends, having a profound effect on the well-being of animals.

Supermarkets — With Americans consuming $900 billion of fresh and processed food a year,[1] supermarkets have a great ability to promote animal compassion by selling local and organic meat and produce, ensuring humane methods by their suppliers and clearly labeling products to keep their customers informed. Whole Foods Market created an "Animal

In 2005, Wild Oats Marketplace became the first major US supermarket chain to commit to buying only cage-free eggs.

Compassionate Label" for its stores, and Marks & Spencer ensures that its suppliers follow the Farm Animal Council's Five Freedoms (see Solution 48).

Restaurants — A busy independent North American restaurant typically serves up to 4,000 meals a month, while a large hotel restaurant serves up to 30,000.[2] They can help animals on a large scale by offering vegetarian and vegan menu items, using local and organic suppliers and informing staff about the source of ingredients. In Washington DC, 125 restaurants and bakeries display a "Proud to Serve Vegetarian & Vegan Meal" decal on their front doors, promoting compassionate choice (see Solution 47).

Agriculture — Nearly 40% of the Earth's land surface is dedicated to agricultural use.[3] Farmers, and all agricultural businesses, can help wildlife, domestic animals and the environment by farming organically, practising humane animal husbandry, preserving greenspace and creating local farming cooperatives. On their 300-acre sheep ranch in the Montana Rockies, the Hayne family enlisted the help of Defenders of Wildlife to help them coexist with the area's grizzly bears (see Solution 34). In Ontario, Tom Manly made the switch from dairy farming to organic crop farming and created Homestead Organics, a busy feed and seed store that has helped drive the growth of organic farming in his area (see Solution 35).

Manufacturing — By offering animal-friendly options to consumers, businesses can raise awareness, broaden their market, drive healthy competition and, most importantly, directly help animals. Mercedes Benz and SAAB both offer leather-free interiors in their luxury cars. Tom's of Maine, already renowned for its animal-friendly products, is now helping wildlife and the environment by powering its manufacturing facility with renewable wind energy (see Solution 41).

Logging — Sustainable forest management is critical to both wildlife and the environment, as the Earth's forests continue to be cleared at a rate of 18 million acres a year.[4] Yet sustainable harvesting is possible on both a small and large scale. Merve Wilkinson has been managing 137 acres of forest on Vancouver Island for 60 years, and his property has more trees on it now than when he began, despite having harvested 2 million board feet of lumber. Collins Pine manages its 295,000 acres of forest sustainably, also maintaining the same standing inventory as they had in 1941 (see Solution 49).

Finance — By investing in socially conscious sources, and informing their clients about ethical investment options, the financial sector can have a profound effect on animals' well-being, both locally and overseas. Citigroup's Salomon Brothers Asset Management teamed up with the Humane Society of the United States to create the Humane Equity Fund, ensuring that money isn't invested in companies that harm animals or their environment (see Solution 41). Citigroup used its financial influence to halt illegal logging by a client in Southeast Asia and worked with Conservation International to fund sustainable businesses in South America and Africa (see Solution 50).

Fashion — With alternatives becoming not only available but "fashionable," many clothing and accessory manufacturers and retailers are offering animal-free options, or turning away from animal products altogether. More than a dozen fashion industry leaders have opted out of carrying products made from animal fur. Some, like Ralph Lauren, have been innovative in dealing with their stockpile of furs, donating them to charities for distribution in developing nations (see Solution 46).

Googling Compassion

Internet giant Google, with the Web's most used search engine, took a stand for animal welfare in 2006, announcing that its staff cafeterias would no longer serve eggs from hens confined to cages. Google's cage-free move is significant — the corporation employs 8,000 people, serving over 300,000 eggs a year, along with 7,000 pounds of liquid egg products.

- American Advertising Federation: www.aaf.org
- Better Business Bureau: www.bbb.org
- Canadian Council of Better Business Bureaus: www.ccbbb.ca
- Caring Consumer: www.caringconsumer.com
- Ethical Media: www.ethicalmedia.com
- PETA Business Friends: www.petabusinessfriends.com

The Power of Government

> There comes a time when one must take a position that is neither safe, nor political, nor popular, but he must take it because his conscience tells him that it is right.
>
> — Martin Luther King, Jr.

Policy-makers at all levels of government can play a major role in the well-being of animals. From municipal bylaws to international treaties, progressive legislation can preserve ecosystems, protect endangered species, ensure the humane treatment of farm animals, provide safe communities for companion animals, find alternatives to animal testing and chart a course to a sustainable, more compassionate global community.

Municipal — Arcata, California, transformed a toxic landfill into a vibrant 75-acre wildlife sanctuary that is home to 300 species of birds and mammals (see Solution 26). Montclair, New Jersey, practises humane pest control with the use of an innovative lighting system to prevent its parks from being overrun with geese (see Solution 30). Chicago, Illinois, was the first North American city to ban the sale of foie gras (see Solution 29). Montreal, Quebec, helps maintain a network of

100 community gardens, providing produce to 10,000 people and greenspace for birds and small wildlife (see Solution 27). Vancouver, BC, let their residents have the deciding vote on whether to keep its Stanley Park Zoo, and they voted no, prompting its closure (see Solution 28). Barcelona, Spain, banned bullfighting in their city, ending a tradition that killed 100 bulls a year (see Solution 28).

State/Provincial — Oregon initiated a progressive plan to restore the state's wolf population (see Solution 65). South Carolina prohibits the exhibition of whales and dolphins (see Solution 54). Fourteen American states ban the ownership of large exotic pets (see Solution 57). Ten Canadian provinces ban penned hunts (see Solution 53). Victoria, Australia, bans the use of glue traps for pest control (see Solution 58). Virginia worked with PETA to implement an innovative solution to beavers causing floods (see Solution 58).

Federal — Germany altered its constitution to include animals, and its Animal Welfare Act is among the strongest such legislation in the world (see Solution 51). The United Kingdom outlawed the hunting of foxes with dogs, ending a long-standing and controversial pastime (see Solution 51). Denmark prohibits the exhibition or performance of wild animals (see Solution 54). Israel, the Slovak Republic and Argentina ban dissections from school classrooms (see Solution 59). Austria bans the use of battery cages on chicken farms (see Solution 62). New Zealand set aside 24.4% of its total land mass as parklands and wildlife reserves (see Solution 63) and prohibits the captivity of, and experimentation on, great apes (see Solution 66). The United States bans the import of wild-caught parrots (see Solution 69). Brazil, with the announcement of two new protected areas, has created a 100,000 square mile rainforest corridor for wildlife and people (see Solution 73).

Global — The European Union, with its 50 member nations, is raising global awareness about animal welfare through groundbreaking international agreements that recognize animals as "sentient beings" (see Solution 91), improve the lives of veal calves (see Solution 62), protect companion animals with the Convention for the Protection of Pet Animals (see Solution 55), ban the testing of cosmetics on animals (see Solution 60), support the organic conversion process for farmers (see Solution 61) and ban the use of antibiotics and related growth promoting drugs in farm animals (see Solution 78).

The government alliance with the most impact on animal welfare on a global scale is the United Nations. With its Environment Programme (UNEP) and conservation focused conventions, the UN, with 189 member nations, is critical to the creation of a global agreement on animal welfare (see Solution 93).

The Convention on International Trade in Endangered Species (CITES) governs the trade in plants and animals, with 168 nations having ratified the treaty, protecting species from extinction and mandating the humane treatment of wildlife (see Solution 94).

- CITES: www.cites.org
- European Union: www.europa.eu
- IUCN: www.iucn.org
- UNEP: www.unep.org
- United Nations: www.un.org
- WSPA: www.wspa-international.org
- WWF: www.wwf.org

Uniting with the NGOs

The most important allies for governments in shaping a more compassionate society are the organizations that dedicate their efforts to animal welfare, conservation and social ethics. Their experience, research and enthusiasm help shape effective legislation, and the groups serve as well-informed liaisons between governments, individuals, schools, businesses and communities. On a global scale, governments create change by working with organizations such as the World Wildlife Fund (WWF) with 4,000 people working in 100 countries, the World Conservation Union (IUCN) uniting 111 government agencies, 800 NGOs, and 10,000 scientists in 181 countries and the World Society for the Protection of Animals (WSPA) with 650 affiliated animal welfare NGOs in 140 countries, and consultative status with the United Nations.

The Power of the Individual

If the people will lead, the leaders will follow.

— David Suzuki

L ove is inherent to all human beings and guides people from around the world to volunteer at animal shelters, become animal control officers, establish animal welfare advocacy groups and take to the road in courageous campaigns to raise awareness. These people — the messengers and emergency workers — are heroes. It's through their efforts that progress is made, and through their voices that the cause of animals is being heard.

The Elephant Guardian
Carol Buckley attended the Exotic Animal Training and Management Program at Moorpark

The Poster Brat

Lawrence Carter-Long was the United Way's "poster child" at the age of five; his signature beginning to a life dedicated to advocacy. An avid observer of movies and the media in his late teens, Lawrence began writing and campaigning for disability issues, social justice and animal welfare. He became a communications coordinator for the Animal Protection Institute, columnist for the Animals Agenda magazine, issues specialist for In Defense of Animals, advisor to NYC's League of Humane Voters and a committee member for the Humane Society's annual Genesis Awards. He also serves as Network Coordinator for the Disabilities Network of NYC, a contributing editor to Satya Magazine, and workshop facilitator in effective communication at universities across the US. In 2003 Lawrence launched his posterbrat.com website for two reasons: because he often forgets what he's been up to, and because "Sometimes a brat is the best thing to be."

College in Southern California and spent 15 years as a circus performer in North America and abroad. In 1974 she met a six-month-old elephant that had been captured from the wild for promotional purposes and fell in love, purchasing the baby and naming her Tarra. For the next 20 years, Carol and Tarra worked together as Tarra Productions, performing in circuses, movies and ads. Carol, realizing that Tarra was reaching an age when she would no longer enjoy public performances, was inspired to create a natural sanctuary for her. In 1995, with the assistance of Scott Blais, who worked for Tarra Productions, Carol purchased 400 acres of land in Hohenwald, Tennessee, and founded the Elephant Sanctuary, a non-profit organization dedicated to caring for elephants that have been retired from zoos and circuses. Carol's mission for the sanctuary was to provide a natural-habitat refuge where elephants could "once again walk the Earth in peace and dignity," and she has been doing that ever since.

The Elephant Sanctuary has grown to 2,700 acres, with three separate and protected natural environments, including a five-acre spring-fed lake, and cares for 21 African and Asian elephants. The Sanctuary is not open to the general public, as Carol ensures the elephants are no longer "on display," but she does invite donors to tour the facility with a VIP Pledge Program and has taught thousands of school children from around the world as an outreach program to raise awareness about wildlife. Carol has implemented educational programs at zoos across North America, training staff in elephant

- The Elephant Sanctuary: www.elephants.com
- Lawrence Carter-Long: www.posterbrat.com
- The Responsible Animal Care Society: www.tracs-bc.ca

management and medical care. One of her long-term goals is to create a reintroduction program for captive elephants into a semi-wild environment in Southeast Asia.

A Friend for the Foals (and Their Moms)

Sinikka Crosland spent part of her childhood in a cottage along the Similkameen River in southern British Columbia. At the age of five, she witnessed a wounded deer fleeing from a hunter. Soon after, haunted by the brief eye contact she shared with the injured animal, Sinikka declared that she was becoming a vegetarian. Although it took some years for her declaration to pass, she pursued her calling of animal advocacy to become the president of the Responsible Animal Care Society (TRACS) in Westbank, BC, and eventually became a leading voice for PMU (Pregnant Mares' Urine) horses across North America.

Premarin (Pregnant Mares' Urine) was one of the most widely prescribed drugs in the world, its production reliant upon 400 PMU farms scattered across western Canada and North Dakota where pregnant mares are confined to stalls. Their urine is collected for use in hormone replacement therapy and marketed by the corporate giant Wyeth Pharmaceuticals. The industry has been fraught with controversy, with charges that the mares are subjected to high levels of stress and suffering, and that over the years more foals have been produced than sold, resulting in their slaughter. The 2002 National Institutes of Health announcement regarding health risks associated with Premarin caused major cutbacks to the industry, leaving tens of thousands of mares and their foals looking for new homes.

Since 1997 Sinikka Crosland and TRACS, together with internationally known horse rescuer Dr. Ray Kellosalmi, have salvaged, rehabilitated and organized adoptions for hundreds of at-risk horses, many from the PMU industry.

Sinikka Crosland and Kismet, who was rescued as a foal from a PMU operation.

Building a Global Movement

All truth passes through three stages. First, it is ridiculed. Second, it is violently opposed. Third, it is accepted as being self-evident.

— Arthur Schopenhauer

It's a lot to comprehend, this imbalance of nature. We've fallen very far out of touch with other species. We've manipulated the life systems of the world to suit our needs at the expense of nearly every other species. The global community has been responsible for animal suffering in almost every arena of our lives. But that's the thing about communities. We accept responsibility together and we find solutions together. We are here as messengers for the community, to tell you of an animal awareness movement that is building all around you. What will it take to succeed?

Love of animals is a universal impulse, a common ground on which all of us may meet. By loving and understanding animals, perhaps we humans shall come to understand each other.

— Dr. Louis J. Camuti

ANIMAL ACRES

Individuals acting from love and faith, knowing that coexistence with animals is possible, and using our talents to make it happen.

Action groups constantly raising awareness about animal welfare, finding solutions to suffering and facilitating change in society.

Schools cultivating compassion in the classroom and in the hearts of children, guided by the principles of humane education.

Cities recognizing animals, wild and domestic, as part of their community and ensuring that their welfare is assured through thoughtful municipal planning and regulations.

Farmers sharing their fields with animals, embracing their connection to the environment and being responsible stewards of the land.

Fishers being accountable for the waters their vessels ply, taking part in a global conservation effort on the sea.

Businesses taking leadership in an ethical, natural economy that respects life and promotes animal awareness.

Governments on all levels, protecting the rights of species through education and legislation, ensuring animals greater respect and dignity.

Developing nations striving for sustainability for their people and the natural world, protecting their animals and wild places from outside interests.

The global community working together, recognizing the connection between all species on Earth.

> The worst sin toward our fellow creatures is not to hate them, but to be indifferent to them.
>
> — George Bernard Shaw

Listen to the Children

In 2006 a group of 650 children from 18 schools along Finland's coast gathered to discuss the fisheries crisis in the Baltic Sea, create a petition for their government and call for sustainable fishing on a global level. The Baltic Sea, one of the world's most endangered ecosystems, has already lost 50% of its commercial fish stocks, including cod, which have declined globally by 70% since 1975 and, at the current rate, face extinction by 2020.[1] The schoolchildren signed a petition, including stories, drawings and poems, and sent it to Finland's Minister of Agriculture and Forests (who is responsible for fisheries) in time for a European Union meeting addressing fishing quotas in the Baltic Sea. The event was sponsored by the World Wildlife Fund in Finland, and the WWF said the children sent a clear message that they want the government to take responsibility: "These children are the decision-makers of tomorrow."

> If only we can overcome cruelty, to human and animal, with love and compassion we shall stand at the threshold of a new era in human moral and spiritual evolution and realize, at last, our most unique quality: humanity.
>
> — Dr. Jane Goodall

PART II

ANIMAL ACRES

The 101 Solutions

1

Be Responsible for your Companion Animals

> Until one has loved an animal, a part of one's soul remains unawakened.
>
> — Anatole France

Within their first six months of life, 40% of all puppies will be searching for a new home; 60% will be homeless within a year.[1] These numbers reflect a failed bond between humans and their companion animals. At first, the bond is fresh and exciting with the cuddly furball, but then something is lost as the role of responsibility begins to settle in. Dogs and cats develop a sense of bonding quickly, and being moved again and again is terribly difficult for them.

Taking on a companion animal is a lifetime commitment. For the life of the animal, they will look to their guardian for trust, nurturing and kindness.

Gimme Shelter

Are you ready for the commitment of sharing your life with a companion animal? Then make your way to your local shelter and find a pet to adopt. The tragedy of millions of unwanted animals winding up in our landfills can only be stopped by this first step. It is senseless to bring new babies into this world to be sold as pets when our shelters and landfills are overflowing with the animals we already have. So do some homework and prepare your home and your life for a new arrival. Then visit your local shelter to meet the wonderful souls so worthy of your companionship.

Spay + Neuter = Happiness

The first reason to spay and neuter your companion animals is obvious: it will prevent them from adding to the staggering overpopulation that already exists.

- Spayed and neutered dogs and cats have healthier lives. Spaying female dogs and cats eliminates the possibility of ovarian cancer and reduces the incidence of breast cancer.[2]

- Neutering male dogs and cats reduces the incidence of prostate cancer.

- Spayed and neutered animals are calmer, friendlier, more affectionate pets.

- Neutered dogs and cats are less likely to roam, fight, run away or be hit by a car.

Be Exotic-less

Owning exotic pets invariably winds up being a bad idea. Most of these animals are the result of a $10 billion-a-year industry supported by illegal trade, with an extremely high rate of suffering and mortality, even if they were bought from a pet store. Wild animals are not domesticated the way cats and dogs have been over thousands of years. They are used to being wild, and captivity generates a lot of undesirable traits. Many diseases are transmitted from captive wild animals

- Alliance for Responsible Pet Ownership: www.adoptarpo.org
- ASPCA (United States): www.aspca.org
- Companion Animal Protection Society: www.caps-web.org
- Pets911: www.1888pets911.org
- SPAY USA: www.spayusa.org
- SPCA (Canada): www.spca.com
- Vegetarian pet food: www.vegepet.com and www.downbound.com

to both domestic animals and humans. And wild animals in captivity are inherently dangerous. Primates of all kinds, along with bears, lions, tigers and large snakes have inflicted many deadly injuries on their guardians and other animals.[3] It's just not in their nature to be held captive.

Eco-Pets

Another part of your responsibility as an animal guardian is to be accountable for your pets' effect on their environment. A single cat can wreak havoc on songbirds in a neighborhood, and many forest creatures, from field mice to deer, are forced to flee from over-zealous, off-leash dogs. When you place a domestic animal in a wild setting, you alter the balance of nature for all species present. Nor is it really fair to keep an animal cooped up inside all the time to prevent it from running amok in the wild. These are important considerations to make before bringing a companion animal home. It's not just your home and your family that are affected by your choices; it's your environment, too.

Naturalanimal storefront in Montreal, Quebec.

DIANA BOKHARI

Can Dogs and Cats Be Vegetarians?

Can your companion animal exist on a vegetarian diet, lessening its impact on the world around them?[4] Companies such as Vegepet and DownBound provide vegan dog and cat foods that meet the nutritional levels established by the Association of American Feed Control Officials.

That being said, dogs are far more carnivorous than humans by nature, and cats are true carnivores. Replacing the nutrients they find from animal sources may be detrimental to their health, and it is a choice that they would be unlikely to make on their own. For optimal health, dogs and cats should also be fed as much raw food as possible, as is their nature, and it helps prevent arthritis, allergies and pregnancy complications associated with cooked commercial pet food.[5]

Diana Bokhari, of Naturalanimal & Pawtisserie Holistic Pet Center in Montreal, suggests that people consider preparing their pets' foods so that they know what goes into it and buy meats from small farmers who treat their animals with kindness.

2

Practise Humane "Pest" Control

You should have compassion and loving kindness for all living beings without exception, from the tiniest insect to the largest being, because all of them, just as you do, wish to be happy and have a desire to experience bliss.

— Yangthang Rinpoche

From ants and aphids to dogs and deer, there is a humane way to deter just about any unwanted creature from sharing your space. Ordinary household items — such as spices, eggshells and paper bags — can be very effectively used for pest prevention. Your best tools in coping with the unwelcome visitors are tolerance, patience and innovation.[1]

Ultrasound

Ultrasound devices deter birds, insects, mice and even larger animals like dogs and deer; they are harmless to the creatures they deter and inaudible to humans. Ask your local hardware store or garden center if they carry them. If not, ask them to order one for you.

Ants

Paprika is the easiest and best natural deterrent for ants. I've used it and it works. Sprinkle a little line of paprika near ant entryways, but be careful not get it wet because it will stain.

Carpenter Ants

Carpenter ants are attracted to two things: wood and moisture. Preventing the combination of these two is a necessity. This means staying on top of things like clogged gutters, leaky plumbing and rotting decks. Piles of wood and overhanging tree branches should be kept away from all buildings.

Cats

Is your cat, or your neighbors' cat, wreaking havoc in your garden? Try Coleus Canina — a plant that is scentless to humans but effective at discouraging cats by imitating the smell of a tom cat's urine.

Fleas

Vacuuming your carpets and combing your companion animals on a regular basis is the key to preventing fleas. Lightly spraying tea-tree oil or lavender across a carpet also helps as a deterrent. Removing the carpets makes it easier to clean the eggs up.

Flies and Mosquitoes

Burn citronella or basil oil near open windows to prevent flies and mosquitoes

US NATIONAL PARK SERVICE

> **Bug fact** — Daddy-long-legs are not spiders! They look like them but don't have two body sections as spiders do. Most important to all arachnophobes, daddy-long-legs can not bite.

Selling Humane Pest Control

- Abundant Earth: www.abundantearth.com/store/naturalpestcontrol.html
- Dreaming Earth Botanicals: www.dreamingearth.com Click on "Pest Control Products - All Natural".
- Eartheasy Natural Pest Control: www.eartheasy.com/live_natpest_control.htm
- Green Culture Pest Control: www.eco-pestcontrol.com
- Promolife Inc: www.promolife.com/products/u_sonic2.htm
- Tree World Inc: www.plantskydd.com

from entering. Citronella candles are fairly effective outside as well, as long as they're close to where you're sitting.

Mice and Rats

Prevent all access to food. Compost can be kept mouse-free by placing a wire mesh under the pile, mixing the pile regularly and covering new compost with yard clippings. Buy a fully enclosed, circular compost bin for food scraps. Humane live traps are very effective for mice and rats. Relocate the mouse or rat at least a mile away — they'll come right back if released in your neighborhood. Emptying live traps can be impractical if you live in an urban area, so rely more on prevention than trapping.

Raccoons

Trim tree branches that allow roof and attic access, seal openings in sheds with ¼" hardware cloth and place a border of lime around your garden. If they're nesting, wait for the litter to be old enough to leave on their own in 6 to 8 weeks.

Slugs and Snails

Any jagged material, such as crushed eggshells or sharp gravel, works well as a deterrent. Encourage predators (such as snakes), pick the slugs off by hand or place plastic rings with outward-sloping sides around your plants. You can get creative with household items to create these rings or buy one of several products now available from garden centers.

Spiders

A spray made with chestnut and clove scents deters spiders. They can also be caught under an upside-down clear glass by sliding a piece of paper underneath and then releasing them outside. If you don't like catching them, there are battery-operated devices that allow you to gently vacuum up spiders, wasps and other crawling and hovering insects and release them outside without harm.

Wasps

Try inflating a brown paper bag and tying it above a doorway, or wherever wasps are unwanted. They think the bag is another wasp nest and choose to avoid the area. I've found this method to be very effective. Many stores now sell an even more realistic looking replica for the same purpose.

Tolerance

The ultimate method of coping with pests is practicing tolerance. Once we get past our fear and move to a level of tolerance, we find that many of the living beings we share our space with aren't actually pests at all. And tolerance, if nurtured, tends to get easier as it grows.

3

Let Go of Reliance on Animal Products

It may take a little extra time, but finding cruelty-free alternatives to mainstream products has gotten much easier over the years — a little inconvenience on our parts isn't much in light of what it means for the animals.

— Phil Murray, Pangea Vegan Products

The simple choices we make throughout the day can reduce suffering in a big way. Not eating animals and not wearing animals is only the beginning. We're also using them in household items, sporting equipment, construction, medicine and cosmetics. Nearly all of this is unnecessary if we think of animals each time we pull out our wallet.

The A to Z List for Compassionate Alternatives[1]

Animal Fats and Oils — in foods, cosmetics:

- Olive oil, canola oil, wheat-germ oil, coconut oil, flaxseed oil, almond oil, safflower oil.

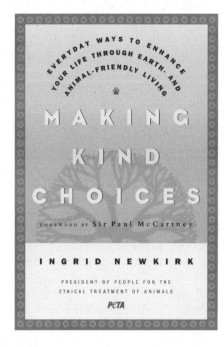

EVERYDAY WAYS TO ENHANCE YOUR LIFE THROUGH EARTH- AND ANIMAL-FRIENDLY LIVING

MAKING KIND CHOICES

FOREWORD BY Sir Paul McCartney

INGRID NEWKIRK

PRESIDENT OF PEOPLE FOR THE ETHICAL TREATMENT OF ANIMALS

PETA

Making Kind Choices, by Ingrid Newkirk. A must-have for compassionate consumers.

Bone Meal — crushed or ground animal bones, used in fertilizers, vitamins, supplements (as a source of calcium) and some toothpaste:

- Plant mulch, vegetable compost, dolomite and clay for fertilizer. Vegetarian vitamins.

Casein, Caseinate, Sodium Caseinate — milk protein, used in non-dairy creamers, soy cheese, many cosmetics, hair preparations and beauty masks:

- Soy protein, soy milk and other vegetable milks. Vegan soy cheese.

Down — insulating feathers from slaughtered geese and ducks, used as an insulator in quilts, parkas, sleeping bags and pillows:

- Polyester and synthetic substitutes, kapok and milkweed seed-pod fibers.

Estrogen and Estradiol — female hormones from pregnant mares' urine, used for reproductive problems, in birth control pills and in Premarin; a menopausal drug:

- Oral contraceptives and menopausal drugs based on synthetic steroids or phytoestrogens (from plants, especially palm-kernel oil). Menopausal symptoms can also be treated with diet and herbs.

Fish Liver Oil — used in vitamins, supplements and in cow's milk fortified with vitamin D:

- Yeast extract ergosterol, and exposure of the skin to sunshine.

Gelatin and Gel — obtained by boiling animal skin, tendons, ligaments and/or bones with water. Used in shampoos, face masks and other

- Animal Concerns: www.animalconcerns.org
- CaringConsumer.com: www.caringconsumer.com
- Compassionate Consumers: www.compassionateconsumers.org

cosmetics, as a thickener for fruit gelatins and puddings (e.g., Jello), in candies, marshmallows, cakes, ice cream, yogurts, on photographic film and in vitamins as a coating or capsules:

- Agar agar, carrageen, seaweeds, pectin from fruits, dextrins, locust-bean gum, cotton gum, silica gel. Marshmallows were originally made from the root of the marsh mallow plant. Vegetarian capsules are now available from several companies. Using a digital camera eliminates the need for gelatin used in film.

Insulin — from pig pancreas, used by millions of diabetics daily:

- Synthetics, vegetarian diet and nutritional supplements; human insulin grown in a lab.

Lard — fat from hog abdomens, used in shaving creams, soaps, cosmetics, baked goods, french fries, refried beans and many other foods:

- Pure vegetable fats or oils.

Monoglycerides and Glycerides — from animal fat, used in margarines, cake mixes, candies, bread, other foods and in cosmetics:

- Vegetable glycerides.

Rennet and Rennin — enzyme from calves' stomachs, used in cheese-making, rennet custard (junket) and many coagulated dairy products:

- Microbial coagulating agents, bacteria culture, lemon juice, vegetable rennet.

Sable Brushes — from the fur of sables (weasels native to Siberia), used in eye makeup, lipstick and artists' brushes:

- Synthetic fibers.

Welcome to Pangea

In business since 1995, Pangea Vegan Products was the pioneer company to offer a comprehensive selection of high-quality, cruelty-free, vegan (non-animal-derived) products. Based in Rockville, Maryland, Pangea offers a vast array of high-quality products, all available online, and 100% vegan. Pangea is one-stop shopping for the compassionate consumer. I've owned a pair of Pangea's No Bull vegan work boots for over three years and happily attest to their quality and durability. www.veganstore.com

Steroids and Sterols — from various animal glands, used in hormone preparation, creams, lotions, hair conditioners and fragrances:

- Plant tissues, synthetics.

Vitamin A — from fish liver oil, shark liver oil, egg yolk and butter; an aliphatic alcohol used in cosmetics, creams, perfumes, hair dyes, vitamins and supplements:

- Carrots, other vegetables, synthetics.

Vitamin B-12 — from animal products or bacteria cultures. Twinlab B-12 vitamins contain gelatin:

- Vegetarian vitamins, fortified soy milks, nutritional yeast and fortified meat substitutes.

Whey — a serum from milk, used in cakes, cookies, candies, breads and cheese-making:

- Soybean whey.

4

Learn to Recognize Animal Suffering

Think occasionally of the
suffering of which you spare
yourself the sight.

— Albert Schweitzer

The first step to ending animal suffering is to recognize it happening. By observing life with a compassionate eye, we can be a voice for those in need. Often we can be the helping hands that might save their lives. This is where advocacy starts — in awareness.

A Friend in Need

Some tell-tale signs of an animal, wild or domestic, that needs your help:

- visible wounds on their body, patches of missing hair, limping or showing pain
- emaciated, clearly visible ribs, other signs of malnutrition
- struck by a car or any other physical injury
- being struck or harassed by anybody, or attacked by another animal
- cowering in fear when you or anyone else approaches them
- confined in extreme weather without shelter

Animal First Aid

The Palo Alto Humane Society, in conjunction with the American Red Cross, has an excellent online guide to animal first aid. It lists animal first aid supplies to have on hand, vital statistics for cats and dogs and detailed handling instructions, along with first aid procedures for cats, dogs, birds, small mammals and reptiles. The guide also reminds us that all injuries involving fractures, bleeding, burns or shock require immediate veterinary care.

A Helping Hand

A wild animal or bird can often be helped by gently moving it to a safe area and leaving it where it can recuperate on its own. It's best to interfere as little as possible with wild animals and birds in their recovery, particularly if they are babies. If it's just a matter of catching and releasing a trapped songbird, or assisting a snake across a road, the simple act of moving them to safety is all that is required. If a wild animal or bird is injured and in pain, it's time to call for help and stay with them to protect them from further injury.

With domestic animals, often just providing a little kindness is enough; like giving a dish of water to a dog that has been left out in the sun. Do not put yourself in between an animal and its guardian. If you suspect a person is abusing their animal companion, contact the proper authority to deal with the matter as soon as possible.

Who to Call

Every region and municipality has different rules for whom to contact for animal welfare and rescue. Some areas rely on their police forces, while others have animal control officers and fish and wildlife agents. Ask questions, and get informed. When you see an animal in pain, vital time can be wasted trying to find someone who can help. The ASPCA website has a section that helps people find local animal services across the United States (see resource list). The SPCA has a similar guide for Canadians. Both websites have guides to finding your local SPCA office to report animal emergencies.

When reporting an incident of animal suffering, it's important to get as many details as possible, such as the location, time and who was involved. This will help the rescue service respond the most efficiently and helpfully.

Know Their Legal Rights

Animals in nearly all regions, both wild and domestic, fall under some legal jurisdiction. Some have significant protection from abuse and neglect, while others have no protection whatsoever. It's up to us, as animal advocates and compassionate citizens, to know what our local legislators can do about animal welfare and assistance. Make a call or send a letter to your municipal and regional government to find out how far you can go, and how far they will go, to help animals in need. If you don't like their answer, request a change in legislation. Both the SPCA and ASPCA have online guides to help you find your local legislators.

Make Friends with Your Shelter

Visit your local animal shelter and veterinary offices and ask for information on rescuing and assisting animals in need. They will give you lots of literature and local contact information. While you're there, you can volunteer to take one of their furry tenants out for a stroll.

Part of being aware of animal suffering is demonstrating compassion yourself. Give your animal companions lots of love and care. And be aware of what's going on around you. Your awareness and compassion will rub off on others.

A rescued lamb at Animal Acres' shelter in Acton, California.

- American Society for the Prevention of Cruelty to Animals (ASPCA): www.aspca.org
- Palo Alto Humane Society Animal First Aid: www.preparenow.org/fa-anim.html
- Pets 911: www.pets911.com
- Society for the Prevention of Cruelty to Animals (SPCA): www.spca.com

5

Switch to a Meatless Diet

Nothing will benefit human health and increase chances of survival for life on Earth as much as the evolution to a vegetarian diet.

— Albert Einstein

One of the simplest, most fundamental ways to reduce animal suffering is to stop eating them. There are so many reasons to do so.

For You and Your Family

Vegetarians live longer than average and suffer less from high cholesterol, heart problems, diabetes, cancer and other ailments linked to the consumption of meat.[1] Vegans consume absolutely no animal products at all and share the health benefits of vegetarians.[2] Meat contains protein and other important nutrients because animals eat plant sources that are high in these nutrients. Vegetarians and vegans go straight to the source.

For the Planet

A 10% reduction in our meat consumption could feed every starving man, woman and

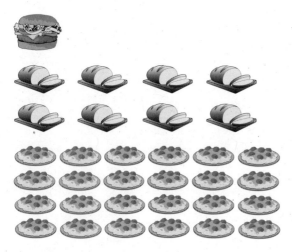

1 hamburger = 8 loaves of bread = 24 plates of spaghetti.

child on this planet,[3] since it takes far more resources to grow food for meat production than it does to feed humans. Twelve pounds of grain go into the production of every hamburger. That's enough grain to make 8 loaves of bread or 24 plates of spaghetti.[4] And it goes way beyond that. Animals (livestock) bound for our dinner tables are sucking up our water supply much faster than nature can replenish it. The Ogallala Aquifer, a gigantic underground body of water that stretches from South Dakota to Texas, is being drained so quickly that, at its current rate of depletion, it will be empty by 2050.[5] The environmental and social impact of this catastrophe to people who live in the US Midwest isn't fully comprehendible, but it will be devastating. What's draining the aquifer so quickly? Mainly cows and pigs destined to become beef and pork. A single pound of beef requires over 5,000 gallons of water to produce. A pound of tomatoes requires just 23 gallons.[6] And it's still more than that. Our forests are in crisis. We have lost 80% of our old-growth forests worldwide,[7] often to clear land to range more cows to produce more beef for North American dinner tables. At the current rate of deforestation, there will be virtually no rainforest left by 2050.[8]

For the Animals

People argue that if you don't eat farm animals there will be no need for them to live, and they won't be born at all. But perhaps not being born at all is better than being born into a life of captivity, overcrowding, manipulation, fear and

- EarthSave International: www.earthsave.org
- *The Food Revolution: How Your Diet Can Help Save Your Life and the World*, by John Robbins, www.foodrevolution.org
- Jo Stepaniak's site: www.vegsource.com
- Physicians Committee for Responsible Medicine: www.pcrm.org
- Vegetarian Resource Group: www.vrg.org
- *The New Becoming Vegetarian*, by Vesanto Melina and Brenda Davis, Healthy Living Publications, 2003. An excellent guide for those who choose to make a dietary shift away from animal products. A comprehensive and wonderful resource for every home.

The New BECOMING VEGETARIAN

THE ESSENTIAL GUIDE TO A HEALTHY VEGETARIAN DIET
complete nutrition information for all age groups
♦ recipes ♦ vegetarian food guide ♦ disease prevention ♦

VESANTO MELINA, MS, RD & BRENDA DAVIS, RD

slaughterhouses. Over 10 billion animals are slaughtered every year in the United States alone. Right now, as you read this, animals are being slaughtered for food at the rate of 317 per second. If you stop eating meat right now and don't eat any more meat for the next year, you will save the lives of 35 animals.[9]

But Don't We Need Meat?

Ask Jo Stepaniak. She's an author and educator who has pursued vegan and vegetarian issues for over four decades and who has raised three beautiful, healthy children on a vegan diet.

Or ask Carl Lewis. One of the most famous and decorated Olympians ever, he won nine Olympic gold medals and he's a vegan.

Or ask actor Alicia Silverstone, rock star Bryan Adams, Dr. Benjamin Spock, US Congressman Dennis Kucinich, actor Ed Begley Jr., singer Fiona Apple, actors Joaquin and Summer Phoenix, actor Keenan Ivory Wayens, artist Peter Max, tennis champion Peter Burwash, three-time Ironman athlete Ruth Heidrich, singer Shania Twain, actor Tea Leoni or marathon runner Sally Eastall. All vegans, every one of them. The list is a lot longer than that. None of us needs to eat meat.

World Meat Consumption[10]

	Annual average per person (lbs)
United States	275
Canada	238
Argentina	215
Italy	199
Germany	181
Brazil	181
United Kingdom	175
Norway	136
Mexico	129
China	115
South Africa	89
All Developed Nations	176

The other end of the scale

Indonesia	18
India	11
All Developing Nations	64

* Note: These figures are for land animals only. Averages include vegetarians, so the actual numbers are higher.

6

Do Without Dairy

Ninety percent of our dioxin intake, which causes cancer and other serious problems, comes from eating dairy.

— Dr. John McDougall, author, nutrition educator and founder of the McDougall Program[1]

The introductory section "Deceptions of Dairy" is an important building block for this solution. Milk, cheese, butter, yogurt and ice cream are deeply entrenched in our lives. Only with a thorough understanding of the suffering of animals, and the detriment to our health that dairy products cause, can we make an informed choice to do without dairy.

For the Health of It

A move away from dairy benefits our health immediately. Once we've been weaned off our

Soy Quick Automatic Soy Milk Maker — This great machine makes soy milk, tofu, rice milk and more.
www.biosupply.com/soy_milk_maker.htm.

mothers' milk, our bodies begin producing less of the enzyme lactase that breaks down and absorbs milk sugar (lactose). Over 80% of people who are descended from Native North Americans, Africans and Asians suffer from lactose intolerance.[2] This results in many people suffering from intestinal problems without knowing what's causing their discomfort. However, people who react to conventional milk are often not allergic to organic milk. Most people have no idea to what extent dairy products are affecting their long-term health. Cow's milk contains no fiber or antioxidants for us, and it's very high in fat: 2% milk is, in truth, comprised of 35% milk fat.[3]

Milk alternatives — There are a wide range of milk alternatives on the market. If your grocery stores doesn't carry them, ask them to, or you can make your own alternatives. Several companies now sell soy milk makers, and the cost of buying one will be easily offset by the long-term savings of not buying cow's milk or soy milk in cartons.

Cheese alternatives — Most of the cheese alternatives on the market contain casein, a dairy derivative, and you're not helping any veal calves, or their mothers, by consuming it. There are a few truly vegan cheese alternatives, but I recommend using a natural substitute. Red Star nutritional yeast sprinkled on just about any dish gives your meal a distinctly cheesy flavour and gives you a good vitamin B_{12} kick at the same time.

Butter alternatives — There's a simple substitute for butter in just about every recipe — vegetable oil. Organic olive oil and canola oil are the healthiest. Vegetable-based margarine makes a good substitute for butter, but check the ingredients for whey (yes, whey is dairy). Earth Balance Natural Buttery Spread is a favorite made from certified organic ingredients with no trans (hydrogenated) fat. Trans fats are created by heating unsaturated fats until they become saturated, as is done in many brands of margarine, and should be avoided, so read the labels carefully.

Ice cream alternatives — Ice cream is the proverbial dairy favorite. Check your market coolers for Soy Delicious, Soy Dream, Rice Dream and other non-dairy frozen desserts. These companies have become so good at making organic natural ingredients taste like conventional ice cream that most people would never be able to tell the difference. They're delicious. If your markets don't carry them, ask them to. You deserve a taste.

Are you still skeptical about eliminating dairy from your diet? Good — skepticism can get you everywhere. Visit the websites and read the books by the doctors listed; all are well-respected doctors who have a wealth of information and many reasons for adopting a dairy-free life.

Got Calcium?[4]

Food Sources with 150 or more mg per serving (RDA 1000-1300 mg/day)*	Calcium (mg)/serving
Blackstrap molasses	342/2 Tbsp
Tofu, processed with calcium sulphate	200-330/½ cup
Fortified soy or rice milk	150-500/cup
Collard greens (cooked)	357/cup
Fortified orange juice	300/cup
Cow's milk (whole)	290/cup
Commercial soy yogurt	250/¾ cup
Turnip greens	249/cup
Tofu, processed with nigari	80-230/½ cup
Kale (cooked)	179/cup
Okra (cooked)	176/cup
Soybeans (cooked)	175/cup
Sesame seeds	160/2 tbsp
Bok Choy (cooked)	158/cup
Tempeh	154/cup
Mustard greens (cooked)	152/cup

*RDA = Recommended Daily Allowance established by the United States Department of Agriculture (USDA) for adults.

- Dr. Neal Barnard: www.nealbarnard.org
- Dr. Colin Campbell: www.thechinastudy.com/authors.html
- Dr. Michael Greger: www.drgreger.org
- Dr. Michael Klaper: www.drklaper.com
- Dr. John McDougall: www.drmcdougall.com
- Dr. Dean Ornish: www.pmri.org

7

Begin in Your Own Backyard

Even with my tight budget and tiny suburban lot, I found that I could do much to attract and benefit wildlife. I have bettered my little corner of the world. That's what creating an urban wildlife sanctuary is all about.

— Backyard naturalist Sydney Smith in the Humane Society's *Wild Neighbor News*

The number one threat facing wildlife today is habitat loss, partly due to ever-expanding urban sprawl. Our communities continue to spread into open fields and deeper into nature, laying down a blanket of green lawns and concrete sidewalks.

These little blocks of real estate we "own" are under our stewardship. We bought the land, and with it we acquired a responsibility. Now is the time to invite nature to return. The first step is to walk outside, breathe deeply, take a close look at the environment we've chosen and try to imagine how it was before we arrived. The prospect of recreating wildlife habitat can seem rather daunting.

Now What?
Fortunately, there are resources to get you started. Several years ago, the National Wildlife Federation ran an article in *National Wildlife Magazine* encouraging people to landscape and garden in a more sustainable, natural way.

- Backyard Gardener:
  www.backyardgardener.com/organic
- Backyard Sanctuary on a Budget:
  www.projectwildlife.org/gardens_backyardsanctuary.htm
- Backyard Wildlife Sanctuary:
  www.wdfw.wa.gov/wlm/backyard
- Naturescape British Columbia:
  www.hctf.ca/naturescape/resources.htm
- Rooftop Gardens: www.cityfarmer.org/rooftop59.html
- Wildlife Gardening: www.wildlife-gardening.co.uk

The response was so overwhelming that they began their Backyard Wildlife Habitat Program, teaching people how to restore habitat and harmony to their backyards, apartment balconies, townhouse patios, workplaces and communities.

Once you've created a new landscape, you can apply to the National Wildlife Federation to have your yard certified as one of more than 38,000 designated sites around the world (www.nwf.org/backyardwildlifehabitat).

The Canadian Wildlife Federation (CWF) also offers a certification program (www.wildaboutgardening.org/en/gab/section5_certify). CWF's Backyard Habitat Certification Program focuses on wildlife-friendly gardening, earth-friendly gardening and naturalized habitat.

The Humane Society of the United States' Urban Wildlife Sanctuary Program (UWSP) helps individuals and communities assess and improve their property for wildlife habitat. You don't need a backyard to enroll; UWSP shows you how to create butterfly gardens and birdfeeders on apartment balconies, and members receive educational material, a sign designating the property as an Official Urban Wildlife Sanctuary and a subscription to *Wild Neighbor News* (www.hsus.org/wildlife/wildlife_and_habitat_protection_programs).

Limit Your Lawn
Lawns offer little in the way of food and shelter for wildlife. By replacing lawns with ground-cover plants, you can build islands of vegetation with as many varieties of native plants and flowers as possible, and create a habitat for wildlife from butterflies to birds.

Keep it organic and make your backyard a pesticide- and chemical fertilizer-free zone. Practice humane pest control (see Solution 2), use compost to fertilize your soil and encourage insect-eating birds to visit.

Work with your neighbors, create large patches of habitat and invite more wildlife into your backyards. Designate areas near your property lines as wildlife corridors, offering undisturbed areas for birds and animals to move through in peace.

Spreading the Word
Callawassie Island, South Carolina, has a population of just 800, yet has 75 NWF Certified Backyard Wildlife Habitats. The island had 54 certified sites, but Dorothy Mosior, and the Ecology Committee, launched a "Friendly Persuasion" campaign, to get people with certified yards to talk to their neighbors about the benefits of creating wildlife habitat. The campaign was successful, becoming a community effort, and in 2006, the island achieved NWF Community Wildlife Habitat certification.

Bird-feeding Basics

Will feeding birds in your backyard discourage them from migrating? Not according to the National Audubon Society. Seasonal changes in the length of day, rather than an abundance of food, determines when birds migrate. So welcome birds into your life by creating as hospitable an environment as possible.

- **Window collisions** — Position bird feeders within three feet of a window. This prevents them from gaining enough velocity to hurt themselves.
- **Collisions with cats** — Forget the warning bells; cats can easily keep them quiet while stalking birds. Place bird feeders at least ten feet away from foliage or where cats can wait in hiding.
- **Squirrel raiders** — Squirrels can leap six feet and climb into just about any feeder. Build your bird feeder on a pole and keep it more than six feet away from a tree or building. An inverted sheet metal cone on the pole should keep the furry acrobats away.
- **Audubon** has an excellent in-depth resource on bird feeding. Visit www.audubon.org/bird/at_home/ bird_feeding.

8

Find Your Niche in Animal Welfare

In 1989 I saw a documentary on television about the traditional slaughter of dolphins and whales in the Faroe Islands. That one small television piece changed my life forever.

— Aaron Koolen, videographer,
Meat Free Media

To create change, your voice must be heard. The greatest representation of how you feel, the truth within your heart, must sing out through your voice. How do you make that happen? By simply doing what you love to do. If you love to paint, paint about animal welfare. If you love to sing, write songs about animal welfare.

Animals in Translation

Author and animal advocate Temple Grandin found her niche and used it to help on a large scale by helping to relieve some of the suffering within meat-packing plants. She used her own experience with autism and her understanding of animals to develop an apparatus that soothes animals on their way to slaughter. Her first step was to create such a machine for herself and then test it on the animals. Her invention was extremely successful, and is now used in nearly half the meat-packing plants in North America. Her innovation led to her being hired as an

auditor, using her unique understanding of animals to guide plant operators in the choices they make. There are still miles to go within the industry, but Temple Grandin has made it a little easier for millions of the animals who have to go through it. She is also the author of two books: *Animals in Translation: Using the Mysteries of Autism to Decode Animal Behavior*, and *Thinking in Pictures*.

Painting 4 Paws

Karen Derrico found her voice through painting. In 2004 she created Painting 4 Paws: Art with a Cause, blending her love of art and animals. Each month, she selects two animals from rescue groups and paints portraits of them. She then places the paintings up for "adoption" on her website (www.painting4paws.com), charging a nominal adoption fee, and includes a certificate and a story about each animal. She then donates a portion of her fee to the rescue organization that provided her animal subject. Her paintings have included many rescued animals, including monkeys, pigs, ducks, horses, cats, dogs and cows. Karen's art, and her goal of finding loving homes for homeless pets, led to the release of her book: *Unforgettable Mutts: Pure of Heart, Not of Breed*.

Food Without a Face

When singer/songwriter Heidi Howe was a teenager, she had an inspiring vegetarian friend who played guitar, and Heidi began learning about music and animals. While studying music in Kentucky, she spent time with a group called

- Animal Concerns: www.animalconcerns.org
- Animal Defenders International: www.ad-international.org/take_action
- Care 2 Make a Difference: www.care2.com
- Earth Island Institute: www.earthisland.org
- Institute for Animals in Society: www.animalsandsociety.org
- North American Vegetarian Society: www.navs-online.org

Youth for Causes, and got inspired to make a difference. She became a vegan in 1995, while beginning her musical career, and was able to donate a portion of the proceeds from her second CD to EarthSave, Louisville. In 2001 she found a way to raise awareness about animals and help EarthSave International, by writing a song called *Food Without a Face*, and launched a national tour by the same name in 2002. The successful tour finished back home in Louisville, with a turkey-free Thanksgiving dinner and concert, hosted by EarthSave (www.heidihowe.com).

Compassion on Camera

Photographer Derek Goodwin became a vegan in 1996 and worked with the Animal Defense League and Rochester Area Vegetarian Society until 1999, when he moved to Massachusetts. It was there he became established as a professional photographer, all the time guided by his commitment to animal welfare. He began photographing several vegan weddings each year, served as photography advisor to *Veg News Magazine* and worked with Dr. Michael Greger to photograph covers for informational nutrition DVDs. He became the co-host and producer of *Vegan Radio*, in North Hampton (103.3 FM), and created a website designed for animal-friendly artists, musicians, writers and craftspeople (www.veganica.com). Since 2001 Derek has been the primary photographer for Farm Sanctuary, using his talents to promote the cause of the animals in their New York and California shelters, as well as photographing the sanctuary's promotional events across the country.

How It All Vegan

Sarah Kramer and Tanya Barnard found their voice for animals by writing a popular cookbook loaded with delicious animal-free recipes and advice for a compassionate lifestyle. Barely a vegetarian household exists without *How It All Vegan* in their kitchen. After the success of their first book, they teamed up again, writing *The Garden of Vegan*. Sarah went on to write a third book on her own, called *La Dolce Vegan*, as well as creating a website dedicated to animal friendly living (www.govegan.net).

9

Campaign until the Cows Come Home

Don't be shy, pluck up the courage and speak for them, please, because the animals need desperately every single one of us.

— Ingrid Newkirk

How do you get your cause heard? You believe wholeheartedly in ending animal suffering, but when you talk to people, a lot of them brush off what you're saying. Family and friends are more likely to listen if they hear it from the media, rather than you. When they see it on TV, or read about it in a magazine, they start to pay attention. Many a well-intentioned person has given up on their cause after having their spirits crushed by a skeptical family member.

So step outside the familiar boundaries, and get your voice heard in a new way.

イシイルカ猟を中止せ
Stop the Dalls porpoise

PLEASE
RESPECT
ALL LIVING
CREATURES.
DO NOT
HARM THEM
BY CRUELTY
OR NEGLECT.

WSPA

Get It in Print

With one newspaper article, you can get your message read by the masses. Find out the editorial guidelines for your local papers, and give them a well-written article outlining clear problems and solutions. Keep it concise and lively.

You can do the same for regional and national magazines, which get great coverage, and usually have their editorial guidelines inside the opening pages. Follow them closely and research your facts very carefully, including strong photographs or illustrations with your article. Once published, it becomes much easier to do it again. Just keep on it.

Nora Kramer spent four and a half months at Farm Sanctuary's New York shelter, working with the animals and helping in the campaign office. The internship changed her life, and she was compelled to write about it; sending an article to *Newsweek*, which they published in 2001. Nora went on to volunteer at PETA for two months and spent two years working for the San Francisco office of In Defense of Animals. She now runs a humane-education program in the Bay Area called The Empathy Project, along with running a website (www.vegsf.com) and moderating the Bay Area Animal Rights Network email list.

Animals on the Airwaves

Getting a message about your cause aired on TV or radio requires that it be built around an event or a story they can cover. It could be a bike ride, a run, a bake sale or an auction. Maybe you can organize a benefit concert for a local animal

Campaigning in the Heartland

Alyson Powers is a voice for farm animals in America's heartland, and a master campaigner. When she moved from the Pacific Northwest to Iowa, she brought her animal welfare dedication with her. When her initial conversations with fellow students at the University of Iowa were encouraging, she began to campaign in earnest for greater awareness of the plight of farm animals. She created the campus-wide Farm Animal Welfare Network (FAWN) and uses print media by placing ads in her campus paper about pending farm animal legislation. Alyson operates information tables promoting a vegetarian lifestyle, passes out literature on factory farming and gives presentations to student groups. Her enthusiasm has caught on, as hundreds of students join FAWN every semester. Her animal welfare initiatives extend beyond campus, as she campaigns tirelessly around Iowa City as an advocate for the animals.

Alyson Powers campaigning at the University of Iowa.

shelter. Phone the news team; try to get an interview and invite them to cover the event when it happens.

Create a press release to promote your event and send it (by mail, email or fax) to the news team. Keep it to one page and include your contact information at the top, followed by the event's title (in upper case), subtitle, date and a clear, concise and inspiring preview.

Get to Know Your Representatives

Your elected representatives can play a huge role. They make laws that affect the well-being of species, and they like to stay in office, so hearing from their constituents can be very persuasive.

There's one important rule when approaching your elected representatives: treat them with respect. Accusations and threats will not get you heard. Give them credit for being intelligent, compassionate beings, who are doing the best they can. Get to know them. Email their office

- Activism for the Mature Motivated Mind: www.animalactivist.com/retired.asp
- Alyson Powers: www.geocities.com/iowafawn
- Helping Hands 101: www.helpinganimals101.com
- PETA's Guide to Letter Writing: www.peta.org/alert/tkit.html
- The Petition Site: www.thepetitionsite.com

or write a friendly, persuasive letter. It just might get them thinking in a way they haven't before.

The next step is to get the thoughts of their constituents to them, en masse, something best done with a petition campaign. Successful petition drives have lain behind many government decisions. The petition has to be clear and specific and include full names and addresses to keep it legitimate.

10

Step onto the Frontlines of Compassionate Activism

> The journey from cruelty to compassion can take thousands of lifetimes — or it can take a single second.
>
> — John Robbins

You want to step a little closer to the edge? This isn't for everyone. In fact, you're well-advised to take a good, hard look at your motives before stepping into this realm. It can't be confrontation you're looking for. We don't need any more hostility on the front lines. What we need are thoughtful, compassionate activists who have the courage to step outside their comfort zones to raise awareness for animals.

A Summer Break to Write Home About

From May to August 2004, 19-year-old college freshman Jeremy Beckham took to the road with his campaign to save primates. Traveling with stuffed monkey companions, bumper stickers, posters, videos and boxes of flyers, he visited eight American Primate Research Centers where government-funded bio-chemical lab research takes place on a large scale. Jeremy set up information tables wherever he traveled, sharing literature and details with passersby. He talked to hundreds of concerned citizens, many of whom were unaware of what was going on in their backyards. He met with reporters and held candlelight vigils. This is compassionate activism on a grand, effective scale.

On the Ice Flows

Rebecca Aldworth was born in Newfoundland and grew up well aware of the Canadian seal hunt and its international reputation as an unnecessary, brutally cruel tradition. After seeing video footage of what was happening on the ice flows of northeastern Canada, she decided she had to do what she could to help the seals. In 2006 she made her eighth trip to the ice flows to document the seal hunt, video camera in hand, sending news from the front lines to media sources all over North America and spreading as much awareness as possible. She is now the Humane Society of the United States' Director of Canadian Wildlife Issues and has become a well-respected leader and compassionate voice in the movement to end the Canadian seal hunt forever.

Set Yourself up for Success

Activists often face considerable risk for their own safety, despite how compassionate and gentle their approach may be. There is a lot of passion on the front lines of any contentious issue, and animal welfare is no exception. Your personal safety, and the safety of those around you, can be greatly supported by good preparation.

Know your cause inside out. Be well informed and ready to communicate.

Be compassionate. No yelling, no judging and no attacking people for the way they choose to support their family.

Seek the guidance of an action group that knows your cause before you try to save the world on your own. They've been there before, and you can learn from their experience.

From Inside the Industry

Pravin Shah wanted to learn more about what goes on inside dairy farms, so he chose farms in the United States and India to visit. In the States, he chose a dairy that sells all its products directly to Ben & Jerry's, which advertises as being an ethical company. What he found, in both countries, was far from ethical. Pravin Shah instantly became a vegan after his dairy visits and began learning all he could about health, nutrition and an animal-free lifestyle. He now dedicates much of his time to sharing his knowledge with others in his role as president of a Jain study center in North Carolina.

Active for Animals

Jeremy, Rebecca and Pravin took a huge amount of courage with them on their journeys to help animals. There is an enormous groundswell happening, but we have a long way to go. As individuals, we can only be successful if we get more people excited about helping animals. We won't do it by pressuring them or scaring them. We can only do it by leading from our hearts and showing them positive solutions to get excited about.

- Center for nonviolent Communication: www.cnvc.org
- Greenpeace: www.greenpeace.org/international/getinvolved
- PETA's Animal Activist: www.animalactivist.com
- Ruckus Society: www.ruckus.org

THE HUMANE SOCIETY OF THE UNITED STATES

Rebecca Aldworth out on the ice with a pup during the 2005 seal hunt in Eastern Canada.

11

Create a Local Animal Welfare Action Group

Never doubt that a small group of thoughtful, committed citizens can change the world. Indeed, it is the only thing that ever has.

— Margaret Mead

There is tremendous value in starting an animal welfare action group. It provides a focal point through which a group of people can concentrate their efforts. Bringing knowledge, experience, ideas, courage and compassion together into one group creates a source of energy that is much greater than people acting individually.

Do Your Research
Starting a non-profit organization takes planning and preparation, just like any other business.

- What service(s) will your group provide for your community?
- Will your group be able to work well with other animal welfare groups?
- Will you have access to the resources you need for your group?

- Will you be a general group, or have a specific focus?
- Can you get your hands on enough material about animal welfare, so your group will know the issues inside out?
- Do you have information on the bylaws that govern the operation of a non-profit group in your region?

Don't rush through the initial research phase. It's critical to your group's success.

Your Initial Gathering
Gather everyone together for your initial organizational meeting. Pick a date and time and ensure that everyone makes it to the meeting. Plan this carefully, listen carefully and let everyone communicate their thoughts. This will be the most important meeting your group ever has because it will be carried forward by the energy you create.

Create a Board of Directors
Your Board of Directors guides your group and shares the work. As you grow and get busier, this core group will keep everything rolling smoothly, so you can focus your attention on helping animals. For this reason, it's important to choose your Board of Directors carefully. Select people who are passionate, reliable and make it out to your meetings.

Write Your Mission Statement
Your mission statement sums up your group. It will become your guiding light,

GALAPAGOS NETWORK/ECOVENTURA S.A

Group Start-up Resources
- Best Friends Animal Society: www.bestfriends.org/nomorehomelesspets/ resourcelibrary/fororganizations.cfm
- Charity Village: www.charityvillage.com/cv/guides/guide4.asp
- Community Media: www.community-media.com/ Start_A_Non_Profit_Group.html
- PETA's Animal Activist: www.animalactivist.com/actguide6.asp
- Starting a Non-Profit Organization: www.managementhelp.org/strt_org/strt_np/strt_np.htm

and you will carry it with you into your role of helping animals.

Pigs Peace Sanctuary (www.pigspeace.org) in Stanwood, Washington, has been providing a save haven for pigs and other animals since 1994, guided by their group's mission statement: "Pigs Peace Sanctuary is a non-profit organization dedicated to providing a safe home for unwanted, abused or neglected animals in need, and is committed to spreading the message of compassion and respect for all animals."

Make It Legal
Get your group incorporated. Register your name and become a government-recognized non-profit organization. It adds credibility to your group and makes it easier to succeed. Your community will trust you, and raising funds will be possible. Contact your federal and state/provincial government offices for the registration forms you need.

Develop a Plan
Just like any organization, your group will need a business plan in order to succeed. Get books out of the library on non-profit societies. Search the Internet. See how it's done and work together to build a plan that matches the needs of your group.

Build a Budget
You group will need a detailed budget. It takes careful financial planning for non-profit organizations to succeed. You aren't in the business of

making a profit, so all the money you raise through donations and other means must be accounted for and spent very carefully.

Build Your Animal-Friendly Team
Now it's time to put together your volunteer team. These are the people who will represent your group within the community and help the animals you've created your group for. It's difficult to turn away anyone who volunteers their time, but "recruitment" is important. You want people who communicate well and who demonstrate compassion and honesty. Select one of your board members to be in charge of recruiting people and to interview every prospective volunteer personally. Don't be afraid to say no. Your group will be carried by these people, and you want them to be an honest reflection of your ideals.

Think Customer Service
Always remember that you're there to offer a service; both to animals and to those who want to help animals. Treat everyone, animal and non-animal, with the utmost in compassion and respect. You're in business to do just that.

12

Connect with Your Community

When our community is in a state of peace, it can share that peace with neighboring communities. What is important is that we each make a sincere effort to take our responsibility for each other and for the natural environment we live in seriously.
— His Holiness, the Dalai Lama

Whether you're a new group or an existing one, a public event is an excellent way to get to know your community. Plan an upbeat and informational event where everyone can mingle and learn about your group. Arrange for a guest speaker, and maybe a performer. Have literature on hand about your group and its causes. Perhaps you can serve refreshments or have a product demonstration from an animal-friendly company. Whatever you do, keep it upbeat and friendly. Cultivate community spirit.

A Life-saving Walk
In 2005 the Atlanta Animal Alliance began its Life Saver Fund to help guardians who are unable to afford unexpected veterinary bills, believing that no companion animal should

have to be euthanized for an otherwise treatable condition. The Alliance began a campaign to support the emergency, life-saving financial assistance to be disbursed to animal agencies throughout the 20-county Atlanta region, as well as to individual guardians. In 2006 they reached out to the community and organized the Atlanta Walk for Animals, an event that included a three-mile walk or run, post-race celebration, contests and prizes for the most creative costumes, with all entrance fees going directly to the Life Saver Fund (www.lifesaverfund.com).

Getting the Word Out
Promoting a community gathering, or simply connecting with your community, comes down to a few basic principles:

- Create a database of contact information for every person and organization who might be interested in your cause.
- Everyone in your group should network with their friends and family, as well as people in their favorite businesses.
- Get to know your media and learn how to get your stories covered.
- Plan poster and flyer campaigns (using recycled paper), but don't drown your community with notices. A few key locations such as bulletin boards and the windows of partner businesses will gain you more respect.

Have a questionnaire ready at your event, allowing people to share their views and ideas. Ask them for their personal expectations and what time and resources they have for volunteering.

An Island of Animal Awareness

The Vancouver Island Vegetarian Association (VIVA) hosts monthly vegan potlucks in and around Victoria, BC. They are entertaining and educational, and the group strives to have a speaker or presentation at each event. The potlucks are open to everyone; the only requirement being that you show up with an animal-product-free dish to share and a nominal fee to cover rental. VIVA will also gladly give culinary advice to those who have no idea how to create a vegan dish. Far from being a hard sell on veganism, the events have become a popular, laid back social activity in Victoria, and VIVA gives out great door prizes donated by partner organizations. See: www.islandveg.com.

- Animal Place: www.animalplace.org/ap_food_for_thought_brochure.pdf
- Hosting a successful food event: www.ivu.org/vuna/guide/guidelinesp.html
- Open Space: www.openspaceworld.org
- Planet Friendly — event planning: www.planetfriendly.net/promote.html
- Sustainable Communities Network: www.sustainable.org/information/susevent.html
- Vegsource events page: www.vegsource.com/talk/events

In a Time of Need

When Hurricane Katrina hit the Gulf Coast in 2005, hearts went out to the people and animals affected by the tragedy. The Dog Adoption and Welfare Group (DAWG) of Santa Barbara, California, jumped into action and contacted the Humane Society of the United States (HSUS), offering their help. Within days, the HSUS told DAWG that their volunteers would be dispatched to the front lines in Mississippi to help stranded animals. DAWG reached out to their community, and within 24 hours, residents of Santa Barbara and Goleta had donated enough supplies to fill a moving van, and four DAWG volunteers were on their way to the Gulf Coast. When they returned home, they brought five rescued dogs and nine cats. Then they returned to the Gulf Coast, bringing back another 12 rescued dogs. While most of the rescued animals were taken in by Pet Orphans of Southern California, DAWG took seven dogs into their own care, asking their community to adopt the "Katrina Seven." The community responded again, giving each of the dogs a new home (www.sbdawg.com/sbdawg/katrinadogs.asp and www.petorphans.org).

Members of DAWG bound for Mississippi with their vanload of donated emergency supplies.

13

Help Animals Touch the Hearts of Humans

We still haven't realized that owning a pet isn't just some kind of hobby.
— Dr. Alan Beck, director of the Center
for the Human-Animal Bond at
Purdue University

In Fairfax, Virginia, the Shilo Project helps animals touch the hearts of humans in a beautiful way, offering juvenile offenders and at-risk youth the opportunity to socialize and interact with rescued, homeless dogs. It operates entirely on the principles of compassion, respect and responsibility. Juvenile offenders and at-risk youth are able to cultivate a healthy and nonviolent relationship with the dogs, while discovering how to make a difference in the lives of homeless companion animals. It brings together young people and homeless dogs, both of whom may not have experienced much affection in their lives. The group got its name from a beloved shelter mutt named Shilo, who touched the hearts of many people.

Therapy Dogs
There are a growing number of specially trained therapy dogs visiting hospitals, nursing homes and mental health centers. Most people are familiar with dogs that assist people with physical disabilities, but these therapy dogs offer something different — they lift the spirits of the people they visit. Therapy dogs have a lasting effect on those they visit, enabling people to reconnect with comfort and love. To learn more, see Therapy Dogs International (www.tdi-dog.org).

From Awareness to Awe
Sadly, many people never enjoy the presence of animals. Regardless of how committed to animal welfare people may be, until they spend time with the animals they are trying to protect, they won't experience the real rewards of their work. The best way to help animals touch the hearts of other people is to let them touch your heart first. Spend time with shelter animals, shower affection on them and let them shower affection on you.

Don't limit it to companion animals. Visit someone's family farm and watch a newborn lamb take its first few wobbly steps. Let a pig sidle up to you to have its underbelly scratched. Offer to comb a horse's mane.

Your heart can be touched just as thoroughly by being in nature. Watching a duck

WENDY KEIGHLEY

Therapy dog Luke of Crosswinds.

land on an icy pond, skid playfully across the surface, plop into a snow bank and dust itself off will touch your heart. Watching a mother deer kiss the soft little nose of her fawn will do much the same. If, as I have, you're fortunate enough to be able to witness a mother orca whale teaching its baby how to swim, you will be truly amazed.

You've Been Touched: Now What?

You could follow the lead of the Shilo Project and develop your own unique path, or you could contact other groups to find out what has worked for them.

You could organize guided hikes in local parks or overnight camping trips into the backcountry.

Be sure such trips are led by a very knowledgeable guide. It's not just about seeing nature — it's about having your heart touched by it.

Trips to an organic family farm are a great way to help children and their families interact with animals. Again, the selection of your guide for such a trip is important. You don't want someone who's going to preach about the virtues of farming or the horrors of factory farming. Such a trip is about touching hearts, not politics.

Animal shelters are also a great way to touch people's hearts, particularly in urban areas. Team up with a shelter and help everyone. Companionship cultivates compassion.

The research shows[1]...

In 1995 Erika Friedman conducted a study at the University of Maryland Hospital involving 392 people. She found that heart attack patients who had dogs were eight times more likely to be alive a year later than those without dogs.

In 1999 the State University of New York at Buffalo conducted a study involving 24 stockbrokers who were taking medication for high blood pressure. The researchers found that adding a dog or cat to their lives helped stabilize and reduce their stress levels.

In 1999 Swedish researchers reported that children exposed to pets during the first year of life had fewer allergies and less asthma.

Furry fact — Cats and humans share a remarkable similarity — they have identical regions in the brain responsible for emotion.

- All Creatures animal stories: www.all-creatures.org/animal.html
- Animals in our Hearts: www.animalsinourhearts.com
- Best Friends Animal Society, animals helping people: www.bestfriends.org/atthesanctuary/humaneeducation
- Daily OM, animals as healers: www.dailyom.com/articles/2005/481.html
- The Shilo Project: www.shilohproject.org/index.html
- Therapy Pets: www.dogplay.com/Activities/Therapy/join.html

14

Create an Animal Shelter

Homeless animals outnumber homeless people at least 5-to-1. Until people take responsibility for their animals by spaying, neutering and putting identification on their pets, there will always be a need for animal shelters.

— Bill Garrett, Executive Director of the Atlanta Humane Society

An animal shelter is a temporary home for animals of all shapes and sizes; a haven where they can find safety, nourishment and kindness when they really need it. Creating a shelter is not a responsibility to enter into lightly. It's a huge undertaking involving lots of research and education, as well as the heart-wrenching task of euthanizing animals (see "From Pets to Companions"). It can also be an extremely valuable and rewarding journey.

Thinking Big

In 1986 Gene and Lorri Bauston found a live sheep abandoned in a stockyard deadpile, and decided on the spot to rescue her and give her a home. They named the sheep Hilda, and she inspired the creation of their animal shelter, Farm Sanctuary. Today, Farm Sanctuary is the largest farm animal rescue and protection organization in North America, with two locations in New York and California. They have over 100,000 members who diligently operate coast-to-coast rescue and rehabilitation programs, as well as raising public awareness and lobbying for tougher legislation to protect farm animals. Farm Sanctuary is a great example of a very successful non-profit shelter that has reduced animal suffering on a large scale.

Shelter from a Storm

People in Britain fleeing from situations of domestic violence and worrying about their pets can turn to the Royal Society for the Prevention of Cruelty to Animals (RSPCA) for help. Instead of leaving their beloved pets behind in a dangerous situation, they can make a phone call, and the RSPCA will arrange safe, temporary shelter for the animals while their human companions find a safe place to stay. The RSPCA's Pet Retreat Program is a great example of a shelter filling a void; one that people frequently forget about.

Now It's Your Turn

If you want to create a shelter that fits your group and the community

DEREK GOODWIN FOR FARM SANCTUARY

Farm Sanctuary in Watkins Glen, New York.

- The ASPCA has several useful publications, including *Keys to a Great Shelter, 101 Great Shelter Ideas* and *101 More Great Shelter Ideas.*
- The American Society for the Prevention of Cruelty to Animals (ASPCA): www.aspca.org
- Animal Acres: www.animalacres.org
- Animal Ark: www.animalarkshelter.org
- Best Friends Animal Sanctuary: www.bestfriends.org/atthesanctuary
- Farm Sanctuary: www.farmsanctuary.org
- Pet Shelter Network: www.petshelter.org

Animal Ark

Animal Ark is a no-kill shelter in Hastings, Minnesota; just a 30-minute drive from the Twin Cities of St. Paul and Minneapolis. While 20,000 cats and dogs are killed every year in shelters and pounds in the Twin Cities,[2] Animal Ark maintains a no-kill philosophy to rescue and adopt, only euthanizing those animals that are terminally ill and suffering. Animal Ark's numerous community programs include responsible pet guardianship education, a mobile surgical van (called the Neuter Commuter) supplying low- and no-cost services to homeless pets, New Chance shelter visits with at-risk youth and adoption services that find homes for 1,000 animals a year.

you live in, you'll need to source out funding, shelter space, bylaws and insurance. This will require much more than good intentions. With careful planning and patience, however, opening a shelter can become a reality.[1]

1. Assess your community's needs. Are there other animal welfare organizations or shelters in your community? If so, will your shelter complement existing services or be a drain on resources for both? Will your community be supportive of an animal shelter?

2. Think twice about the enormity of your endeavor. Assess your resources and be sure you're up to it. If you have doubts, your efforts might be better spent assisting an existing shelter.

3. Get experience by volunteering in a shelter — it's the best training you can have.

4. Form a team of knowledgeable allies. This might include veterinarians, a lawyer, local business people and potential sponsors.

5. Hit the road, go on a tour and visit as many shelters in as many regions as you can. Ask lots of questions.

6. Decide what type of shelter you want. Learn about the services of different shelters that offer varying levels of service and care for animals.

7. Create a mission statement and a plan. This is the foundation of your shelter; make sure it's a strong one.

8. Look into fundraising and get a clear picture of your required budget. Develop relationships with as many fundraising sources as possible and plan fundraising events.

9. Spread the word far and wide about what you're planning. Network: let everyone know what you're up to.

10. Remember the animals you want to help — keep them in mind at all times.

15

Create an Animal Food Bank

Oh God of homeless things look down and try to ease the way of all the little weary paws that walk the world today.

— Author unknown

Your group can offer temporary relief to hungry animals everywhere by creating an animal food bank. There are thousands of homeless pets in every city that could use your help, people suffering from financial hardship who are having trouble feeding their pets and farm animals, and wild creatures that aren't able to find the food they need during extreme weather. A little help in a time of need goes a long way.

A Food Banking Success Story

In 1993 Renee Carleton was volunteering by transporting homeless pets to visit with prospective adoptive families in Southern California and decided to find a solution to the prohibitive cost of feeding rescued animals. She found many warehouses throwing away damaged containers of food and began collecting the food to distribute to shelters and rescue groups. The warehouses were happy to get rid of the excess food, and soon Renee's car wasn't big enough, and she had to borrow trucks from friends. Her service grew rapidly over the years, and the trucks were replaced by an 18-wheeler, along with warehouse space, a forklift and volunteers

to help transport all the donated food. Renee formed the Pet Food Bank, with all equipment and services being donated, and by 2006, they were receiving up to 80,000 lbs. of pet food in a single week. The Pet Food Bank now distributes food to over 50 animal rescue organizations in Southern California and Mexico.

Where to Start

Assess the needs of your community and get a feel for what kind of support they will give you. Once you have a clear idea of the service you can establish, it's time to grasp a clear vision of why you're doing this. It can seem disheartening to bring food to homeless animals in a city where they just keep reproducing and the problem seems never-ending. Yet this little bit of relief for each animal is extremely important. One square meal goes a long way.

Organizations that provide nourishment to animals in need rely almost entirely on their communities to provide the food. You'll need to network with everybody, from the public to schools, churches, the media, veterinary offices, grocery stores — basically every business and organization in your community needs to know you exist. Let your community know you have a continuous need for appropriate animal food. Use every means of communication at your disposal and let everybody know that cash donations are welcome, too. It's just a little easier to get support if people are donating the food itself.

Contact large pet food distributors and tell them what you're doing. Let them know you'll

- Alley Animals: www.alleyanimals.org
- The Pet Food Bank: www.thepetfoodbank.com
- Seattle Humane Society:
  www.seattlehumane.org/fooddrive.shtml
- Shelter Source food bank resources:
  www.sheltersource.org/banks.htm

give them credit for their donations and then watch what happens. This is great PR for them, and they can afford to send you a lot of food.

Know where your food donations are best utilized and keep track of them. You will have regular requests for food, and you must make sure you're supporting your community fairly. That's why strong relationships and reliable records are important. If you have the luxury of a regular abundance of food arriving at your doorstep, you can allot surplus amounts to local animal shelters, feral cat and dog support, farm support, wildlife support and emergencies.

A Note on Nutrition
You will receive food donations that are inappropriate for animals. Probably a lot of them.

If you aren't able to gratefully turn them away (they might just show up when you're not around), unopened items like cookies, pasta or flour can be donated to a human food bank. Some of the food you receive may seem incongruous to give to a dog or cat, and certainly not the most nutritious. Nevertheless, these are often starving animals, and they aren't going to be very picky. Keep in touch with your local veterinary office and ask about any nutritional concerns you may have. You'll also want a chart of animal nutritional tips to refer to.

Alley Animals

Alley Animals, in Baltimore, Maryland, takes to the streets every night to bring meals to the city's four-legged homeless. Traveling in pairs by car and ready for anything, the courageous volunteers visit hundreds of city alleys in a single night, feeding as many as 3,000 homeless cats and dogs. They are also ready to rescue animals in desperate need, taking them to safety and getting them medical attention if necessary. This service relieves the animals' hunger for another night, helping them to survive in an inhospitable world.

16

Offer Humane Education

Tell me — and I forget
Show me — and I remember
Involve me — and I understand.
— Ancient Chinese proverb
on education

Children are indeed our future. All the progress we make today in animal welfare will be in their hands one day. They will create the laws, build our communities and shape our consciousness. Each one of them will also be a consumer, making choices either out of compassion and awareness, or out of convenience and indifference. Your group can make a huge difference by having one person offering education, spreading humane values and fostering animal awareness in our children.

The International Institute for Humane Education (IIHE) was founded in 1996, creating the first-of-its-kind humane education and certificate program in the US. With its headquarters in Surry, Maine, IIHE is affiliated with Cambridge College in offering a M.Ed. with a concentration in Humane Education, including in-depth instruction in education and communication, human rights, environmental ethics, animal protection and cultural issues. IIHE has trained hundreds of humane educators, reaching thousands of students through its distance-learning certificate and degree programs, workshops and publications. Zoe Weil, the founder of IIHE, is the author of several books, including *The Power and Promise of Humane Education*. She defines "humane education" as examining the challenges facing our planet, exploring how we might live with compassion and respect for everyone and inspiring

Children getting acquainted with rescued animals as Animal Acres.

Inspired Education

Carrie Lang and David Berman were 12-year-olds attending different schools in Philadelphia when they took an after-school class with humane educator Zoe Weil. The students were inspired to gather their friends and form their own animal welfare group, Students for the Protection of Animal Rights and the Environment (S.P.A.R.E.). S.P.A.R.E. grew to include over 100 students, arranging lectures in their schools, educating other students, participating in animal rights campaigns and volunteering at non-profit organizations.

- American Humane: www.americanhumane.org
- Animalink: www.animalink.ab.ca/HumaneEducation
- The Institute for Animal Associated Lifelong Learning: www.aallinstitute.ca
- International Institute for Humane Education: www.iihed.org
- Petakids: www.petakids.com

people to "live examined, intentional lives so that what they do today helps the planet, animals and all people tomorrow."

Natural Allies

Children are intrinsically drawn to animals. From the time they're babies, they are fascinated by all creatures great and small. From butterflies to blue jays, chimpanzees to piglets, kids love to explore the living world around them. It's through lack of contact with animals that misunderstanding begins. If they observe other people's lack of respect for animals, they will close themselves off from their innate compassion. Left to their own devices, and raised in an environment that fosters compassion, most children will thrive on their connection to the natural world and treat animals with kindness and respect.

Establish Trust

To be welcomed as a humane educator, you will need to establish trust in your community by holding events, doing work that results in benefits for animals and people and by demonstrating compassion in action.

When you approach a school for the first time, bring references, such as a letter from the local animal shelter for which your group raised a thousand dollars with a charity drive, media articles about your compassionate approach to animal awareness or testimonials from a seniors' center where you organized companionship with pets from a local shelter.

Keep it compassionate, upbeat and inspiring. Touch their hearts with moving stories and ideas about living with kindness towards animals. Most importantly, know your issues. You will be working alongside teachers and parents who know their facts, and you will certainly be challenged if it appears you are vacillating.

For the Little Ones

- Host a library hour, reading books with a humane theme.
- Present a puppet show in kindergarten or elementary school, inspiring kindness and respect for animals.

For Middle and High Schools

- Visit classrooms and teach about the issues.
- Mentor a school club.
- Arrange field trips to places where animals are exploited and places where they are cared for.
- Offer summer courses at camps/schools where summer programs are available.
- Teach a Religious Education class at a church/synagogue/mosque.
- Offer an after-school class, hosted at a school or at your group's offices.

For Adults

- Offer a continuing education class showing films and leading discussions.

17

Educate the Legislators

> We need to abolish certain forms of exploitation, not regulate them. We need to recognize that animals, like humans, have certain interests that can't be traded away.
>
> — Dr. Gary Francione

Much animal suffering can only be ended through legislation. There are small legal victories all the time, and, while progress is slow, it is steady. For society to embrace the need for respect and individual rights for all creatures, we need to see it developing through legal channels. Animal rights have to become law. The people who create laws are our elected representatives. They deal with laws all the time: that's part of what they're in office to do — create the legal guidelines we live by.

Action Groups and Balance

Our goal must be to work with our legislators, and not against them. The role that action groups can play in the creation of legislation can not be stated enough. Almost every law ever created came about because a lobby group of one kind or another campaigned for it adamantly. Some of the groups lobbying for legislation are large corporations with an agenda of their own. That's why it's so important for progressive

action groups to keep working with the legislators. If they only hear the persuasive words of corporate wealth, the laws they create may not bode well for animal welfare. It's essential that progressive action groups maintain the balance. We must stay in touch with our legislators and keep them informed about animal welfare issues.

Share Knowledge, Not Opinions

Building a positive relationship with legislators grows from honest communication and shared ideas. But here's the important part: you're the animal welfare expert in this relationship, not them. Explain the facts as you know them to be, not just how you feel about them. When legislators talk to someone from the National Cattleman's Beef Association, for instance, they need to have your knowledge running through their minds, not your opinions. Legal decisions are (or should be) based on facts, so make sure you've got your facts together.

Protecting the Mississippi Cats

In 2003 Natchez, Mississippi, resident Annette Byrne heard a horrific story of a cat being tortured and the perpetrator being arrested but released since the state had no laws protecting cats. Annette took the matter to Senator Bob Dearing, who spent the next three years lobbying for cats to be included under a law that already protected dogs from malicious treatment. Finally, after a long process of watching the legislation pass the Senate, but fail in the House, the Senator's efforts paid off in 2006, when Governor Haley Barbour signed the Senate bill in law, forcing those convicted of harming cats or dogs to spend up to six months in jail, pay up to $1,000 in fines and cover veterinary bills. "It's a relief to me," Annette said of the new law. "With a lot of people's help, we finally got it."

Know Your Legalities

Before you propose laws or amended legislation with your elected representatives, make sure you know the existing laws. Study every law in your area that has anything to do with animal welfare until you understand them and know what rights you have within the laws. Your understanding will mean everything to the animals you're protecting.

Rattling the Cage: Toward Legal Rights for Animals, by Steven M. Wise. A very important and deeply moving plea for legal rights for animals. A must-have for the library of action groups that should be read by everybody.

In Old St. Louis

The St. Louis Animal Rights Team has been campaigning successfully since 1985; leading the efforts for new animal welfare legislation both in Missouri and across the United States. On their own, and with the cooperation of other groups, they have lobbied to enact several animal protection laws, including having cockfighting banned in Missouri, establishing safer air travel for animals, creating a sanctuary system for chimps and establishing a committee to develop alternatives to testing commercial products on animals. None of this would have happened without the relationship they've built with legislators over the years.

- Doris Day Animal League: www.ddal.org
- In Defense of Animals: www.idausa.org
- The Institute for Animals in Society: www.animalsandsociety.org
- Rutgers Animal Rights Law Project: www.animal-law.org
- St. Louis Animal Rights Team: www.start4animals.org

Find your legislator:

- Government of Canada Directory: www.canada.gc.ca/directories/direct_e.html
- United States House of Representatives: www.house.gov/writerep

18

Find Your Big Issue and Run with It

People need a focus. Understand everything you can about the problem. If you are not already one, become an expert.

— Gregory Castle, Best Friends Animals Society

There are no results without focus. What's your Big Issue? Which aspect of animal suffering gets you fired up every time you think about it? As specialists, you can affect incredible change.

Paws Across the Border

Paws Across the Border was created after its founder, Debbie Segal, took a trip to El Paso, Texas. Crossing the border into Ciudad Juarez, Mexico, she saw the heart-wrenching sight of countless numbers of dogs and cats living in great suffering. Over 100,000 stray cats and dogs live in Ciudad Juarez, and no spaying or neutering services have been available before now.

Paws Across the Border began their spaying and neutering clinics in 2003 and have been working with the animals and the people of the region ever since. In addition to the clinics, they educate local people, train local medical staff, emphasize good health habits for companion animals and work to eliminate unwanted animal births in the area.

The organization has been very successful and plans to expand to other areas of Mexico to help manage the very high populations of stray animals. They are seeking volunteers from across the country to help them develop their clinics, bringing much-needed relief to a pet population in critical trouble.

Don't Reinvent the Wheel

When your group has found its focus, take the time to find out what similar groups around the world have done. If you cast your net far enough, you will find others who are dealing with the same issue who will be able to talk to you and will have valuable tools for you to use. Stay in touch with others who are working on the same issue, even if they're in another state or country. This will help you keep abreast of new legalities, victories and challenges and you'll come up with ideas together.

Whatever your Big Issue is, learn everything about it you can.

PAWS ACROSS THE BORDER

The Paws Across the Border medical team at work in Nogales, Mexico.

Following the Whales Home

Alexandra Morton followed a childhood dream of studying animals, and after recording orca whales in captivity in Los Angeles, she became fascinated with learning more about how orcas communicate. In 1979 she traveled to northeastern Vancouver Island, where the captive orcas once called home, to find their families; an essential part of her study since each family of the area's whales has a unique dialect. Alexandra fell in love with the area called the Broughton Archipelago and moved to a tiny floating community that has been her home ever since. In 1981 she founded the Raincoast Research Society (originally called Lore Quest) to study the acoustics of BC's orcas. In 1987 the first commercial salmon farm opened in the area, causing widespread ecological damage to the Archipelago (see Solution 40), and Raincoast dedicated its efforts to an unprecedented study on the impact of salmon farming. Alexandra and her team continue their conservation work today, recording whale and dolphin activity and raising awareness about the impact of farming Atlantic salmon in British Columbia.

If you need certification or special training, go for it. The animals are depending on you.

Welfare, Rights, Rescue or Habitat Protection?

There are many different ways in which action groups help animals but most fall into one of four categories. Figure out which defines your work and stick with it. Focusing on one area conserves your energy, time and resources. Make your focus clear in your mission statement.

- Bat Conservation International: www.batcon.org
- Endangered Species Coalition: www.stopextinction.org
- HelpHorses.com: www.helphorses.com
- International Primate Protection League: www.ippl.org
- Migrating Birds Know No Boundaries: www.birds.org.il
- Paws Across the Border: www.pawsacrosstheborder.org
- Pisces: www.pisces.demon.co.uk
- Raincoast Research Society: www.raincoastresearch.org

1. Animal Welfare — works to prevent suffering and cruelty:
   - Monitors the living conditions of all animals.
   - Educates the public about animal welfare.
   - Works for legislation that protects animals, both wild and domestic.
2. Animal Rights — works to end all animal exploitation:
   - Lobbies for the legal rights of animals as sentient beings.
   - Acts as a voice for animals exploited through captivity, experimentation, sports, food.
3. Animal Rescue — works to assist animals in immediate need of care:
   - Provides hands-on action through shelters, farm animal rescue, animal food bank distribution, veterinary care and animal first aid.
   - Educates the public in handling animal emergencies.
4. Habitat Protection — works to protect habitat for all species:
   - Initiates conservation projects.
   - Protects endangered species.
   - Monitors global exploitation.
   - Educates the public about the need for ecosystem biodiversity.

19

Practice nonviolent Activism

If you want to be respected for your actions, your behavior must be beyond reproach ... this is how you gain the respect of others.

— Rosa Parks

Animal suffering will only be ended through compassion. This is more than just a philosophy — it is a universal truth. Violence does not end violence. At best, it crushes it into submission until it can arise again.

We have to foster a willingness to change. People have to make the choice to end animal suffering. It cannot be forced upon them. Your group provides a voice for the animals, and through your actions, people will gain awareness. By assuming the role of ambassador for animals, you take on a responsibility. If your actions are compassionate and inspiring, people will equate animal welfare with hope. If they are violent, people will equate animal welfare with violence. It spreads very quickly.

Suffering and Cruelty

The nonviolent attitude can be explained by means of two words: "suffering" and "cruelty." "Suffering" suggests a state of pain or sorrow that needs attention. No violence has to happen for suffering to exist. "Cruelty" suggests intent. Cruelty is a product of violence.

That's why an effective action group talks about animal suffering, not animal cruelty. People can relate to suffering, and there is an automatic willingness to help. Cruelty puts people on the defensive, lest they be held accountable.

The majority of animal suffering is caused by a lack of awareness. Give people a chance to react to this new awareness as they see fit.

A nonviolent Voice

Marshal Rosenberg's book, *nonviolent Communication: A Language of Life*, serves as a wonderful tool for people who wish to use their voice more effectively. Rosenberg's book is a result of his experience as founder and educational director of the Center for Nonviolent Communication, and he has organized peace programs in many war torn areas of the world, including Rwanda, Croatia and the Middle East. This book is highly recommended for its effectiveness in breaking violent patterns in the way we think and debate with others. If followed by action groups, his methods of communication could benefit everyone — including animals.

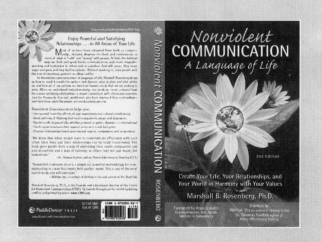

- Center for Nonviolent Communication: www.cnvc.org
- Compassionate Kids: www.compassionatekids.com
- The Institute for Animals and Society: www.animalsandsociety.org
- The Ruckus Society: www.ruckus.org
- A Season for Nonviolence: www.agnt.org/snv02.htm

Creating a Compassionate Ruckus

The Ruckus Society is a non-profit organization that has earned a reputation as a leader in training for nonviolent activism. Ruckus has trained thousands of activists in the use of nonviolent direct action. Condemned by some as fostering violence, Ruckus's goal is quite the opposite. They foster strong communication skills, media skills, leadership and courage to stand up to oppression with a clear, compassionate voice.

Ruckus hosts Action Camps, which are week-long intensive training programs for community members, students and campaign organizers to develop activism training through theoretical and strategic workshops. Ruckus also hosts "micro-Ruckus" programs, which give interactive training in nonviolence, media communications, political/theater arts in action and fundraising.

A nonviolence Pioneer

In 1960 James Lawson was a student at Vanderbilt University in Nashville, Tennessee, where he began conducting nonviolence training workshops. He launched a series of sit-ins to end racial segregation in downtown Nashville businesses, and formed the Student Nonviolent Coordinating Committee (SNCC), a group that played a major role in the US civil rights movement. Despite the SNCC's commitment to peaceful direct action, James Lawson was expelled from Vanderbilt. He continued his campaigns for social justice and was supporting

black sanitation workers in Memphis with Martin Luther King in 1968 when Dr. King was assassinated. Lawson moved to Los Angeles in 1974, where he still works for social justice, continuing to train activists in nonviolence.

During the 2006 graduation ceremony at Vanderbilt, the university officially apologized for its treatment of James Lawson.

An Oxymoron?

Some people consider "nonviolent activism" to be a contradiction in terms. Imagine it becoming quite the opposite. Hold a vision in your mind of the day when people look forward to your demonstrations because you're entertaining, courageous and inspiring. Your activism sheds light through the shadows of uncertainty, spreading peace.

Imagine a time when you are face to face with the leader of the people against whom you are demonstrating. Forget about your differences and realize how many similarities you have. They have a family like you. They have causes they feel passionate about like you. They have been thrust into this moment like you. Imagine if they asked you how you were holding up, if you wanted to take a walk and talk about things. Maybe the two of you could work this out on common ground. Just imagine.

Now act on it.

20

Work with Other Groups

We all have the same goal — to help animals. But in the past we focused on minor differences instead of on what we could accomplish if we worked together.
— Bob Rohde, president of the Dumb Friends League

In 2005, 17 local, state and national animal advocacy groups united to form the California Animal Association (CAA), a first-of-its-kind alliance in the US and a wonderful collaborative voice for animals in the state. The CAA draws on the strength of 275,000 Californians from individual groups, working in support of companion animals, farmed animals, exotic animals, animals used in research and wildlife. The CAA holds monthly meetings to discuss progress on one legislative initiative during each two-year session, rotating the focus of the legislation among different animal species. Member organizations are the American Anti-Vivisection Society, Animal Legislative Action Network,

Animal Place, Animal Protection Institute, Association of Veterinarians for Animal Rights, California Animal Defense and Anti-Vivisection League, California Lobby for Animal Welfare, Doctors for Kindness to Animals, Farm Sanctuary, In Defense of Animals, Last Chance for Animals, Orange County People for Animals, People for the Ethical Treatment of Animals, The Paw Project, United Animal Nations, United Poultry Concerns and Viva! USA.

Uniting for Animals

The cohesive efforts of the CAA give a strong legal voice to animals in California and serve as a model for other groups to follow in working together. Combining forces is incredibly effective and will play a huge role in the evolution of a more compassionate society.

There are animal welfare groups all over the world. Finding them is as easy as doing an Internet search or checking the links pages of your affiliated organizations. Build a database and invite a member of your group to maintain it. Someone else could be in charge of contacting other groups to establish relationships. Cast your net far and wide. Make sure you're in touch with all the animal welfare groups in your own area. Working with them, you can really get things done. Find out what your mutual visions are and create shared campaigns. It lends a

BUDD CHRISTMAN/NOAA

lot of credibility to an event when two or more groups work together.

Just as individuals have differences, so do action groups; find your common ground before you work together. You're all in this to end animal suffering, so you have a great start. But perhaps the other group has a more confrontational style of activism than you're comfortable with. Meet with them ahead of time and discuss this, so that you're all on the same page when you work together.

Connecting Online

One great way to work with other groups is to establish an online forum or listserv where everyone can share ideas. David R. Woolley, writing for the Association for Community Networking, says that successful online forums must have four essential elements: a clear purpose, experienced hosts, interested participants and good software.[1]

Invite a member of your team to moderate the forum and maintain communication between

the groups. This streamlines communication and lets the groups get on with the work at hand.

Create a Coalition

If your group plays a specific role in animal welfare, find other organizations that are doing the same thing and create a coalition. Organize regular conferences with the members of your coalition, online or in person, to establish common goals and work toward effective solutions.

- Animal Alliance of Canada: www.animalalliance.ca
- Asilomar Accords: www.asilomaraccords.org
- Canadian Coalition for Farm Animals: www.humanefood.ca
- European Coalition to End Animal Experiments: www.eceae.org
- United Animal Nations: www.uan.org

The Asilomar 2004 Accords

In August 2004 animal welfare leaders representing 23 groups met in California to create a unified force with a single goal: to significantly reduce the euthanasia of healthy and treatable companion animals in the United States. By bridging the various philosophies of the different groups, the combined efforts were able to establish goals and chart a course for the future. And, thus, the Asilomar Accords were drafted establishing 14 guiding principles, led by the mission of working together to save the lives of healthy and treatable companion animals.

The Asilomar Accords set a wonderful precedent for animal welfare groups working together. In the words of the agreement's guiding principles:

We, as animal welfare stakeholders, agree to foster a mutual respect for one another. When discussing differences of policy and opinion, either publicly or within, and among, our own agencies, we agree to refrain from denigrating or speaking ill of one another. We will also encourage those other individuals and organizations in our sphere of influence to do the same.[2]

21

Create Animal-Friendly Classrooms

> Teaching children abstract concepts like compassion can be easier, more engaging and more fun when animals are a springboard for discussion.
>
> — Traci Bryant,
> Humane Society University

Schools are where our future generations gather to learn about the world around them. A few simple choices within classrooms, through the actions of the teachers and the support of parents, can go a long way to creating an animal-friendly society.

KIND News

One vehicle for kindness in school systems is the monthly publication *KIND News*, produced by the National Association for Humane and Environmental Education (NAHEE). KIND is an acronym for Kids In Nature's Defense, and has added a fourth R to the three Rs: **R**espect for animals. It is available to classrooms across North America, providing students with articles, stories, puzzles, celebrity interviews, best books and videos and project ideas from grades K-6 that inspire positive actions for animals. Lincoln Elementary School students in Roselawn, Indiana, were inspired by *KIND News* to make posters, talk to other classes and collect supplies for their local

- Animal Adoptions: www.adoption.co.uk
- BBC Kids online: www.bbc.co.uk/nature/animals
- Farm Sanctuary: www.farmsanctuary.org
- National Arbor Day Foundation: www.arborday.org
- National Association for Humane and Environmental Education: www.nahee.org
- National Wildlife Federation: www.nwf.org/kids
- Save the Manatee Club: www.savethemanatee.org
- WWF Schools for Wildlife: www.wwfcanada.org/satellite/wwfkids

animal shelter. Students at Austin Elementary in Harlingen, Texas, collected and recycled plastic ring tops from soda cans to prevent seagulls and other animals from becoming tangled in them. *KIND News* is distributed to 38,000 classrooms and can be obtained through NAHEE's Adopt-a-Classroom program for $30 in the US and $50 in Canada (www.kindnews.org).

A Humane Environment

Let your ideas spread out across your classroom. Walls, desks, blackboard trim, the ceiling and even the floor can be covered in creations for animals, including colorful collages from magazines, photos from an animal shelter field trip or paintings of favorite animals.

An aquarium filled with tropical fish or a photo display from a zoo or circus may do nothing to inspire animal awareness. Instead it teaches children that removing animals from their natural environment and confining them to captivity for our entertainment is acceptable. Explain the difference between zoos that act as sanctuaries and those that breed animals and sell their surplus to hunting ranches. Discuss humane animal husbandry and how it differs from factory farming. Promote shelter adoption over buying from a pet store and explain why. Tell them about animal-free circuses. Show them alternatives to animal products.

Adopt an Animal or a Forest

Help your class do some research and find an animal species or area of the world that they all agree needs help. Then contact a group that provides animal adoptions or find a local wildlife rehabilitator and raise funds for their efforts. Create an adoption "shrine" in your classroom, with photos and drawings about your adoptee. Have your class stay on top of the news about their adoptee and discuss their concerns with them.

Rebekah's Animal Friends

Rebekah Harp, a special education teacher and guidance counsellor at Enterprise Learning Academy and Bethune Elementary School in South Jacksonville, Florida, uses the companionship of animals to connect with students. Her Pet Partnership Programs are renowned around campus and have the enthusiastic support of school staff. Six times a year, Leonardo (a Chihuahua who was rescued when he was six months old) hosts a talk show with Rebekah on Enterprise's closed-circuit television network, where students open up to him about their issues and ask for advice. Two other dogs conduct a Polite Pug Patrol around campus, awarding certificates, buttons and pictures with the dogs to students who model courtesy and kindness. Again, it's all captured on closed-circuit TV. Rebekah also finds that her dogs help children read; students who are too shy to read in front of a class will often sit in a quiet area with one of the dogs and read to them, boosting their confidence to read in front of others. All of Rebekah's lesson plans have an animal theme. She operates a Jr. Humane Society Club, which organizes pet food drives, spay/neuter campaigns, fundraises for emergencies such as Hurricane Katrina animal relief, campaigns

against the Canadian seal hunt and puts on theater performances to raise awareness about animals. She also stages an annual Endangered Species Safari, in which classrooms research endangered species and put on a skit about them. Students are given a safari visa, so they can travel from one classroom to another to see every skit. Rebekah has been voted teacher of the year at both schools, and in 2006, she was honored as NAHEE's National KIND Teacher.

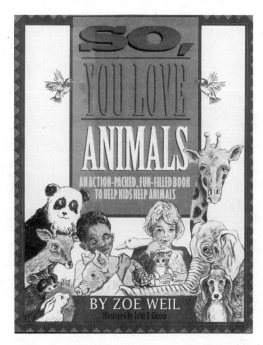

So, You Love Animals, by Zoe Weil. An entertaining, informative guide to animal welfare for kids. A great addition to any school library.

22

Help Children Voice Their Compassionate Choice

Kids need to address real needs in their community — to think, plan and actually make a difference.

— Barbara A. Lewis

Mrs. Jan Flanagan's sixth-grade class at St. Edwards School in Waterloo, Iowa, was working on a service-learning project with the Cedar Bend Humane Society when they discovered something that needed their support. They found out about Bill SSB3086, which would classify animal fighting in Iowa as a felony. At the time, Iowa was one of only three states that still allowed dog fighting, and the 12-year-olds from St. Edwards jumped at the chance to do something about it. Without any instruction, they began a letter-writing campaign to Iowa representatives. So impassioned was their plea that

they even got a visit from Iowa Senator Bill Dotzler, who praised the children's efforts and expressed surprise that they had found the time and enthusiasm to make such a difference.

The students' letter-writing campaign was successful, and Iowa became the 48th state to ban animal fighting. After her class's campaign and subsequent legislation, Jan Flanagan said, "I hope they remember that they have a right to be listened to, and what they do makes a difference."

Jan's words were as important as the legislation banning animal fighting. Not only did an entire state take a compassionate step forward, but a whole class of children learned an empowering lesson. Children have a right to be listened to, and their actions can make a difference.

Cultivating Creativity

Children gain confidence and awareness by watching creative ideas come to life, especially when it's an idea they've come up with themselves. That's why it's so important to let students follow through with their ideas. Teachers and parents can provide access to information about animals, encourage them to learn more and support their efforts, helping

CHASE PICKERING/JANE GOODALL INSTITUTE/JANEGOODALL.ORG

Participants in Roots & Shoots' Youth Leadership Immersion Experience trip in Peru.

them realize that they can make choices that make a big difference.

Roots & Shoots

In 1991 a group of 16 students gathered around Dr. Jane Goodall on her front porch in Dar es Salaam, Tanzania. The students were fascinated by animals and the environment, and they asked Dr. Goodall what they could do to learn more about topics that their school didn't cover. She sent them back to school with a mission: to find other interested students and take action. Thus, the Roots & Shoots program was born. With the guidance of the Jane Goodall Institute, and the enthusiasm of young people worldwide, Roots & Shoots has spread to over 90 countries and more than 7,500 registered groups.

All Roots & Shoots groups are dedicated to three goals: caring for animals, the human community and the environment. In schools, Roots & Shoots participants organize workshops, conferences and after-school clubs. Students and teachers from elementary school through university use education materials and special events to raise awareness and effect change both locally and globally.

Roots & Shoots succeeds because of the efforts of youth like the 12 members who attended the first-ever Children's Earth Summit in Soweto, South Africa, in 2002. Among the five delegates who drafted the body's final declaration[1] was 16-year-old Roots & Shoots member Jessica Rimington of Cape Cod, Massachusetts. The declaration was presented to United Nations Secretary-General Kofi Annan.

Roots & Shoots also succeeds because of the efforts of the dedicated groups of 2 to 2,000 members, working together for a more compassionate, sustainable world. You can get involved with Roots & Shoots by visiting www.rootsandshoots.org.

- Children of the Earth United: www.childrenoftheearth.org
- Compassionate Kids: www.compassionatekids.com
- Earth's Birthday Project: www.earthsbirthday.org
- The Giraffe Heroes Project: www.giraffe.org
- PAKT Foundation: www.paktfoundation.com
- Peace Corps Kids World: www.peacecorps.gov/kids
- Seeds for Change: www.seedsforchangehumaneeducation.org

Compassion from the Farm

Cultivating Compassion: Teachers' Guide and Student Activities, created by Farm Sanctuary, includes lesson plans, handouts and activities to inform and inspire kids about farm animals. It is warm-hearted and humorous, while guiding kids through the difficult subject of farm animal welfare. Designed for elementary (grades 3-5), intermediate (grades 6-8), and secondary students (grades 9-12), *Cultivating Compassion* can be ordered from Farm Sanctuary: www.farmsanctuary.org/media/pr_teach_guides.htm.

23

Work Together to Preserve and Restore Habitat

What do parents owe their young that is more important than a warm and trusting connection to the Earth?

— Theodore Roszak

In the Russian Far East and northeast China, there lives a bird called the scaly-sided merganser. These colorful waterfowl have been increasingly threatened over the past few decades, as the forests they nest in have been steadily cleared. It is estimated that the little-known bird's population is down to about 4,000. But the scaly-sided merganser is getting some help. Their population decline has slowed, due to the efforts of school children. With the support of Russian authorities, students in the area have been making nestboxes for the vulnerable bird, and substitute homes in several key river and forest areas are now protected by the government. The kids have created over 140 nest boxes, and many are already being used by the mergansers.

It's easy to get kids fired up about the environment and the species that share the natural world with us. Help them spend time outdoors with a field guide in hand, and they quickly become budding ornithologists and wildlife

- Action for Nature: www.actionfornature.org
- Adopt-A-Beach School Assembly Program: www.malibufoundation.org/tmffe004.htm
- Earth Day Network: www.earthday.net
- Schools Go Green: www.schoolsgogreen.org
- The Sierra Club — Youth Services: www.sierraclub.org/youthservices
- Sierra Youth Coalition: www.syc-cjs.org
- Young Environmentalist Actions: www.globalresponse.org/kidsactions.php

conservationists. Whether through a city park or a park trail far from home, children benefit greatly from spending time in nature. And children benefit nature too, if they're given a chance.

Conservation in Every Class

- In Shop, kids can make nest boxes, bird feeders or toad houses (a cool, dark home where toads rest, feeding on the pests that plague people's plants).
- In Science, kids can learn about the ecosystems that animal species depend on, and develop models that make a positive difference.
- In Math, kids can be given practical problems involving animals, humans and society.
- In Art, kids can be given projects that depict conservation and animals. Try holding art classes out in nature, using real-life examples.
- In Social Studies, kids can learn about the impact affluent cultures have on wildlife and its habitat, looking at solutions enacted by some cultures and obstacles faced by others.
- In Gym, take it outside — way outside. If there are forest, mountain or park trails nearby, hold your class outside. Go for a hike and discuss conservation along the way.

Recycle in Your Classroom

A classroom recycling program can be more far-reaching than you might think. From disposable lunch packaging alone, every student in North America adds a half-pound of garbage to land-fills every day; for a school of 350 students, that's 175 pounds.[1] Multiply this by every school in the region, and you have an enormous problem. Garbage winds up in landfills, displacing wildlife habitat, leaching toxic liquid into the soil and water and producing greenhouse gas (methane) that contributes to global warming.

In November 2004, students in the Sierra Youth Coalition at the University of Saskatchewan in Saskatoon performed a waste audit on a busy lunch area of their campus. They searched through eight bags of garbage, from one lunch period, and split it into four categories: recyclables, compostables, necessary waste and unnecessary waste. Their audit showed that actual garbage accounted for only 5% of the total and easily fit into one small bag. The remaining 95% could have been avoided through reducing and recycling.

If you want to do a waste audit, there are many good models online.

Children gather on the beach to spell 'Thank you' to Mexico.

MALIBU FOUNDATION FOR ENVIRONMENTAL EDUCATION/CALIFORNIA COASTAL COMMISSION/AERIAL ARTIST JOHN QUIGLEY

Adopt-A-Beach

Students in California have been taking part in the Earth Day Adopt-A-Beach Kids Clean-Up since its inception in 1994. On Earth Day in 1998, 4,500 kids took part in a joint distress call from beaches in Los Angeles and San Francisco, standing on the beach and forming the letters SOS for aerial photographs. Their message, Save Our Seas, supported the United Nations declaring 1998 the International Year of Oceans. In 2000 the clean-up kids were at it again, this time creating a whale's tail and spelling out the word Gracias to Mexico for keeping grey whale habitat free from development.

The Malibu Foundation's Adopt-A-Beach program has three stages. First, a teacher workshop, including a slide show of previous events, and recycling lesson plans for students. Then the Foundation hosts a school assembly, discussing recycling and the importance of conservation, followed by a Recycle-A-Thon to raise funds for the extra buses required for the event. Finally, the annual Earth Day Clean-Up with a trip to the beach to where the Foundation has hosted over 30,000 students for the hands-on event.

24

Create a Humane Biology Classroom

I personally don't feel dissection is necessary in my class if there's an alternative ... too many pigs die to teach students a lesson that could have been learned on the computer.
— Travis Burnham, high school teacher

Six million animals are dissected in school classrooms every year in the United States.[1] Many schools allow students to opt out of classroom dissections, but for most, it remains mandatory. Students are demanding alternatives, however, and so are their teachers. Research shows that computer modeling gives better learning results and costs far less than the management of live rabbits, pigs, cats and rats.

Scientists with the Humane Society of the United States Biology Consultancy Service have developed a program that helps teachers introduce humane dissection alternatives into their classrooms, custom-designed to fit the curriculum. The Humane Biology Classroom program software packages replicate dissection procedure and, using animation, teach students everything about biology without taking a single life. The NORINA database, from the Norwegian

Reference Centre for Laboratory Animals and Alternatives, provides a huge database of alternative options for humane classrooms, including loan programs, free products and free demos.

From inexpensive models to elaborate computerized mannequins, alternatives are available almost everywhere to help students learn about the dissection of skin and internal organs without inflicting suffering on animals or causing anxiety in students. Software programs that offer alternatives to dissection are becoming more and more effective and will hopefully replace classroom dissections altogether. Audio-visual methods also provide an excellent understanding of biology. A good video can give a student far more information in 30 minutes than he or she can possibly gain by the same time spent in dissection.

Ethically Sourced Animal Cadavers
This term "ethically sourced" means that animals used in laboratories are not being bred and raised for the purpose of dissection. Instead, programs can be set up between schools and area farms and veterinary clinics. Animals that have died from accidents or illness, or that have been euthanised for good medical reasons, could be donated to schools for classroom dissections. Such a program requires that a school treat the cadavers with respect and dignity. Although still using animals, it takes advantage of tissues and organs that would otherwise be wasted.

Clinical Practice

Students pursuing a medical career clearly need hands-on instruction before they operate on living creatures, whether human or animal. For veterinary education, clinical observation is a proven effective alternative to dissection. Students can learn by observing, and once a demonstrated level of medical understanding has been reached, they will be eligible to enroll in a training program through a veterinary clinic, for hands-on education.[2]

A Day No Frogs Shall Die

In 1987, 15-year-old Jennifer Graham made headlines in her home state of California and across the country when she took a stand against dissection. Jennifer refused to dissect a frog that had been killed for that purpose and was given a low mark in class for her objections. So she took the matter to court and, in doing so, brought the case for opting out of classroom dissections into the public eye. In Jennifer's case, the court ruled that she shouldn't have to dissect any animal that hadn't died of natural causes. The decision was a big one because it led the state of California to pass a law that upholds the right of students under 18 to refuse to participate in "harmful" or "destructive" uses of animals in education.

> They won't learn much with their eyes closed, because they're disgusted.
> — Amy Richards, student,
> Little Chute, Wisconsin

- American Anti-Vivisection Society: www.aavs.org/home.html
- Digital Frog: www.digitalfrog.com
- European Coalition to End Animal Experiments: www.eceae.org/factsheets/A5_Dissection.pdf
- Humane Animals in Education: www.hsus.org/animals_in_research/animals_in_education
- Norwegian Inventory of Alternatives (NORINA): http://netvet.wustl.edu/norina.htm
- Physicians Committee for Responsible Medicine: www.pcrm.org/resch/anexp/elem_sec_alternatives.html
- Student Rights Option: www.psyeta.org/studentrights.html

Taking a Stand in Las Vegas

In 2002 the Clark County School Board in Las Vegas, Nevada, voted in favor of allowing students to opt out of dissections, given parental support, after a successful petition drive by eighth-grader Laurie Wolff. Two years earlier, in sixth-grade, Laurie had chosen not to participate in a worm dissection that made her feel uncomfortable, and the A student received a C for her choice. Realizing that there were more dissections ahead of her in secondary school, and with the urging of her grandmother, Laurie created the petition for her classmates and presented it to the school board (the sixth-largest in the US) at a 2001 meeting. The board voted unanimously on the amendment, giving 244,000 children the right to choose.

25

Offer Vegan and Vegetarian Choices in School Cafeterias

It's made it a lot easier for me to be a vegetarian, and the food is really interesting.

— Eliza Martin Simpson,
grade 10 student at
Rockland Country Day School

With ever more information at their finger-tips, students are learning the effect their choices have on their health and the world around them. And that may be why children aged 8 to 15 are switching to vegetarian diets at twice the rate of adults. Overall, the number of people in the United States who have switched to a vegetarian diet has passed 12 million,[1] or 4% of the total population. In Canada the rate is similar, with 1.2 million vegetarians,[2] or 3.5%. The food giant, Kellogg's, reports that 30% of its customers are asking for vegetarian options.[3] Teenage girls are leading the wave. Surveys find that between 11% and 24% of American girls are vegetarians.[4] Teen boys lag behind: only 5% of male teens are choosing to forego meat.[5]

The USDA and Your School

The US Department of Agriculture (USDA) is supporting more vegetable-based diets in school cafeterias. As recently as the 1980s, they stated that meat was essential for kids to get the required amount of protein, iron and zinc. Only 30% of the protein in school cafeterias could come from vegetable sources, and sources other than meat had to be fortified with zinc and iron. The USDA withdrew all such requirements in 2001, stating that their research was based on old data and has been proven false.[6] As many healthy vegetarians know, there are plenty of complete protein and essential nutrients in a well-balanced, vegetable-based diet. The soy industry celebrated wildly at the USDA's change of heart, and the beef industry cried foul.

What might a student find on a new cafeteria menu? At the Au Naturel vegetarian station at Pomona College in Claremont, California, you can order anything from spicy Spanish potatoes with green beans and sprouts to pita bread stuffed with sautéed veggies, potatoes and peanuts. Au Naturel's business is up 20-30%.

Get It Started

Work with other students, teachers and parents to request a change. Suggest your school hire a registered dietician to evaluate the cafeteria's menu.

Switching to a vegetable-based diet is a triple-win situation. It save the lives of animals, eases our impact on the environment and improves our overall health, helping to reduce the epidemic of obesity, which is a good argument to use among people who might otherwise resist.

An Edible Schoolyard

In 1994 Chef Alice Waters teamed up with the principal and teachers of King Middle School and parents in Berkeley, California, to create the Edible Schoolyard. Using an abandoned lot next

- Edible Schoolyard: www.edibleschoolyard.org
- Kids Gardening: www.kidsgardening.com
- Two Angry Moms: www.angrymoms.org
- USDA Dietary Guidelines: www.cnpp.usda.gov/DietaryGuidelines.html
- The Vegetarian Resource Group: www.vrg.org
- Veg For Life: www.vegforlife.org/kids.htm

to the school and raising $10,000 for the start-up, the Edible Schoolyard has grown into a vibrant garden and kitchen program with a full-time staff of six and the involvement of every child in the school. Students and adults work together to plant, maintain and harvest the garden. Their cooperation extends to the kitchen, where students prepare meals from seasonal recipes, clean up together and return the food scraps for compost to the garden after every kitchen class.

For the Health of It

In 2006 England announced new nutrition guidelines, effectively banning junk food from school cafeterias across the country. The move followed a campaign by renowned TV chef Jamie Oliver, who called for the government to improve the quality of school meals. The new standards must be in place in all primary schools by 2008, with secondary schools following a year later. Students will be served a minimum of two portions of fruit and vegetables with every meal, and deep-fried foods can only be served twice a week. Burgers and sausages made from "meat slurry" or mechanically recovered meat

are banned from school cafeterias altogether, along with sweets such a chewing gum, taffy, liquorice, marshmallows and deep-fried chips.

The Edible Schoolyard at King Middle School in Berkeley, California.

Going Veggie in Congers

Rockland Country Day School, a private school in Congers, New York, serves their students meals prepared by a local vegetarian restaurant. The move came as an effort to combat the increase in childhood obesity. Rockland's cafeteria offers a wide variety of plant-based selections provided by Main Essentials in nearby Haverstraw. Rockland also began an organic vegetable garden, which provides produce for their cafeteria, and changed the food in their snack machines. Granola, pretzels and soy-based cookies replaced candy bars, chips and Pop-Tarts; and water, juice and seltzer-based sodas replaced Coke and Pepsi.

26

Create Habitat for Wildlife

We encourage all our customers to shut their lights off at night to save birds, electricity and money — all at the same time.

— David O'Brien, president of Toronto Hydro Corporation, and partner in the City's Lights Out Toronto campaign

Buried under the concrete sea of our cities, there beats a heart that once thrived everywhere. If we give life to its soil, nature will return. Almost everybody likes to see wildlife — birds, deer, butterflies — sharing their community. Most people recognize the effect that our exploding population is having on their environment and the creatures that share it with them. When a whole community, led by its city planners and legislators, makes the effort for a common cause, the results can be enormous.

From Waste to Wildlife

In 1964 the City of Arcata, California, built a dike along 40 acres of Humboldt Bay, creating an oceanside landfill. By the 1970s, the landfill had contaminated local neighborhoods, and toxic leachate was reported in Humboldt Bay. The Department of Health condemned the site, and the landfill was closed in 1973.

After several years of planning, new life was brought back to the degraded marsh area in 1981 with the funding and creation of the 75-acre Arcata Marsh and Wildlife Sanctuary, a flourishing ecosystem encompassing the old landfill.

In Arcata, meanwhile, a proposed wastewater pipeline was being criticized for its cost and vulnerability in an area that was at risk from earthquakes and tsunamis. Arcata citizens rallied for an integrated wastewater treatment process within a natural system, a task force was assigned to the project and a complete wetland wastewater treatment system was authorized for the Arcata Marsh.

What appears to be a lush, vibrant ecosystem is actually a complex system of treatment that has become a model for other cities that are intrigued by Arcata's success. Wastewater travels from the city, through gravity and pumps, to arrive at the Marsh's headworks, from where a system of clarifiers, digesters and oxidation ponds guide it through both mechanical and natural treatment systems.[1]

Over 300 species of birds and mammals, 100 species of plants

From toxic landfill to vibrant wildlife habitat — the Arcata Marsh and Wildlife Sanctuary.

ETHAN SMITH

and 6 species of fish call the Arcata Marsh home. Arcata residents use the Marsh's trail system for bird watching, jogging, cycling and finding solace, and teachers and parents show children how science and nature work together. Nearby Humboldt State University uses the Marsh for its biology, environmental engineering, botany and wildlife management programs, and tourists from around the world visit the Marsh because of its unique integrated system.

Bridges for Bats

When the Congress Avenue Bridge in downtown Austin, Texas, was reconstructed in 1980, the bridge's engineers had created the perfect home for Mexican freetail bats. The crevices under the bridge began attracting thousands of bats to roost, and Austin's residents reacted with great concern, calling on the city to eradicate the bats. That's when Bat Conservation International stepped in, assuring Austinites that bats are gentle, sophisticated creatures that pose no risk to humans unless handled. What really changed

the view of the residents, though, was learning that the booming bat population was capable of eating up to 30,000 pounds of insects every night.

Today Austin embraces the Congress Avenue Bridge colony, numbering 1.5 million bats, as the largest of its kind in North America. An observation center has been built adjacent to the bridge, drawing 100,000 people annually to watch the colony take to the sky every night at sunset.

A Little Help from Our Friends

Most successful municipal conservation initiatives involve the combined efforts of city officials and local wildlife groups. Contact local groups and work with them to map your city's wildlife habitat, drawing up plans to create more habitat, making your parks and greenways a place for all creatures to safely pass through or call home.

- Bat Conservation International: www.batcon.org
- Friends of the Arcata Marsh: www.humboldt.edu/~ere_dept/marsh/FOAM
- Lights Out Toronto: www.toronto.ca/lightsout
- National Park Service Center for Urban Ecology: www.nps.gov/cue/
- Wildlife Society: www.wildlife.org

Lights Out Toronto

In 2006 Toronto, Ontario, became the first city in the world to implement a migratory bird protection policy. Lights Out Toronto is the combined effort of city council, an organization called the Fatal Lights Awareness Program (see Solution 82) and others who work to turn off the lights in the downtown core. It's estimated that nearly 10,000 birds are killed by collisions with lit structures in the city every year. The City of Toronto worked to get the program running in time for the spring 2006 migratory season.

27

Encourage Urban Farms

If the investment were made in urban agriculture, it could bring full employment to a community, great improvements in nutrition, and a sense that we've got a mission.

— Ken Dunn, founder of
Chicago's Resource Center

Urban farms are traffic stoppers. They spring up out of vacant lots, where, in the midst of a concrete landscape, an abundance of greenery bursts proudly forth, resplendent with fresh, colorful vegetables and dedicated individuals weeding and watering their plots of land.

Community Gardens — Oases in the Inner City

The Resource Center in Chicago, Illinois, launched its first community garden in 1975, founded by Ken Dunn. With encouragement and support from the city, the group now runs four community gardens and provides fresh produce to its members, as well as to area markets, restaurants and passersby.

The gardens produce a wide variety of crops, from tomatoes and greens to potatoes and turnips. They generate income, offer a sense of self-worth and provide fresh organic produce that is nearly impossible to find in Chicago's poorer neighborhoods. LaDonna Redmond, president of the Institute for Community Resource Development in West Garfield says; "It's a real chore to get a salad. We can purchase illegal drugs, weapons, Nike trainers and junk food, but we can't get a salad."[1]

With the city's support, the urban farms could expand far more. Chicago has over 6,000 acres of unused land that could support 42,000 full-time jobs, if it were cultivated.

In a city like Chicago, converting an abandoned lot to a thriving community garden costs about $20,000,[2] which is why cities need to help with the process. With the involvement of city planners, start-up and operational committees, citizens' co-operatives and funding drives, urban farms can be very viable and support themselves.

Growing It Right in Montreal

The City of Montreal has created over 100 community gardens throughout its metropolitan area, encompassing 15 municipalities. With 8,000 plot allotments, Montreal's urban farms produce food for over 10,000 people. The City's garden programs have been in operation since the 1970s, and the gardeners and the City

Growing Peas and Peace

In San Antonio, Texas, the Avenida Guadalupe Garden bursts with life from what used to be a parking lot in one of the toughest neighborhoods, managed by two master gardeners and 200 fourth- and fifth-graders. Planted, weeded and harvested by the students, the garden produces a bounty of broccoli, beans, squash, greens and other vegetables, giving the children a newfound respect for the earth and for themselves.

Across town, Rodriquez Park used to hold the distinction of being the most vandalized park in the county. That was before 30 juvenile offenders constructed a large neighborhood vegetable garden and served as mentors for some 70 younger children. Excitement about urban gardening has risen in these troubled neighborhoods, and crime is falling, so much so that San Antonio's police officials have begun funding urban garden projects in other hard-hit areas of the city.

continue to work hard to make them more accessible to the public and more ecologically oriented. Montreal has been recognized as having one of the best urban farming programs in North America by the American Community Gardening Association. The City takes responsibility for providing soil, manure, fencing, water, tools, toilets, clubhouse/tool sheds and ongoing maintenance and employs horticulturalists to liaise with the garden groups. As in most cities with community garden programs, the plots are in great demand: Montreal's gardens need to grow by 25% to include everyone on the waiting list.

For the Animals: Urban Farms in the UK
Meanwood Valley Urban Farm in Leeds, England, has played a leadership role among Britain's many successful city farms, opening the first certified organic city farm in 1987. Meanwood is a green oasis, providing a thriving organic market, gardens and educational programs for visitors. The farm, a member of the Rare Breeds Survival Trust, helps to conserve endangered breeds of cows, sheep, pigs, goats, chickens and waterfowl.

Reach Out to the Community
Contact your local community organizations, find local organic farming advocates and set up a meeting to discuss your city's

potential for urban farms. Talk to other cities who have established programs, learning from their successes and obstacles, and put together a planning committee to strategize and fund a start-up program or expand an existing one.

- American Community Gardening Association: www.communitygarden.org
- City Farmer: www.cityfarmer.org
- Meanwood Valley Urban Farm: www.mvuf.org.uk
- Montreal's Community Garden Programs: www.cityfarmer.org/Montreal13.html
- Resource Center of Chicago: www.resourcecenterchicago.org
- The Urban Farm: www.urbanfarm.org

A community garden in Victoria, BC.

28

Ban Performing Animals Events

> This sends a very strong message to the circus industry that what they consider to be fun and entertaining is ... duping the public for profit.
> — Dr. Allison Stanley, Santa Ana, California

All around the world, people are beginning to look beneath the surface of the circuses, rodeos, aquariums and zoos where animals are forced into captivity for entertainment. The purveyors of these events adamantly defend their exhibitions, insisting that their animals are having a great time, but slowly but surely, people are becoming aware of the suffering and indignity these animals endure.

A Step Forward in Orange County
In Santa Ana, California, city council has officially banned wild and exotic animal performances. In 2004, by unanimous vote, the mayor and council answered a call from the community and agreed that animal circuses are inhumane and pose a risk to both the animals and the general public.

Circus shows that use animals are no longer welcome in Israel's busiest urban center, either. After a successful campaign by animal welfare lobby groups in 2005, Tel-Aviv's mayor

- Animal-Free Circuses:
  www.circuses.com/pdfs/AnimalFreeCircuses.pdf
- Born Free Foundation: www.bornfree.org.uk
- Captive Animal Protection Society:
  www.captiveanimals.org
- Cities with legislation prohibiting animal performances:
  www.circuses.com/pdfs/AnimalActs_Legislation.pdf
- Dawnwatch: www.dawnwatch.com/entertainment.htm
- Performing Animal Welfare Society: www.pawsweb.org

instructed his municipality to avoid any future contracts with circuses involving performing animals. This move is an evolution from Israel's previous law banning wild animal acts and now protects all animal species from being used for human entertainment in the city.

Burlington, Vermont, Sao Paulo, Brazil, Windsor, Ontario, Rio de Janeiro, Brazil, Kamloops, BC, and Redmond, Washington, have all followed suit. It's time for all cities to make this move.

Consider the Alternatives
Still want a circus to come to town? There are plenty of highly entertaining circuses that don't use animals that are just as exciting and a lot more humane. Montreal-based Cirque du Soleil is one of the best-known circuses in the world, wowing international audiences with their spectacular productions. There's also California's Earth Circus, Hawaii's Hiccup Circus, Laser Vaudeville in Colorado, the Mexican International Circus, Ontario's Little Russian Circus, No Fit State Circus in Wales, Circus Oz in Australia and Cirque Plume in France.

A Victorious Vote for the Bulls
In Barcelona, Spain, the city council has also taken a courageous choice and listened to its conscience and its electorate. In defiance of what many consider to be Spain's national pastime, the City has banned bullfighting. Nearly 250,000 people signed the petition that led to the 2004 vote.

Every year, over 100 bulls were killed during the bullfighting exhibitions. However, a city

council spokesperson says there has not been a large bullfighting following in the region since the 1960s.[1] Apparently, those who watch the events are generally curious tourists. Nonetheless, the move has angered supporters of the sport who have vowed to fight the new law.

Many rodeo events, such as calf roping, cause intolerable suffering, injury and death to animals. At the world's most famous rodeo — the Calgary Stampede — more than 50 animals died between 1986 and 2006 from injuries sustained during the event.

Put It on the Ballot

In 1997 the city of Vancouver, BC, let their citizens have the final say on the fate of a public zoo by holding a referendum. Organized by the group Friends of Stanley Park, the question was asked whether or not Vancouverites supported the Stanley Park Zoo, and to the surprise of both sides, people voted 54% in favor of closing the zoo. Flowerbeds and walkways now greet visitors where over 50 animals were once held in captivity.

The move reflects Vancouver's concerns over animal welfare. Thanks to public pressure, performing animal circuses have been banned, along with the capture of wild whales and dolphins for the city's aquarium. The aquarium lives on, however, and remains a center of controversy for animal welfare advocates, city councilors and many residents.[2]

Maui Gives Whales Their Freedom

In 2002 Maui County Council passed a bill banning the captivity of cetaceans. Maui is world famous for its wild whales and dolphins, a reputation that will continue, thanks to the timely legislation being introduced before the construction of a new resort and aquarium in Maui.

Aquariums, particularly marine mammal circus acts, are bound to disappear as the public is educated and revolts against it.
— Jean-Michel Cousteau

29

Create and Enforce Animal Welfare Bylaws

> It's not going to cost the taxpayers a single nickel. It's simply outlawing the product of a cruel and inhumane practice.
>
> — Joe Moore, Chicago Alderman, on his city's legislation banning the sale of foie gras

Cities can play a huge role in animal welfare by writing and enforcing bylaws and ordinances that protect all species within the municipality. All animals deserve humane treatment, and city councils have the power to ensure they get it.

Humane Choices in Italy

Reggio Emilia is a prosperous tourist town in Italy that has one of the toughest animal protection bylaws anywhere. Animal rights groups and many residents champion the precedent-setting legislation as monumental and heroic, while many restaurateurs and even pet owners have reacted with outrage.

- Under the bylaw, introduced in 2004, lobsters can no longer be boiled alive. The bylaw calls the practice useless torture. This changes everything for restaurants that have lobster on the menu.
- Pet owners are criticizing the bylaw since they have to ensure that sociable caged birds

are kept in pairs, with enough width in their cages to accommodate five times their wingspan and three times their height.

- The city has hired a full-time employee to look after stray cats.
- Hunting with dogs is prohibited.

Reggio Emilia's bylaw covers everything from pet shops to amusement parks. To animal advocates who have spent years rallying for the humane treatment of their four-legged and feathered friends, it seems like common sense. They figured out that boiling lobsters alive is a horrible practice a long time ago.

Animal Friendly Bylaws Abound

In Turin, Italy, residents can be charged up to $650 for failing to walk their dogs. The northern Italian city takes its animal welfare very seriously and also has progressive legislation banning the mutilation of animals for esthetic motives, such as tail-docking. The city's *La Stampa* daily reported, "In Turin it will be illegal to turn one's dog into a ridiculous fluffy toy."

In Boulder, Colorado, people with pets are no longer their "owners." In all city literature, the word is now "guardian," suggesting responsibility and respect, instead of simple ownership.

San Francisco, California, has also adopted the word "guardian" for pet owners. Their recreational pathways and outdoor areas have been designed with animals in mind, as well as people. There are 24 designated off-leash Dog Play Areas across the city, ranging from 0.3 to 21 acres in size.

- Carriage Horses:
  www.animalrightsflorida.org/CarriageHorses.html
- The Humane Society of Canada:
  www.humanesociety.com
- The Humane Society of the United States: www.hsus.org
- Model Municipal Bylaws:
  www.cfhs.ca/law/model_municipal_bylaws
- World Society for the Prevention of Cruelty to Animals:
  www.wspa.ca

Relief for Carriage Horses

The suffering that carriages horses are subjected to in cities around the world is often overlooked. The constant pounding of their hooves on the pavement, inhaling exhaust fumes from city traffic, stops and starts under heavy loads and temperature extremes make it a miserable job. In New York City, four horses died from heat exhaustion on a single day.[1] The average working life of a North American carriage horse is less than four years, after which the majority are worn out and sent to slaughter.[2]

London, Paris and Toronto have all banned horse-drawn carriages. Santa Fe, New Mexico, rejected a proposal for carriage-horse operation, stating that the city "should not advocate any type of operation which could result in the abuse of horses." In 1994 when the Biloxi, Mississippi, city council voted unanimously to ban horse-drawn carriages, they received thousands of letters and calls commending their decision,[3] prompting one councilor to say, "I didn't know it was that hot an issue, but we have literally gotten mail from every place imaginable."

Cities with carriage-horse operators should agree on a temperature-extreme bylaw whereby horses would be given a break until more moderate temperatures resume, between 25°F and 75°F (-4°C and 24°C), while taking wind chill and humidity into consideration. Sacramento, California, has already introduced temperature restrictions for carriage horses, after a campaign by the Carriage Horse Concerns Coalition. Bylaws should also ensure that carriages operate solely within park boundaries or designated pedestrian streets and make it mandatory for operators to be licensed and adhere to high safety standards and compassionate care of their horses. Each horse should have a maximum eight-hour workday and a day off after three days of work, unshod on pasture, to relieve hoof stress and allow for freedom of movement.

Chicago, Illinois, has banned the sale of foie gras. When Chicago City Council passed the ordinance in 2006, they set a precedent by becoming the first major North American city to ban the sale of the luxury ingredient, which involves the cruel practice of force-feeding geese and ducks through a pipe.

ETHAN SMITH

30

Make Humane Pest Control Part of City Planning

> Given the choice, most people would prefer to resolve wildlife conflicts in a humane manner, but they usually have no idea what to do.
>
> — Dr. John Hadidian, Humane Society wildlife biologist

What about the animals you don't want around, such as the rats, crows, raccoons and wasps? A city can play an important preventative role in pest control, by educating citizens that the vast majority of the little creatures they encounter pose no threat to them or their homes and are beneficial guests.

Casting Light on the Problem

The township of Montclair, New Jersey, has a brand new light show in two of its parks. Very early in the morning, just before dawn, a laser light show begins dancing through the grass of Edgemont Memorial and Yantacaw Brook parks. But it isn't intended for the local residents — it's intended for the geese.

Montclair has a huge goose problem. The geese don't think it's a problem, but the residents do. A thick layer of goose droppings

Pesticide free sign in Hamilton, Ontario.

carpets both parks on a regular basis, causing quite a mess for park users and a potential health risk.

Other communities have been less inventive in dealing with the geese, euthanizing them to lower their populations. But Montclair sought a more humane approach, choosing the services of a local laser company. The low lights dancing over the grass deter the geese from landing, causing no more harm than the annoyance of rescheduling their morning flight.

Geese have excellent memory, similar to that of a nine-year-old child,[1] and will pattern their morning visits around the lights. In order to be effective, the lasers have to be moved around and lit at different times to persuade the geese to move their morning visits farther from the community.

Feral Felines

Hampton, Virginia, has a cat problem. The region has an over-population crisis, and feral cats have created large colonies to survive. The city responded by creating legislation to curb the problem by setting strict rules for cat guardians; including not letting cats venture outside at all unless they have been licensed, vaccinated and sterilized. The city issued firm guidelines for the courageous people who have taken on the responsibility of caring for the wild cat colonies.

Going Pesticide-free in Canada

Over 60 communities across Canada have pesticide restrictions, including the major centers of Toronto, Vancouver, Montreal and Halifax, with

30% of Canadians living in communities with such bylaws.

The Ontario College of Family Physicians says a growing body of studies show pesticides cannot be considered safe at any level of exposure, and a 2002 Environment Canada study found that water in the Don and Humber rivers was contaminated with pesticides coming from Toronto lawns, with amounts exceeding Ontario's water-quality guidelines for aquatic life.[2] With many studies confirming the danger of pesticides to humans, animals and the environment,

cities coast-to-coast are creating bylaws to stop an out-of-control situation. A 1993 Ontario government survey found that professional applicators alone were applying 2.8 million pounds of pesticides for cosmetic reasons, accounting for just 21% of the provincial total of outdoor pesticide use.[3]

City residents in areas with pesticide bylaws are adapting quickly. Within three years of Halifax's 2002 bylaw, 93% of its residents had stopped using pesticides altogether. In Toronto, where pesticide use was reduced by 97% between 1998 and 2002, public opinion polls suggest that 80% of residents support the bylaw.[4] Businesses are behind the bylaws, too. One of Toronto's premier golf courses, The Granite Club, reduced its costs by $40,000 by cutting its pesticide use in half, and it still has pristine greens. In 2003 the Canadian Center for Pollution released a report finding that pesticide bylaws in Quebec have resulted in an economic boom for the organic lawn-care industry.

Pesticides are:

- Harmful to human health. Of the 30 most commonly used pesticides, 19 are known carcinogens (cancer causing), and 13 are linked with birth defects.[5]

- Particularly harmful to children, pregnant women, the elderly and those with chronic illnesses.[6]

- Hazardous to companion animals. Dogs and cats that spend time in public parks and backyards are vulnerable to pesticide poisoning and long-term illness.

- Hazardous to wildlife. Deer, raccoons, squirrels, birds, butterflies, snakes, insects and fish are all vulnerable.

- Contaminating soil, water and air. A 2005 study by the Environmental Working Group, analyzing 22 million tap-water samples from across the US, found 260 contaminants; 141 of which have no safety regulations.[7]

- Abundant Earth: www.abundantearth.com/store/naturalpestcontrol.html

- Humane pest control information: www.absoluteponds.com/links/pestcontrol.html

- Pigeon control: www.animalaid.org.uk/h/n/CAMPAIGNS/wildlife/ALL1348

- Trapping alternatives: www.idausa.org/facts/gluefacts.html

- PiCAS UK Limited: www.picasuk.com/alternatives.htm

31

Return to Family Farming Values

How I make my living has to fit in with my goals as a caretaker of the land. When I leave this ground, I want it to be in better shape than when I arrived.

— Larry Thompson,
Oregon organic farmer

Small farms are disappearing in North America, having fallen deeply into debt paying for genetically modified seed, pesticides and chemical fertilizers, and are being replaced by a few corporate production machines. The big companies are able to drive prices of conventional food too low for small farms to stay afloat in the aggressive industry. Between 1974 and 2002, the number of corporate-owned farms in the US increased by more than 46%,[1] while family-owned farms continue to decline, now accounting for just 44% of total farmland.[2]

Family farms in the US are going out of business at a rate of 330 farms per week.[3] Many of the farms are taken into corporate ownership, with the big companies taking over the land when small farms go bankrupt. And much of the farmland falls to development. According to the Environmental Protection Agency, 3,000 acres of productive US farmland is lost to development every day.[4]

Opting out of "Conventional"

By going organic (see Solution 33), conventional farms change the nature of the game. No longer

- Ecological Farming Association: www.eco-farm.org
- Farm Aid: www.farmaid.org
- Local Harvest: www.localharvest.org
- NOFA: www.nofavt.org
- Organic Valley Family of Farms: www.organicvalley.coop
- Stoneyfield Farm: www.stonyfield.com

are they committed to paying for the agrichemicals produced by the same corporations who threaten to take over their land. The demand for organics is increasing by 20% a year, and family farmers who have made the transition are finally making a profit.

Vermont is leading the way in North America for organic transitioning. With the help of state officials, who hire people to spur conversion, and organizations like the Northeast Organic Farming Association (NOFA) of Vermont, which assists and oversees the conversion process, organic dairy farms reached 10% of the market share by 2006, and NOFA expects the number to double over each of the coming years.

In North Troy, Vermont, Rick Letourneau fell so deeply into debt as a conventional dairy farmer that he had to sell his cows and was burning his furniture to heat his house. He began the conversion to organic in 2000, and by 2003, his 36 dairy cows were bringing him a profit. With financing from a local bank, which would only lend money to farmers becoming organic, and farm contracting work on the side, Rick continues to improve his 85-acre farm and add more cows to his herd. Rick says the cows are happier and healthier now, too. Before the conversion, he spent $200 a month on vet bills. After going organic, he went three years without a vet visit.

Family Farms on a Big Scale

How can a large farm operate on family-farm values and yet still remain competitive in today's consumptive market?

Stoneyfield Farm in New Hampshire is committed to family-farm values, producing quality organic dairy products. Guided in part by the fact that the average mouthful of food travels 1,200 miles,[5] Stoneyfield has done its best to reinvent the idea of farming locally on a large scale. They work closely with supermarkets, farmers markets and community-supported agriculture to promote a return to community farming and cut down on mass transportation and packaging.

Stoneyfield began operation in 1983 with 11 jersey cows and a yogurt recipe that would become their trademark. Throughout their growth, they remained committed to family-farming values, placing their community, their animals, the environment and the planet ahead of profits. They give 10% of their profits to their Profits for the Planet program, funds that are distributed to organizations such as the Sustainability Institute, Children's Health Environmental Coalition, Nesenkeag Cooperative Farm and the Rainforest Foundation.

They have an aggressive program for recycling and reusing materials, saving an estimated $100,000 annually and preventing hundreds of tons of waste from entering landfills. They are also committed to environmental packaging (they even have a toothbrush made from their recycled materials), oppose bovine growth hormone (they will not work with any other dairies that use rBGH) and support climate change initiatives and educational programs for students and other farmers.

Stoneyfield's efforts have been recognized with the Green Cross Millennium Award for Corporate Environmental Leadership.

SINIKKA CROSLAND

Faith in the Family Farm

Peter Decker and Tina Durrance believe in the future of family farms; so much so that they sold their autobody shop in Florida and spent $500,000 to start an organic dairy farm in Vermont. From their New Venture Farm in Barton, Peter says the move is a great investment: "I can work from home, it's cheaper on gas and my employees — the cows — always show up for work."

32

Practice Humane Animal Husbandry

Animals are only farm animals when they've been domesticated by us. Otherwise, they'd be just what their ancestors were — wild animals, ranging across the wide open spaces, foraging for food and shelter. But we changed all that. Now farm animals live and work in close proximity to us, according to rules we set, and the moment they're past their peak productivity, we get rid of them. This is a relationship we've created for farm animals that is quite beyond their choice. Much of the time, the relationship involves incredible discomfort and suffering. But it doesn't have to be that way. It is possible to practice humane animal husbandry. We can coexist with our farm animals; being grateful and respectful for the role they play in our lives.

He [grandfather] believed that having the animals relaxed and comfortable right up to the time of slaughter was not only humane, but produced a better quality product. I suppose that has never been proven scientifically, but it's conventional wisdom in my family.

— Jim Rickert

It's even possible to let them enjoy their days; looking forward to interaction with humans rather than fearing them.

A Humane Example in Northern California
Prather Ranch is a 15,000-acre cattle ranch near Mt. Shasta that proudly proclaims its cattle as being "Certified Humane Raised and Handled." Jim and Mary Rickert run their large organic ranch guided by principles that ensure their cows are treated with respect and dignity. The Rickerts have been around cows all their lives. Jim says he got his first lesson in responsible animal husbandry when he overfed a calf given to him as a present by his grandfather, and it died. The incident shook Jim up and taught him the importance of careful treatment for farm animals.

Since 1993 the Rickerts have dedicated their time to creating a low-stress life for their cattle and a deep understanding of their herd. All of their cows are born and raised on their farm. They are also slaughtered in the Rickerts' processing plant on the ranch; preventing the need for stressful transportation to overcrowded plants elsewhere. The practices the Rickerts follow are inspired by the work of animal scientist Temple Grandin who developed

FARM SANCTUARY

humane methods of handling and slaughter, reducing the animals' suffering as much as possible.

All the cows on Prather Ranch have access to fresh spring water and are never fed animal-based proteins, antibiotics or growth-stimulating hormones. As Jim Rickert said, "Our philosophy is that responsible stewardship of the land is a priority. By doing so, we are in a win-win-win situation: the animals live in ideal conditions, we use ecologically sound and sustainable methods, and consumers can serve our beef with confidence that it is a pure product."

Sharing the Land
Stefan and Doreen Sobkowiak produce apples and animals from Miracle Farms in Verdun, Quebec. They share the land in their no-spray orchard, allowing sheep, chickens, turkeys and guinea fowl to roam through lush grass around their apple trees. The land has been in trees and grass since the mid-1980s and is dedicated to permaculture practices and humane animal husbandry.

In Castor, Alberta, James and Katherine Griebel of Prairie Wool Organics are dedicated to the well-being of the animals that share their farm. They're proud to proclaim their certified organic, pasture-raised beef and free-range chickens as being free of pesticides, synthetic hormones and antibiotics. The three-generation farming family is guided by principles of low-stress treatment of animals.

Michael and Diana Austin moved to their 160-acre Misty Mountain Farm in West Virginia in 2001, taking over a rundown, 100-year-old homestead, and have been working hard to reintroduce a healthy ecosystem. They use rotational and multi-species grazing to return fertility and balance to their pastures. They are dedicated to the humane treatment of their cattle, goats, turkeys and chickens, recognizing the importance of a successful relationship between the land, the animals and themselves.

The Five Freedoms — from the Farm Animal Welfare Council

Freedom from Hunger and Thirst
Freedom from Discomfort
Freedom from Pain, Injury or Disease
Freedom to Express Normal Behavior
Freedom from Fear and Distress

- AWI — humane husbandry criteria: www.awionline.org/farm/standards.htm
- Canadians for the Ethical Treatment of Food Animals: www.cetfa.com
- Farm Animal Welfare Council: www.fawc.org.uk/freedoms.htm
- HSUS standards for livestock and poultry: www.eap.mcgill.ca/LPAW_1.htm
- Humane Farm Animal Care: www.certifiedhumane.com/story.html
- Prather Ranch: www.pratherranch.com

33

Go Organic

Organic farming systems have been designed to produce food with care for human health, the environment and animal welfare.

— Alissa Cook, Soil Association

Ever since the introduction of agrichemicals, nature has been thrown off-balance. Pesticides have killed many of the birds that once lived in fields, resulting in more insect problems, heavier pesticide use and the contamination of soil and water. Farm animals have been injected with growth enhancers and medication to boost production and ward off disease, resulting in antibiotic-resistant bacteria and the global spread of highly contagious illnesses such as mad cow disease[1] and avian flu.[2]

Organic for All Species

In 2005 Oxford University's Wildlife Conservation Research Unit concluded a five-year study, the most comprehensive to date, of 180 farms in the UK, finding that organic farms support 85% more plant species than their conventional counterparts, as well as more birds, bats and spiders.[3] Other studies have found 44% more birds in organically farmed land, with twice as many skylarks and butterflies.[4]

Organics are also better for animal reproduction. Studies have shown female rabbits having twice the level of ovum production when eating organically, while those fed conventional food had a decline in fertility over three generations. Chickens given organic feed increased their egg production by 28%.[5]

Animals Prefer Organics[6]

Animals themselves are showing us that organic food is better for us.

- Wild geese prefer to eat in fields of organic canola rather than genetically modified (GM) fields.
- Raccoons often raid organic cornfields, but ignore GM crops.
- Deer will choose organic crops if they are across the road from GM crops.

From Gnodstadt to Baden

The Pfennings were a farming family in Europe at least as far back as the 1600s, and when agrichemicals were introduced 100 years ago, they embraced the new technology and applied it to their land. But, by 1950, Wilhelm Pfenning was becoming concerned about his health and was questioning the nutritional value of his German farm's produce. His first attempts at chemical-free farming were unsuccessful, so he went back to "modern" farming and committed himself to learning all he could about alternatives. Between 1965 and 1978, the Pfennings lobbied for a return to chemical-free agriculture. Their efforts were met with resistance from their community at first, but their village of Gnodstadt began to come on board, and the local bakery became a thriving business on the strength of their organic sourdough bread. In 1978 the Pfenning's farm fell into the proposed path of the new A7 Autobahn roadway, and they decided to look to the future; moving their family of six to Canada. Today the Pfenning Organic Farm in Baden, Ontario, is one of Canada's largest suppliers of organic produce, with 100 acres of organic vegetables and 30 seasonal employees working alongside the family.

- Tests have shown cows to sniff and ignore GM corn, when a trough of organic corn is nearby.
- Similar tests on pigs have seen them devouring organic feed while leaving GM feed behind.
- Lab rats refused to eat GM FlavrSavr tomatoes, eventually developing stomach lesions when force-fed them. The tomatoes went on the market in 1990, but humans didn't like them much better, and their production was discontinued.

Why Panic, Go Organic

There's change on the horizon — sales of organic products have increased by more than 20% every year since 1997.[7] In 2003 US sales of organic foods passed $10 billion.[8] Canada's sales, increasing similarly, passed $1 billion in 1999.[9] Worldwide, annual sales of organic products are estimated at more than $20 billion.[10]

Leadership in New England

Travis and Amy Forques are leading an organic revolution in New England, and their efforts are spreading across the country. In a region where many farmers were despairing about the future (123 dairy farms folded in 1999 alone), Travis and Amy began the conversion to organic farming on their 240 acres near Alburg Springs and were determined to involve other farmers. Travis spent two to three hours every night helping farmers understand how organic farming would bring stability to their farms, protect the environment and contribute to their communities.

As a result of his efforts, 22 farming families now farm organically on 6,000 acres, with over 1,350 dairy cows between them. The collective sells its New England Pastures organic milk across the northeastern States, and the farmers are all part of the Organic Valley cooperative of organic dairy farmers, the largest of its kind in North America. There's a long list of farmers waiting to join the Organic Valley Vermont milk pool. Travis said, "They know organics is a lifeline, and they want in."

ETHAN SMITH

- Canadian Organic Growers: www.cog.ca
- International Federation of Organic Agriculture Movements: www.ifoam.org
- Organic Farming Research Foundation: www.ofrf.org
- Organic Valley: www.organicvalley.coop
- Pfenning's Organic Farm: www.pfenningsorganic.com
- Soil Association: www.soilassociation.org
- USDA Organic Program: www.ams.usda.gov/nop

34

Share Your Habitat

We've let the grass grow back and allow all kinds of wildlife. Yet we're able to support as many cows as he (the previous owner) did, and we're making a good profit doing it.

— Tim Tew, Montana rancher

Farmland and ranchland cover more than half the American landscape. Combined with increasing urban sprawl, this is dramatically affecting wildlife habitat. Decreased water quality, dwindling food supplies and pollution are also taking a heavy toll on wild animals that use agricultural land.

Something has to change, because without the natural balance that a diversity of species provides, agricultural land will soon no longer be able to support life of any kind.

An Answer for the Skylark

In the United Kingdom, a group of farmers has been volunteering with the British Trust for Ornithology (BTO) in a study to find ways to help farmland bird species. Intensive farming practices

since the 1970s have driven many species, most notably the skylark, to "threatened" classification. But the study has found a solution in the practice of delayed stubble plowing.

Conventionally, crop stubble is plowed under soon after harvesting, leaving fields with little or no vegetation until reseeding happens the following spring. Delaying stubble plowing until the early spring creates a vast food source for the skylark and their avian friends. Dr. Juliet Vickery, BTO's Head of Terrestrial Ecology said, "Stubble fields are like giant bird-tables across the countryside; they contain seeds spilled as the crop was harvested, and also weeds. So if the stubble fields disappear, so does a key food source."

Over the ten years of the study, the results of delayed stubble plowing showed a clear population recovery for several species of birds and a decrease in the decline of others. The skylark and ten other species all benefited from the study, giving hope for the practice to work elsewhere.

On the Open Prairie

Mary and Jim Norton own 200 acres of farmland in New Hartford, Iowa. The land has been in Mary's family since 1893 when it was a vast sea of native prairie grasses, wildflowers and a thriving diversity of wildlife. Since that time, the state of Iowa has seen the original prairie land dwindle to less than one percent.

US NATIONAL PARK SERVICE

Mountain lion (cougar).

On the Norton's Prairie Hill Farm, however, the prairie is being restored, because Mary and Jim have spent 30 years recreating its natural habitat. Stands of native plant species, including bluestem grass, yellow prairie coneflower and purple prairie clover now abound in the fields. The native plants have become so abundant that the Nortons are able to share seed with their neighbors and local schools to begin new areas of restoration. Prairie Hill Farm includes ponds, woodlands and riparian buffer strips, offering habitat for many wildlife species that now live and travel through their land.

Livestock Guardian Dogs

Livestock guardian dogs are trained to ward off predators, offering a unique way for farmers to share their land. These dogs have been bred for centuries to protect farm animals. In Italy shepherds have been protecting their flocks from bears and wolves with Maremma dogs for 2,000 years, and today there are 7,000 of the big dogs at work in the country. The most common guardian dog in North America is the Great Pyrenees, known for its size, courage and reliability. Successful guardian dogs are responsible, intelligent and formidable enough to scare off the largest predators. The dogs work wonderfully on small farms and large ranches, thriving on the space to move around and preventing the need for ranchers to shoot or poison wolves, coyotes, cougars and bears.

- Guardian dogs for livestock protection: www.all-animals.com/groveland/dogs.html
- Livestock Guardian Dogs: www.lgd.org
- National Sustainable Agriculture Information Service: www.attra.ncat.org
- Ranching with Grizzlies: www.defenders.org/ defendersmag/issues/spring05/grizzly.html
- USDA Wildlife Habitat Incentives Program: www.nrcs.usda.gov/programs/whip

Sharing Habitat in Big Sky Country

Leanne and John Hayne have a 3,000-acre family sheep ranch in northwestern Montana, in the shadows of the Rocky Mountains. Their ranch borders grizzly country, where the bears are making a comeback, thanks to conservation efforts by Defenders of Wildlife and ranchers like the Haynes. The Haynes don't consider the bears intruders and do their best to give them their privacy. They've partnered with Defenders of Wildlife to install electric fencing around sheep bedding grounds and 400 acres of their pasture, and Defenders helps other ranchers to use Karelian bear dogs to condition the bears to avoid certain areas. As Defenders' Minette Johnson said, "Preventing conflicts is our best bet for building tolerance among local folks and helping the bears recover."

35

Switch to Food Crops for People

Inch by inch, row by row
I'm going to make this garden grow.
All it takes is a rake and a hoe
And a piece of fertile ground...

— **Pete Seeger**

Every farmer who switches to growing food crops for people reduces animal suffering, preserves the environment and potentially helps to reduce world hunger, since ten pounds of plant protein is needed for every pound of meat,[1] protein that could be fed directly to people.

10 hectares of land will produce enough:[2]

Meat to feed 2 people

Corn to feed 10 people

Grain to feed 24 people

Soybeans to feed 61 people

ETHAN SMITH

Of Beef and Hunger

In India the average person consumes 11 lbs. of meat a year. In Britain, one of the wealthiest nations, it's 175 lbs.[3] In the US it's 275 lbs. of meat, mostly beef. Americans' appetite for beef is huge, resulting in the sale of 6.7 billion burgers a year.[4]

There are nearly three times as many farm animals in the world as there are people: 16.8 billion. Even the most efficient animals consume much more protein than they produce. Cows are the worst, with a 10:1 ratio. Pigs are right behind at 9:1, with chickens at 5:1. All the excess nutrients are lost as manure. Livestock in the United States eat enough wheat and soy beans to feed one billion people annually; almost one-sixth of the world's population.[5]

Since North Americans don't have enough farmland to raise all the beef we eat, we use other nations' farmland to grow our beef for import. The more meat we produce, the more hunger exists.

Meat and the Environment

Producing meat takes a much harder toll on the environment than do food crops for people:

- A pound of beef requires three-quarters of a gallon of oil to produce it. By the time a beef cow reaches its adult weight of over 1200 lbs., it will have "consumed" 283 gallons of oil,[6] producing 2.8 tons of carbon dioxide (CO_2) emissions over 5 years.[7]

- Its manure will produce 20 lbs. of nitrous oxide (N_2O) annually,[8] a greenhouse gas that is 296 times more powerful than CO_2.

- Its digestive system will produce 285 lbs. of methane (CH_4) annually,[9] a greenhouse gas that is 23 times more powerful than CO_2.
- When you add these together, a beef cow will produce 6.8 tons of CO_2 equivalent a year, more than an average family car.[10]
- The average meat eater is responsible for 3.8 tons of CO_2 equivalent a year from eating beef.[11]
- 90% of the packaging used in meat production is not recycled.[12]
- A pound of beef requires 2,500 gallons of water to produce it, leading to water depletion. The Ogallala aquifer is losing 13 trillion gallons of water a year; some wells in Northwest Texas are already running dry.[13]
- The waste from a cow, which is 130 times greater than it is from a human, sometimes contaminates water systems and soil with disease-bearing organisms.[14]

One-Stop Farming in Ontario

Tom Manley's family farm, near the small town of Berwick, Ontario, made the switch from dairy to cash crops in 1988 and became certified organic. Tom went to farmers, friends, family and strangers and managed to raise the start-up funding he needed.

It was a tough sell, getting funding and finding support for his business idea: a one-stop business for feed for animals and people, seeds for fields and gardens and organic fertilizers. Most importantly, it would all be organic in a time when the word still raised eyebrows. Today, Homestead Organics is a hub of activity in an area that once lacked an organic infrastructure, and Tom spends most of his time answering questions from other farmers and spreading the word about organic agriculture.

Molly Thorkildsen and Will Bonsall began farming "veganically" over 20 years ago. Their Khadighar Farm, near Farmington, Maine, uses no animal products whatsoever, including in its fertilizers. Molly and Will prefer this method of farming because of the inefficiency and waste associated with relying on manure that comes from animals high on the food chain. Khadighar Farm is on a path of self-sufficiency, and veganic farming is helping them meet that goal. They grow a wide variety of vegetables, fruits, grains and legumes, using solar-powered irrigation, extensive terraces and ramial (deciduous wood) chips for mulch.

- Ask Farmer Brown: www.askfarmerbrown.com
- Energy Bulletin — farming sustainability: www.energybulletin.net/1202.html
- Fertilizing without manure: www.navs-online.org/voice/plant.html
- Genetic engineering and world hunger: www.greens.org/s-r/19/19-01.html
- Organic Consumers Association: www.organicconsumers.org
- Plants for a Future: www.pfaf.org/leaflets/whyplts.php

36

Fish Sustainably

More than 90% of the world's living organisms are found in the ocean,[1] creating a cradle of life that sustains our planet. Yet uncontrolled fishing worldwide is vacuuming up life faster than it can reproduce: 85 million tons of wild fish were pulled from the oceans in 2005.[2] The United Nations Environment Programme (UNEP) and World Conservation Union have warned that overfishing, along with pollution and climate change, are pushing marine life to a point of no return.[3] The world's most heavily fished species have declined by 75% over the past 100 years.[4] The numbers are worse for large fish like tuna, marlins, swordfish, cod and sharks, all of which have seen population declines of 90% since 1950.[5]

Follow the Rules of the Sea and Report Those Who Don't

UNEP estimates the value of Illegal, Unreported and Unregulated (IUU) catches to be between

- Audubon Seafood Lover's Guide:
  http://seafood.audubon.org
- Fishonline: www.fishonline.org
- Marine Conservation Society: www.mcsuk.org
- MSC certification: http://eng.msc.org
- Smart Gear Competition: www.smartgear.org
- Sustainable Seafood:
  www.eartheasy.com/eat_sustainable_seafoods.htm
- *The End of the Line: How Overfishing Is Changing the World and What We Eat*, by Charles Clover, New Press, 2006

Rather than being satisfied with the big fish, people are now routinely going after many of the little ones, too. Although the situation is not exactly analogous to eating one's seed corn, the result may be equally catastrophic.

— Daniel Pauly, director of the Fisheries Centre at the University of British Columbia

$4.9 billion and $9.5 billion annually.[6] A third of all IUU fishing occurs beyond national jurisdiction. It happens on both small and industrial scales, in both inshore waters and on the high seas. IUU fishers often use "flags of convenience," flying different national flags to avoid detection and circumvent regional guidelines. IUU fishing hurts fisheries and conservation initiatives. It hurts the people who depend on fisheries for food and jobs and causes coastal economies to collapse.

Fish On-Target

Global bycatch — the unwanted sea life caught by fishers — amounts to 20 million tons annually, accounting for 25% of the global catch.[7] Industrialized fishing vessels use increasingly advanced equipment to catch as many fish as possible, throwing away what they don't want. Only 1% of the world's 3.5 million fishing vessels are classified as industrial vessels, yet they have the capacity to catch 60% of the world's fish.[8] Industrial bycatch causes the continuous death of off-target fish, marine mammals, birds and sea turtles, as well as damaging gear and wasting time for fishers.

Become a Steward of the Sea

The Marine Stewardship Council (MSC) is an international non-profit organization, based in the UK, dedicated to reversing overfishing and the decline of fisheries. It was established in 1997 by the world's largest seafood buyer,

Unilever, and the World Wildlife Fund. Operating independently since 1999, the MSC is supported by over 100 organizations in 20 countries. Their product label rewards environmentally responsible fishery management and practice, based on a set of standards developed by scientists, fishery experts and environmentalists. Fourteen fisheries have obtained MSC certification, and over 300 seafood products bearing their blue label are available for consumers around the world. MSC certification is based on four guiding principles:

- The maintenance and re-establishment of healthy populations of targeted species;
- The maintenance of the integrity of ecosystems;
- The development and maintenance of effective fisheries management systems;
- Compliance with relevant local and national laws, as well as international understandings and agreements.

How Consumers Can Help

Ensure your grocer is carrying eco-friendly fish. Check the MSC website for companies in your area that sell MSC-certified fish. In Canada, Whole Foods Market sells wild-caught Alaskan salmon with the MSC label, as do several companies in the US, including Whole Foods, Safeway, Odyssey and Wildcatch.

Rewarding Innovation

Get involved with the World Wildlife Fund's Smart Gear Competition, which rewards innovative ideas in reducing bycatch. The 2006 grand prize of $25,000 went to Michael Herrmann, who developed a magnet attached above a fishing hook to deter sharks, which have a keen sense of magnetic fields.

Global fishing over 50 years (marine fish catches in million tons)[9]

	1953	1980	2003	Increase (%)
Pacific Ocean	7	32	44	+ 528
Atlantic Ocean	11	24	21	+ 90
Indian Ocean	1	3	9	+ 800
All Oceans	20	60	75	+ 275
Human Population (billions)	2.5	4	6	+ 140

37

Find Alternatives to Longlining

A moratorium would give us the time to put proven conservation measures into place to keep the leatherback from dropping off into oblivion forever.

— Robert Ovetz,
Sea Turtle Restoration Project

Longlines are a type of commercial fishing gear designed to catch swordfish and tuna, with lines up to 80 miles in length, carrying up to 10,000 hooks. Unfortunately, they also tend to catch everything else in their path. Many species are wounded and killed by commercial longlining, including endangered turtles, seabirds and an estimated 4.4 million marlins, sharks and marine mammals annually.[1] Fisheries are making progress in better designing long-lines to reduce the amount of bycatch — the unwanted fish and other marine life that end up on the lines — but the only effective means of curbing longline mortality is to get the lines out of the water from where they're doing the most damage.

Peril of the Leatherbacks

Approximately 40,000 sea turtles are caught and killed by longline operations every year.[2] The Pacific population of leatherback sea turtles is now so threatened that scientists estimate the gentle giants could be extinct within 15 years. The female nesting population has dropped by 95% since 1980.[3] For a creature that has been around for over 100 million years, this is a big deal, which is why 705 international scientists from 83 countries are urging the United Nations to implement a moratorium on all longline fishing in the Pacific. In 2005 the UN General Assembly adopted a resolution urging governments and fisheries management groups to take immediate steps to protect endangered sea turtles and seabirds.[4]

Peril of the Albatross

An estimated 300,000 seabirds, including 100,000 albatrosses are caught and killed by longline fishing hooks every year.[5] Albatrosses are being killed faster than they can reproduce, with the number of their 21 species threatened with extinction increasing from 7 in 1994 to 19 in 2004.[6]

In 2005 Prince Charles and yachtswoman Dame Ellen MacArthur joined forces to raise awareness for the plight of albatrosses, lending their voices to the Royal Society for the Protection of Birds for an urgent campaign to

NATIONAL UNDERSEA RESEARCH PROGRAM/NOAA

save the world's largest seabird. "The albatross lives in the middle of nowhere," said Dame Ellen, who credits the big birds with keeping her company on round-the-world trips. "They don't affect man, but man is affecting them."

Relief along Both Coasts

In 2003 NOAA Fisheries enacted a ban on longlining in a 133,000 square-mile area off the southeast US coast, which was followed by a complete moratorium within 200 miles off the coasts of Washington, Oregon and California. The National Coalition for Marine Conservation is now lobbying for a complete ban on longlining everywhere in the Pacific.

Getting the Facts

In Hawaii longline vessel owners and operators are required to attend an annual workshop to learn more about protected species and the threat posed by commercial fishing. Seabird, sea turtle and marine mammal biology and identification are discussed, along with interaction and avoidance measures. Various fishing gear alternatives are discussed, and first aid for injured sea life is demonstrated.

The workshops don't remove the threat posed by longlining, but they do allow fishers to learn the facts and the latest preventive measures, which is a step in the right direction. It is up to individual fishers to do their part now by modifying their gear and adopting less-invasive methods of fishing.

Alternatives to conventional longlining involve a number of gear adjustments, including:[7]

- Adding weights to sink bait faster
- Towing buoys behind the fishing vessel
- Towing artificial lures behind the vessel as a distraction
- Use of a diversion steamer line (tori line)
- Blue-dyed bait (which birds can't see)
- Strategic offal discarding (this means not indiscriminately dumping fish guts into the water)
- Side-setting of fishing lines with the use of a bird curtain between the fishing gear and the stern of the vessel
- Fishing at night when most seabirds are less active

Turtle fact — Female green sea turtles will swim as far 800 miles to mate but will return to nest on the very beach where they were born.

- National Coalition for Marine Conservation: www.savethefish.org/position_statements.htm
- National Marine Fisheries Service: www.nmfs.noaa.gov
- Save the Albatross: www.savethealbatross.net
- Sea Turtle Fact Sheet: www.sharkysdive.net/sea_turtles_fact_sheet.htm
- Sea Turtle Restoration Project: www.seaturtles.org

38

Find Alternatives to Bottom Trawling

Bottom trawling is like a farmer tearing his trees out by the root to get their fruit.
— Tom Raftican, United Anglers of Southern California

Commercial fishers use large nets, dragged along the ocean floor, to scoop up shrimp, groundfish species and everything else that happens to be in the way. Bottom trawling is devastating to many forms of marine life, most notably the endangered sea turtles that get caught up in the nets and die. Before attention was drawn to their plight, 55,000 sea turtles were being killed by shrimp nets every year in US waters alone.[1]

Down on the Floor

Far more than sea turtles are affected by bottom trawling. Delicate coral reefs, resplendent with

MIKE WHITE/NOAA

A coral reef — untouched.

life, sea sponges and thousands of tiny bottom-dwelling species also live on the ocean floor, along with crustaceans and groundfish, but the nets catch and tear apart everything in their path. The result is the destruction of entire ecosystems that have been millions of years in the making. The practice has been likened to chasing a rabbit with a bulldozer. And it's happening throughout the world's oceans, 24 hours a day.

- The estimated area that is swept annually by trawl gear is equivalent to 50% of the world's continental shelf area, or 150 times the area of forest that is clearcut worldwide each year. Sometimes, the same area is trawled many times a year.[2]
- During one year of a fishery trawling in the high seas south of Australia, observers recorded 10,000 tons of coral being brought up in the trawlers' nets. By contrast, the fishery reported a catch of 4,000 tons of orange roughy — their target species.[3]
- In the North Pacific, 44 tons of cold-water coral are taken as bycatch by bottom trawlers every year.[4]
- A single pass from a bottom trawl can cause damage to corals, sponge and other essential marine habitat which can take decades, or centuries, to recover.[5]

International Outcry

A thousand scientists, along with many NGOs and individuals, have pleaded with the United Nations to call for a halt to bottom trawling. The UN responded in 2004 by expressing concern over the results of bottom trawling in the world's oceans and asked countries to consider a temporary ban on the practice until the problems have been looked at. Yet bottom trawling continues unchecked. Russia, New Zealand and nine European countries lead the way, sharing 95% of the industry between them.[6]

In 2006 the World Wildlife Fund (WWF) released a report co-written with the wildlife trade-monitoring network, Traffic, warning that deep-sea fish and their habitat are being "plundered" to extinction by trawling. Simon Cripps, of WWF's marine programme, said, "It's got to stop, we've got to do it quickly. There is hope, if we can get management put in place."[7]

Trawling for Answers
There are two answers:

- A voluntary moratorium by the fishers themselves, who need to recognize the damage they are doing.

- A worldwide imposed moratorium called for by the United Nations and enforced by every nation.

Until the matter has been explored for better long-term answers, the practice must stop. For every vessel that lifts its nets off the ocean floor, the marine creatures that live there will breathe a collective sigh of relief.

- Blue Ocean Institute: www.blueocean.org
- Bottom trawling: www.akmarine.org/ourwork/conserve-fisheries-marine-life/impacts-of-bottom-trawling
- Caribbean Conservation Corporation: www.cccturtle.org
- Living Oceans Society: www.livingoceans.org/fisheries
- Save the High Seas: www.savethehighseas.org
- Sea Turtle Excluder Devices: www.nmfs.noaa.gov/pr/species/turtles/teds.htm

A Solution for Sea Turtles

The invention of the Turtle Excluder Device (TED) has brought some relief to the beleaguered sea turtle. TEDs are large grids of metal bars with an opening at the top or bottom attached to a shrimping net, allowing room for a sea turtle to escape while containing the shrimp and fish. By law, all US shrimpers and all countries providing shrimp to the US must use TEDs.

But TEDs have had their challenges. They continue to trap the larger loggerhead and leatherback sea turtles. New regulations require the TED escape hatches to be larger in the Atlantic and the Gulf of Mexico, but the biggest challenge is lack of enforcement. Outside US waters, it's simple to remove the TED from the shrimping nets to make bottom trawling easier, and governments in Central and South America lack the resources to enforce regulations. The turtles are also frequently killed when the TED equipment malfunctions or die from repeated capture. The TEDs were created with good intentions for sea turtles, but they are a stop-gap solution for only one species and not a comprehensive answer to bottom trawling.

39

Stop Inhumane and Unnecessary Fishing Practices

In the United States, over 17 billion fish are killed for food every year; 245 million in the name of sport.[1] By any measure, the methods used to kill sport fish are horrifying. Fish are hooked, speared, clubbed and suffocated. Inflicting cruelty like this on a land animal would quickly bring felony charges against the perpetrator.

Do Fish Suffer?

Suggesting that fish feel pain creates a heated debate with sport fishers and those who love eating fish. To animal welfare advocates, fish deserve as much respect and care as any other species. What has changed is the voice of scientists, who, after extensive research, have reached an overwhelming agreement that fish *do* feel pain and have brains that are far more complex than we ever imagined.[2]

One for the Lobsters

Clearwater Seafoods in Nova Scotia listened to the concerns of its customers and now trains its fishers and staff in the humane handling of lobsters, including individual saltwater holding cells to minimize stress, and an instant shock method of killing them rather than the traditional boiling water. Clearwater's industry-leading move paid off in 2006, when Whole Foods Market named them as the exclusive supplier of lobster meat for their North American grocery chain.

It's like running pedestrians down with your car. When they get up and brush themselves off, you roll down the window and say, "OK, you can go now. I just wanted to see if I could hit ya!"
— Comedian Ellen DeGeneres, on catch-and-release fishing

The scientific literature is quite clear. Anatomically, physiologically, and biologically, the pain system in fish is virtually the same as in birds and animals.
— Dr. Donald Broom, scientist at Cambridge University, and animal welfare advisor to the British government

No Kindness in Catch-and-Release

Nobody does a fish a favor by impaling it on a hook and releasing it. Playing a fish on the end of a line and exposing it to air greatly reduces its chance of survival. About a third of all fish exposed to air for just 30 seconds die after being released. Fish left out of the water for 60 seconds have a mortality rate of over 70%.[3] Many deep-water fish also have air bladders that inflate when brought to the surface too quickly, killing the fish. Then there are the injuries sustained during the hook impaling and removal. A single fish may be caught repeatedly in the same area, leading to its demise. Think a fish is dumb to keep biting the same hook? Not really. The hook is disguised as food, and the fish will keep trying to eat to survive.

Stop Shark Finning

Sharks often get caught in tuna and swordfish nets, but, instead of releasing them, fishers cut off their fins and dump the shark overboard. A shark with no fins will soon die or be eaten by other sharks, but a bowl of shark-fin soup in Asia can sell for over $100. There is a growing awareness about the practice, and 63 countries

- Animal Aid — fishing:
  www.animalaid.org.uk/images/pdf/fishfact.pdf
- Cetacean Bycatch Resource Center:
  www.cetaceanbycatch.org/gear_gillnet.cfm
- Coral reefs and dynamiting:
  www.starfish.ch/reef/conservation.html
- Fish and pain: www.organicconsumers.org/organic/
  043003_fish_pain.cfm
- Fishing Hurts.com: www.fishinghurts.com
- Pisces: www.pisces.demon.co.uk

have joined to ban shark finning in the Atlantic Ocean.[4] Shark populations have been dwindling, particularly in the North Atlantic, where the porbeagle shark has lost over 90% of its population since the 1960s.[5] Until now, there has been no protective legislation whatsoever. Tens of millions of sharks are killed every year, but the exact number is impossible to record since no laws govern their catch.

Norway Is Nice to Fish

How is it that the country that leads the world in the export of fish also leads in the humane treatment of fish? As with all EU countries, Norway's animal welfare laws include fish. Norwegians take the treatment of fish very seriously. Their country is the first in the world where citizens, the government and the fishing

NOAA

industry have worked together to end the suffering involved in sport fishing. In 2003 legislation went into effect, banning ponds where people could pay to catch fish. Norwegian conservationists and legislators are also teaming up to create laws to end catch-and-release fishing.[6]

In North America, fish have no protection whatsoever. Canada and the United States have flatly ignored all requests by conservationists, scientists, NGOs and individuals who have repeatedly pleaded for the extension of animal welfare laws to include fish. Canada and the United States' reluctance are heavily related to the protection of their economies. But if Norway, the world leader in fish exports can do it, every nation can.

40

Stop Fish Farming

The more aquaculture there is, the more disease there will be.

— Callum Roberts,
marine conservationist,
University of York, England

Fish farming, or aquaculture, is the world's fastest-growing food industry, with farmed fish and shellfish accounting for 30% of all seafood consumed, up from 10% in 1980.[1] On the surface, fish farming appears to be the perfect solution to overfishing and destructive fishing practices on the open sea. It's profitable, too, with the average salmon farm producing 50,000 tons of salmon annually, worth $10 million in retail sales.[2]

For the Fish

A fish farm is a floating feedlot, with a series of cages made from synthetic nets acting as a giant sieve to keep fish in, while allowing their waste to drop into the ocean. In a large farm, as many as 1.3 million fish are raised in a caged area the size of four football fields.[3] Farmed fish spend their lives in cramped quarters, subject to injury from their cages and each other, suffering a mortality rate of 10% to 30%[4] and a blindness rate of 40%.[5]

A Matter of Waste

Open net cages release untreated sewage directly into the ocean, discharging contaminated feed, toxic chemicals, artificial colorants (farmed fish are dyed so their meat will resemble that of their wild cousins), antibiotics and leaked oil into the surrounding marine ecosystem. A large fish farm produces the sewage equivalent of a city of 20,000 people. In the Clayoquot Sound's UNESCO Biosphere Reserve on Vancouver Island, with a human population of 1,500, the area's fish farms produce as much sewage as a city with 150,000 people.[6]

Great Escapes

A 2002 study by the Royal Society of London found that repeated escapes from salmon farms could lead to the extinction of wild salmon populations worldwide, because interbreeding reduces the population's fitness and ability to survive.[7] In 2002, 600,000 salmon escaped from a single farm in the North Atlantic's Faroe Islands, bringing the worldwide total of recorded fish farm escapees for that year to 2 million.[8] In 2004, 1 million farmed salmon escaped in

Led by Greenpeace, a flotilla of boats protesting the industry's expansion along the west coast surrounds a fish farm in B.C.'s Broughton Archipelago.

- Farmed and Dangerous: www.farmedanddangerous.org
- Living Ocean Society: www.livingoceans.org
- Oceans & Sustainable Fishing: www.davidsuzuki.org/Oceans.
- Raincoast Research Society: www.raincoastresearch.org
- Sea Around Us: www.seaaroundus.org
- Watershed Watch Salmon Society: www.watershed-watch.org

Chile, bringing that year's total above 2 million, as well.[9] Researchers in Norway have found as many as 80% of the fish from some rivers to be descendants of fish farm escapees.[10]

The Health of the Ocean

Crowding thousands of fish together also facilitates the rapid spread of parasites, such as sea lice and kudoa (soft flesh syndrome), and infections such as bacterial kidney disease. The kudoa parasite costs British Columbia's salmon farming industry $30 million to $40 million annually.[11] With open cages, these diseases spread easily to wild fish. Sea lice infestations have been recorded as being 70% higher than normal among wild salmon in close proximity to fish farms, while still exceeding natural levels up to 18 miles along the salmon's migration route.[12]

Peter Mantle owns a wild salmon and sea-trout fishery in Delphi, Ireland. He first saw the effects of sea lice in 1989 after salmon farms were introduced to the area. "Sea-trout fishing was sustainable and eco-friendly," said Mantle, "but the salmon farms killed it off within a decade."

Fish Pharmacy

Antibiotics, pesticides and fungicides are all used against disease outbreaks on fish farms. Since antibiotic use is a relatively new practice, its consequences on surrounding marine life are not yet known. What has been discovered is an increase in antibiotic-resistant bacteria in the sediment under fish farms, in the farmed fish and in other marine life surrounding the farms.[13] Three of the most common pesticides used in fish farming — ivermectin, cypermethrin and azamethiphos — are toxic to marine life around fish farms, but further studies are needed to understand their full impact.[14]

Environmentally Friendly Aquaculture

Closing in on Environmentally Sound Aquaculture: A Fresh Look at the Economics of Closed-Containment Systems is a report compiled by the David Suzuki Foundation, Conservation Strategy Fund, Friends of Clayoquot Sound and the Raincoast Conservation Society in British Columbia. The joint project explores the economic rationale for shifting the environmentally unsustainable, open-net-cage aquaculture industry towards a more sustainable, closed-tank, land-based model.

David Suzuki Foundation scientist Heather Deal has also produced a report, *Sustainable Shellfish*, examining the environmental impacts of commercial shellfish farming and offering recommendations for farmers and policy-makers.

41

Offer Suffering-free Options

People like knowing that the way they shop makes a difference.

— Dave Sudarsky, the Vegetarian Site

Many people will choose products that don't involve animal suffering if they're given the chance. When a business offers a suffering-free option, customers feel empowered to make a compassionate choice, and those who were unaware of the suffering involved may ask for humane options in the future. As well as helping animals, suffering-free options also drive business.

Leatherless Choices

It takes the hides of four cows to upholster the interior of one Mercedes car, but now luxury car buyers will be able to end that practice.[1] Mercedes Benz has become the latest major automobile manufacturer to offer a leather-free option in all their new vehicles, joining another company, SAAB, in responding to growing social consciousness. Meanwhile, Toyota has taken the stand of not offering leather interiors in their successful gasoline-electric hybrid, the Prius.

Take Me out to the Ball Game

People for the Ethical Treatment of Animals (PETA) compiles an annual Top10 list of vegetarian-friendly major-league baseball stadiums. SBC Park in San Francisco took PETA's honors in 2005 and 2006, making a great Portobello mushroom burger, grilled veggie kebabs, vegetarian sushi and the local favorite — edamame (salted soy bean pods). Busch Stadium in St. Louis is also on PETA's Top10 list for their veggie options and for legendary Cardinal manager Tony LaRussa; a vegetarian who does extensive work educating people about the overpopulation problems of cats and dogs.

From Wheels to Runners

New Balance, Nike, Reebok, Adidas, Brooks, Converse and Saucony have all heeded the call of their customers and offer leather-free shoes. When I walked into a New Balance store in Victoria, BC, and told them I was vegan and needed a pair of good shoes, the staff were very helpful, demonstrating their company's commitment to ethical choices.

Offering leather-free options goes beyond being animal-friendly. Leather tanneries also wreak havoc on the environment and have been linked to cancer and respiratory infections.[2]

Cruelty-free Investing

Since 1995 Rocky Mountain Humane Investing (RMHI) has been dedicated to socially responsible investing. The Colorado-based company was a pioneer in creating a screening system for animal testing and humane issues, empowering its clients to make humane choices in choosing mutual funds. RMHI's founder, Brad Pappas, established the first effective animal issues screening in 1990 and has shared the system with investment managers across the US. RMHI screens and rejects investments for any industry that involves animal experimentation, factory farming, animals in entertainment, environmental degradation or weapons production.

Health Care with Heart

When Tom and Kate Chappell founded Tom's of Maine in 1970, they were committed to creating natural products for personal health care. They have become leaders in the industry, offering a

- Carbon Neutral Living: www.carbonneutral.com
- Cruelty-free products:
  www.animalinks.net/intros/aniprod.html
- Green Earth Travel: www.vegtravel.com
- PETA's Caring Consumer:
  www.caringconsumer.com/searchcompany.asp
- PETA's Top 10 Ballparks: www.goveg.com/feat/ballpark
- Rocky Mountain Humane Investing:
  www.greeninvestment.com

Tom's of Maine's Ainsworth Wind Generating Facility in Nebraska.

wide range of products that are free of animal ingredients. They started their company by themselves with a $5,000 loan. Today they have 170 employees, and their animal-friendly products can be found in 40,000 retail outlets around the world. With a commitment to animals and the environment, in 2006 the Tom's manufacturing facility made the move to renewable wind energy. This change will reduce carbon dioxide emissions by 750 tons a year, the equivalent of removing 138 cars from the road.[3]

Sharing the Great Outdoors
Mountain Equipment Co-op (MEC) got its start in 1971 when a group of students huddling

together in a tent during a winter storm decided they needed a place to buy quality outdoor gear that they couldn't find in conventional stores. Today, MEC is the largest supplier of quality outdoor gear in Canada, operating as a co-operative with 2 million members from 190 countries. The company is committed to preserving nature for people, animals and the environment. They offer grants to conservation and recreation programs and use environmentally conscious choices in their stores; striving for zero waste, energy conservation and commitments such as never using paper or wood from old-growth trees.

Traveling with Conscience
Green Earth Travel is a Maryland-based travel agency that offers a variety of options for people who care about the environment and animal welfare. Founded in 1997 by Donna Zeigfinger, a member of Humane Society International, the company organizes vegetarian package tours, ecotours, animal rights group trips and custom independent tours around the world.

42

Ask Your Suppliers to Follow Humane Animal Practices

Animal welfare audits allow slaughter operations to demonstrate their commitment to good handling practices and meeting their customer's requirements.
— Gary Smith, Silliker Inc.

When companies take an interest in offering suffering-free alternatives for their customers, they usually have to do a little research and are often shocked at what they discover. The owners of a market that prides itself as providing healthy deli food to its customers may visit the processing plant where meat comes from and be stunned at what they see. A health and wellness store may discover that the body-care products they sell are the result of painful animal testing.

Animal-Friendly Fast Food

There is a growing trend in the fast-food industry to ensure that suppliers follow humane handling and slaughtering methods. In an industry where suffering is synonymous with speed, this is a step in the right direction. Burger King and Wendy's led the way in Canada and the United States. Then McDonald's climbed on board, followed by Domino's. All four companies now demand that their suppliers adopt a higher level of animal welfare standards and conduct unannounced animal welfare audits of the slaughterhouses they work with.

Animal welfare advocates, health care professionals and many parents may cringe at an endorsement of the fast-food industry, but this couldn't be more important. Millions of animals die every day to sustain fast-food consumption, and ensuring that they're being slaughtered humanely does help relieve suffering.

The Testing Specialists

Silliker is an international network of accredited testing laboratories that serves the food processing, retail, food service, pharmaceutical and cosmetic industries, based in the US and operating in ten countries. They provide animal welfare audits to companies for beef, pork and poultry slaughter operations, using a team of auditors who have been extensively trained in humane practices for housing, handling, transportation and slaughter. The Silliker audit for beef and pork was developed in collaboration with Dr. Temple Grandin, of Colorado State University, whose groundbreaking designs for more humane slaughterhouse systems are in use around the world.

Uniting for One Cause

Several leading clothing companies have taken a stance against the practice of mulesing, a method of collecting wool that involves the mutilation of lambs, which is common among wool farmers in Australia.[1] Animal welfare action groups brought the realities to the world's attention, and now

Create Your Own Purchasing Rule

The Body Shop created its own Purchasing Rule: We encourage ingredient suppliers to stop animal testing. We will not purchase any ingredient that they have tested or retested on animals for cosmetic purposes since at least 31st December, 1990.

By sticking to their rule and playing a leadership role in the cosmetics industry, the Body Shop was the first international cosmetics company to be approved under the Humane Cosmetics Standard (known the Corporate Standard of Compassion in the US), operated by a coalition of animal welfare action groups.

many leading clothing companies are demanding changes. Nordstrom has told Australian suppliers that it will give purchasing preference to guaranteed non-mulesed wool, and they have been followed by the UK retailer George, Timberland, Indigenous Designs, Benetton and American Eagle. Six leading fashion designers in India are boycotting Australian wool until measures are taken to make the industry more humane.

Humane Health Care from Avalon

Avalon Organics is dedicated to the health of people, the environment and animals. Their line of health care products is all vegetarian, and they only buy from suppliers who share their commitment to sustainable, humane practices,

FARM SANCTUARY

including the rejection of any testing on animals. They reject any by-products of the meat and fishing industries, such as gelatin and collagen, and other ingredients that involve animal suffering. Some of their products do include animal-derived ingredients such as milk, honey, beeswax and lanolin, and they ensure that these suppliers follow humane practices.

Educate Yourself

Education is essential to learn how your products are being made and how animals (and people) are treated along the way. Simply asking your suppliers is unlikely to get you the truth, so you have to dig deeper. Give them a chance to get involved. A company's relationship with its suppliers is very important, so propose the idea to them and invite them to work with you toward a more humane society.

Local animal welfare advocacy groups will probably be a good source of information and will advise you what to look for and what questions to ask.

- The Body Shop: www.thebodyshopinternational.com
- Corporate Standard of Compassion: www.leapingbunny.org
- Humane Cosmetics Standard: www.eceae.org/english/hcs.html
- Silliker Inc.: www.silliker.com
- Slaughterhouses audits: www.organicconsumers.org/foodsafety/factoryfarm.cfm

43

Teach Animal Compassion to your Staff

We believe companies, like individuals, must assume their share of responsibility as tenants of Planet Earth.

— John Mackey, CEO,
Whole Foods Market

Compassionate employees reduce animal suffering, whether they work hands-on with animals or not. By being well-informed about animal welfare, they can help customers make choices that benefit all species. The first step in cultivating animal compassion is to give your staff happiness and pride in their work.

Wholehearted Whole Foods

Whole Foods Market has 183 stores across Canada, the US and Britain and employs over 39,000 staff. As a leader among natural foods

markets, they have been educating and empowering their employees since their inception in 1980, and 2006 marked the ninth year in a row that they were ranked as one of the 100 Best Companies to Work For by *Fortune* magazine. In 2003 they founded a new project called the Animal Compassion Foundation, which operates as a non-profit organization with its own board of directors, and is funded by Global 5% Days, when Whole Foods dedicates 5% of their net profits to non-profit or educational organizations. The Foundation's mission is to provide education and research for ranchers, meat producers and their staff so that they can achieve a higher standard of animal welfare, while still maintaining their economic viability. The Foundation gives them the opportunity to learn from innovative animal husbandry techniques that create ideal conditions for their animals, using standards developed by Whole Foods Market and animal welfare advocacy groups such as PETA, the Humane Society of the United States and Animal Rights International.

The standards set out by the Foundation also include such issues as predator control. Livestock must be protected from predators using exclusion and non-lethal methods such as livestock guardian dogs. Humane methods are used for all pest control, including rodents; live traps must be checked daily.

Compassionate Staff

Although compassion is an individual choice, a company can provide its staff with the knowledge and support to cultivate kindness.

The Four Elements of Humane Education for Businesses[1]

1. Provide accurate information so that your staff understand the consequences of their decisions as consumers, citizens and representatives of your company.

2. Foster the three Cs: Curiosity, Creativity and Critical thinking, so that your staff can evaluate information and solve problems.

3. Instill the three Rs: Reverence, Respect and Responsibility, so that your staff will act with kindness and integrity.

4. Offer positive choices that benefit oneself, other people, the Earth and animals, so that your staff feel empowered to help create a more humane world.

Employees can be empowered with a sense of purpose and pride in having helped make the lives of animals a little easier. This informed awareness spreads far beyond those who come in contact with animals. Businesses throughout the retail and manufacturing sectors use, and sell, animal products and by-products. By being aware of what they're promoting, and what alternatives they might offer, employees can make a big difference to animals.

How to Get Started

- Take a look at the resources and see which have tools that apply to your business.
- Contact local animal welfare groups and ask them for ideas on staff training.
- Talk to staff training facilitators and ask them to design an animal compassion training session.
- Be creative; you're building a training program that other businesses may use for their own programs.
- Keep it positive and focused on solutions. Create excitement and make it fun.

Protect Your Staff from Burnout

Teaching animal compassion benefits animals and the people working with them.

- Animal Compassion Foundation: www.animalcompassionfoundation.org
- Canadian Federation of Humane Societies: www.cfhs.ca
- Compassion Fatigue: www.animalsinour_hearts.com/fatigue/whatis.htm
- Humane Society University: www.humanesocietyu.org
- National Association for Humane and Environmental Education: www.nahee.org
- Whole Foods Market: www.wholefoodsmarket.com

"Compassion fatigue" is a name given to the burnout experienced by people who work in fields that require continuous emotional stress, and is often applied to those who work in animal shelters or rescue organizations. But compassion fatigue can also afflict anyone continuously affecting the life of an animal, from those in the food industry responsible for slaughtering them to the veterinarians responsible for saving their lives. As Diane Less Baird, president of Angels for Animals, a pet shelter and education center in Greenford, Ohio, said, "You can only hold so many animals in your arms, and feel the life go out of them, without it starting to suck the life out of you."

44

Find Alternatives to Animal Product Testing

> Having assessed the current degree of scientific knowledge, the company does not foresee any situation in which animal testing might be necessary in the future.
> — Spokesperson for Mary Kay

At some point in our cultural history, somebody decided it was a good idea to test newly manufactured products on animals before use by humans. If the product caused illness or death in the animal, the manufacturer would start over, make a new prototype and test it on another animal. On and on until the test animals showed the desired reaction to the product. They then determined that their product was safe for use by humans.

Even to the untrained eye, the practice seems a little unfair to the animals. And, since laboratory animals differ from humans in their genetic makeup, do the tests have any validity? Not enough to convince the scientific community or any government body. There isn't a single country in the world that requires that household products or cosmetics be tested on a living being before marketing them to humans. There are laws requiring that such products be safe for human use, but nowhere is it legislated that animals must be used for testing.

Cruel and Inconclusive

Acute toxicity testing for consumer products began in the 1920s, and some of the same methods of testing on animals are used today, such as the LD50 test which measures the lethal dose (LD) at which 50% of a group of animals will die. Increasing amounts of a substance are administered through the mouth, nose or skin of test animals until it becomes fatal, in order to arrive at a "safe" level for human use. LD50 tests have been criticized for decades by animal welfare advocates and by people in the scientific community who recognize the ineffectiveness of the test, which research has shown to have just 65% accuracy when predicting toxicity in humans.[1] The rats, mice, guinea pigs and rabbits that are used in product testing are easily accessible and have no way to defend themselves from an inefficient and archaic practice that is still used only out of convenience. It's time for that to change.

There Are Alternatives

Alternative methods of testing are becoming increasingly available:

- Tissue culture techniques are leading the way, as companies move from in-vivo (animal) testing to in-vitro (in glass) tissue testing.
- Eyetex and Skintex are in-vitro procedures that replicate conditions for human skin reactions and can measure the toxicity of over 5,000 different materials.

- Alternatives to Animal Testing:
  www.allforanimals.com/alternatives1.htm
- American Anti-Vivisection Society:
  www.aavs.org
- The Coalition for Consumer Information on Cosmetics:
  www.leapingbunny.org
- Humane Society — product testing:
  www.hsus.org/animals_in_research/animal_testing
- International Foundation for Ethical Research:
  www.ifer.org
- National Anti-Vivisection Society: www.navs.org

- Lab-grown cells and organs. Scientists are developing better cells and organs all the time, and they're already being used for cosmetics testing. EpiPack and Testskin are two such products.

- Improvements to testing methods. A woman no longer has to make a trip to a doctor to test for pregnancy, which has traditionally involved killing a rabbit or frog. A simple over-the-counter kit can be used to do a chemical analysis of her urine, and no animals have to die.

- Human clinical tests: medically monitored clinics where humans volunteer to test the effectiveness and safety of a product before it goes on the market.

A Greater Consciousness in Aesthetics

In 1989 the cosmetics industry giant Mary Kay announced a moratorium on all animal testing until a review of animal testing practices was complete. Now they've announced that they've gone animal-testing-free forever.

Mary Kay is the largest cosmetics company to sign the Corporate Standard of Compassion for Animals, a stringent internationally accepted standard established by the Coalition for Consumer Information on Cosmetics.

The following companies have all opted out of testing on animals: The Body Shop, Beauty Works, Dr. Bronner's, Calder Valley Soap Company, Color My Image, Dead Sea Magic, French Transit, Kiss My Face, Maxim Marketing, Montagne Jeunesse, Pro-Tech Pet Health, Revlon, Tom's of Maine and Yardley.[2]

The internationally recognized Leaping Bunny logo, developed by The Coalition for Consumer Information on Cosmetics, helps businesses verify their commitment to animal-free product testing.

Grape Juice That's Good for Everybody

In 2006 Welch's, the company most famous for its grape juice, announced that they will no longer fund any animal experiments, previously done at three universities, to inflict health problems on animals before feeding them juice to determine its health benefits. Such practices are not required by law but are still used by other drink manufacturers.[3] Sunny Delight, Old Orchard, SunSweet, Tampico, Cascadian Farms, Newman's Own, Bolthouse Farms, Jamba Juice and Campbell's V8 juices are among many companies that have signed a statement of assurance for People for the Ethical Treatment of Animals, stating that their products do not involve testing on animals.[4]

45

Don't Sponsor Events Involving Animal Suffering

> It is the reckless infliction of terror, pain, exhaustion, suffering and death on an animal that has been our faithful partner and companion through the ages.
>
> — Dr. Andrew G. Lang, ASPCA, on the Omak Stampede's Suicide Race

Companies can have a huge impact on animal suffering by the way they use their advertising dollars. Sponsorship is a powerful tool, and when an influential company makes careful choices about who they want to sponsor, it draws a lot of attention. Events that traditionally involve a lot of animal suffering, like rodeos and animal circuses, depend on sponsorship to get off the ground. By refusing to sponsor events that involve cruelty, a company makes a strong statement about its principles.

Coke Withdraws from Rodeos

At the corporate level, Coca-Cola has withdrawn its advertising dollars from all rodeos. For the time being, the soft drink giant still allows local bottlers to sponsor rodeos if they choose to, but the company's corporate offices will no longer do so. Corporate advertising is where the big money is, and the move by Coke sends a message that there is something seriously wrong with the way animals are treated in rodeos.

No Bull in Mexico

PepsiCo, the parent corporation of Pepsi, Frito Lay, Tropicana, Quaker and Gatorade, has withdrawn its sponsorship from all bullfighting events in Mexico. This move is huge because the corporate giant was the largest sponsor of bullfighting events in the country.

Credit for Compassion

The credit card giant MasterCard has ended its sponsorship of Ringling Bros. and Barnum & Bailey circuses, joining VISA and Sears, Roebuck & Co. The move by MasterCard came after animal welfare groups had been campaigning for them to do so for some time, showing continual evidence of the suffering that the companies' animals were subjected to.

Going the Extra Mile

How about creating your own animal-friendly event? Businesses of any size can promote their business while helping animals by hosting an event such as a Walk for Animals day, getting families out to raise money for local animal shelters and animal welfare organizations. You could also raise funds for animals overseas, helping to protect an endangered species or supporting the efforts of an animal rescue organization.

- Contact local animal welfare organizations and ask for ideas.
- Ask for, and volunteer to join, a planning team and give them a budget to work with.
- Invite other businesses to join you, creating more publicity, more advertising and helping more animals.
- Get the word out to your community.
- Invite the planning team to distribute the funds you raise, so that it goes to the animals it was intended for.

- Animal Defenders International: www.ad-international.org
- Animal News — sponsorship: www.animalnews.com/sponsor_opps.html
- Performing Animals Welfare Society: www.pawsweb.org
- Showing Animals Respect and Kindness: www.sharkonline.org

The Leader in Fast-food Compassion?

Burger King became the first fast-food giant to offer a veggie burger to those wishing to make a compassionate choice. Now they've become the first to opt out of circus sponsorship, withdrawing their support from UniverSoul Circus. General Mills and Ford Motor Company have also withdrawn their sponsorship.

Withdrawing from the Race

Wal-Mart and Crown Royal have withdrawn their cash sponsorship of the Omak Stampede and Suicide Race in Omak, Washington, responding to public concern for horses in the event. The suicide race involves a mass-start to gain speed, a plunge down a 210-foot slope into the Okanogan River, a swim across the river and a sprint uphill to the finish line. Between 1982 and 2004, 21 horse deaths were documented in the event, 3 of which were in 2004.[1]

Reality Call

In 2005 animal welfare advocates alerted the four sponsors of the reality TV show, *Celebrity Circus*, to the mistreatment of the animals involved in the production. When the TV giant Endemol, the company behind *Big Brother*, unveiled its *Celebrity Circus* in Portugal, video footage was captured and included an elephant being repeatedly jabbed in the face with a metal spike to force it to perform.[2] Film from 11

LAZAR VAUDVILLE

Animal-free and wildly entertaining, the cast of Lazar Vaudville circus dazzles audiences around North America.

Portuguese circuses was presented to the sponsors, RE/MAX, Cofaco, Credial and Bayer, all of which withdrew their support.

One for the Sled Dogs

Spectrum Brands responded to public concern over one of their subsidiaries' sponsorship of the Iditarod in 2006, announcing that they would withdraw their corporate sponsorship at the end of the year and would no longer be associated with the event. The Iditarod, a 1,000-mile sled dog race in Alaska, draws international concern over the extreme conditions and long distances the dogs are subjected to while their owners vie for a cash prize. Since its beginning in 1973, more than 120 dogs have died in the event, sometimes dubbed the "Ihurtadog."[3]

46

Stop Selling Fur in the Name of Fashion

It takes 40 animals to make one fur coat, but just one informed person to make a difference.

— Heidi Prescott, Humane Society of the United States

The winds of change are drifting through the fashion industry. As more and more people become aware of how senseless it is for living beings to be killed for their fur, companies and industry leaders are switching to fur-free products. To the relief of animals and their advocates everywhere, the industry would appear to be on the verge of a total transformation to one guided by compassion. There is no compassion in killing a living creature so that a human can wear its skin for fashion, but there is great compassion in choosing to stop doing so.

A Changing Industry

The fashion leader Ralph Lauren pulled the plug on his company's fur sales in 2006. The Polo Ralph Lauren Corporation had been considering eliminating fur sales for some time but made the move after company executives watched undercover video footage of the cruelty endured by animals in Chinese fur farms, which produce more than half the finished fur garments imported for sale in the United States.[1] To clear out its fur inventory, the company is donating 1,200 of its brand new, fur-trimmed coats to charities in developing nations.

Ralph Lauren joined a growing list of companies that are opting out of a chapter of their industry's history that has become synonymous with suffering. In 2006 the Canadian fashion leader Jacob, with 200 stores across the country, announced that it was going fur-free, following the move by Bedo, Gadzooks, J. Crew, Selfridges, Zara, Junonia, Forever 21, Suzy Shier, Bela Voce, SABA, Gap, Banana Republic, H&M and others.

Faux Furry Alternatives

There are many alternatives to fur, made from both natural and synthetic fibers. Whether customers are looking for warmth, comfort, fashion or all-out luxury, there are readily available materials to produce what they're looking for.

COALITION TO ABOLISH THE FUR TRADE

A mink gnaws at his cage. Farmed mink comprise the majority of the 40 million animals killed worldwide for the fur industry.

Your company can proudly wear a fur-free label and still meet the needs of its customers. By maintaining your attention to quality while making compassionate choices, you'll most likely increase your customer base by welcoming those who had been concerned about animal suffering. So announce your new stance proudly and carry all the alternatives you can.

Going Polar Fleecy

Polar fleece may be the ultimate alternative to fur. It's warm, comfortable, stylish and very effective. Made from polyester, it's hydrophobic, wicking moisture away from the body and keeping you warm and dry. It's lightweight, easy to care for and comes in all shapes, sizes and colors. It doesn't shrink, doesn't fade, and its versatility is unmatched by any other activewear material. There are over 100 varieties of polar fleece, many of which are made from recycled plastics such as pop bottles, keeping plastic out of our landfills.

Donate Your Old Furs

If you want to stop selling furs but still have a bunch in stock, donate them to people in need. Wherever people are struggling to stay warm through cold weather, your unwanted furs will be a blessing. Work with local shelters and arrange a plan for donation and disbursement. Your donation can even be tax-deductible.

People for the Ethical Treatment of Animals (PETA) will collect unwanted furs, send them overseas to people in need in freezing temperatures and give you a tax-deductible receipt (PETA, Fur Campaign, 501 Front Street, Norfolk, Virginia, 23510).

- Coquette Faux Furriers: www.coquettefauxfurriers.com
- Fur and alternatives: www.fundforanimals.org
- PETA's fur campaign: www.furisdead.com
- Polar Fleece: www.getcreativeshow.com/crafting_sewing_conference_center/craft_sewing_seminars/polarfleecefacts.htm

Fur the Environment

In a declining industry, furriers are now claiming that wearing fur is more environmentally friendly than its synthetic alternatives. This is not true. It takes 60 times more energy to produce a fur coat from ranch-raised animals than a fake fur.[2] Furs are loaded with chemicals to keep them from decomposing; waste from fur farms is extensive, contaminating vital groundwater; and carcasses from the skinned animals wind up being dumped into landfills.

What about furs that are trapped rather than farmed? Traps are placed indiscriminately throughout trapping areas and continually catch non-target animals, which are then discarded. There is nothing green about the fur industry.

47

Put Compassion on Your Menu

There was a time when waiters rolled their eyes at people who asked for vegetarian options, but now we purposely cater to those who are vegetarians for whatever reason. Vegetarianism is here to stay.

— Rhys Lewis, executive chef,
the American Club

According to the National Restaurant Association, a whopping 54 billion meals are served annually in American restaurants and cafeterias.[1] Human beings spend a whole lot of time and a whole lot of money ordering food. With those kinds of numbers, restaurants can play a huge role in promoting animal awareness and welfare.

Vegetarian Starter Kit for Restaurants

Servers and chefs in nearly every restaurant in the world have had to put up with pesky vegetarians asking for animal-free meals over the years. But now the days of eye-rolling are dwindling because vegetarian menu items are becoming a major part of the industry.

Your menu itself can demonstrate compassion toward animals, not just by offering salads and veggie burgers but by indicating which items contain animal products and which don't. You can take it a step further and use your menu to explain how your restaurant views all life as being precious and chooses food from humane sources.

By serving organic food, you'll be helping animals, the environment and people. Farm animals suffer less on organic farms with access to the outdoors and a life free from routine injections of antibiotics, hormones and growth stimulants. Animals on organic farms are fed organic feed, so they aren't subjected to residual pesticides. Wild animals and birds suffer less, too, since organic farms avoid pesticides that contaminate their habitat.

Educate Yourself and Your Staff About Vegan

For a restaurant to serve an ethical menu, its staff must become familiar with what vegan and vegetarian means. Vegan is more than a food choice: it's a lifestyle. Vegans don't consume, wear or promote any animal products or by-products. This means no cheese, eggs, butter, seafood or meat. But that's not as restrictive as it sounds. Combine any legume or plant protein source with a grain like rice or whole wheat pasta, along with veggies and a light soy or peanut sauce, and you've got a complete and delicious vegan meal. This is a must-know for restaurants, because more and more people are going animal-free every day.

Cheesy Choices
Many diners are also choosing to avoid cheese, whether out of concern for their health or awareness of the suffering in the dairy industry. All too often, chefs will pile on heaps of cheese as a substitute for meat. There are plenty of alternatives to cheese that add great flavor and provide a complete meal. The most commonly used is soy cheese, but most soy cheese is made with casein, a dairy by-product. There are several mock cheeses such as those from Galaxy Foods that don't include casein. Ask your suppliers to find a soy cheese without casein. Crushed cashews make a wonderful substitute on top of pasta, and Red Star nutritional yeast makes a vitamin B$_{12}$-rich and nutritious topping for just about anything.

Compassion in the Capital

In Washington DC, the animal welfare group Compassion Over Killing distributes colorful decals to eateries that want to proclaim themselves animal-friendly. Over 125 restaurants and bakeries display the decal in their front window, including the Washington Deli, which offers over 20 animal-friendly menu options, including vegan "cheese" pizza, mock meat subs and a vegan breakfast menu. Their menu has been such a hit that their sister deli, Pumpernickel Bagelry and Caterer, has followed suit.

- The Enchanted Broccoli Foresty by Mollie Katzen
- *Entertaining Vegetarians* by Celia Brooks Brown and Jan Baldwin
- *Everyday Vegan: 300 Recipes for Healthful Eating* by Jeani-Rose Atchison
- *How it all Vegan!: Irresistible Recipes for an Animal-free Diet* by Sarah Kramer and Tanya Barnard
- *Simply Vegan: Quick Vegetarian Meals* by Debra Wasserman and Reed Mengals
- *Vegan World Fusion Cuisine: Over 200 Award-winning Recipes* by Mark Reinfeld and Bo Rinaldi
- *Vegetarian Starter Kit for Restaurants* by Physicians Committee for Responsible Medicine: www.pcrm.org/health/rvsk
- *Viva la Vegan!: Simple, Delectable Recipes for the Everyday Vegan Family* by Dreena Burton

48

Restock Your Shelves with Kindness

Whole Foods is helping to create a paradigm shift in the way farm animals are treated. We don't want incremental change that leaves the industrial farming model still operable. We are committing to a revolution.
— John Mackey, Whole Foods Market

Supermarkets are the driving force behind factory farming, so their role in animal suffering is enormous. Factory farms have become production juggernauts because supermarkets demand more and more food to keep up with consumer demand. Somewhere along the line, the animals have been forgotten. By slowing down enough to take responsibility for the suffering behind their products, supermarkets could have an enormous effect on the welfare of animals.

Labeling Kindness

Whole Foods Market took the lead by creating an "Animal Compassionate" label for products on their shelves. Throughout its history, Whole Foods Market has set high standards for animal welfare. The comfort, safety and health of all the animals involved in their products is monitored through continuous feedback with their suppliers, regular third-party audits, inspection of each suppliers' operations and an annual affidavit from each producer describing its animal raising and handling practices. Products which meet the highest standard in animal welfare receive their Animal Compassionate label. Whole Foods Market states that animal treatment should be the first criteria in the development of standards.

In the UK the supermarket giant Marks & Spencer maintains its high animal welfare standards by monitoring exactly where all their animals used for food come from, how they've been fed and how they've been treated. M&S works closely with their suppliers, ensuring that they follow the Farm Animal Council's Five Freedoms:

- Freedom from hunger and thirst
- Freedom from discomfort
- Freedom from pain, injury and disease
- Freedom to express normal behavior
- Freedom from fear and distress

M&S has also banned the use of growth-promoting antibiotics, meat, bone meal and genetically modified ingredients from the diets of animals used for food.

Britain's Sainsbury's shares a similar commitment to farm animal welfare, using the Five Freedoms for their animals used for food. They also keep their production local, buying 95% of their meat from UK suppliers, enabling them to monitor and audit them. In 2004 they began their first Freedom Food certified line, following guidelines set by the Royal Society for the Protection of Cruelty to Animals. Their commitment to animal welfare is ongoing, as they review each new nonfood product they carry. In their clothing line, they don't sell real fur, and they monitor the welfare of animals used for their feathers, suede and wool.

- Compassion in World Farming: www.ciwf.org.uk
- Earth Fare: www.earthfare.com
- Farm Animal Welfare Council: www.fawc.org.uk/freedoms.htm
- RSPCA: www.rspca.org.uk
- Whole Foods Market: www.wholefoodsmarket.com
- Wild Oats Natural Marketplace: www.wildoats.com

Feathery Fact — All those funny sounds chickens make aren't just gibberish. Chickens have over 200 distinct sounds to communicate with each other.

Waitrose is another UK supermarket with a commitment to animal welfare. In 2006, for the second year in a row, they were named Britain's most farm-animal-friendly supermarket by the Compassion In World Farming Trust (CIWF). Each year, CIWF does an exhaustive survey to determine how well farm animals are raised, transported and slaughtered for leading supermarkets. Waitrose was particularly praised for its treatment of pigs, ducks, laying hens and farmed fish.

Support Local Producers

The main reason why animal welfare has fallen by the wayside is that the large supermarkets chains are buying from producers who give the largest volume at the cheapest rates. This results in huge amounts of meat and animal by-products coming from a few selected suppliers, hundreds or thousands of miles away, making it nearly impossible to have any control or understanding of where the products come from.

By buying from a variety of local producers, a supermarket can sell fresher, healthier food and have a much lighter effect on the environment. They can also communicate more easily with their suppliers, maintain animal welfare standards and visit their facilities to understand their operations. It's a win-win situation for everyone, including the animals.

Cage-Free Compassion

There is probably no animal that is subject to as much suffering as the laying hen in a factory farm, stuffed into a tiny cage with up to eight other birds and barely able to move for its short life. Public pressure and increased awareness has brought the plight of battery cage hens to the forefront of the supermarket industry however, and several major markets are doing something about it. Working with animal welfare groups like the Humane Society of the United States, more supermarkets are selling cage-free eggs, including Trader Joe's, Wild Oats, Bon Appetit and Earth Fare.

Making organic produce accessible to consumers helps animals, people and the environment.

49

See the Forest for the Trees

In one tree we counted the number of birds, and there were eight species nesting in one year. It was an apartment building, you could say.

— Merve Wilkinson, Wildwood

The forest industry is responsible for the habitat loss for thousands of species around the world. At the current rate of deforestation, most of Earth's ancient forests will be gone within the 21st century,[1] along with the habitat the forests provide to so many species.

For the forests to be preserved for wildlife, while still meeting the human demand for forest products, logging companies must adopt a whole new vision of how they operate. Sustainable forest management involves careful selection of the trees to be harvested, following ecological principles, while allowing for continued habitat for wildlife and maintaining the integrity of forest ecosystems.

An Island of Sustainability

Merve Wilkinson is pretty much a legend to residents of Vancouver Island, British Columbia, and his logging methods have been a source of inspiration to thousands who visit his sustainably managed forest every year.

Merve has been practising sustainable forestry on 137 acres for most of his life; managing both his 77 acres at Wildwood and his neighbor's 60 acres. When he bought his land in 1938, over 1.5 million board feet of Douglas fir, grand fir and red cedar towered over him. After training in forest management based on Swedish methods, he began cutting the trees selectively, paying attention to the forest while keeping an open mind for new ideas. The results of his methods prove the wisdom of his approach. By 2000 Merve had logged 2.1 million board feet from the forest, and yet the standing volume was 1.65 million board feet; ten percent more than when he started. Merve's Wildwood is a multi-age, multi-height, multi-species forest, quite the opposite of standard commercial lumber harvesting in British Columbia and other areas. Merve speaks strongly against the industrial logging model,

Wildwood Tree Farm on Vancouver Island.

HAROLD WOLF

"Rows of trees are not forests. They represent blind stupidity and a one-track mind."

As a result of his methods, Wildwood has retained its old-growth characteristics and is a haven for small forest creatures. Merve understands what diversity means to a forest and leaves snags for wildlife, such as pileated woodpeckers. The results of his work, the success of his methods and the wisdom that a lifetime of sustainable forestry has given him are a model that many other foresters look up to.

A Council for the Forests

The Forest Stewardship Council (FSC) is an international network that certifies and promotes the sustainable management of the world's forests. Created in 1990 by a group of foresters and environmental and human rights organizations, FSC was officially founded in 1993 in Toronto, Ontario, with representatives from 26 countries.

Headquartered in Bonn, Germany, the council sets international standards and provides a trademark with which consumers worldwide are able to support responsible forest management. By 2006 over 73 million hectares in 72 countries had been certified according to FSC standards. In 2005, 5.5 million hectares of land in Northeastern Alberta, owned by Alberta-Pacific, became the largest FSC-certified forest in the world, and in 2006 Random House Group became the first consumer publishing group to be awarded FSC certification, with all their titles being printed on FSC-certified paper.

- Ecoforestry Institute: www.ecoforestry.ca
- Forest Stewardship Council: www.fsc.org
- Silva Forest Foundation: www.silvafor.org

Large-scale Sustainability

The family-owned Collins Pine Company operates 295,000 acres of forests in several locations across the United States and does so sustainably. The company began operation in 1941, managing its forests on a multi-age, sustained-yield basis, using a forest management philosophy that continues today in its Almanor Forest in Northern California. Collins began with a standing inventory of 1.5 billion board feet. After nearly 70 years, having removed enough trees to build 133,000 homes, the forest still holds 1.5 billion board feet of timber. The forest remains vibrant and alive with a wide diversity of multi-age canopied trees providing homes to an abundance of birds and other forest dwellers, where blue heron rookeries, black bears and bald eagles enjoy the natural meadows and clean waters of the forest. Collins was the first privately held forest company in the United States to be certified by the Forest Stewardship Council. As the Sierra Club's Seth Zuckerman put it, "This is a forest that has never known a clearcut ... where foresters tell the mill how much timber it may have, and where the forest itself tells the foresters."

50

Use Your Influence for Preservation and Compassion

> Wall Street is outpacing Washington in the fight to end destructive forestry.
>
> — Brant Olson, Rainforest Action Network

Almost all companies have clients who depend on them for business. The operational methods of your clients, however, may be harming animals, even if they are totally unaware of it. A simple statement by your company could make a big difference in the lives of thousands of animals.

Kudos for Citigroup

Citigroup began supporting sustainability in 1996, when they partnered with Conservation International to find new ways to encourage ecologically sustainable small businesses in Brazil's Atlantic Forest. In 2004 the US-based bank took a stand for conservation, warning the Malaysian logging company Rimbunan Hijau that it must stop its illegal logging methods in South East Asia.[1] Citigroup's CEO told the company that, if it wanted to continue as a client, it must comply with a strict set of environmental policies. The move by Citigroup was part of their commitment to a new code of corporate social responsibility policy that they adopted after a lengthy campaign by the Rainforest Action

- Citigroup: www.citigroup.com/citigroup/environment
- Goldman Sachs: www.gs.com
- IKEA: www.ikea.com
- The Natural Step: www.naturalstep.org
- Proctor and Gamble declaration: www.pg.com/science/ria_hs_partnership.jhtml
- Rainforest Action Network: www.ran.org

Network (RAN). In 2006 Citigroup announced its New Environmental Initiatives policy, committing the world's largest bank to protection of the world's endangered ecosystems and prohibiting its investment in any extractive industry (logging, mining and oil and gas) in primary tropical forests. As part of the initiative, Citigroup audits its climate-changing investments and contributes capital to renewable energy projects.

Going Green at Goldman Sachs

In 2005 global investment giant Goldman Sachs took over a portfolio of defaulted mortgages for 680,000 acres of wilderness in Tierra del Fuego, Chile, and donated all of the land to the Wildlife Conservation Society.[2] The move by the $60 billion investment firm was part of the Center for Environmental Markets that it established in 2005, committing $1 billion to renewable energy projects, prohibiting investing in industrial activity in ecologically sensitive regions and recognizing the rights of indigenous peoples.

Goldman Sachs (GS) CEO Hank Paulson asked RAN for help, and his company worked closely with the conservation group, along with other NGOs, in the creation of its environmental policy. GS owns major fossil-fuel-driven power plants in the United States where it works to reduce greenhouse gas emissions and publicly reports its progress.

Leaders in Alternatives

In 2006 Proctor & Gamble created a declaration with the Humane Society of the United States

Leaders in Furniture and Sustainability

The IKEA Group of Companies, founded in 1943, has 150 stores in 22 countries. The home-furnishing giant, which purchases raw materials from 50 countries, prohibits the use of wood from intact natural forests, except those certified by the Forest Stewardship Council (see Solution 49). In 1990 IKEA adopted The Natural Step for its environmental policies and by 1992 had created its Environmental Action Plan, with 25 of the company's senior managers attending a seminar led by representatives from TNS, Greenpeace and several other conservation organizations. IKEA has phased out the use of PVCs from furniture, wallpaper and home textiles; minimizes the use of formaldehyde in its products; and uses only recyclable material for its flat packaging. IKEA employees have access to an Eco-Facts database, and some have begun local environmental working groups. IKEA is committed to farm animals, as well, ensuring that all food sold or served in its stores is the result of humane animal husbandry in the rearing, transportation and slaughter of animals. Their code of conduct[3] sets clear guidelines for legal operations, working conditions, environmental and forest management practices of every supplier.

IAN McALLISTER/RAINCOAST.ORG

(HSUS), committing to the elimination of consumer product safety testing on animals. The two organizations first teamed up in 2001, when Proctor & Gamble received a Humane Award for Corporate Champions from the HSUS for its commitment to the advancement of testing alternatives. In 2005 the two organizations provided bursaries for students and scientists from around the world to attend the 5th World Congress on Alternatives and Animal Use in the Life Sciences in Berlin. Also in 2005, HSUS supported the establishment of the annual Proctor & Gamble European Animal Welfare and Alternatives Awards.

Assess Your Sustainability

To lead by example and use your influence for conservation and animal welfare, your company must be part of the solution. Conduct an assessment of your organization and industry sector, identifying your impact on animals and the environment. Organizations like The Natural Step can help you by teaching sustainability as a business opportunity rather than a liability, providing a strategic framework for success for your conservation plan and giving you access to a global network of sustainability experts and business leaders committed to a common purpose.

51

Include Animal Rights in Your National Constitution

Austria is taking the role of pioneer. This new law will give both producers and consumers a good feeling, and it lifts animal protection to the highest level internationally.

— Wolfgang Schuessel, Austrian chancellor

It's time for all nations to revisit their constitutions and ensure that they serve and protect all species. Animals are an integral part of a country, along with its culture, heritage and environment. The constitution should set a sustainable path for generations to come that includes healthy forests, clean skies and a future where all species are treated with respect and dignity.

Animal Awareness in Austria

In 2004 Austria's parliament gave overwhelming approval to legislation that makes the nation one of the world's toughest protectors of animal rights. The new anti-cruelty laws make it illegal for animal guardians to crop their dogs' ears or tails, raise their chickens in cages or keep exotic animals for circus acts. Violating these and other stipulations of the new legislation will net offenders heavy fines and possible seizure of their animals. Extreme cases of animal cruelty carry fines as high as 15,000 Euros (US$18,000).

The new legislation will include the appointment of an animal rights ombudsman to oversee the treatment of animals on farms and in zoos, circuses and pet shops. Chicken farmers who invested in new cages shortly before the legislation will have until 2020 to switch to free-range fencing.

Charting a Course in Germany

In Germany the Federal Ministry of Consumer Protection, Food and Agriculture is guiding the country to a pioneering role among European nations. In 2002 Germany added the words "and animals" so that their constitutional law now reads, "The state takes responsibility for protecting the natural foundations of life and animals in the interest of future generations."

The consequences of this change include:

• Prohibition against the conventional keeping of laying hens in battery cages from 2007 onwards.

Creating Constitutions

World Animal Net (WAN) is an international organization representing over 1500 affiliated societies that launched its Constitution Project to facilitate the recognition of animals as sentient beings by including animal protection in international, national and regional constitutions and charters. WAN calls for:

1. The United Nations to create a charter for the protection of animals.

2. The Council of Europe to create a general convention covering animal ethics and animals in entertainment.

3. The European Union to take practical steps to implement its Animal Welfare treaty protocol.

4. All national governments to introduce animal welfare into their constitutions (if they haven't already done so).

5. All regional governments and town councils to do the same.

- Animal Aid: www.animalaid.org.uk
- Animal Legal Defense Fund: www.aldf.org
- Eurogroup for Animal Welfare: www.eurogroupanimalwelfare.org
- European Parliament: www.eurogroupanimalwelfare.org/intergroup/intergroup.htm
- International Fund for Animal Welfare: www.ifaw.org
- World Animal Net: www.worldanimal.net/constitution.htm

- Tighter restrictions on the use of animals for testing cosmetics and non-prescription drugs.
- Responsibility of farmers to provide their animals with room to move freely, with adequate lighting and temperature.
- A requirement for all people caring for animals for commercial purposes to provide proof of their knowledge and skill about animal husbandry.[1]

Germany's Animal Welfare Act states that everyone has to take responsibility for animal welfare, from farmers and animal guardians to researchers and consumers. The government's commitment extends to its neighbors, encouraging other European Union countries to follow suit.

DEREK GOODWIN FOR FARM SANCTUARY

A Step Forward in Switzerland

In 2005 the Swiss parliament strengthened its animal welfare laws to protect the dignity and well-being of animals. The new law limits animal transportation to six hours from the loading point and bans the import of cat and dog skins, the castration of piglets without anesthetic (as of 2009) and any form of ritualistic slaughter.

The new legislation didn't go as far as Swiss Animal Protection, Switzerland's largest animal welfare organization, wanted, which was for the inclusion of legal representation in court, and provisions on dangerous dogs.

Official Status in France

In 2005 France gave animals official status for the first time under the country's 200-year-old civil code. The move followed a report that recommended that animals be recognized as protected property, as living and sentient beings. In 2003 France passed a bill that added an Environmental Charter to its constitution, recognizing that: "The rise of humanity was made possible through the existence of natural resources and the balance of nature," and declaring that, "Every person has the duty to participate in the conservation and improvement of the environment."[2]

52

Abolish Trophy Hunting and Cruel Hunting Practices

Sport hunting — the killing of wild animals as recreation — is fundamentally at odds with the values of a humane, just and caring society.

— Humane Society of the United States

Every year 40,000 black bears are killed by hunters in the United States,[1] and another 40,000 are killed in Canada.[2] Grizzly bears have been driven from 99% of their habitat in the US[3] and 60% in Canada. Experts estimate that for every bear killed legally, another bear is killed illegally, often to smuggle bear parts — including the gall bladder, bile and paws — to Asia, where a gall bladder can sell for $10,000.[4]

Across North America, over 2,000 mountain lions (cougars) are killed by trophy hunters every year,[5] along with thousands of wolves, moose, elk, bighorn sheep, deer, mountain goats, caribou and other species. Trophy hunting removes the strongest animals and causes the remaining population to diminish in size and become more vulnerable to disease and predation. Sport hunting of predatory species causes an imbalance of nature when species such as deer become overpopulated and strip their habitat of available food.

Governments need tougher laws to protect wildlife, allowing subsistence hunting while discouraging hunting for sport and creating much stricter penalties for those convicted of poaching. By promoting alternatives such as ecotourism — encouraging cameras rather than rifles in the backcountry — everybody can benefit from greater revenue, stable wildlife populations and a healthy environment.

Victory for the Foxes — Finally

It has been a long and tiring campaign for animal welfare advocates, but the cruel practice of fox hunting with dogs has been outlawed in England, Scotland and Wales. Fox hunting has a very long history in the United Kingdom where, for centuries, hunters on horseback have traveled across the countryside with their hounds to flush out and kill foxes. Despite fierce support, there has been an equally dedicated campaign to end the hunt because of its consequences for the foxes. As far back as 1949, a bill was introduced to end the hunt, followed by repeated campaigns over the decades. It wasn't until 2002 that the movement gained significant momentum, when Scotland banned

IAN MCALLISTER/RAINCOAST.ORG

hunting with dogs. England and Wales weren't far behind. In February 2005, a new hunting act came into effect, and the centuries-old practice of hunting with dogs was officially outlawed.

Freedom from Hunting in Captivity
In 2005 Ontario became the eighth Canadian province to ban penned hunting (see Hunting: Subsistence vs. Sport). Between 200 and 400 animals, mostly wild boar and deer, were being hunted on the province's game farms annually.[6] The farms are still allowed to raise animals for meat, but they are no longer allowed to offer hunting. In Canada, only Saskatchewan and Quebec continue to permit the hunting of wild animals in captivity. In the US, there are over 1000 game farms in at least 28 states.[7]

No Trophy Wolves in Wyoming
Gray wolves in the northern Rocky Mountains of Wyoming are protected by the federal endangered species list, and they'll be staying that way for now. In 2006 Wyoming officials appealed to the US Fish and Wildlife Service to delist the wolves, based on concern about predation on domestic animals, allowing trophy hunting in some areas, while classifying them as predators that could be shot on site elsewhere. But federal officials rejected the proposal, standing behind conservation efforts and saying that the population was not adequate to move ahead with delisting for the state's 250 wolves.

- Defenders of Wildlife: www.defenders.org
- National Wildlife Federation: www.nwf.org
- NSPCA: www.nspca.co.za Click on "wildlife".
- PETA factsheet on captive hunting: www.peta.org/mc/factsheet_display.asp?ID=53

Listen to the Voices of the People

Hunting is big business, with American hunters spending $20 billion annually and reporting the kills of 100 million animals;[8] 84% of the hunters target big game animals such as deer and elk.[9] Most states actively recruit women and young people into hunting by hosting youth hunts, often held on National Wildlife Refuges. Yet, despite the apparent strength of the industry, public interest in recreational hunting is dwindling. The US Fish and Wildlife Service reports a steady drop in the number of hunting licenses issued each year, with 1.3 million fewer licenses issued in 2000 than in 1980.[10] Only 5.4% of Americans hold a hunting license, and public opinion polls by the Associated Press and *LA Times* indicate that a majority of the population is opposed to recreational hunting.[11] In 1999 the Animal Protection Institute hired pollster Decision Research to conduct an extensive telephone survey of 800 American households; 76% of those surveyed saying that an animal's right to live free of suffering should be as important as a person's right.[12]

53

Outlaw Cruel Sporting Events

Animals should not be killed in the name of human entertainment. In the 21st century, bullfighting should be confined to the history books.
— The Dalai Lama

There are some very cruel sports that are happening legally in our backyards and around the world every day. Governments have traditionally turned a blind eye to sports such as dogfighting and cockfighting, but the times are beginning to change. Due to the efforts of animal welfare groups and individuals who have campaigned tirelessly for decades, laws are finally being created to end the cruel practice of pitting animals against each other.

Enforce Your Legislation

Dogfighting and cockfighting are now illegal in most US states. Oklahoma became the 47th state to ban cockfighting, and its anti-dogfighting legislation is some of the toughest in the country. Both practices, along with blood sports such as bear-baiting, are illegal in Canada and are becoming increasingly illegal around the world.

In 2006 Mississippi's governor signed a new bill outlawing hot dog rodeos, an event where pit bulls and other dogs are put in pens with wild pigs that have had their tusks sawn off.

- American Humane: www.americanhumane.org
- Anti Bullfighting Cause: www.stopbullfighting.org
- HSUS — dogfighting: www.peoriahs.org/hsusanatomy.htm
- In Defense of Animals — animal fighting: www.idausa.org/facts/fighting.html
- Last Chance for Animals: www.lcanimal.org/cmpgn
- Okalahoma Coalition Against Cockfighting: www.bancockfighting.org

Spectators place bets on how long it will take for a dog to pin down the pig. Events like hot dog rodeos usually take place in isolated rural locations, but are beginning to become the focus of much-needed legislation.

The problem lies with enforcement. Although cruel sports are a felony in many jurisdictions, they still continue. Dogfighting in the US is widely practised, particularly in states where it is only a misdemeanor, not a felony. Dogfight operators make such high profits that the fines are simply counted as part of their operating expenses. Beyond a slap on the wrists, governments must follow through with sentencing that has a meaningful effect, from jail terms and much stiffer fines to sensitivity counseling.

Legislation must also apply to the spectators. It is now illegal to watch blood sports in 40 states. In 2005 authorities in Tennessee raided what was billed as the largest cockfight in the country, arresting 144 people and seizing 300 roosters. Conviction for spectators at a cockfight can bring up to a year in jail and fines of $2,500.

Humanity in Hungary

In 2005 Hungary's parliament banned cockfighting and the breeding or sale of animals for fighting. The move was part of new anti-cruelty legislation that moves animal torture from a misdemeanor to a felony, punishable by up to two years in prison.

Influence Your Fellow Governments

While governments in North America and parts of Europe are waking up to the cruelty of animal fighting sports and moving to ban it, most of the world has no such legislation. In France blood sports are illegal, except in locales where an "uninterrupted tradition" exists for them. In Japan dogfighting is still a legal, and very common, pastime. In much of Asia and many developing nations around the world, there is no anti-cruelty legislation of any kind. Dogfighting has made a big comeback in Afghanistan since the fall of the hard-line Taliban rulers, and it is also a common, although illegal, event in Pakistan.

Governments that are working to end animal suffering must tell their neighbors and trading partners that anti-cruelty laws are important. Good relationships between governments are important, but so is the well-being of the species we share this world with.

WSPA

The Sun Will Set on the Matadors

When the Spanish region of Catalonia, including the City of Barcelona, made history in 2005 by banning bullfighting (see Solution 28), it may have started the end of this cruel tradition. Leah Garces of the World Society for the Prevention of Cruelty to Animals said, "We commend the courage that the Catalan people have shown … they are taking a stand against animal cruelty that has no place in the modern world."

There is nothing sporting or fair about bullfighting. The bulls are seriously wounded before they enter the ring so that they pose little threat to the matador. Despite the claims of bullfighting aficionados, the matadors do little but finish the bull off. Often they aren't even able to do that, and an "executioner" is called in to put the bull out of his misery.[1]

Spain, Mexico and South America are the only areas of the world that host bullfighting events on a regular basis. The profits that keep these events happening, though, come from curious European and North American tourists.

54

End Exploitation for Entertainment

Their world becomes a maze
of meaningless reverberations.
— Jean-Michel Cousteau,
on dolphins in captivity

Governments must protect all species within their borders, and few are more deserving than those held captive and forced to perform for the amusement of others in zoos, animal circuses, rodeos and aquariums, where the animals regularly suffer indignity, injury and death. Despite impassioned arguments by those who obtain their living from animal performances, there is nothing humane about this tradition. It's time for us to evolve beyond it.

Following Scandinavia's Lead

Denmark was seemingly ahead of its time when the Danish government adopted a Law of Protection of Animals in 1962, creating a federal prohibition against performances with wild animals throughout the country. Because of the longevity of Denmark's stance, the Danes have established themselves as the most progressive people in the world when it comes to protecting animals from exploitation. Their Scandinavian neighbors have been watching: in 1974 Norway

passed a law that banned the exhibition of wild animals in public places, and Finland and Sweden have brought in strict rules that govern which animals can be exhibited in performing animal acts, although not as inclusive as Denmark's.

Rising to the Occasion

The choices made by the Scandinavian countries and by some municipalities around the world are slowly having an effect:

- Canada no longer allows orcas or beluga whales to be captured and exported.[1]
- Switzerland has a federal prohibition on animal performances.
- Singapore has banned the use of wild animals in circuses and traveling shows.
- India has banned the use of tigers, bears, monkeys, panthers and lions for entertainment of any kind.
- Costa Rica has banned the use of wild animals in circuses.
- Nova Scotia has banned the captivity of primates, bears, marine mammals, cetaceans, amphibians or fish species for animal performances.
- Israel has banned the importation of dolphins for use in marine parks.
- Brazil has banned the use of marine mammals for entertainment.
- South Carolina has banned all exhibits of whales and dolphins.

Across the United States, Canada, Great Britain, Europe, Asia and Australia, many municipalities

- Animal Liberation — rodeos:
  www.animalliberation.org.au/rodeos.php
- Born Free: www.bornfree.org.uk
- Captive Animals' Protection Society:
  www.captiveanimals.org
- European Anti-Rodeo Coalition:
  www.anti-rodeo.org/english.htm
- Fight Against Animal Cruelty in Europe — rodeos:
  www.faace.co.uk/rodeo.htm
- Zoocheck Canada: www.zoocheck.com

have adopted legislation against performing animal acts (see Solution 28). In British Columbia more than 20 municipalities have adopted such legislation, although its neighbor, Alberta — home of the world famous Calgary Stampede, doesn't have a single one. Municipal support for animal welfare creates an opportunity for a provincial or state government to create province or state-wide legislation which ends the traditions of traveling circuses, rodeos, zoo performances and aquarium shows.

Such legislation can create anger among people who grew up with these pastimes, so a government must take the time to inform its citizens with public service announcements, school programs, lectures, information sessions and publications.

Animal-Free and Wildly Successful

Cirque du Soleil (French for "Circus of the Sun") was founded in Quebec in 1984 by two street performers and has become one of the world's best-known circuses without the use of any animals. The famous troupe uses elements of street performance, along with rock music, opera, ballet, trapeze artists, jugglers, contortionists and a wide variety of international guests; combining all the talent into a spectacular show that has entertained audiences around the world. They don't use any soundtracks, relying on live music, and have created their own language, called "Cirquish," using it to illustrate their colorful storylines. The international success of Cirque du Soleil is evidence that the most entertaining events of all can rely on human talent alone and need not exploit a single animal.

No Captivity for Whales

In 1996 the Vancouver Aquarium announced it would never again capture cetaceans from the wild, and in 2001, its staff bade farewell to their last remaining orca (killer whale), when Bjossa was shipped to Sea World in San Diego. The move underscored the problem of keeping whales in captivity — they belong in the ocean. Bjossa saw five other orcas, including three of her own calves, die while in captivity, and she herself died just six months after the move. Between1965 and 1999, 56 orcas were captured from the waters around Washington and British Columbia, and 54 of them have died, living an average of just 5 years.[2] In the wild, a male orca can reach 50 years of age and a female can live to be 80. Worldwide, between 1965 and 2005, 136 captured orcas have died, along with 20 born in captivity.[3]

Dolphins belong in the open sea.

55

Create Legislation for Companion Animal Safety

In 2006 a five-year-old New York City dog named Bebe received statewide attention when the person accused of beating him was given a restraining order. Bebe had been left in the care of the perpetrator, and when his guardian returned, he found his 14-pound Bichon Frise limping and in pain from being beaten. The court order, with the restraining order to stay 100 yards away from the victim, was the first of its kind in the state, after New York's governor signed a new bill into law, allowing companion animals to be included in orders of protection.

New York's legislation, as well as serving as a deterrent, is significant because it protects animals from being returned to situations where they may be abused again; a person convicted of beating a pet can be sentenced to a year in jail.

This is not seen as silly or crazy any more. It has touched a nerve with legislators, judges and all sorts of others who consider animals part of the family.
— Joyce Tischler, Animal Legal Defense Fund

Pet Protection in North America

Both Canada and the United States have blanket animal welfare laws which loosely cover all animals. In Canada companion animal safety falls under an animal welfare section of the Criminal Code. An animal guardian can be charged with violation of the Criminal Code by a police officer or a special constable who may be a humane society employee.

In the United States, companion animals are covered by the USDA's Animal Welfare Act, although it doesn't cover reptiles, birds or rodents and only loosely covers cats and dogs. Retail breeders and pet shops selling domestic animals are not covered, but some fall under state or municipal legislation, leaving it up to groups such as the American Humane Association and the Humane Society of the United States to work with local and state officials to enforce the law.

In both countries this means that it's up to animal welfare groups to stay on top of what's happening and report any violations to authorities to enforce the rules — if there are any rules. With more companion animals than people, state and federal governments should not wait for animal welfare groups to tell them where the problems are. They should work with these groups to find solutions to the problems and suffering that companion animals have to put up with everyday.

In the United States alone, there are nearly 77 million cats and 65 million dogs. Add to that all the other pets like birds (17

BOB WALSH

million), reptiles (9 million), small mammals (16 million) and fish (190 million). According to the US Food and Drug Administration, there are a grand total of 378 million companion animals to 280 million people.[1]

Required Legislation
Federal and state/provincial laws must have strong enough teeth to prompt individuals to be responsible for their companion animals. The legislation must be thorough, and it should protect all domestic species, focused on the following areas:

- Population control — the enforcement of laws governing spaying and neutering.
- Registration — laws for the legal guardianship and responsibility for all animals.
- Physical safety — laws ensuring a safe and humane home for companion animals, including the ability to charge a guardian

who leaves an animal locked in a sealed car on a hot summer day.
- Animal trade — laws protecting animals from being sold to puppy mills, experimentation labs or blood sport operators.

As with many of these government solutions, public education is critical. Governments should help animal protection groups run educational programs and distribute information to guardians about the loving care of their companion animals.

In both the United States and Canada, legislation to improve the standards for companion animals (and animal welfare in general) has languished on the back burner for years. The proposed bills keep getting bumped to the back of the line when items of greater perceived concern arise. With more companion animals than people on our continent, we need to move these bills back where they belong: to the front of the line. This will only happen with persistent effort by governments working with animal welfare groups to write effective legislation.

The European Union Way

In the EU, the Convention for the Protection of Pet Animals lays out basic principles for each country to follow, stipulating that nobody can cause a pet unnecessary pain, suffering or distress, and that no one abandons a pet. It gives rules for who can own a pet, includes rules for commercial breeding and boarding and gives guidelines for animal sanctuaries. Most importantly, it helps prevent abuse.[2]

- Canadian Federation for Humane Societies: www.cfhs.ca
- Companion Animal Protection Society: www.caps-web.org
- Humane Society for Companion Animals: www.hsca.net
- National Dog Registry: www.nationaldogregistry.com
- Petsmart Charities: www.petsmart.com/charities
- Worldwide Directory of Animal Shelters: www.adoptapet.com

56

Write Legislation to Help Animal Abusers and Their Victims

People who abuse animals need help, as well as their victims. They need help so that they won't reoffend and so they will become more aware of their interconnectedness with other species. Simply fining abusers or giving them a jail sentence often does nothing to help, except giving the animals a brief reprieve. We need to find a way to reach people convicted of animal cruelty, so that they gain more understanding and find a way to open their hearts to kindness instead of cruelty.

States of Awareness
In the US, 27 states allow the courts to order counseling for animal abusers so that they can learn from their actions and gain a better awareness of the species around them. Colorado, New Hampshire and Virginia require alleged offenders to post a bond to cover the cost of holding the victimized animals during adjudication. These are positive steps that can make a difference.

Anicare Model for Treatment of Animal Abuse logo.

> The courts are beginning to take animal cruelty seriously now that it is more widely understood as a rehearsal crime. Anyone who hurts animals has the potential to move on to people.
> — Dr. Stephanie LaFarge, American Society for the Prevention of Cruelty to Animals

In Oregon anyone convicted of knowingly abusing animals can be handed a $100,000 fine, while in Louisiana an animal abuser can be sentenced to up to ten years of hard labour.

In Canada animal abuse is covered under the Criminal Code, and the maximum fine is $2000, with a possible two-year ban on owning an animal. The federal laws have not been changed in over 100 years, but an anti-cruelty bill was introduced in parliament in 1999. It has been stalled ever since, with two governments having changed the name of the bill seven times. As of 2006, Bill C-50 was still stalled, while animal welfare groups pushed for its acceptance.[1]

Effective legislation and tough penalties are great deterrents for animal abuse, but the help that comes with counseling is just as important.

A Model System
Simply mandating counseling for animal abusers is too vague. The counseling must be of a pattern that has a proven track record, such as the AniCare Model for Treatment of Animal Abuse; the first professionally developed intervention program for animal abusers over the age of 17. There's also AniCare Child for children who abuse animals. The programs, the result of a partnership between the Society & Animals Forum and the Doris Day Animal Foundation, have been used in 30 states, Canada and Mexico.

AniCare works closely with each client, giving him or her exercises and guidance for each particular situation. Their programs are guided by seven underlying themes, which become familiar to the client: accountability, respect/freedom, reciprocity, accommodation, empathy, attachment and nurturance. AniCare collects questionnaires from their clients, to build a better understanding of the profiles of people who abuse animals, and gives their findings to professionals and the general public in order to generate more understanding, with the hope that one day all cruelty to animals can be ended.

AniCare was born out of a California law that made animal abuse a felony. Along with the legislation came the awareness that those convicted needed counseling and there was nothing in place to help them. "We thought we'd better provide a treatment," said Ken Shapiro, who co-founded the program.

AniCare has been so successful that the Society & Animals Forum is giving training workshops to mental health agencies and professional groups across the United States and Canada, and many courts stipulate the AniCare Model for the treatment for convicted animal abusers.

- AniCare Model of Treatment for Animal Abuse: www.psyeta.org/AniCare.html and www.psyeta.org/anicarechild.html
- Animal Place: www.animalplace.org
- Animal Rights Law Project: www.animal-law.org
- Doris Day Animal Foundation: www.ddaf.org
- Friends of Animals: www.friendsofanimals.org

An Eerie Correlation

Research shows a correlation between animal abuse and family violence. One study showed that in 88% of the American homes where childhood physical abuse was present, so was animal abuse.[2] A study of women who were seeking shelter in a safe house showed that 71% of the women had partners who had abused or killed their companion animals.[3] The ASPCA's Joseph Pentangelo said, "Pets are often caught in the cycle of domestic violence."

Intentional cruelty to animals is rarely, if ever, an isolated incident born of a complete lack of understanding. It is nearly always indicative of more serious issues below the surface. The sad truth is that it's much easier to abuse an animal and get away with it, so animals become the unfortunate target of a person's anger, when their loving companionship could be the very thing that is lacking in that person's life.

57

Outlaw the Captivity and Ownership of Large Exotic Animals

> I can't tell you how many frantic calls we receive, asking for us to take their exotic pet because they can no longer provide proper care.
> — Tony Vecchio, Oregon Zoo

It is estimated that between 10,000 and 20,000 large cats, including tigers, lions and bobcats, are being kept as pets in the United States.[1] Although the US Department of Agriculture requires licenses for exhibitors, dealers and researchers, no such rules govern the individual ownership of these and other large exotic animals. The exact number of animals in private possession is unknown, since no licensing is required.

Over Their Heads

Buying a baby tiger or a bear cub may seem like a fun idea, but it doesn't take long for the situation to get out of control. Tiger cubs grow up to be 600-pound adult tigers that require 20 pounds of meat a day.[2] Many owners find themselves overwhelmed by their new "pets," who eat them out of house and home. They also learn that they require a huge amount of care and attention, and soon they are calling their local authority for help: either to remove their pet or have it put down. All too often, the authorities are called to homes where large cats, snakes and other exotic animals have been mistreated, malnourished and left in enclosures that are far too small for their health.

So Far from Home

Tigers don't belong in back yards in Nevada; nor do boa constrictors belong in cages in Manitoba. These creatures have been taken from their natural environments and forced to exist in cramped conditions, far from home. They have not been domesticated for thousands of years like cats, dogs and cows. They will spend most of their lives trying to escape from captivity, and their health will decline the longer they are away from their natural habitat. Despite adamant support by those who keep large exotics as pets, the practice is inhumane for the animals, as well as being expensive and often very dangerous.

Captivity and Tigers Don't Mix

Over and over, conflicts between large cats and their owners result in tragedy. Since 1990, 6 adults and 2 children have been killed by tigers in the United States, and more than 80 people have been seriously mauled.[3] Every year animals escape and are killed by authorities, and a huge number simply die in captivity. This isn't the way it should be.

No Exotics in New York

In 2005 New York State passed a law banning the ownership of exotic pets. The legislation

- ASPCA-exoticpets: www.aspca.org, search for exotic pets
- Avian Welfare Coalition: www.avianwelfare.org/issues/pets.htm
- Captive Wild Animals Protection Coalition: www.cwapc.org/education/API_3_Reasons.html
- Scales and Tails: www.scalesandtails.com/ban_exotic.html
- USDA Position on Exotic Pets: www.aphis.usda.gov/ac/position.html

prohibits the possession, import, sale and barter of many species, including big cats, monkeys, large reptiles, bears, wolves, venomous snakes. It allows those who already own large exotic animals to continue to do so until the end of their pets' natural lifetime, providing they adhere to strict guidelines governing their care. With the new law, New York became the 14th US state to ban the ownership of large exotic pets. A further 8 states have a partial ban on certain species,

and 13 states regulate the ownership of exotics. But in 15 states, and in all provinces of Canada, there are no laws governing their ownership.

The solution is easy. Federal, state and provincial governments must ban the possession and trade of large, exotic animals used as pets and enforce the ban. There is no valid reason for the captivity of these animals. The practice is a danger to both the animals and their owners, and our governments must ban the practice.

Respect for Reptiles

Large snakes are some of the most popular acquisitions in the billion-dollar exotic pet trade, but few people realize what they're getting into. Some snakes, such as the Burmese python, can grow to over 20 feet long and weigh 200 pounds. Snake owners repeatedly find themselves in over their heads and have nowhere to turn, as most zoos won't take the unwanted reptiles. Of all large exotics, reptiles have the highest rate of mortality. Close to 90% of all reptiles die in their first year of captivity, largely due to loneliness, misery and a loss of the will to live.[4]

Desert glossy snake.

58

Cultivate Coexistence with Problem Animals

Our homes and roadways were once their homes, and therefore, it is our obligation to do all we can to coexist peacefully with them.
— Stephanie Boyles, wildlife biologist

Governments need to help people cope with unwanted animals, and this goes far beyond cockroaches and mice. Coyotes, bears, deer, ravens, feral dogs and cats, raccoons, hawks and porcupines all suffer from a general lack of understanding. All have been considered frightening, annoying and disposable.

They were here first. It was us who arrived and made their homes our own. Wild animals interfere with our lives because we have broken their natural balance, and governments can do a lot to restore what has been lost by cultivating awareness.

- Create greenspace and protect wilderness (see Solution 63). The more natural areas animals have to live in, the less they'll bother people's homes, so create wildlife corridors where they can travel easily.

- Don't let people take wildlife control into their own hands. Create a hotline for humane, responsible animal response teams and make sure everyone knows the number.

- Establish humane ways of responding to animal issues and share the information with schools, businesses and individuals.

- Ban the use of cruel pest control methods such as glue traps and poisoning.

A Little Relief Down Under

The Australian state of Victoria has passed legislation that bans the use of glue traps (trays or sheets of paper coated with an adhesive that instantly immobilizes any small animals or birds on contact). Although used around the world, glue traps are widely criticized by animal welfare groups and concerned citizens. In Australia alone, professional trappers kill 250,000 rodents every year in glue traps. The number becomes much larger when you include people who use the traps around their homes. But that's all changed in Victoria. When state officials adopted the ban, they cited the extreme injury, distress and suffering that animals are subjected to in glue traps. The ban comes with a $1,000 fine for anyone caught using the traps.

Working Together for Beavers

The state of Virginia had a problem with beavers, which had become pests in the eyes of residents who had to deal with their presence along highways, building dams that caused expensive and dangerous flooding. People for the Ethical Treatment of Animals (PETA) came to the rescue, working closely with Virginia's Department of Transportation (VDOT). A simple device was installed to prevent the beavers from causing flooding, and the project was so successful that VDOT funded a year-long study by PETA wildlife biologist Stephanie Boyles to establish the criteria for eight of the non-lethal beaver management devices to be deployed along Virginia highways. Thanks to the State's support, and to their willingness to work with PETA, a large number of beavers have been spared the painful death of underwater traps.

IAN McALLISTER/RAINCOAST.ORG

Preventing Predator Conflicts in BC

In British Columbia it's illegal to feed dangerous wildlife, such as bears, cougars and coyotes, or to deposit any substance that might attract them. This is important legislation in a province where 905 black bears and 49 grizzlies are destroyed by Conservation Officers every year[1] after the animals have become reliant on human food sources. While some animals are relocated successfully after becoming habituated (BC relocates around 250 bears every year), many become a "problem" in their new territory, while some travel hundreds of miles to return to where they came from. Proper waste management and public education are the keys to conflict prevention before habituation occurs.

The Return of the Swift Fox

When settlers arrived in the Great Plains, they sought to eradicate wolves and coyotes from preying on their domestic animals, indiscriminately poisoning their habitat. This led to the demise of the swift fox, already low on the food chain and preyed upon by coyotes, eagles and trappers. So, even though the tiny fox eats only small animals and bugs, posing no economic threat to ranchers, they were believed to be driven to extinction from Montana by 1969 and remain on the Species at Risk list in Canada. In 2006 a swift fox den was discovered in Montana's Fort Peck Reservation, and now a conservation effort is under way, with the Native American Fish and Wildlife Society and Montana's Fish, Wildlife, and Parks Service working together to reintroduce the swift fox to its former habitat and protect its natural corridor that runs from Wyoming to southern Saskatchewan. Since the 1980s, 800 of the tiny foxes, each weighing only four to six pounds, have already been reintroduced to southern Saskatchewan, as ranchers realize them to be allies instead of pests.

- Care for the Wild International: www.careforthewild.org
- Humane Society of Canada: www.humanesociety.com
- National Wildlife Federation: www.nwf.org
- Progressive Animal Welfare Society: www.paws.org

59

Make Dissections in All Schools Optional

Many students have an ethical, religious or aesthetic distaste for animal dissection. ... State policy should provide for a choice for students.

— Senator Ryan Deckert, Oregon

Students should never be forced to take part in an action that runs deeply against their ethical beliefs or which they find to be abusive. Nor should they be penalized for opting out of such actions. The life of an animal is spared every time a student chooses to opt out of a classroom dissection, and yet, in classrooms far and wide, students are told that dissections are mandatory.

There are plenty of alternatives to classroom dissections (see Solution 24). Students can easily learn biology without cutting into the body of an animal, so there is no reason for dissections to be mandatory. All schools should offer the alternative methods, and dissections should be optional everywhere. It's the right thing to do not just for the animals, but also for the students. It sends a message that their choices

count, and they do not simply have to conform to tradition.

Climbing on Board

There is no federal legislation in North America to help students opt out of dissection in their classrooms. There is, however, a movement developing among state and provincial governments. Twelve states have passed legislation allowing students to opt out with no penalty, and more have legislation pending, although it has been turned down in several states. In Canada, it's up to individual school districts to create policies regarding classroom dissections. While some districts, such as Nova Scotia's South Shore, have created progressive policies regarding dissection alternatives, many have avoided breaking with tradition.

Get Involved

A government's involvement in providing alternatives can be enormously helpful for schools and school boards. There are often misconceptions about the cost of providing dissection alternatives which deter schools from trying to stretch their budgets. The reality is, after the initial cost of purchasing the videos and computer simulation software, the long-term expenses are far less, since the materials can be used over and over again, while frogs can only be dissected once.

US NATIONAL PARK SERVICE

Saving Money for Schools[2]

Cost of dissections for 3 years, for a school with 3 classes of 30 students performing 3 dissections a year: $10,044.90

Cost of using a combination of alternatives for the same students over 3 years: $2,680.50

Total savings over the 3-year period by using alternatives: $7,364.40

- All Creatures — dissections: www.all-creatures.org/adow/cam-lab-diss.html
- Humane Education Advocates Reaching Teachers: www.teachhumane.org
- International Institute for Humane Education: www.iihed.org
- International Society for Animal Rights: www.isaronline.org
- National Humane Education Society: www.nhes.org

Governments and policy makers can:

- Learn about the alternatives, tell school districts about their choices and discuss ways to implement them.
- Create a budget to provide alternatives for school districts and help them with the transition.
- Assign a task force to research the best educational alternatives.
- Write a law supporting the right of students to opt out of classroom dissections.
- Support a humane-education network.
- Create animal-free biology classrooms.

An End to Dissections

Governments can take the extra step and ban classroom dissections altogether, eliminating the need to provide alternatives for some students, and animals for dissection for others. Adapting biology classrooms for the alternative methods reduces the long-term cost for school boards and creates a more humane society in which animals are no longer exploited and where children learn respect and responsibility for the lives of their fellow creatures.

There is no need to provide animals for classroom dissection, even for students intent on pursuing biology at college.[1] Dr. Nedim C. Buyukmihci, Professor of Ophthalmology at the University of California, Davis, calls classroom dissections a "rite of passage" rather than a well-thought-out method of teaching: "I can unequivocally state that the experience of dissection is totally unnecessary for the biologically minded pre-college student."

Governments Giving Students a Choice

Classroom dissections have been optional in several countries and banned in others. Israel, the Slovak Republic and Argentina have banned these dissections altogether, while in Italy and India, they have been made optional. In the UK, all students under 16 can opt out of dissections, although some schools still attempt to make them mandatory; students and their parents have to insist on the student's right to choose. In Queensland, Australia, both primary and secondary students are able to choose alternatives to dissections.

60

Find Alternatives to Animal Experimentation

> As the scientific community discovers legitimate alternatives to using animals, we embrace them.
>
> — Dr. Helen Diggs,
> UC Berkeley's Animal Care Facility

With an estimated 24 million animals being used every year in American laboratories (see "Laboratory Labyrinth"), it is time that governments made themselves accountable for what happens during animal experimentation. It is no longer tolerable to allow this amount of suffering to continue unchecked, while there are alternatives that can make it unnecessary. When suffering of this magnitude happens, it's time to step in:

1. **Establish** a task force to seek alternatives. Learn from both sides and from credible sources.

2. **Enact** legislation to govern the procedures that take place, with tough, effective penalties if violated.

3. **Assist** laboratories and research teams to use alternatives to animal experiments.

Finding Alternatives

The use of animals in laboratories is a complex issue that needs urgent solutions. Lab animals have played a critical role in the development of important medical procedures and have, quite against their will, shown us the necessity of testing chemicals for toxicity. We live in a world full of man-made chemicals that affect the health and environment of all species, and vigilance for their safety is essential. Fortunately, there is a global community of scientists who are working to find effective alternatives to the use of animals in laboratories. Their work is benefiting animals, and the improved accuracy of the alternative methods is benefiting both humans and the environment. Many alternatives already exist:

For product testing:

- In-vitro initial screen for anti-cancer compounds, already adopted by the National Cancer Institute.

- Episkin — reconstructed human in-vitro epidermis for the evaluation of the corrosiveness of pharmaceutical and chemical compounds.

- Computerized chemical structure-activity relationship (SAR) — knowledge-based expert systems that allow for the prediction of safety and toxicity of new compounds.

- Toxicogenomics — utilizing DNA chips to identify patterns of gene-change characteristics of specific toxicity endpoints. This method should ultimately replace nearly all current animal-based tests.[1]

For research:

- I-MAb Gas Permeable Tissue Culture Bags — used to produce monoclonal antibodies for research diagnostic and clinical purposes.

- British Union for the Abolition of Vivisection: www.buav.org
- Ethologists for the Ethical Treatment of Animals: www.ethologicalethics.org
- European Alliance to End Animal Experiments: www.eceae.org
- International Primate Protection League: www.ippl.org
- Medical Research Modernization Committee: www.mrmcmed.org

- Human cadaver cross-sections and CAT scans[2] — used by the National Library of Medicine Visible Human Project, along with computer programs to develop new surgical techniques.
- Mathematical models and computer simulations — for use in physiology, cardiovascular, pharmacology and neurosciences.
- Human cell and tissue cultures, to identify disease processes and treatments.[3]

All of these alternatives are recognized by the scientific community and are in limited use across North America and Europe. Government and independent teams set up to look at the use of the alternatives are chronically under-funded, however, and unsupported by the research industry.

Moving Ahead in Europe

The Council of Europe has created the European Convention for the Protection of Vertebrate Animals Used for Experimental and other Scientific Purposes[4] to reduce the amount of animal suffering in laboratories. The convention has two primary focuses: finding alternatives to animal experimentation, thereby reducing the number of animals used, and finding ways to limit the discomfort that lab animals are subjected to. The convention is a moral agreement, rather than a legal one. It is recognized by the European Union, however, and its provisions are easily adoptable as legally binding by EU member nations. The convention is an important step forward and presents a path to a future where animal-free laboratories may be possible.

ETHAN SMITH

An End to Cosmetics Testing

In 2003 the European Union reached an agreement to immediately ban the testing of cosmetics on animals and the marketing of such products whenever alternatives are available, and they announced a complete ban of all cosmetics testing on animals by 2009, allowing time for alternatives to be put in place. The ban includes a wide range of products from shampoos and lotions to deodorants and mascara. While some nations including the UK and Germany had already banned the testing of cosmetics on animals, none had taken this extra step of banning the importation of animal-tested cosmetics from other countries.

61

Promote Organic Farming

> It should come as no surprise that the demand for organic, pesticide-free foods has skyrocketed in recent years.
>
> — Rush Holt, New Jersey Congressman

Organic farms stimulate biodiversity, while preserving the air, soil and water for all creatures great and small, and provide life-sustaining, nutritious food for everyone involved (see Solution 33). They have been found to support 57% more species of life than their conventional counterparts, including 44% more birds,[1] and their use of natural pest control methods eliminates the need to test pesticides on animals.

Worldwide, biodiversity is in decline, air quality is deteriorating, topsoil is vanishing, and water is becoming more polluted. Government initiatives to increase biodiversity have focused on establishing protected areas, but these areas only cover 10% of the Earth's surface, compared to 40% that are used for agricultural purposes.[2] With so much of our land committed to agriculture, the use of chemicals and the move to monoculture crops is having a heavy impact on global biodiversity.

In 2001 an ecological study of 14 grassland sites from 8 countries verified that plant communities fare better when they consist of complementary teams of species, rather than being dominated by a single species.[3] This simple truth is the key to biodiversity and life on Earth.

Supporting Conversion in Europe

The best way for governments to promote organic farming is to help farmers during the transition. All European Union nations support the conversion process for farmers, some quite extensively. The EU allocates $130 million annually for the development of organic farming, four times more than the rest of the world.[4] Austria, Finland, Germany, Sweden, Switzerland and Denmark provide generous funding of their own and have targets and action plans. The EU's Common Agricultural Policy (CAP) no longer pays subsidies to organic farmers based on volume; instead, it gives out subsidies based on "cross compliance," when farmers respect environmental, food safety, animal and plant health and animal welfare standards, as well as keeping their farmland in good agricultural and environmental condition.[5]

In 2004 the European Commission's Action Plan of Organic Food and Farming created a strategic policy for the growth of the organic sector across Europe and supported the sector's contribution to CAP.

Transition Relief in the US

In the US the Organic Transitions[6] program provides grant funding to projects that help farmers with organic production and marketing. In 2006 Congress increased its funding from $1.8 million to $5 million,[7] cutting $100 million from other

- European Action Plan of Organic Food and Farming: www.orgap.org
- International Federation for Organic Agriculture Movements: www.ifoam.org
- Organic Agriculture Centre of Canada: www.organicagcentre.ca
- Organic Crop Improvement Association: www.ocia.org

agricultural programs and reflecting the growing consumer demand, with sales of organic produce surpassing $10 billion for the first time in 2003 (see Solution 33).

Global Growth of Organics

In 2001 organic agriculture surpassed 24 million acres (10 million hectares) of land worldwide, and by 2006, 76 million acres of land had been certified organic, with 623,000 organic farms in 120 countries. In total area, Australia leads the way with 29 million acres of organic farmland,[8] while Austria and Switzerland have the highest percentage of agricultural land dedicated to organics.

Organic farming in the US is regulated by the Department of Agriculture (USDA), providing a certification label for the rapidly growing organic market, aided by a growing number of certification agencies. In Canada the organic farming industry has a voluntary Canada Organic Standard, which is not yet supported by legislation.[9]

Despite the rapid growth of the global organic market, only 2% of the world's agricultural land is certified organic. For the sustainability of our planet, and all species that share our world, we need government policies that will get our farmland off pesticides, remove genetically modified organisms (GMOs) from our food and preserve the integrity of our ecosystems.

We need to commit to a goal of 100% organic agriculture. A study of over 200 agricultural projects in the developing world, where poverty and hunger is the most severe, found that, for all of the projects, yields increased by an average

SHEL NEUFELD/WILDARTPHOTOGRAPHY.COM

of 93% when converted to organic. Organic farming is producing nearly twice as much yield in the poor, arid areas of the world where hunger is the most severe. A team from the University of Michigan tested the results on a global model, studying total conversion to organic methods, finding that organic methods yielded 4,381 calories per person, which is 75% more than is achieved today.[10] We can feed the whole world by going organic.

Organic farming as a percentage of total agricultural area.[11]

Austria	13.5	Norway	3.9
Switzerland	11.3	Australia	2.7
Finland	7.3	France	1.8
Sweden	6.8	Canada	0.7
Italy	6.2	China	0.6
Czech Republic	6.1	Brazil	0.3
Denmark	5.7	Mexico	0.3
Germany	4.5	United States	0.2
United Kingdom	4.3		

62

Write Legislation Protecting Farm Animals

> Large numbers of animals, especially farm animals, are exempt from true protections and are allowed to suffer provided their pain is considered necessary.
>
> — Brian Sherman, Australian lawyer

When policy-makers consider animal welfare legislation, they tend to stop short at the uncomfortable issue of farm animals. It's relatively easy to rally support for endangered wildlife and laboratory animals, but farm animal welfare threatens the very way we eat. We know there's suffering on our dinner plates, but nobody wants to look at it, so it continues to be accepted as "the way things have to be."

In the United States, 10 billion farm animals are killed every year in the meat, egg and dairy industries — nearly twice the human population of the world, and 500 times more than the 20 million animals that die in laboratories.[1]

Current legislation in the US supports existing farming practices, despite their cruelty. States which have anti-animal cruelty laws generally have exemptions when it comes to "common farming practices."[2] In other words, you can't subject an animal to cruel and unnecessary suffering unless it's a farm animal.

Hope for Farm Animals Around the World

- Britain has a law that protects breeding sows from overcrowding, and a law against the mistreatment of veal calves, including denying them iron and roughage, a common practice in the US, where it is said to produce a more desirable product.

- Austria's 2005 law, accepted by every member of parliament, banned the use of battery cages on chicken farms. Austria's laws require that every province must appoint a lawyer on behalf of animals in court cases to ensure that all animals, including farm animals, are treated humanely.

- New Zealand's Animal Welfare Act of 1999 ensures that chickens live in as much comfort as possible, with adequate space, ventilation, temperature control, light and water. The legislation includes detailed management guidelines, such as temperature limits during transportation and hourly inspections on the chickens' welfare during hot weather.

- Norway's Animal Welfare Act prohibits the debeaking of chickens, geese and ducks and bans the castration of piglets without anesthetics; tail-cutting or tooth-clipping of pigs; and the use of veal crates or holding stalls for calves.

FARM SANCTUARY

- Queensland, Australia, has legislation that protects laying hens, forbidding the stacking of vertical cages unless each hen has adequate space to move around and protection from excreta falling from the cage above her.

- Ontario has a law in the Health of Animals Act that segregates farm animals by compatibility during transportation. Animals of different sizes, or which may cause injury to others, cannot be transported together.

- Florida regulates the treatment of pigs during pregnancy, ensuring that pregnant sows are not confined to cages, crates or other enclosures that restrict movement. Nor can they be tethered in a way that prevents them from turning around freely.

- California has legislation that ensures humane treatment for animals that cannot stand or walk without assistance. Only USDA-inspected facilities can purchase or sell such animals, and care must be given during their transportation.

- Animal Legal and Historical Center: www.animallaw.info
- Animal Legal Defense Fund: www.aldf.org
- Canadian Coalition for Farm Animals: www.humanefood.ca
- Compassion in World Farming: www.ciwf.org.uk
- Farm Animal Reform Movement: www.farmusa.org
- Food Animal Concerns Trust: www.fact.cc
- Humane Farming Association: www.hfa.org

Standing Up for Veal Calves

In the European Union, where all 25 member nations are uniting to improve the life of farm animals, life got a little easier for veal calves in 2006 when a Europe-wide ban took effect on the confinement of calves over the age of eight weeks in veal crates. Younger calves can still be kept in crates, but they must have adequate space to move around. In addition, feed for all calves must contain sufficient levels of iron, and fiber must be introduced after two weeks of age.

In Israel the government has also passed legislation to ease the suffering of veal calves. The new regulations ban the practice of keeping calves in solitary confinement, while setting improved standards for ventilation and footing material. The new standards will be fully in place after a three-year transition period, but one aspect took place immediately; that veal calves be supplied with an unlimited supply of drinking water at all times.

63

Address Global Climate Change

The challenge is either to build an economy that is sustainable, or to stay with our unsustainable economy until it collapses. It is not a goal that can be compromised. One way or another, the choice will be made by our generation, but it will affect life on Earth for generations to come.
— Lester Brown, Earth Policy Institute

To end the suffering of farm animals, we can pass new legislation. To end the suffering of animals in labs and zoos, we can introduce new standards and requirements. But how do we prevent the future suffering of polar bears, who are losing the very ice they depend on to hunt? How do we prevent the future suffering of elephants, who may lose the water they need to drink? Climate change haunts their future like an ominous storm that they — *but not we* — are powerless to prevent.

Our planet's life is sustained by a fragile miracle that evolved over millions of years, long before humans appeared. Some say the Earth is so large that it is impossible for humans to influence this ancient flow of temperature, atmosphere and ocean. They are wrong. It took many million years for the human population to reach one billion by 1800. In the next 200 years, thanks to the Industrial Revolution, it exploded to 6.5 billion, and is still growing. The Industrial Revolution was almost entirely powered by fuel from ancient trees and plants, and it is their released carbon that is the primary cause of global climate change that threatens us all — humans and animals alike — with such enormous consequences.

The task for governments is to guide our civilization through the dangers we have created and help us craft a world that either no longer needs fossil fuels or where the ancient carbon is captured and made safe before it can escape into the atmosphere.

ETHAN SMITH

- Climate Ark: www.climateark.org
- Climate Group: www.theclimategroup.org
- *Stormy Weather: 101 Solutions to Global Climate Change*, by Guy Dauncey with Patrick Mazza, New Society Publishers, 2001: www.earthfuture.com

This may seem a stupendous task, but it is possible to spin it around, so that instead of being enormously difficult, it becomes a natural evolution to another industrial age. The first is powered by those ancient fossil fuels, as a one-off gift from the past; the second is powered by the renewable energy of sun, wind and tides, laying the foundation for a far healthier, secure, sustainable future.

In 2006 the government of California set its sights on this future by making a commitment to reduce the state's greenhouse gas emissions by 25% by 2020 and 80% by 2050. The tools they are using include incentives for more solar and wind energy, more use of biofuels and regulations designed to move all automobiles towards far lower greenhouse gas emissions and all buildings and appliances towards far greater energy efficiency.[1]

Sweden, likewise, has made a national commitment to turn things around, so that by the year 2020, citizens will no longer depend on oil to fuel their vehicles or heat their homes. They too are looking to more use of sustainable energy from wind and waves, biofuels and greater efficiency, so that less energy is needlessly wasted. Their goal is to replace all fossil fuels with renewables before climate change damages their economy and world oil scarcity leads to price rises.[2]

There are many sources of information that describe the technologies, policies and strategies that are available to governments, once they decide to adopt the turnaround path.

- There are cars in Zurich that are fuelled by gas from household compost wastes.
- There are electric vehicles that can be powered by the sun and wind, and plug-in hybrid vehicles that operate as electric vehicles for local trips and can also use liquid fuel for long distances.
- There are plans for enormous solar thermal collectors in the deserts of North Africa, transmitting power to Europe.
- There are cities that have seen a dramatic increase in cycling, thanks to a mix of intelligent policies and good cycle lanes.
- There are companies that have made the commitment to become fully sustainable by 2020, with all their energy coming from sustainable sources.
- Sweden uses nationwide carbon taxes, with the income being used to reduce other taxes.
- Other countries use "cap and trade" policies that require companies to either reduce their emissions or trade them for reductions elsewhere.

The challenge to governments is not knowing what to do: it is gathering the commitment to do it and then carrying the public behind you, so that your work is not undermined by those who are unwilling to face the inconvenient truth that climate change is with us and must be addressed as a matter of the greatest urgency.

64

Preserve Wilderness

> If future generations are to remember us
> with gratitude rather than contempt,
> we must leave them more than the
> miracles of technology.
>
> — US president Lyndon B. Johnson,
> upon signing the Wilderness Act in 1964

The natural world evolved over millions of years, unaltered by civilization, maintaining its ecological balance, ensuring biodiversity and sustaining life through its forests, mountains, grasslands, jungles, wetlands and alpine meadows. But today, wilderness is vanishing from our world, the victim of logging, agriculture, oil and gas development and urban sprawl.

Globally we are losing 39.5 million acres of forested land per year; we have lost a fifth of all such land since 1950. Seventy-six countries have no frontier forests left.[1] It needn't be this way, however. Forests can be managed sustainably (see Solution 49); agricultural land can be managed organically; we can share farmland with wildlife (see Solution 34); renewable energy initiatives can reduce oil and gas exploration; and urban sprawl can be restricted, setting aside land for wildlife.

An Act of Preservation

In 1964 President Lyndon Johnson signed The Wilderness Act, creating America's National Wilderness Preservation System, protecting 9.1 million acres of forest and declaring wilderness "as an area where the Earth, and its community of life are untrammeled by man, where man himself is a visitor who does not remain."

Forty years later, land designated as wilderness in the US has grown to 106 million acres,[2] 4.7% of its land mass. There are 655 million acres of federal public land in the US, so 549 million acres remain available for preservation. In 2002, however, the Bush administration announced that federal land managers will no longer study or recommend lands for future wilderness protection.

Committing to Conservation

Canada is the world's second-largest country (behind Russia). Its 3.8 million square miles comprises 7% of the world's land surface, including vast wilderness areas that are home to 300,000 species of plants and animals.[3] By 2003, 155 million acres had been protected as national parks, reserves, or "sustainable use management" areas,[4] covering 6.3% of Canada's landmass, while deforestation is happening at 224,000 acres per year.[5]

Yellowstone to Yukon

The Yellowstone to Yukon Conservation Initiative (Y2Y) is a Canada – US network of 800 organizations and individuals who are working together to preserve nearly 2,000 miles of Rocky Mountain wilderness, from Yellowstone National Park in the south, to Peel River, Yukon Territory, in the north. Y2Y's scientists and

- Algonquin to Adirondack Conservation Association: www.a2alink.org
- National Park Conservation Association: www.npca.org
- Sierra Club: www.sierraclub.org
- Sierra Club of Canada: www.sierraclub.ca
- Wildlife Conservation Society: www.wcs.org
- Yellowstone to Yukon Conservation Initiative: www.y2y.net

conservationists are working with conservation groups, communities and governments to promote the preservation of this vast international bioregion.

Algonquin to Adirondack

The Algonquin to Adirondack Conservation Association (A2A) is another Canada – US joint project dedicated to the preservation of the largest natural land connection in eastern North America, from Lake Superior to the Atlantic Ocean. A2A's conservation area stretches from Adirondack Park in New York State to Algonquin Provincial Park in Ontario, a corridor that is heavily populated by wildlife and humans. A2A works with landowners, conservationists and policy-makers to promote the vital importance of sustaining natural connections between forests, wetlands and national boundaries.

Meet the UN Goal

In 1987 the United Nations suggested that, in order to preserve the Earth's ecosystems, the amount of land under protection would need to be tripled from the global level of 4%. They asked each nation to set aside 12% of its land mass. To make the UN goal successful, the total protected area must be of sufficient size to support biodiversity and migration. In North

Learn from New Zealand

New Zealand takes its wild places very seriously: 16 million acres, 24.4% of the total land mass, is dedicated to parkland and wildlife reserves,[8] including 14 national parks.

This is what governments must do to preserve wilderness: protect, protect, protect. Have the political courage to preserve more land, so that it will still be wild and inspiring in a thousand years' time.

America, 70% of the protected areas are less than 500 acres.[6] The land must also be fully habitable to a wide variety of species. In 2006 the British Columbia government announced it had raised the protected area to 1.8 million hectares (4.4 million acres); accounting for 13.8% of its land mass, surpassing the UN goal. However 29% of BC's park system comprises alpine tundra,[7] prompting criticisms of the Province's "rock and ice" conservation.

65

Protect Habitat for Endangered Species

> If the spotted owl situation is not an emergency, then nothing is.
>
> — Devon Page, Sierra Legal Defense

An endangered species is one that faces a substantial risk of extinction, and has a population base too low to sustain itself without immediate assistance. The World Conservation Union estimates that 5,200 species of animals — including birds, mammals, reptiles, amphibians, fishes and invertebrates — are currently facing extinction. By 2100 if the current rate is allowed to continue, two-thirds of all animal and plant species on Earth will be extinct.[1]

How will we explain that to our grandchildren? What will we say if they meet us in the afterlife? That we simply didn't care?

Primary Causes

There are three primary causes of extinction, all of which governments can have a direct effect on.

- Habitat destruction — resulting from human population growth, urban sprawl, agriculture, forestry and extractive industries.
- Exploitation — from over-hunting, over-fishing, trapping and the international trade in animal parts.
- Introduction of exotic species — disturbing the balance of nature and often resulting in species dying off. This includes the arrival of domestic animals in wild areas.

Endangered Legislation

In 1973 the United States introduced its Endangered Species Act, a piece of legislation unlike any seen before, stating that the government would do everything in its power to prevent the extinction of any species within its borders. To this day, the Act lives on, despite considerable controversy. Repeated attacks by special interest groups continue, including from within the government: the Bush administration has tried repeatedly to make it more favorable to the oil, logging, fishing and hunting industries.[2] Yet 30 years later, the Act still exists, thanks to huge support from individuals, organizations and politicians.

On the Great Plains

There are only two herds of genetically pure bison roaming the Great Plains of the United States: one in northeast Montana, and one in Wind Cave National Park, South Dakota. All other

- Committee on the Status of Endangered Wildlife in Canada: www.cosewic.gc.ca
- Endangered Species Coalition: www.stopextinction.org
- US Endangered Species Act: www.fws.gov/endangered/esa.html
- US Endangered Species Program: www.fws.gov/endangered
- World Wildlife Fund: www.worldwildlife.org

Hope for the Kakapo

There's a little-known and critically endangered species of parrot in New Zealand's offshore islands called the kakapo. These plump nocturnal birds can't fly, but they are able to climb tall trees. Kakapo populations dropped to near 50 during the mid-90s and were in danger of becoming a footnote in history until a team of volunteers and the New Zealand Department of Conservation created a program to boost their numbers. Staff and volunteers are continuously monitoring the parrots' nests, ensuring that they remain undisturbed and warm while the parent kakapos leave to find food.

bison in the US are contaminated with cattle genes, leaving the American bison vulnerable to extinction.[3] The World Wildlife Fund is working with conservation groups and state governments to reintroduce bison throughout the Great Plains, while preserving native grasslands and restoring the natural prairie.

Canada's Act

In 2003 Canada's Species at Risk Act[4] was proclaimed, giving hope to the country's 516 animal and plant species that are facing extinction. A Committee on the Status of Endangered Wildlife in Canada was created to identify species at risk, and the government is responsible for legally protecting all species on federal land which the Committee identifies as being at risk. The Act identifies the major threats to wildlife populations, including climate change and environmental contamination, and outlines protective guidelines for species at risk. However, Canada's Act has been widely criticized by conservation groups for being ineffective; only protecting wildlife on federal lands and being bypassed for economic reasons.[5]

BC's Endangered Species

The province of British Columbia, covering 95 million hectares (234 million acres) hosts the greatest biodiversity in all Canada, but it has no Endangered Species Act. A clear example is the spotted owl — an endangered species that saw its population decline by 84% between 1995 and 2005. In 2002 the Province appointed a Spotted Owl Recovery Team, and three major logging companies agreed to suspend activities within areas identified as critical habitat. This move led to increased logging in adjacent areas, and government biologists were only able to find six pairs of owls in 2005.[6]

The spotted owl, like the rest of BC's 1,364 at-risk animal and plant species, needs legislation to protect it, with adequate attention and funding.

A Federal or Provincial Problem?

Under Canada's Species at Risk Act, if a province doesn't take adequate action to protect a species, the federal government can step in using an emergency provision. In the case of the spotted owl, several environmental groups called for them to do so, but in 2006, the federal government declined to intervene,[7] placing the spotted owl in further peril and diminishing the effectiveness of the Act. In order for legislation to be successful, federal and state/provincial governments must work together. Endangered species know no political boundaries.

66

Ban the Import of Endangered Species

> The greatness of a nation can be judged by the way its animals are treated.
>
> — Mahatma Gandhi

The global trade in wildlife and wildlife products has grown from $3 billion a year in the 1980s to $10 billion just two decades later.[1] Consumers, many of whom have little knowledge about how endangered the species are, look for live animals as exotic pets, as well as for body parts such as ivory, fur, bones, claws and bile. Some are looking for rare plants or exotic lumber, which impact animals by depleting their natural habitat.

Enter CITES

In 1973 the United Nations Convention on International Trade in Endangered Species of Wild Fauna and Flora (CITES) was signed, and by 2006, 154 nations had signed on to regulate the trade of 5,000 animal and 25,000 plant species. Of the 30,000 species that are threatened by international trade, 800 have been moved to CITES' Appendix I, meaning their trade has been banned worldwide. CITES does not police international trade, leaving it to individual countries to enforce the treaty and place sanctions on the violators (see Solution 94).

A Day No Elephants Shall Die?

Through the 1980s, 770 tons of ivory was exported annually from Africa, causing the deaths of 75,000 elephants a year.[2] In 1989 the trade of ivory was banned worldwide by CITES, but in the three years before the ban, 300,000 elephants were killed in Africa, leaving just 625,000 alive on the continent.[3] Accessibility to automatic weapons by hunters and lack of protection from governments fueled the hunt during the 1970s, and prices for ivory climbed from $3/lb to $125/lb, before the CITES ban effectively ended the industry. Had it not done so, African elephants would probably be extinct today.

Elephants are far from out of danger, however. In 2006 Taiwan confiscated 5 tons of ivory being smuggled in from Tanzania. In the same month, authorities in Hong Kong seized 3.9 tons of ivory being smuggled in from Cameroon.

One for the Parrots

A quarter of all existing parrot species are threatened with extinction, making them the most endangered bird family on Earth.[4] In 1992 the US wrote the Wild Bird Conservation Act, banning all imports of wild-caught parrots. By doing so, it

US NATIONAL PARK SERVICE

reduced the global trade of parrots by 44%. Worldwide, however, the trade of wild parrots continues, with Japan leading the way. The trade captured 600,000 birds in 1999.

Relief for the Beluga Sturgeon

The beluga sturgeon, native to the Caspian and Black Seas, and used for caviar and cosmetics, was placed on the IUCN endangered species list in 2004. The US warned eight exporting nations to commit to immediate recovery programs, and when no progress had been reported within a year, they banned the import of all beluga sturgeon products as of 2005.

No to BC Grizzly Trophies

In 2004 the European Union banned the import of grizzly bear hunting trophies from British Columbia. The ban, agreed to by all EU member nations, puts international pressure on the Province of BC to boost conservation efforts for grizzlies, while reducing the incentive for Europeans to hunt bears in BC, since they were unable to bring home their heads and hides.

Guarding Their Habitat

Developed nations must track imported products from their source, ensuring that the mining, logging, fishing and farming are conducted legally, with minimal harm to wildlife and its habitat.

In 2003 the Environmental Investigation Agency alerted governments and traders in North America, Europe and India that illegal talc (used in cosmetics) and marble mining in the Jamwa Ramgarh Wildlife Sanctuary and Sariska Tiger Reserve was destroying vital tiger habitat, forcing India's 3,000 remaining tigers closer to extinction. Western traders agreed to stop buying talc from the sanctuary areas, and India's government closed 53 illegal mines.

Getting Tough on Smugglers

The illegal trade in animal parts is estimated to be as high as $8 billion per year.[5] Governments need to ensure that penalties meet the crime, while dedicating time and funds to finding solutions. In 1999 government authorities in Canada and the US worked together to prosecute an Ontario couple who had illegally imported over 800 tropical birds and were smuggling them into the United States. The Ontario Court of Justice sentenced them to a combined 15 months in jail, a fine of $125,000 and 40 hours of community service.[6]

- Convention on International Trade in Endangered Species: www.cites.org
- Environmental Investigation Agency: www.eia-international.org
- IUCN Redlist: www.iucnredlist.org
- Journal of International Wildlife Law and Policy: www.jiwlp.com
- North American Commission for Environmental Cooperation: www.cec.org

67

Preserve Your Predators

We have to go deeper and change our perception of predators. It is already taking place with the wolf and grizzly.

— Ian Ross, wildlife researcher

Humans have demonized predators for centuries. Scary stories of wolves, bears and mountain lions (cougars) have been sending chills down people's spines for a very long time. The early settlers in North America did everything they could to wipe out predatory species. Wherever predator populations have fallen dramatically, deer, elk and other prey species have experienced a boom-or-bust imbalance. There is only one way to maintain a healthy biodiversity: by preserving the predators.

While Canada has regional hunting seasons for predators, most of the US has no such restrictions for wolves, bears or cougars — people can shoot whenever they see one. Over 2,500 mountain lions are killed by sport hunters in the western states and provinces every year, making hunting the leading known cause of death.[1]

Once the most widely distributed mammal in the world, the wolves are now extinct across Western Europe, in Mexico and in much of the United States. In Yellowstone National Park, the wolves had all been eradicated by 1926. The loss of the Park's keystone species allowed elk to feed in open fields and riverbanks. This caused riverbank erosion and drove the beavers from the rivers, creating ecological imbalance throughout the Park. After a 70-year absence, 31 gray wolves were reintroduced into Yellowstone in 1995 and 1996. Their success has been celebrated by the National Park Service, and by the year 2000, 216 wolves were calling Yellowstone home, with 24 packs and 14 breeding pairs. As the elk retreated to the woodland to avoid the wolves, trees returned to the riverbanks, and the beavers returned to their rivers. The whole ecosystem depended on the top predator — the wolf.

The Oregon Wolf Plan

In Oregon wolves have been hunted to extinction, but the State now has a plan to restore them. In 2005, despite pressure from outside forces, the Oregon Fish and Wildlife Commission adopted a progressive plan, led by a 14-member advisory committee. The Oregon Wolf Plan charts a course for other states to follow, outlining specific steps to restore and preserve wolf populations, while addressing the concerns of citizens:

- Guaranteed protection for wolves that migrate naturally to Oregon.
- Management tools to address conflicts with livestock and elk/deer populations.
- The use of non-lethal control methods as the first response to conflict, while allowing wolves to be killed if caught in the act of killing livestock.
- Prohibiting open or general season wolf hunts.

- California Wolf Center: www.californiawolfcenter.org
- Predator Conservation Alliance: www.predatorconservation.org
- Predator Conservation Trust: www.predatorconservation.com
- Predator Defense: www.predatordefense.org

IAN MCALLISTER/RAINCOAST.ORG

- Allowing the translocation of wolves within the state to ensure conservation goals are met in east and west Oregon.
- Creating a fund to pay for wolf-caused livestock losses, and to assist producers with non-lethal methods of preventing conflicts.

More Help for the Wolves

North Carolina has successfully reintroduced red wolves into its mountains after free-for-all hunting had reduced the population to a few remaining animals. In 1980 a group of wildlife experts captured 14 remaining wolves and began a conservation effort. The wolves spent seven years in captivity before being introduced to the wild in the Alligator River. Today there are over 100 red wolves in the wild, and in 2004, a record 55 wolf pups were born to 11 litters.

A Call for New Legislation

Bears, mountain lions, lynx, wolves, coyotes, wolverines, eagles, hawks, sharks, orcas and otters are all North American predators, and each plays a vital role in its ecosystem. In a 1995

Dispelling the Myth

One of the most frequent charges against predators is that they are a primary cause of livestock loss for ranchers. In reality, predators account for only a tiny fraction of mortality. In one year alone, in the Northern Rockies, ranchers reported livestock losses of 100,000 animals due to weather, illness and birthing complication. In the same region, over a 13-year study, there were 505 reported cases of livestock deaths due to wolves,[3] representing 0.04% of the annual livestock mortality.

study, the World Wildlife Fund's Paul Paquet found that preserving the habitats of grizzlies, lynx and wolves would directly benefit 372 of the 381 additional land animals in the southern and central Canadian Rockies.[2]

There is no legislation in place to protect these keystone species. Wolves and grizzlies are aided by the Endangered Species Act in the US, but legislation is needed to protect predators before they become endangered.

68

Protect Our Primate Cousins

> There is really no justification for forcing these amazing creatures to suffer for our amusement or gain.
>
> — Jane Goodall

Chimpanzees share 99% of our DNA. They resemble us in so many ways. They are intelligent beings who express emotion and have a strong sense of community. Scientists all over the world who have spent decades working with the great apes are calling for them to be given basic rights similar to humans.

The great apes (chimpanzees, gorillas, bonobos and orangutans) belong to the hominid family, just like humans. And yet our cousins are languishing in zoos, circuses and private captivity all over the world and are subjected to suffering and torture in research laboratories. If humans were penned up for no crime of their own, put on public display for the amusement of other species and subjected to horrible experiments in laboratories, people would not stand for it. Taking a highly sentient creature like a human being or a great ape out of its natural surrounding and forcing it into a life of captivity and cruelty should be a serious crime.

The first step to protecting our primate cousins is to create a charter of rights unique to great apes that covers every facet of their lives. There are many scientists and researchers who would be more than happy to contribute.

The second step is to write legislation to support the charter, specific to your country and the great apes that live there.

The third step is education, by funding conservation groups to educate citizens about the importance of helping the great apes.

Follow the Leaders

In 2000 New Zealand became the first country to give the great apes special rights, setting forth tough new guidelines. Great apes can no longer be held in captivity without a court's ruling, and none can be used in experiments, other than those that benefit the apes themselves. This is an enormous step forward for great apes and a leap in consciousness that has begun to spread.

A Call for American Chimps

Chimps have consistently demonstrated their ability to solve mathematical problems, plan for future events, utilize tools in problem solving and express a wide range of emotions, including depression, anxiety, pain and empathy. With these similarities to ourselves, how could we subject them to torture in the name of medical research? And yet people in the United States still do so on a regular basis. With 1,300 chimpanzees housed in research laboratories, the US is one of the few remaining countries to conduct biomedical research on chimps.

In 2000, weeks after the Great Ape Conservation Act was signed into law, the US passed the CHIMP Act, creating a system of non-profit sanctuaries for chimpanzees that have been retired from experimentation. The Act has been welcomed by some, because it improves the lives of chimps once held captive in research labs, and criticized by others, because it legitimizes their continued use in labs.

Orangutans get their name from the Malay people, who call the fascinating primates "people of the forest." Orangutans have powerful long arms stretching seven feet from fingertip to fingertip, perfectly suited for swinging from branches. They have opposable thumbs, just like humans, as well as opposable toes.

Sweden, Germany, Britain and the Netherlands have all banned the use of great apes in biomedical research. Their legislation stops short of actually granting special rights to great apes or helping apes being held in captivity, but it is an important step in the right direction. Sweden has also included gibbons in its protection.[1] Britain does not test on great apes but continues to test on other primates, such as macaques and marmosets.

Great Ape Conservation Act

In 2000 the United States signed the Great Ape Conservation Act into law, establishing a federal fund for projects in Africa and Asia that conserve great apes in their natural habitat. The Act channels funds to conservation initiatives that work to find solutions to the problems of human encroachment, logging and hunting for the bushmeat trade, which exacts a heavy toll on the wild great ape populations (see Solution 85).

- Chimpanzee Fact Sheet: www2.bc.edu/~piscatel/chimpanzee.htm
- Great Ape Legal Project: www.aldf.org
- Great Ape Project: www.greatapeproject.org
- International Primate Protection League: www.ippl.org
- Jane Goodall Institute: www.janegoodall.org

Orphaned orangutan babies in Borneo.

Chimpanzee family.

69

Work Together to Protect Global Fisheries

> It only takes a drop of oil about 2.5 centimeters (1 inch) in diameter to kill a seabird.
>
> — Jon Stone, Environment Canada

Global fisheries are in a state of crisis, and governments must act. With over-fishing, habitat destruction, pollution and bycatch rates of 25% continuing largely unchecked, cooperation between nations is urgently needed.

Stop Subsidizing the Problem

Government fisheries subsidies around the world amount to $15 billion annually, equaling 20% of the value of the world's total catch.[1] Subsidies lead to over-capacity, over-fishing, destructive fishing practices and unfair advantages for the most heavily subsidized fisheries.

In 2002 a group of eight nations including the US formed an alliance at the World Trade Organization's Ministerial Conference, calling for an end to the unsustainable subsidizing of global fisheries. Calling themselves "Friends of Fish," the alliance underlined the imbalance created when a heavily subsidized fishing fleet, like those from Spain, fish in the waters off a poorer nation like Fiji, while Fiji's unsubsidized fishers are unable to sell the same fish competitively in the European market. The debate continues, with a growing number of nations trying for a global consensus, while Japan and Korea remain strongly opposed. Japan subsidizes its fishing fleets more than the United States and the European Union combined.[2]

Monitor Dirty Fishing

In 2004 after an extensive campaign by conservation groups, the United States doubled the funding going into the federal fisheries observer program from $14 million to $29 million, so that more observers — usually marine scientists — could travel with fishing boats to monitor what gets caught and what gets discarded. Most dirty fishing practices go unseen, but an estimated 16 billion pounds of fish are wasted worldwide every year.[3] With marine scientists on board, problems can be accurately determined and improvements made.

Reduce Pollution

In 2005 the European Parliament wrote legislation resulting in criminal sanctions against companies and individuals found dumping oil and other hydrocarbons at sea. The move followed the discovery that oil tankers were

A 600 lb tuna caught in the mouth of a fish trap.

DANILO CEDRONE/UN FAO

- Conservation Fisheries: www.conservationfisheries.org
- National Fisheries Conservation Center: www.nfcc-fisheries.org
- Oceana: www.oceana.org
- Pacific Fisheries Resource Conservation Council: www.fish.bc.ca
- World Fisheries Trust: www.worldfish.org

routinely dumping large quantities of oil into European waters during cleaning procedures. The legislation will also help put an end to the dumping of oil and other wastes by the fishing industry, cruise ships and recreational boaters. According to research by Oceana, 20 million tons of oil and other waste materials are dumped in Europe's waters every year.

The International Convention for the Prevention of Pollution from Ships (MARPOL) targets the dumping of oil, and several countries including the US, Australia and the UK are cracking down on it. In 2003 the US issued $7 million in fines and more than two years in prison in seven cases on the West Coast. Canada, China and India have been criticized for their lack of enforcement. Canada prosecuted only 24 cases between 1994 and 2001, yet intense shipping traffic in Atlantic Canada causes the death of 300,000 seabirds each year, nearly the same number that perished from the1989 Exxon Valdez oil spill in Alaska's Prince William Sound.[4]

Ban Ocean Fish Farming
Fish farming is one of the world's fastest growing food sectors, despite being plagued with problems of contamination from concentrated waste, disease, sea lice, escaped fish competing with wild fish (see Solution 40) and health risks to consumers. A 2004 study concluded that farmed salmon had such elevated levels of PCBs, dioxin and other cancer-causing contaminants, that consumers should limit themselves to one eight-ounce portion a month.[5]

Tuna Driftnets Are Too Destructive for the EU

In 2002 drift-netting for tuna by European Union nations became illegal in the Atlantic and Mediterranean. The EU adopted the legislation after research found the nets were catching 48 different species along with targeted tuna in the north Atlantic, and 74 species in the Mediterranean, including unacceptable numbers of cetaceans, marine mammals, birds and reptiles.[7] The EU is assisting member nations and their tuna fisheries to find alternatives and move away from the destructive practice.

Alaska has banned ocean fish farming and has no plans to join US initiatives to boost the aquaculture industry to $1 billion by 2025.[6]

Work to Strengthen the Law of the Sea
The 1994 United Nations' Convention on the Law of the Sea (LOS) has been ratified by 145 countries but has not slowed the destruction of the world's oceans (see Solution 98), due in part to the United States' reluctance to sign the treaty and to the failure of governments to establish standards and effective legislation. Join the effort, work together, strengthen LOS and save the sea.

70

Use Your Purchasing Power to Help Animals

We believe it's time to have basic humane standards for food purchased with tax dollars.
— Christopher Shays, US Congressman

In Canada the federal government is the leading buyer of goods and services, spending over $10 billion annually on everything from office paper to automobiles.[1] In the US the federal government spends $200 billion annually, making it the world's largest customer for goods and services, and all levels of government combine to spend more than $1 trillion.[2] Government purchases account for 18% of the American Gross Domestic Product.[3]

Government purchasing power has the potential to help animals on a grand scale by purchasing animal-friendly products, leading by example and prompting the private sector to follow suit.

Buying Green

Most states and provinces have some level of green purchasing, whether it's committing to the use of recycled paper or investing in renewable energy initiatives. The US government uses 30% post-consumer waste office paper, saving seven trees for every ton of paper and helping to preserve wildlife habitat. All environmentally conscious purchasing contributes to the well-being of animals and people.

Massachusetts has been employing a green purchasing team since the early '90s, and the State's spending on recycled goods had increased from $3 million annually to $68 million in 2001, with a further $18 million on environmentally friendly products. Their vehicle fleet includes 37 zero-emission electric vehicles and 82 powered by natural gas, and they have a statewide Integrated Pest Management (IPM) program to reduce pesticide use.

The municipal government of Santa Monica, California, receives calls from all levels of government around the world because of its successful model for green purchasing and its commitment to being a "sustainable city." The City replaced 90% of its cleaning products with non-toxic alternatives, adopted an IPM program, bringing relief from pesticides to animals and people and converted 75% of its 500-vehicle fleet to alternative energy sources.

Ethical Purchasing

Environmental initiatives and green purchasing are very important, but animals need us to go a step further. Create a purchasing team dedicated

Setting Ethical Standards

US Congressman Christopher Shays is Co-Chair of the Congressional Friends of Animals Caucus, a group that lobbies from within the government for the humane treatment of all animals. In June 2006 Shays and Congressmen Peter DeFazio introduced the Farm Animal Stewardship Purchasing Act (HR5557), groundbreaking proposed legislation that sets animal welfare standards for those supplying food to the federal government through the military, federal prisons, school cafeterias and all government programs. HR5557 would ensure adequate shelter, comfort, freedom of movement, access to food and water and prompt veterinary attention for all farm animals.

- Compassionate Consumer: www.compassionateconsumers.org
- Congressman Shays and HR5557: www.house.gov/shays/issues/animal/index.htm
- Massachusetts Environmental Purchasing Program: www.epa.gov/epp/pubs/mass.pdf
- Policy Recommendations: www.ethicalconsumer.org/aboutec/manifesto.htm
- Santa Monica Green Energy Purchasing: www.santa-monica.org/epd/residents/Energy/green_energy.htm

to animal welfare and use the power of government purchasing to help lab animals by buying products that haven't been tested on animals. Buy from food suppliers that use humane animal husbandry and farm organically. Avoid buying animal products wherever possible, asking suppliers for alternatives such as leather-free car interiors and clothing.

Ethical purchasing is a new arena for governments to venture into. Be a pioneer. Government involvement in the research and purchasing of ethically sourced goods and services stimulates the market, driving prices down, and prompting innovative ideas and interest in animal welfare, making humane choices affordable for companies, schools and individuals.

Say No to the GPA

The World Trade Organization (WTO) presents an obstacle to green purchasing initiatives by governments around the world. Driven by a mission of globalizing the world economy, the WTO has created the Government Procurement Agreement (GPA) that prohibits obstacles to international trade imposed by government purchasing policies and could effectively ban the purchasing of environmental and animal-friendly goods.

Including the United States and Canada, 37 countries have signed the agreement. The GPA has been used by the WTO to ask Japan to reduce its testing for pesticides on imported produce, the US to relax its clean air standards and Europe to wait on a ban for the import of genetically modified foods until they could prove conclusively that they are harmful to human and environmental health.[4]

Take a leadership role in opposing the GPA and work to persuade other governments, at all levels, to do the same. The agreement is a dangerous step for animals, the environment and the Earth.

IAN MCALLISTER/RAINCOAST.ORG

71

Replace Animal Trade with Ecotourism

The memories the group will take away from our trip are not the challenge of Kilimanjaro, or the excitement of safari, but meeting the people and culture of Africa, which has been one of the most moving and profound experiences of my life.

— Gavin Bate, Adventure Alternative guide,
quoting a letter from clients

Replacing hunting and the animal trade with ecotourism is a conservation strategy that holds great promise. It protects wild animals, helps the economies of developing nations and allows visitors from around the world to see wildlife in its natural surroundings. Animals are always more beautiful in the wild.

Globally, tourism generates $6 trillion a year,[1] and ecotourism is one of its most rapidly growing sectors. Exciting, dynamic and conservation-minded, it allows people to travel with a conscience.

From Rifles to Binoculars

Uganda has begun the process of changing from animal trade to ecotourism. The Ugandan economy has traditionally been heavily involved in the trade of wild animals, getting much of its national income from the sales of animals. But the government is transforming the landscape. In 2002 President Museveni called for an immediate ban on the export of wild animals and began promoting the nation in a new way. With the help of the UN's Global Environment Facility, and ecotourism projects centered in

- Animal Protection Institute: www.morebeautifulwild.com
- CarbonNeutral Company: www.carbonneutral.com
- Ecotourism Portal: www.ecotourism.cc
- Ecotourism Resources: www.vorion.com/what-is-ecotourism.html
- Global Environment Facility: www.gefweb.org

Bwindi Impenetrable and Mgahinga Gorilla National Parks, Uganda is preaching conservation and telling the world of the natural beauty of its land. With 18,000 recorded animal and plant species, the country has one of the highest rates of biodiversity in the world.

A Whole New Economy in Indonesia

Gunung Leuser National Park is a 1.9-million-acre conservation area in North Sumatra, home to 129 species of mammals, including orangutans, tigers, elephants and rhinos. It is also an area in which illegal logging has been rampant with 15% of the park having been deforested. In 1998 the Leuser region was declared a conservation area, and three governing bodies began working with the residents of nearby Namo Sialang Village to switch from logging to ecotourism as a means of income. The park is a perfect setting for such an industry. Mt. Leuser Peak, towering 10,000 above sea level, provides a haven for mountain climbers, along with rivers for whitewater rafting, hot springs, lakes and caves. Namo Sialang villagers got involved, developing a master plan for the park and forming their own tourism committee, called Tangkahan Tourism Institution. The village has been granted authority to manage the tourism project, setting its own entrance fees, and an income distribution program.

A New Sanctuary in the Philippines

In 1998 whale sharks were discovered in plankton blooms near the Philippine fishing village of Donsol. The gentle giants quickly attracted the attention of tourists, media and the government, who were interested in capitalizing on the new marine residents. They also attracted poachers, who quickly killed seven of the whale sharks. The waters off Donsol were subsequently declared a sanctuary, and whale shark hunting was banned throughout the Philippines. The World Wildlife Fund got involved, working with local authorities and Donsol residents to establish the Whale Shark Research and Conservation Project, while finding ways for residents to practice conservation and benefit from responsible ecotourism. Regulations, fees and training were organized, and residents became boat operators, tour guides and dive leaders. In 2003 Donsol hosted 3,175 registered visitors to the sanctuary and was able to finance the construction of a tourism office dedicated to whale shark tours.

Carbon-Neutral Traveling

Flying is a major factor in global climate change, contributing 358 million tons of CO_2 from international flights in 2003.[2] By the very act of flying, ecotourists could be contributing to the extinction of the animals they're going to see.

In 2005 Ecoventura, an adventure tourism company in the Galapagos Islands, became the first travel company in South America to achieve CarbonNeutral status, monitoring and offsetting the CO_2 emissions that it is responsible for. For every ton of CO_2 it creates, Ecoventura contributes to climate-friendly projects that will save or absorb one ton of CO_2, including a renewable solar lighting project in India and Sri Lanka, a methane storage project in the US and a sustainable forestry project in Chiapas, Mexico.

All tourists should travel in a carbon-neutral manner: if we do not, our pleasure will contribute to our planet's climate chaos.

Exploring the Galapagos the Ecoventura way.

GALAPAGOS NETWORK/ECOVENTURA S.A

72

Practise Sustainable Forestry

Logging has pulled the plug on tropical forest wildlife.

— Dr. John Robinson, Wildlife Conservation Society

Forests in developing nations are being harvested at an increasingly unsustainable rate, eliminating wildlife habitat and driving many species to extinction. These important reservoirs of life are being cleared at the alarming rate of 32 million acres a year (an acre a second).[1] Of these, 14 million acres are pristine primary forests, with no visible signs of human activity, that are being cleared for lumber and agriculture. This global rate of logging is completely unsustainable and very dangerous for animals, people and life on Earth. It has to change.

Cameroon's Gift to the Earth

To the Baka people of southern Cameroon, Jengi — the spirit of the forests — is their guardian, in a lush 6-million-acre rainforest that is home to 50 large mammal species, including elephants, gorillas and chimpanzees, as well as 300 bird, 121 fish and 250 butterfly species. Yet the forest has been exploited by industrial and illegal logging, poaching, the bushmeat trade (see Solution 74), illegal mining and the trapping of parrots (see Solution 88). In 1998 the government of Cameroon worked with the World Wildlife Fund (WWF) to establish three protected areas, covering 1.7 million acres of forest, one of which, in Lobeke, was designated by the government as its "Gift to the Earth." The project has been named the Jengi Initiative and involves:

- A monitoring program for conservation and biodiversity trends
- Global Positioning System equipment and map reading for logging company employees
- Collaborative agreements with logging companies to work toward sustainability and certification
- Community hunting zones to address subsistence hunting needs.

Going Green in Guyana

In 2006 WWF Guyana, the Guyana Forestry Commission and Barama Company Ltd. announced that 1.4 million acres of Barama-owned forests have met the standards of the Forest Stewardship Council (FSC), making it the largest natural tropical forest in the world to obtain FSC certification. The Council sets international standards of sustainable operation that include responsible environmental, social and economic forest management (see Solution 49). WWF's role in Barama's Guyana operations is to

NASA

- Forest Stewardship Council: www.fsc.org
- Tropical Forest Conservation Act: www.state.gov/g/oes/rls/fs/2003/22973.htm
- United Nations Forum on Forests: www.un.org/esa/forests/documents-iff.html
- WWF Forestry Campaign: www.panda.org

train employees in low-impact logging practices, improve factory safety operations and monitor Barama's adherence to FSC standards.

Community-based Forestry in Brazil

In 2002 the Chico Mendes Association in Acre, Xapuri, became the first community-based forestry operation in Brazil to obtain FSC certification. The economy of Acre was supported by latex from rubber trees and Brazil nuts, but a growing population had depleted both, and residents knew they had to respond to a growing demand from outside for forest products. The community created its own forestry management plant, meeting production goals, while sustainably harvesting wood from its 2,000 acres of tropical forest. The community association's guiding principle of forest management is to leave one "child" and two "grandchildren" for every tree they harvest.

FLEG and Illegal Logging

In 2001 ministers from East Asia, Europe and the US met in Indonesia for the East Asia Forest Law Enforcement and Governance (FLEG) conference, agreeing to take immediate action on illegal logging and its international trade. Since the conference, with the efforts of conservation groups, Tanjung Puting National Park in Indonesia has received attention for the plight of orangutans in the Park, a powerful illegal logging infrastructure has been dismantled and ships carrying stolen timber have been seized.

Burning More Efficiently in Kenya

In Africa 90% of the population uses fuel wood for cooking, leading to deforestation, erosion and the loss of habitat for wildlife. It was women in Kenya, who do most of the wood gathering and cooking, who came up with the design for the Kenya Ceramic Jiko; an hourglass-shaped stove with a ceramic liner that directs the fire's heat directly to a pot, rather than losing it through the sides of a conventional stove or into the air around an open fire. A consortium of craftspeople, called Jua Kali ("hot sun" in Swahili) worked with government and international aid groups, and today the Jiko has found its way into 1 million homes across Kenya, saving money, time and resources.[2]

Despite these victories by countries following the governance of FLEG, illegal logging continues across East Asia and around the world and needs to be stopped: for people, animals and the environment.

Pick up the Phone

Call the World Wildlife Fund's Forestry Campaign and ask if they can help you develop a partnership with them to convert your forests to FSC management. This is the single best way to preserve your forests for the future and still return an income from them.

73

Create New National Parks and Wildlife Sanctuaries

Creating a vibrant national park system provides an ecosystem with vital biodiversity, a safe home for animals and a park system that people can be proud of. Yet there are significant obstacles in a developing nation's path to conservation, including pressure for development from the rural poor, developers and oil companies, as well as poaching and illegal logging. It takes money to find solutions, and many countries are too plagued with economic problems

TOM CLAYTOR/CLAYTOR.COM

Before, the elephants used to move in a single file because it was a danger zone. Since the conservation program started, you can see them spreading into Il Ngwesi, Tassia and Lewa because they feel safe.
— Peter Kiyaa, on the creation of the Lewa Wildlife Conservancy in Kenya

and debt repayments to the developed nations to spend time preserving wildlife habitat.

New Parks in Brazil

In 2005 Brazil declared two new major protected areas; the 8.3-million-acre Terra do Meio Ecological Station, and the 1.1-million-acre Serra do Pardo National Park, both in the eastern sector of the central Amazon. The two new parks are part of Brazil's Amazon Region Protected Areas (ARPA) initiative, and their size is critical to the survival of several wildlife species, including jaguars, macaws and harpy eagles. Brazil has effectively created a vast ecological corridor, providing 64 million acres of protected rainforest for wildlife and indigenous peoples, amounting to 6% of the remaining 1 billion acres of Amazon rainforest. Since logging began in the 20th century, the Amazon has lost 200 million acres of rainforest.

It Begins with the People

More than a billion people live in biodiversity hotspots that support 75% of the world's most endangered mammals, birds and amphibians and yet cover just 2.3% of the Earth's surface.[1] This critical habitat can only be protected if its human residents are included in the conservation plan, preserving and restoring the ecosystems that provide farmers and forest dwellers with food, fuel, medicine, clothing and shelter.

Offer training in sustainable agriculture and permaculture, and help communities benefit from an improved ecosystem. Get involved in ecotourism (see Solution 71), providing funding for conservation efforts and employing local residents through park entrance fees and guided tours. Contact conservation groups such as the World Wildlife Fund and Conservation International to help develop conservation strategies. They have the experience and resources to develop a sustainable plan, and they can help establish effective local conservation groups.

Ganzi Prefecture, in China's Sichuan Province, is home to 880,000 people and 550 mammal and bird species. In 1998 thousands of people and animals in Ganzi were killed when the Yangtze River flooded, with land erosion from extensive logging blamed for the severity of the flood. The Chinese government ordered a halt to logging in the area, and in 2004 a network of environmental activists and concerned Ganzi residents formed the region's first environmental group. Green Khampa worked with 500 monasteries across Ganzi to collect information on its dedicated natural sacred spots and presented the information to Conservation International China's Sacred Land Protection program, which maps the biological value of thousands of sacred sites and works with governments to promote their legal protection.

- African Conservation Foundation: www.africanconservation.org
- Conservation International: www.conservation.org
- World Wilderness Congress: www.8wwc.org
- World Wildlife Fund: www.panda.org

Innovative Ecology

Connect with companies in your country and abroad, inviting them to sponsor the creation of a national park. A company can "adopt" an acre of forest or an entire park, with the understanding that all money will go directly to its conservation.

Bio-prospecting fees can be also be charged to scientists for allowing them to develop products from plant species. Costa Rica was the first nation to have such an agreement, allowing the US company Merck to identify plants with pharmaceutical value, returning the profits to conservation initiatives. Swiss fragrance company Givaudan made a similar deal with Madagascar in 2001, finding plants with new aromatic qualities and reconstituting the aroma for commercial products back in Europe. A portion of profits from all 40 new products goes directly to local communities and conservation efforts in Madagascar.

Conservation in the Himalayas

The mountain country of Bhutan is almost a secret, and its citizens like it to stay that way. They keep quiet about politics and stay as far as possible away from the haste of the rest of the world. High up on the "Roof of the World," Bhutan comprises 29,000 square miles of pristine mountains, undisturbed greenery and a vast array of wildlife. With exotic creatures like golden langurs, red pandas, snow leopards, Himalayan brown bears and tigers, little-known Bhutan is a haven for wildlife. Its conservation plan is impressive — nearly two-thirds of the country has been dedicated as a nature preserve.

74

End the Commercial Bushmeat Trade

We, in the developed world, have a direct role (in the bushmeat trade) through our exploitation of those countries, and in the waters adjacent. This is an international problem.

— Justin Brashares,
University of California, Berkeley

The illegal hunting of wild animals, commonly referred to as "bushmeat," has become the number one threat to wildlife populations in Africa. The Jane Goodall Institute reported that 15 species, including chimpanzees, will be lost by 2020 if the bushmeat trade continues at today's pace.[1] The value of the illegal trade is about $50 million annually, with more than one million metric tons of bushmeat being taken from the Congo Basin alone, every year.[2]

Animals have been part of forest dwellers' diets for a very long time, and hunting has been a relatively sustainable practice, but the population of bushmeat consumers has increased, and illegal hunting has become profitable for those who lack an alternative income, bringing a hunter from $300 to $1000 a year.[3] The hunters sell the meat to distributors or loggers who sell to markets. While wealthy people in the cities pay high prices for exotic gorilla or snake meat, most bushmeat is consumed by families who can't afford the more expensive, commercially raised meat.

The logging industry is fueling the bushmeat trade by cutting through previously impenetrable forest, providing easy access for hunters and transport between markets. It's not unusual for a logging truck to carry 450 pounds of bushmeat for resale at the next market down the road.[4]

Uniting to Find Answers

The Bushmeat Crisis Task Force (BCTF) was established in 1999 by 28 conservation organizations, including the Jane Goodall Institute, to protect the species threatened by illegal hunting. BCTF gathers information, educates groups, governments and corporate decision makers and raises public awareness, with a primary role of sharing information so NGOs, scientists and governments can find solutions together. In 2002 BCTF ran a series of workshops held at wildlife colleges in South Africa, Tanzania and Cameroon, setting up a bushmeat curriculum for each college.

Caring for the Orphans

1n 1992 the Jane Goodall Institute established the Tchimpounga Sanctuary in the Kouilou region of the Republic of Congo. Tchimpounga has become a refuge for chimpanzees orphaned

Bushmeat's Connection to the Sea

Along the West African coast, people have traditionally supported their families by fishing. In the 1970s governments along the coast sold offshore fishing rights to foreign fishing conglomerates, mostly from Europe, and over the past three decades, fish stocks have declined by over 50%. With their waters seriously overfished and unable to feed themselves, villagers have had to turn inland to find food, and this has led to an increase in the bushmeat trade, as coastal people kill whatever land animals they can find for subsistence and income. Since heavy foreign fishing began in the region, 41 species of mammals have seen their populations decline by 75%.[5]

- Ape Alliance — bushmeat: www.4apes.com/bushmeat
- Bushmeat Crisis Task Force: www.bushmeat.org
- Bushmeat Project: www.bushmeat.net
- CITES — bushmeat: www.cites.org/eng/prog/bushmeat.shtml
- Jane Goodall Institute — bushmeat: www.janegoodall.org/africa-programs/objectives/controlling-bushmeat-trade.asp

from the bushmeat trade and, by 2006, was housing 115 young chimps. Between 2004 and 2006, Congolese authorities delivered 40 new orphaned chimps to the sanctuary, most of which had been confiscated from hunters trying to sell them to the pet or entertainment trade after having killed their parents.

The Ngamba Island Sanctuary was established in 1998 and is another safe refuge for orphaned chimps located in the Entebbe region of Uganda. Ngamba is managed by the Chimpanzee Sanctuary and Wildlife Conservation Trust; an alliance of five international conservation groups. By 2006 Ngamba was home to 42 orphaned chimps.

Return to a Sacred Past
The Mount Kupe forest in southern Cameroon is home to many rare and unique animals, including eight primate species and a bird called the Bush Shrike, which was thought to be extinct until 1989. The forest was also held sacred by nearby villagers, since they believed it to be the home of their spirits, and killing an animal from the forest was considered to be killing an ancestor. In the 1970s, an influx of new people from the surrounding grasslands led to logging and poaching and the erosion of the sacred beliefs, and hunting for the bushmeat trade became prevalent; fueled by the strong wildlife population that had benefited from the forest's sacred past. Today 16 villages surround Mount Kupe, with 140,000 villagers who depend on the forest for food, water, medicine and building materials.

This Bosman's potto in Zaire is among the many primate species, along with ungulates, birds, and rodents commonly killed for the bushmeat trade.

Enough of the sacred beliefs lived on, however, and enough people were upset by the illegal hunting that a group of village chiefs united in 2004 to establish the Nyasoso Ecotourism Group. Financed by village development associations under the guidance of the World Wildlife Fund, it is an anti-poaching group, providing park rangers throughout the forest and protecting its inhabitants.

75

Take a Stand Against International Whaling

Whales have complex family structures similar to ours, and their high intelligence has always been a mystery to us. Most people around the world understand that hunting whales and dolphins is fundamentally wrong, and that we must protect these graceful beings.

Since 1986 whale-hunting has been illegal, although Japan kills hundreds of whales every year, using a loophole in the international moratorium by calling their hunt "scientific research." Norway does the same, saying it's their tradition and they'll keep on doing it, regardless of world opinion. Since the International Whaling Commission (IWC) moratorium was announced in 1986, 25,000 whales have been killed.[1]

Japanese polls show a decline in the consumption of whale meat, yet the government of Japan struggles to keep its whaling industry afloat, trying to promote whale meat products with the creation of blubber ice-cream, the publication of whale meat cookbooks and the

In a relatively short time Kaikoura has gone from a depressed little town to one of the leading marine mammal tourism destinations in the world. It's not nuclear physics: how many times can you kill a whale? How many times can you watch one?

— Melino Maka, Tongan Advisory Council

performance of a pro-whaling musical. Japan cannot claim tradition as a reason for whaling — commercial whaling on a large scale began only after World War II to help feed an impoverished, war torn nation.

Japan has been harshly criticized for "buying" the alliance of developing nations and persuading them to join the IWC to vote in favor of commercial whaling. Despite Japan's denial, they have built an alliance of small countries that use their votes to support Japan, including impoverished island nations such as Tuvalu, Palau and Grenada, along with African nations such as Guinea and Benin, and Asian countries including Mongolia. By all accounts, Mongolia does not have a very big whaling fleet — or even a coastline.

At the IWC's annual convention in 2005, many of the developing nations that were

- Cetacean Society International: www.csiwhalesalive.org
- International Whaling Commission: www.iwcoffice.org
- International Wildlife Coalition of Brazil: www.via-rs.net/iwcbr
- Sea Shepherd Society: www.seashepherd.org
- Whale and Dolphin Conservation Society: www.wdcs.org
- Whale Protection: www.whaleprotection.org

WSPA / EIA

Harpoon boat.

Ethics and Sustainability in Brazil

The waters of South America were once dominated by Japan's whaling fleets, which have hunted the coasts of Argentina, Peru, Chile and Brazil for decades. But in 1985, when José Sarney was elected as Brazil's first civilian president since the '60s, he promptly ended the killing of whales in Brazilian waters.[4] Since then, Brazil has been committed to marine conservation, creating the National Action Plan for Research, Conservation and Management of Marine Mammals in 1994. In 2000 Brazil began the new millennium by creating a whale sanctuary along 90 miles of the Santa Catarina coastline, restricting all commercial fishing and industrial activity. Southern right whales that were once hunted to near extinction in the region have returned and are breeding and calving in the sanctuary's bays.

invited to the table by Japan failed to show up. Of those present, three out of four failed to vote, causing Japan to lose its bid to lift the moratorium. But they came much closer in 2006, after recruiting the support of 15 nations from Africa, Central America and the Caribbean. This caused a split vote, which was only just enough to keep the moratorium in place. Before the meeting, Japan paid $1 million to the tiny nations of Tuvalu, Nauru and Kiribati.[2] The small African nation of Togo arrived two days late for the meeting to vote with Japan and brought their membership fees in a paper bag — $13,000 in Japanese Yen.[3]

Humpback whale breaching.

Take a Stance

The IWC's moratorium must be sustained, and smaller nations must show that they won't be bought by Japan. Talk to your neighbors, talk to Japan's "allies" and persuade them to prevent a return to commercial whaling. Unite to form your own alliance; one that recognizes the importance of protecting whales, and one that will not be bought by wealthier nations.

Listen to public opinion. In 2006 the World Wildlife Fund conducted a survey of the ten

Caribbean countries that have repeatedly voted in alliance with Japan at the IWC's annual meetings and found that the majority of people in every country were opposed to the killing of whales. WWF's Dr. Susan Lieberman said Caribbean people are clear that their governments are not voting on their behalf, despite their claims of doing so: "Commercial whaling will not help alleviate poverty nor help coastal communities. It doesn't matter how many times you state it, it doesn't make it true."

76

Outlaw Sport and Trophy Hunting

> The public response has been overwhelming on an issue that is loaded with emotion and sentiment.
> — Marthinus van Schalkwyk

Sport and trophy hunting is big business in many developing nations, especially across Africa. Trophy hunters from the West bring their wallets and buy extravagantly priced hunting licenses. In several African nations, governments have figured out how to get the most from their wealthy visitors, imposing minimum stay requirements of up to three weeks for every hunting license issued, guaranteeing that the hunters will spend plenty of money.

The lucrative source of income is a very sad reality for the animals involved, as well as for the residents of these nations. The populations of target animals are dropping sharply, and entire ecosystems are becoming unbalanced as the top predators are removed. When the lions are killed, their prey animals become overpopulated, stripping the landscape of its vegetation. As elephant populations fall because adult males are killed for their tusks, the herds lose their largest, healthiest breeding males.

Wealth and shooting accuracy don't go hand in hand, and many animals are painfully wounded by would-be marksmen, purely to provide a trophy for someone's mantelpiece.

Kudos for Kenya

Kenya has taken steps to end trophy hunting, after seeing lion populations across Africa drop by nearly 50% over the past 30 years. Through the Convention on International Trade in Endangered Species (see Solutions 64 and 94), Kenya is pressing other governments to give African lions the highest level of protection, as they have in Asia, where only a few hundred Asiatic lions remain. The European, Middle Eastern and Cape lions were long ago hunted to extinction. Despite their reprieve in Kenya, trophy hunting for lions is still a lucrative business in Tanzania, South Africa, Zimbabwe, Namibia, Botswana and Zambia. Kenya's stance on lion conservation is very much resisted by the neighboring government in Tanzania, which says a ban on hunting lions doesn't make economic

Photographer Tom Claytor with an orphaned elephant in South Africa.

sense. Although half of Kenya's lion population lives within the protection of national parks; the remaining lions are very vulnerable to sport hunters and villagers who see them as a threat to their livestock. Lions are also frequent casualties during times of political unrest.

A Matter of Economics

Countries that issue highly expensive trophy hunting permits can afford to pay for anti-poaching initiatives, giving them control over animal populations and the appearance of having a sustainable conservation plan, despite rampant trophy hunting. Tanzania has implemented aggressive anti-poaching measures in the Serengeti National Park; and since 1995 the park has recorded a population explosion among its elephants and lions, with elephant numbers doubling to 120,000.[1]

Despite the lucrative income that trophy hunting permits, ecotourism offers more to a country's economy than hunting. In South Africa, hunting brings in 660 million Rand ($91 million) annually, while accommodation at just one location in Kruger National Park brings in 300 million Rand ($42 million) annually[2] from people coming to photograph the animals. South Africa recognizes the rapid growth of ecotourism and has established the Centre for Ecotourism at the University of Pretoria. Ecotourism employs far more people than hunting outfitters do and leaves wildlife populations undisturbed for future visitors. It allows money to flow into conservation, social programs and education.

- International Wildlife Coalition: www.iwc.org
- League Against Cruel Sports — trophy hunting: www.bloodybusiness.com
- Wildlife Conservation Society: www.wcs.org
- Wildlife International: www.wildlife-international.org

Changes Coming for South Africa

In South Africa, in 2004 alone, 6,700 gun-toting visitors killed 54,000 animals, including 200 lions, 5,500 kudus and 45 leopards, along with baboons, giraffes, elephants, hippopotamuses, mongooses, porcupines, warthogs and zebras.[3] South Africa has responded to the huge numbers by clamping down on trophy hunting, after being advised by a panel of conservationists who studied hunting practices on game ranches. There captive hunting facilities use crossbreeding and genetic manipulation to produce animals such as zonkeys (zebras bred with donkeys) and albino lions, giving wealthy hunters the opportunity to kill increasingly exotic animals. Marthinus van Schalkwyk, Minister of Environmental Affairs and Tourism, himself a keen hunter, said, "This is something that no civilized country can continue to tolerate. We want to stop the approach of 'anything goes' in terms of hunting and crossbreeding." In 2005 the South African government committed to banning the hunting of animals raised in captivity, as well as those living in the vicinity of national parks.[4]

77

End Wildlife Farming

Game farming is one big field experiment that has failed. It's time for governments to admit they were wrong, and shut this industry down.

— Colin Maxwell,
Canadian Wildlife Federation

Wildlife farming has become a widespread practice in many developing nations, with wild animals being taken from their natural habitat and forced to live in captivity for hunting, breeding for zoos and private purchase. Stripping wild animals of their freedom and imposing a life of captivity on them is cruel, regardless of the purpose. On top of the suffering, disease is often spread between the newly captured wildlife and domestic animals, and sometimes to people. Wildlife farming also undermines the preservation of biodiversity and the richness of a country's cultural heritage.

Bear cub in a bile farm cage.

Vietnam Stands up for Bears

In 2005 Vietnam announced that it was closing down the country's bile farms, where thousand of bears lived in captivity for the harvesting of their bile for medicinal purposes. Government officials in Hanoi signed an agreement with the World Society for the Protection of Animals (WSPA) that will see over 3,000 bears gain freedom from the cramped quarters they were living in. Bear farming was already illegal in Vietnam, but the government hadn't been cracking down, and the business had been flourishing, exporting the bile for use in everything from traditional medicine to shampoo and wine.

While bear bile has been proven to combat certain ailments such as fever and liver complaints, herbal and synthetic alternatives are readily available, so there is no strong case for continuation of the farms. With the Vietnamese bear farms shut down, only North Korea, South Korea and China still allow the practice of farming bears for their bile, with hundreds of bear farms across the three countries.

What About the Freed Animals?

Can farmed wildlife be reintroduced to the wild? Sadly, the answer is often no. Animals that have been stripped of their wild instincts, particularly those born in captivity, are often unable to survive in the wild, and their mortality is high. In response to the problem, the Vietnamese government and WSPA have committed themselves to open a bear rescue center in the southern Cat Tien National Park, where they can be gradually introduced back into the wild, under the supervision of park staff.

Amazoonica is an animal refuge deep in the rainforest of Ecuador that serves as a transition place for displaced wildlife. The center opened in 1993 and is staffed largely by volunteers who care for a wide variety of mammals, reptiles and birds. Most of the animals come from concerned individuals who bought the animals from the commercial or illegal animal trade, or were confiscated by police. Staff are able to reintroduce about a third of the wildlife into its native habitat, while another third remain in half-captivity; free to leave but choosing to stay. Those that cannot be released live out their lives at the center and help fund the refuge by drawing visitors to it. In 1999 Amazoonica's founders opened the doors to the Liana Lodge; a small ecotourism hotel that supplies income for the rescue center, as well as funding environmental education programs at the nearby Ahuano school.

The high-priced Indian star tortoise.

- Amazoonica: www.amazoonico.org
- Born Free Foundation: www.bornfree.org.uk
- Conservation International: www.conservation.org
- Traffic Network: www.traffic.org

Turtle Trouble in Asia

The insatiable appetite for turtle in China and other Asian nations is creating a disaster for the turtles, which have been around for 200 million years. Over half of the 90 freshwater turtle species across Asia are now listed as endangered or critically endangered by the World Conservation Union. The industry has become enormous, both for food and for traditional medicine, and some 20 million freshwater turtles and tortoises are consumed in China every year.

Some species bring huge profits for their producers, such as the Indian star tortoise, at $24,000. Anything goes when catching turtles, from trapping and netting to spearing and hunting with dogs. But none of these methods can keep up with the demand, which is why turtle farming has begun on a large scale. Countries across Southeast Asia ship tons of the farmed turtles to China, and the Chinese themselves farm half a dozen species intensively. Most of the farms are secretive places where selective breeding produces the most expensive turtles possible for the Chinese market. As Peter Paul van Dijk, a biologist with Conservation International, said, "These farmers are not advertising that they are sitting on millions of dollars worth of turtles. The fact that you have three layers of barbed wire and six vicious German shepherds patrolling the grounds suggests there is something valuable there."

78

farm Sustainably

Factory farming methods are creating a web of food safety, animal welfare and environmental problems around the world, as large agribusinesses attempt to escape tighter environmental restrictions by moving their operations to less developed countries.

— Danielle Nierenberg, Worldwatch Institute

Industrial animal agriculture is the fastest growing means of animal production in the world, with developing nations set to become the global leader in meat production by 2020.[1] Factory farming methods developed in the United States, applied to heavily-populated nations in Africa, Asia, Latin America and South America, have caused global meat consumption to double since the 1970s, with meat and dairy consumption in developing nations increasing three times faster than in the industrialized nations.[2] From 1970 to 2000, the average Chinese citizen's annual consumption of meat increased from 22 pounds to 110 pounds,[3] a fivefold increase in just 30 years.

Tending to the land in South Africa.

A Global Warning

The enormous increase in the consumption of meat in developing nations is causing widespread suffering for the animals, while contaminating the air, water and soil and posing a threat to the health of both animals and people. The World Society for the Protection of Animals released a report in 2005 warning that the crowded and often unsanitary conditions in factory farms, when introduced to tropical countries, create the ideal breeding grounds for disease and could become a serious global health crisis. The WSPA points to Avian Flu and other zoonotic diseases that can be transferred from animals to people, warning that cases of Bovine Spongiform Encephalopathy (BSE), Nipah virus and food poisoning will continue to increase unless developing nations adopt more sustainable farming practices. The report calls for a halt to the expansion of factory farms, the adoption of humane and sustainable forms of farming and a global ban on the use of antibiotic growth promoters and production-enhancing hormones.[4]

India and Its Burial Vultures

In India the population of vultures has dropped by an alarming 99%. The large carrion eaters play a vital role in the country, feeding on the carcasses of dead animals, minimizing the spread of disease and being part of the tradition of sky burials for the Parsi people, who for thousands of years have taken their dead to a Tower of Silence and have ceremoniously given their loved ones to the vultures.[5]

- International Federation of Organic Agriculture Movements: www.ifoam.org
- Natural Resources Institute: www.nri.org
- Well Being Journal — Organic Agriculture: www.wellbeingjournal.com/ OrganicAgriculture.htm
- Worldwatch Institute: www.worldwatch.org/node/4241

Farmers can watch the sky when trying to locate a cow that is giving birth. Vultures will circle high above a cow in labour waiting for the afterbirth (placenta).

The loss of vultures was tracked to the veterinary drug diclofenac, an antibiotic being administered to cattle and water buffalo. Autopsies on the vultures determined that one-twentieth of the normal dose of diclofenac given to cattle was lethal to vultures, and the Indian government finally took action, banning the production and sale of the drug in 2006. It will be replaced by meloxicam, which scientists say is safe for birds. The path to recovery for the vultures will be slow, since they don't breed until they're five years old and only produce one egg per year.

Vulture populations have also dropped by 97% in Pakistan and 90% in Nepal. Nepal followed India's move in 2006 and banned the use of diclofenac, replacing it with meloxicam. All three countries have been the focus of an alliance of conservation groups trying to save the vultures in Asia from extinction.[6]

Responding to a Crisis in Malaysia

In 1998 a new disease causing sudden death among pigs in intensive farming operations in Peninsular Malaysia was observed to be very similar to the viral encephalitis that was affecting pig farm workers. The virus was named "Nipah," and by 1999, 105 human deaths had been recorded, along with the culling of 1 million pigs. The pig farming industry in Malaysia was devastated by the virus outbreak, with 1,000 of the area's 1,800 pig farms going out of business.

Eyes on Europe

Developing nations can follow the lead of the European Union, which in 2006 banned the use of antibiotics and related drugs to promote growth in livestock. Similar legislation was introduced in 1998, but the new legislation goes much farther, recognizing the social, ethical and environmental consequences of antibiotic growth enhancers. Restricting antibiotic use in animals is extraordinarily important, since feeding growth-enhancing antibiotics to animals for extended periods promotes the development of antibiotic-resistant bacteria, which can easily be passed on to humans through the consumption of meat.[8]

The Malaysian government responded by prohibiting the operation of pig farming in previously infected areas, establishing designated Pig Farming Areas far from residential areas and monitoring farming operations around the country.[7] Malaysia has also banned the discharge of animal manure into surface waters nationwide.

79

Go Organic — Not GM

An end to seed saving would lead to the disappearance of the genetic diversity our ancestors have left us, and which we have a responsibility to leave to future generations.

— **Open letter from African NGOs to the ministers at the 2006 Convention on Biodiversity**

Multinational agriculture corporations such as Monsanto (see "Animals in the Boardroom") promote biotechnology as the answer to world hunger, by getting farmers to use genetically modified (GM) seeds that are controlled by the patenting company. The opposite has become true, as farmers in developing nations get farther and farther into debt using unreliable seeds that require the use of expensive chemicals. In India farmers who spend 100,000 rupees per acre using GM seed get a 10,000 rupee return at the end the growing season, resulting in a debt increase of 90,000 rupees ($2,000) per acre every year.[1] When Monsanto brought its Bt cotton to India, they promised that it would double yields for farmers. Instead there was a 90% decline in yields, and farmers who depended on the GM seeds fell more deeply into debt.[2] In 2005 the Indian government banned the use of Monsanto's Bt cotton in the southern states of Andhra Pradesh because of its ineffectiveness and its contribution to increased debt in the region. GM crops are handcuffing farmers in developing nations around the world, forcing them to buy new seeds and expensive chemicals every year, while contaminating soil, air and water and causing health risks for farmers and consumers.

Nations Unite to Reject Terminator Seeds

Terminator technology uses genetic modification to sterilize seeds, forcing farmers to buy new seeds every year, rather than saving seeds from their own crops. There was strong global opposition to the granting of the first US Terminator patent to Delta & Pine Land in 1998, out of fears that multinational agro corporations would quickly dominate the world market, making it impossible for poorer countries to continue farming independently. In 2000 the Convention on Biodiversity agreed to a moratorium on Terminator technology, but six major corporations, led by Monsanto and Dupont, pressed on, and all have obtained US patents for their version of Terminator seeds.

At the 2006 Convention, the United States, Canada, Australia and New Zealand promoted a "case-by-case" assessment of the moratorium, opening the door for Terminator to re-enter global agriculture.

JOAN WALSH

The proposal was condemned by Zambia and Uganda, both of which took a strong stance against the controversial technology, supported by nations from across Africa, Asia, Latin America and Europe, ensuring that, for the time being, Terminator seeds will stay out of their fields.

The Voice for the Seed Savers

Physicist, author and activist Vandana Shiva has been a pioneer of the seed-saving movement, helping farmers organize to reject GM crops and return to organic farming. She has assisted grassroots organizations with organic farming campaigns in Asia, Africa, Latin America and Europe and has fought for changes in the globalization of agriculture and food. She established the Navdanya movement in India, dedicated to a return to nonviolent farming and protection of biodiversity, the environment and indigenous culture. Navdanya's Asha ke Beej (Seeds of Hope) program provided indigenous seeds to 6,000 farmers to convert to organic agriculture in a campaign that covered 250 villages and 10,000 people.

After the events of September 11, 2001, Vandana Shiva recognized that the world had changed and that a new system of education based on love and sustainability was needed, so she founded the Bija Vidyapeeth (School of the Seed) college at Navdanya's organic farm in Doon Valley, India. With a mission of education for Earth citizenship, Bija Vidyapeeth teaches short courses on sustainable agriculture, training in conversion to chemical-free farming, reinventing nutrition, and women and seed sovereignty (in much of India, 60% of the farming operations are run by women[3]).

- Bija Vidyapeeth: www.navdanya.org/bija/index.htm
- Navdanya: www.navdanya.org
- Organic Consumers Association: www.organicconsumers.org
- Seed Savers: www.seedsavers.net
- The Sustainability Report: www.sustreport.org/news/edge_pollute.html

A Seed Satyagrah

In 2005, 3,000 tribal women from Orissa, India, gathered to build a bonfire of hybrid and genetically modified seeds, calling it the start of a seed "satyagrah," Mahatma Gandhi's policy for nonviolent resistance. Orissa Nari Samaj (ONS) is a tribal women's organization with 200,000 members appealing to the Indian government to declare Orissa an organic state and scrap plans for a controversial seed bill that would endanger indigenous seeds and the livelihoods of farmers in Orissa. ONS has already declared 200 villages in the state as organic villages and has cultivated indigenous seeds in 17,000 acres. Before their bonfire, the women exhibited 1,000 indigenous seeds at a conference in the village of Siddharth.

80

Listen to the Dalai Lama

My religion is very simple. My religion is kindness.

— His Holiness the Dalai Lama

The Dalai Lama has called for an end to the illegal trade of wildlife between India, Tibet, Nepal and China. The exiled Tibetan leader is working with the charities Care for the Wild International and the Wildlife Trust of India to raise awareness about the harm illegal hunting and trading of animals is causing. He launched the awareness drive in 2005 by appealing to Tibetans to remember their Buddhist faith: "We Tibetans are basically Buddhists; we preach love and compassion towards all other living beings on Earth. Therefore, it is the responsibility of all of us to realize the importance of wildlife conservation."

Tibetans are becoming increasingly involved in the bloody trade in animal parts through the Himalayas, and the campaign team has distributed leaflets and videos throughout Tibetan refugee settlements around India, as well as preparing anti-poaching messages for television and radio.

Part of the team's concern is the new rail line between the Tibetan capital of Lhasa and Beijing, which will make it much easier for poachers to transport skins and other animal parts. Both charities are thrilled to have the Dalai Lama on board, because his words carry a great deal of weight with Tibetans. It is hoped that his message will reduce the problem before it spirals out of control.

"It is in the Pali and Sanskrit tradition to show love and compassion for all living beings," the Dalai Lama said. "It is a shame that we kill these poor creatures to satisfy our own aggrandizement."

A Bonfire for the Animals

In February 2006 Tibetans took to the streets in support of the Dalai Lama's campaign and the Buddhist tradition of non-violence to all living beings. Cheering and chanting Buddhist sermons, the brightly attired Tibetans burned piles of endangered animal skins. About three billion Yuan ($300 million) worth of skins were destroyed in various parts of Tibet. A film of the mass burning was screened before 1,000 Tibetans at the main temple of the Dalai Lama, and within days, Tibetans were taking to the streets with fires of their own; burning the skins of tigers, foxes and otters.

Changing with the Times

Egypt, which has no animal welfare legislation, was heavily criticized after video footage of

A Letter for the Chickens

In 2004 the Dalai Lama wrote a letter to Yum Brands, the parent company of Kentucky Fried Chicken, appealing to the fast-food giant to halt plans to open outlets in Tibet, and explained that the mass slaughter of chickens violated Tibetans' traditional values. Following the publicity surrounding the letter, Yum Brands abandoned its plans of expanding into Tibet, saying it appeared the move wouldn't be "economically feasible."

In his letter, the Dalai Lama wrote, "I have been particularly concerned with the suffering of chickens for many years. It was the death of a chicken that finally strengthened my resolve to become vegetarian."

- Bhutan's Gross National Happiness: www.bhutanstudies.org.bt/publications/gnh/gnh.htm
- Buddhism and Animals: www.anaflora.com/articles/oth-sharon/animal-bud.html
- Care for the Wild International: www.careforthewild.org
- Government of Tibet in Exile — the Dalai Lama: www.tibet.com/DL
- Tibetan Conservation Awareness Campaign: www.tibetinfonet.net
- Wildlife Trust of India: www.wildlifetrustofindia.org

extreme cruelty in slaughter-houses was made public in 2006. That same year, Cairo hosted a Farm Animal Slaughtering and Transportation conference, attended by the Compassion in World Farming Trust, the Egyptian Society of Animal Friends, the Society for the Protection of Animal Rights in Egypt, Egyptian slaughter-house owners and officials from the Department of Agriculture. The delegates expressed their shock at the video footage, with two doctors from Egypt's Al-Azhar University joining NGOs in a call for reform. Mr. Masoud Khawaja, President of the UK's Halal Food Authority, said that Islam calls for compassion and mercy to animals, adding that technology exists that was not available when the Qur'an was revealed to the Prophet. It is up to us, he said, to deduce from the core teachings how we should use that technology.

In the Central Asian Kyrgyz Republic, a big fur hat tells the story of an illegally-killed, endangered snow leopard.

COURTESY OF SNOW LEOPARD TRUST

Bhutan's Commitment to Happiness

Bhutan measures its progress in terms of Gross National Happiness (GNH), which reflects the health and well-being of the country, rather than the traditional Gross National Product (GNP) measure of economic wealth. The Himalayan nation hosted a GNH international conference in 2004, drawing 82 participants from 20 countries. The GNH model answers the call for a more realistic measure of progress, rather than the one-dimensional GNP. Gross National Happiness helps animals by placing a high emphasis on the preservation of natural habitat. Two thirds of the country is protected wilderness (see Solution 73).

81

For the Amazon Rainforest

> They always put social experiments in the easiest, most fertile places. We wanted the hardest place. We figured if we could do it here, we could do it anywhere.
>
> — Paolo Lugari, founder of Gaviotas

The Amazon River basin has the world's greatest diversity of life. It is the source of a fifth of its fresh water, and home to a third of all animal and plant species. Its 1.2-billion-acre expanse crosses nine international borders. For 500 million years, the Amazon has been one of the most vital sources of life on Earth.[1] Today its vast sea of greenery is pockmarked by logging roads, burning brush piles, ranches, oil wells, mining and hydro-electric dams. The world's hunger for more food and resources is causing the unsustainable harvest of the rainforest; creating lumber, grazing land, electricity and employment, while causing a critical loss of biodiversity, wildlife habitat, erosion, drought, displacement of indigenous peoples and global climate change. In the 1970s, the Trans-Amazonian Highway opened the area up for loggers, settlers and commercial interests. By the 1980s, the Brazilian rainforest was being cleared at a rate of 5.5 million acres per year.[2] By 2006, 15% of the Amazon had been cleared, up from just 2.4% in 1970, and scientists warn that if current trends continue, 40% of the rainforest will be agricultural grasslands by 2050.[3]

During 2005 and 2006, record drought years for the Amazon, rivers and lakes dried up and millions of fish perished, prompting Brazil to declare a state of emergency across 230 villages in the regions that rely on boats to gather food, fuel and medicine. The drought conditions are a new and frightening crisis in the Amazon and appear to be directly linked to record-high water temperatures in the Atlantic and Gulf of Mexico and destructive logging.[4]

The answer to rainforest destruction isn't as simple as imposing an end to logging. Between 2000 and 2006, small-scale subsistence agriculture accounted for 33% of all deforestation in the Amazon, while cattle ranching, industrial agriculture and logging (legal and illegal) accounted for 63%.[5]

Eyes on Brazil

Brazil encompasses 60% of the Amazon basin, including 20 million people, with 220,000 belonging to180 different indigenous tribes.[6] However, the problem

The Murici forest in Alagoas, Brazil, covers just 37 square miles, yet is home to 289 bird species; 15 of which face extinction as surrounding sugarcane plantations and cattle grazing encroach on the fragile ecosystem.

of deforestation is not due to overpopulation, but rather inequality of land ownership. A small number of land barons own nearly half the arable land in Brazil, and the government has managed the situation by allowing farmers forced from their land to move into the rainforest.

But there's new hope for the Brazilian rainforest. The government has teamed up with the World Wildlife Fund and other organizations to create the Amazon Region Protected Areas (ARPA) initiative (see Solution 73); working toward a goal of 121.6 million acres of protected rainforest by 2010 — an area larger than California. In 2006 Brazil announced a sustainable logging initiative, setting aside 3% of the country's rainforest for closely monitored harvesting, undermining illegal logging and providing income to rural Brazilians. The Brazilian government announced progress in 2005, when deforestation of the Amazon fell by 37% from 2004.[7]

Protect-an-Acre

The Rainforest Action Network's Protect-an-Acre program provides grants to indigenous communities in the Amazon to protect their forest homes. RAN helps the communities gain land title with the grants, giving them ownership and allowing them to control how their forests are preserved. The program also establishes protected reserves, develops economic alternatives, creates community organizations, gives environmental education and teaches communities how to resist pressure from commercial interests. Established in 1993, the program raises money

worldwide and in 1998 alone protected 150 thousand acres of rainforest.

In 2005 RAN provided a $5,000 grant to a group of Huaorani women of the Ecuadorian Amazon to facilitate a three-month peace camp in protest of an access road being built through Yasuni National Park by oil company Petrobras. After the successful campaign, Petrobras abandoned the road construction in 2006.

- Friends of Gaviotas: www.friendsofgaviotas.org
- Rainforest Action Network: www.ran.org
- Rainforest Foundation: www.rainforestfoundation.uk.org
- Rain Tree: www.rain-tree.com

A Place Called Gaviotas

Deep in the barren savannahs of eastern Columbia, 200 people live in a small village called Gaviotas. In a South American country fraught with political, environmental and economic strife, Gaviotas is a true oasis of life. There is no police force, no weapons and no mayor. But there is free housing, a school, solar and wind generated power and organic farms. They've built their own biodiesel plant that runs on pure vegetable oil. They gather together for their meals and have created the true definition of intentional community. Perhaps most incredible of Gaviotas' accomplishments is the recreation of a lush, indigenous rainforest, planted by the village's residents. Over a period of three decades, the people of Gaviotas have planted millions of trees; bringing back the rainforest and proving that sustainability is possible anywhere in the world.

82

For Migratory Birds

> We don't know as much about birds as we think we do. You have to be a bird to know what they're up against.
>
> — Chandler Robbins, ornithologist, Patuxent Wildlife Research Center

Since bird lovers may have skipped ahead to this solution, here's a question: Where, on Earth, would you find the highest concentration of migratory birds? Surprisingly, it's nowhere in North or South America. It's in Israel. With its unique geographical location at the junction of three continents, Israel is blessed with the presence of some 500 million migrating birds every year; the skies literally fill with vast flocks of birds, many species mingling together into a gigantic tapestry of colour and motion. It is truly a birder's paradise.

Of Course, There's a Catch

The downside of having enormous congregations of migrating birds in the sky is that it creates havoc for air traffic of the human kind. Every year in Israel, thousands of birds are killed by collisions with aircraft. This is also gut wrenching for the pilots and causes damage to the aircraft. Israel has an active air force, and its fast moving planes are particularly prone to collisions with birds, especially in the spring and fall.

Radar to the Rescue

Israel has found a solution in a radar network set up at weather stations across the country that maps the flight of birds. The Latrun Radar compares data with this network and gives accurate data about the number of birds, their flight direction and height and speed of travel, which is given to pilots and air traffic control centers throughout the region. Radar networks such as Latrun could easily be employed in other areas with heavy air traffic where there are migrating birds.

Fatal Lights

Experts estimate that as many as 100 million birds are killed by collisions with man-made objects in North America every year.[1] The mortality rate is particularly high during nighttime migrations, when birds, guided in part by

Stopover Conservation

Twice a year, millions of birds make the incredible migratory journey across the hemisphere, some trips spanning 10,000 miles. Some of the birds fly for 24 hours a day, and their stopovers are essential, as they literally drop out of the sky to find food and rest. The migration corridor across the Gulf of Mexico is one of the largest on Earth, with many birds crossing the entire 600-mile expanse without a break. Others take the longer journey around it, making the oak and pine forests surrounding the Gulf crucial to the travelers' survival. The forests are the focus of the Nature Conservancy's Gulf Wings Project, which works with authorities and partner organizations in the US and Mexico to protect critical migratory habitat through land acquisition, educational programs, field research and the promotion of ecotourism.

constellations, are attracted to lights from skyscrapers, radio towers, lighthouses, monuments and other lit structures, including greenhouses. The birds either strike the object or fly about it in confusion, often dropping from exhaustion. Inclement weather exacerbates the problem, as does the presence of predatory animals like cats that wait around the lit structure for an easy meal.

In 1993 the Fatal Lights Awareness Program (FLAP) was formed in Toronto, Ontario. FLAP volunteers work with the public, businesses and municipal and provincial authorities to raise awareness about the plight of migrating birds. During spring and fall migrations, they patrol Toronto's streets in the early morning hours, collecting dead birds and rescuing injured ones. Injured birds are given a warm, dark place to

recuperate, and medical attention if needed. Dead birds are transported to the Royal Ontario Museum for research and educational purposes. In 1998 FLAP worked with Ontario Hydro and convinced them to switch from spotlights to rapidly flashing strobe lights on six of their major generating stations, with bird collisions decreasing sharply. In 2006 FLAP helped Toronto become the world's first city to initiate a migratory bird protection program, launching Lights Out Toronto (see Solution 26).

Feathery fact — The American golden plover is so efficient it can fly for 48 continuous hours on less than two ounces of body fat. The small sandpiper summers in the far north, from Alaska to Baffin Island, and winters in South America.

LEO SWARTZ/WETLANDS INTERNATIONAL

- Fatal Lights Awareness Program: www.flap.org
- Migrating Birds Know No Boundaries: www.birds.org.il
- National Audubon Society: www.audubon.org
- National Wildlife Federation — migratory birds: www.nwf.org/migratorybirds
- Nature Conservancy: www.nature.org
- Royal Society for the Protection of Birds: www.rspb.org.uk

83

For Tigers

There has been a shift in attitude over the last few years, and Chinese authorities have removed the tiger and its parts from the national list of approved medicinal ingredients.[1]
— Sally Nicholson, WWF

Tigers play a critical role in the diversity of their complex ecosystems and the heritage of Asia, where they are the national animal of India, Malaysia, North Korea, South Korea, Nepal, Bangladesh and China (sharing the unoffical title with the panda). One hundred years ago, there were100,000 tigers in the wild, with a range that covered Russia, Siberia, Iran, Afghanistan, India, China and Southeast Asia. Since then, the wild population has dropped by 95%, down to just 5,000 remaining in the wild, with three of the nine tiger subspecies falling extinct, and the remaining six being placed on the endangered species list. One of the six may be declared extinct soon; as the last recorded South China tiger in the wild was shot and killed in 1994.[2]

Wild tigers continue to be killed illegally for their skins and for many body parts that are used in traditional Asian medicine, while their habitat continues to vanish with increased human activity. Being solitary creatures, tigers need a lot of land to live in, with the males often having a territory of 70 square miles.[3] More people moving into their range has led to conflicts with farmers and villagers, contributing to the big cats' decline. By 2006, wild tigers occupied only 7% of their historic range.[4]

Help from WWF in India
In 1997 the World Wildlife Fund (WWF) initiated the Tiger Conservation Programme, working with governments, raising public awareness and political will, monitoring conservation efforts and campaigning globally to raise funds and awareness. With international support, the number of protected areas in India, home to 80% of the world's remaining tigers, climbed from 7 in 1997 to 21 in 2006, including tiger reserves, national parks and wildlife sanctuaries.

Around India's tiger reserves, retaliatory poisoning by farmers, whose cows had been preyed upon, was killing more tigers than poachers

SAVE THE TIGER FUND

were. In 1997 WWF began assisting farmers with compensation for lost cattle, paying out for a confirmed kill within 48 hours and preventing retaliatory action against the tigers. The compensation has been successful, with WWF reporting a steady decrease in poisoning deaths.

The Sundarban Mangrove in West Bengal, a world heritage site, is home to the Sundarban Tiger Reserve. The reserve's tigers have earned a reputation as being predatory on humans — in the 120 reported cases of tigers straying into surrounding villages since 1990, 6 cases have been documented of tigers attacking people. This has raised fear among villagers, resulting in the shooting deaths of tigers, both in villages and within the reserve.[5] In response, WWF has initiated a training program for tranquillizing and relocating stray tigers into the deep forest. They also promote ecotourism as a source of sustainable income for the villagers, building the Mangrove Interpretation Centre at Sajnekhali and making it less necessary for them to venture into the tigers' habitat to support themselves.

The Satpuda-Maikal landscape in Central India covers 9.6 million acres. Home to 500 tigers, it includes five tiger reserves, five national parks and seven wildlife sanctuaries. The area is a vital corridor for wildlife migration, but it is under continual threat from poaching, forest fires, increasing pressure from cattle and a growing human population that leads to conflicts with tigers. WWF has identified nine key migration corridors, making them the focus of a wide-ranging conservation effort for tigers, herbivores and the smaller predators who share the

habitat, while training field staff to monitor conservation efforts, watch for forest fires, prevent poaching and raise awareness among residents.

- Sumatran Tiger Trust: www.tigertrust.info
- Tigers in Crisis: www.tigersincrisis.com
- WWF India: www.wwfindia.org
- WWF Tigers: www.worldwildlife.org/tigers

Tigers and TCM

Traditional Chinese medicine (TCM) has been an indispensable part of Chinese culture for 3,000 years, using natural plants, minerals and animal-based ingredients as a holistic approach to health care. Many species used in TCM, including tigers, are protected by national and international laws, but the global interest in TCM has prompted an increase in poaching and illegal trade in parts from endangered species. In the 1990s, WWF began its traditional Chinese medicine program, working with TCM practitioners to raise awareness about the plight of endangered species and to promote alternative treatments that use sustainably harvested (usually herbal) ingredients. In 2003 WWF reported that the availability of endangered species products in TCM shops had significantly decreased in North American cities. In China, the major market for endangered species-based medicine, the government made a landmark agreement in 1999 to work with WWF and other conservation groups to end the use of endangered species products in TCM, while pledging $3.75 million to do research on alternatives.[6]

84

for Canadian Harp Seals

We must all work together to send a message that Canada must end this hunt in order to save the reputation of the seafood industry there.
— Tom Worthington, Monterey Fish Company, one of over 300 American companies boycotting Canadian seafood in protest of the annual seal hunt

The ice floes off Canada's East Coast are the scene of intolerable cruelty every year, as hundreds of thousands of harp seal pups are bludgeoned to death so that their furs can be sold to the fashion industry overseas. The Canadian government's seal harvest plan is widely viewed as unsustainable and is condemned by many other countries, including the United States.

- The fishermen who conduct the seal hunt net only 5 % of their annual income from the hunt, belying the Canadian government's stance that it is an essential part of eastern Canada's economy.[1]

- In Newfoundland, where 90% of the seal hunters live, the annual hunt accounts for less than 1 % of the province's gross domestic product.[2]

- The Canadian government claims that harp seals are overpopulated and pose a threat to the fishing industry, stating that the population has tripled since 1970. That claim is misleading, since two-thirds of the seal population was wiped out by overhunting in the 1950s and '60s, with the increase simply reflecting a return to normal.[3]

Any justification for the slaughter of seal pups has passed. If the seal hunt was once a necessary evil to sustain people who had no other means of survival, that necessity is gone. Today the seal hunt sustains the fashion industry, and the means by which the fur is harvested is horrific. This annual slaughter can only be stopped if individuals, action groups and governments work together to pressure the Canadian government to end the seal hunt forever.

GLOBAL ACTION NETWORK

An Offer Too Good to Accept?

In February 2006, PRAI Beauty CEO Cathy Kangas offered Canadian Prime Minister Stephen Harper $16 million (the amount reported as seal hunt profits from 2005) to call off the 2006 hunt before it began. Kangas said she would also initiate eco-tourism retraining programs to support a new economy for northeastern Canada. The Canadian government refused her offer.

- Coalition to Abolish the Fur Trade: www.caft.org.uk/factsheets/commercial-seal-hunting.html
- HarpSeals.org: www.harpseals.org
- Humane Society of the United States: www.hsus.org
- International Fund for Animal Welfare: www.stopthesealhunt.com
- Sea Shepherd: www.seashepherd.org

Strength in Numbers

The world is angry about the seal hunt. From the far reaches of the globe, letters pour into the Canadian Prime Minister's office. Over 80% of Europeans, 79% of Americans[4] and 70% of Canadians[5] polled say they oppose the hunt.

Contact the Prime Minister

If we shower the Canadian Prime Minister with letters, e-mails and phone calls, he may get the message that the seal hunt is intolerable: Office of the Prime Minister, 80 Wellington St., Ottawa, ON, Canada K1A OA2, 1-613-992-4211, pm@pm.gc.ca.

In the United States, contact: The Ambassador, Canadian Embassy, 501 Pennsylvania Ave. NW, Washington, DC 20001, 202-682-1740, canada@canadianembassy.org.

Elsewhere in the world, contact the nearest Canadian embassy — see www.dfait-maeci.gc.ca/world/embassies/menu-en.asp.

Boycott Canadian Seafood

A growing number of individuals, schools, companies and governments around the world are boycotting Canadian seafood until the hunt is ended. More than 120,000 people have signed the pledge at www.protectseals.org, and the boycott is having an effect. In 2005 Canadian exports of snow crabs to the United States dropped by over $150 million; nearly 10 times the value of the seal hunt and a 36% drop since the seafood boycott began.[6] As Dr. John Grandy of the Humane Society of the United States said, "The Canadian government and the fishing industry need to decide whether maintaining a seal hunt is worth the cost to the country."

Don't Vacation in Canada

Skip your holiday to Canada and tell them you'd love to visit once the seal hunt is ended: Canadian Tourism Commission, 55 Metcalfe St., Suite 600, Ottawa, ON, Canada K1P 6L5, 613-946-1000: www.canadatourism.com (Contact Us)

Newfoundland and Labrador Tourism: P.O. Box 8700, St. John's, NL Canada A1B 4J6, 1-800-563-6353: tourisminfo@gov.nl.ca

Contact these fashion companies that use seal fur and skin

Annika Heinadottir	annika@dottir.dk
Birger Christensen	www.birger-christensen.com
Gucci	www.gucci.com
Marni	www.marni.com
Odette Leblanc Collection	www.ilesdelamadeleine.com/odette
Petit Nord	petitnord.com
Prada	www.prada.com
Versace	www.versace.com

85

For the Great Apes

The great apes are our kin. They are self-aware and have cultures, tools, politics and medicines ... we have not treated them with the respect they deserve.

— Kofi Annan,
former United Nations Secretary-General

All of the great apes — chimpanzees, orangutans, bonobos and gorillas — are endangered species. In 2004 the World Conservation Union recorded the loss of 3,000 Borneo orangutans, 2,000 eastern lowland gorillas and 1,000 Sumatra orangutans in a single year.[1] The eastern lowland gorilla's population fell by 70% from 1994 to 2004. Of the *Hominidae* biological family, humans are the only species not threatened with extinction this century. Our relatives urgently need our help.

An Historic Union

Nowhere is the plight of the great apes more prevalent than in the Democratic Republic of

Congo (DRC), where civil war has led to economic instability, poverty, hunger and the dramatic loss of great apes. In 2006 the United Nations Environmental Programme (UNEP) warned that all great apes in the DRC, as well as neighboring Rwanda and Uganda, face extinction in the near future.[2] UNEP's Klaus Toepfer cited the bushmeat trade (see Solution 74), excessive logging (both legal and illegal) and the spread of disease for the crisis: "It is one minute to midnight for the great apes."

But there is hope, thanks to the efforts of some of the pioneers of primate research. After 40 years of individual pioneering work, the Dian Fossey Gorilla Fund International and the Jane Goodall Institute united with Conservation International in 2005 to create a 7.4-million-acre conservation corridor in the DRC, from Maiko National Park and the Tayna Gorilla Reserve to Kahuzi-Biega National Park. The area is home to 5,000 eastern lowland gorillas and 10,000 chimpanzees. The project involves the leaders (mwami) of eight local tribal nations, permitting sustainable farming and limited hunting but prohibiting the killing of any endangered species. The partnership includes educational programs for sustainable agriculture and projects to improve health care and family planning. The initiative protects a vital corridor for great apes, while improving life for the tribes that live in the region.

The Orangutan's Best Friend

Biruté Galdikas has dedicated her life to helping the orangutans. With the help of Dr. Louis

Remembering a Great Ape Friend

Dian Fossey spent over 20 years studying gorillas, founding the Karisoke Research Center in Rwanda in 1967. A National Geographic cover story in 1970 brought international publicity to her cause of saving the mountain gorilla from extinction, and she continued to promote and practise "active conservation," leading and funding anti-poaching patrols. In 1985 she agreed to the making of *Gorillas in the Mist*, a movie based on her book of the same title, which would further the cause of the great ape conservation worldwide. Months after signing the movie contract, Dian Fossey was murdered in her cabin in Rwanda, killed by a weapon she had confiscated from poachers. After her death, the Dian Fossey Gorilla Fund International lived on, dedicated to the protection of gorillas and their habitat through research, anti-poaching patrols, education and support of local communities.

- Conservation International: www.conservation.org
- Dian Fossey Gorilla Fund International: www.gorillafund.org
- Great Ape Project: www.greatapeproject.org
- International Gorilla Conservation Programme: www.mountaingorillas.org
- Jane Goodall Institute: www.janegoodall.org
- Orangutan Foundation International: www.orangutan.org

JANE GOODALL INSTITUTE/JANEGOODALL.ORG

Leakey, she set up Camp Leakey in Borneo in 1971, where she has studied orangutans for over 30 years. In 1986 she created Orangutan Foundation International (OFI) with a mission of saving orangutans and their habitat in Indonesia and Malaysia. OFI operates the Orangutan Care Center and Quarantine Facility, tending to orphaned orangutans and preparing them for a reintroduction into suitable protected habitat. OFI conducts educational programs for communities, offers grants to students to conduct studies and funds ground patrols of protected areas.

Orangutans are still in great danger of extinction, due to economic collapse of the region, rampant destruction of habitat and recent natural disasters. Since the mid 1980s, 80% of their habitat has been lost. Experts fear that orangutans could be gone from the wilds by 2015.[3]

A Solution for All of Us

Biruté Galdikas, the Jane Goodall Institute and the Dian Fossey Gorilla Fund International have done legendary work in the effort to halt the rapid decline of great ape populations in the wild. So what about the rest of us who live in areas where the great apes exist only in captivity?

The first step is monetary. All conservation organizations rely on continued funding, and the more funding they're given, the more great apes will benefit. One can even become a Chimp Guardian. The Jane Goodall Institute's Chimp Guardian program includes a certificate of guardianship, photos, a biography of your chimp and regular reports on its welfare, as well as updates from the field. The second step is to spread the word.

86

For Orcas

You name it, the whales had it — PCBs, pesticides
and at least one type of brominated flame-retardant.
— Hans Wolkers, Norwegian Polar Institute,
on the results of tissue samples taken from
ten live whales (by dart) in 2005

The global population of orcas (killer whales) is unknown, though estimates place 80,000 in the Antarctic, with another 20,000 around the world. They are at the top of the ocean's natural food chain, preying on birds, fish, sharks and other marine mammals, yet there has never been a documented case of an orca killing a human. Commercial hunting of orcas ended with the 1981 moratorium on hunting whales (see Solution 75), although Japan continues to kill them every year in the name of "research." Yet the real threat to orcas is not hunting, but toxic waste, amplified noise and whale watching harassment.

A Toxic Brew

Orcas accumulate high levels of toxins, such as PCBs and flame-retardants in their blubber, having inherited the contamination of every other species along the food chain.

In 2004 the Stockholm Convention on Persistent Organic Pollutants officially banned PCBs and several other chemical substances known to persist and bioaccumulate through the food chain, but many are difficult to get rid of,

- Orca Lab: www.orcalab.org
- Orca Network: www.orcanetwork.org
- Orca Relief Citizen's Alliance: www.orcarelief.org
- Seaflow: www.seaflow.org
- Whale and Dolphin Conservation Society: www.wdcs.org

breaking down very slowly. The Convention does not cover many toxins such as Deca-BDE; a flame-retardant commonly used in plastics and upholstery, that can affect fetal development.[1]

When the Exxon Valdez ran aground in Prince William Sound in 1989, a resident pod of orcas was caught in the ship's oil spill. Eleven members of the pod were never seen again, and three washed up dead. Tissue samples from the beached whales showed some of the highest levels of industrial contaminants ever found in marine mammals.[2] By 2004 the pod had dwindled to seven orcas and hadn't reproduced since the spill.

The pod received special protection from the US government in 2004, after a campaign by seven conservation and native groups asked the National Marine Fisheries Service for help. The AT1 pod is now covered by the Marine Mammal Protection Act and a government study to help the whales has been launched.

Acoustic Smog

The noise from commercial shipping, cruise liners, the military and recreational boats is masking the natural sounds of the ocean, and marine mammals are unable to escape from it. Whales use their highly sensitive hearing to communicate under water, and they are suffering physical injury and death from the extreme sound. The US navy's LFA Sonar uses extremely loud underwater blasts, one of the loudest noises ever created by man. It actually kills some whales that happen to be nearby, while others beach themselves to get away from the sound.[3]

Onto the Endangered Species List

In early 2006, there were 90 orcas living in the three resident pods that frequent the Puget Sound in Washington, and the Strait of Georgia in British Columbia; a decline of 20% since 1995.[8] In 2001 the southern resident orcas were declared an endangered species by Canada's Committee on the Status of Endangered Wildlife and are therefore covered by the country's Species at Risk Act, making it a federal offence to kill, harm or harass them. In 2005 the region's orcas also received protection in Washington State under the US Endangered Species Act, the highest available under the law.

In the summer of 2006, three orcas disappeared from the southern pods and were believed to have died. One was a nursing mother, whose baby was being cared for by her aunt. The loss of the three orcas occurred at the same time as two whales vanished from a resident pod further north along the BC coast, prompting widespread concern over the future of the remaining population.

The case against LFA Sonar use is clear, and an international ban is being called for by conservation groups around the world, but eliminating ear-splitting sonar activity won't end the constant drone of noise from ships. One solution lies in the retrofitting of ships with better designed, quieter propellers that will lower noise while using less energy, saving fuel and reducing maintenance costs.[4]

IAN McALLISTER/RAINCOAST.ORG

Whale-watching Frenzy

Worldwide, whale-watching has become a billion-dollar industry, with 9 million participants in 87 countries.[5] During the summer, as many as 145 whale-watching boats per day[6] speed around the San Juan and Southern Gulf Islands between Washington and British Columbia, hoping to get a good look at the resident orcas. Three separate studies in the area have shown a connection between population decline and boat activity.[7] Orca Relief Citizen's Alliance president Mark Anderson said, "In an environment of declining salmon, the presence of the whale-watch fleet decreases sonar efficiency by 95% to 99%, while increasing food requirements. The resulting starvation forces the whales to draw down toxin-laden blubber, and they die."

Orca Relief proposes three solutions to the impact of whale-watching:

- Whale weekends — give the orcas two days off from whale-watching boats.
- Shorter days — limit whale viewing hours to between10 a.m. and 2 p.m.
- Give them more space — expand the current 100 yard rule to 400 yards.

87

For Dairy Cows and Their Calves

Corporate demand for increased profits has really hurt dairy cows.

— Sheridan Thomas, Progressive Animal Welfare Society

The dairy industry has built itself into an intensive production machine, with 200 million cows worldwide producing 500 million tons of milk annually.[1] It is done by isolating dairy cows in cubicles, keeping them continually pregnant and removing their calves immediately after birth to be raised in veal crates or slaughtered. With distended udders, mastitis, lameness, anxiety and perpetual pregnancy for the mothers, and painful immobility in dark crates for the calves, the result is a huge amount of continuing misery (see "Deceptions of Dairy). The natural lifespan of a dairy cow is around 20 years, but most dairy cows are slaughtered by age 5[2] because they no longer produce enough milk or have become too lame to support their own

A Jersey tends to her newborn calf; the first heifer born at the University of New Hampshire's organic research dairy.

weight. They are literally worn out. Their male calves, considered unsuitable to be raised for beef, are either slaughtered or forced into confinement for a short life of becoming veal.

Cows are very social creatures who enjoy life most when they are around other cows. By allowing cows the opportunity to interact with each other, while ensuring a certain level of comfort, their suffering can be greatly reduced.

Four Steps to Compassion

- Allow dairy cows to have access to the outdoors, with housing in straw-bedded sheds.
- Allow new mother cows to spend time with their calves during the first 24 hours after birth, since the initial bonding is important for both mother and baby.[3]
- Replace all veal crates with straw-bedded, group-rearing systems. Allowing calves to move around in an open area with other calves will give them a much more comfortable existence where they can interact and play with other calves, especially after being separated from their mothers.
- Allow both cows and their calves to spend more time around the people who are caring for them. This is such a simple part of animal welfare, yet it's overlooked all the time. Domestic animals enjoy spending time around their caregivers, so be their caregivers. Keep a brush around and take the time to groom them. The more time you can spend with them, the better — cows thrive on social contact.

- Apple Family Farm: www.applefamilyfarm.com
- Aurora Organic Dairy: www.auroraorganic.com
- Food Animal Concerns Trust: www.fact.cc
- Humane Farming Association: www.hfa.org

Accountability at Apple Family Farm

In the US alone, four million male calves are born to dairy farms every year.[4] This is a result of having to keep cows continually pregnant to produce milk and a harsh reality for well-meaning farmers who see no recourse but to sell the males to feedlots for veal production. This was the reality for the Apples as well, a fourth-generation farming family in McCordsville, Indiana, who pride themselves on the humane treatment of their pasture-raised, hormone and antibiotic-free cows, sheep and chickens. Fifteen-year-old Brayden Apple was responsible for the care of the farm's calves, and he could no longer face the thought of where the male dairy calves went after selling them at the feedlot. So the Apples took the raising of the male calves into their own hands, feeding them their mothers' milk, raising them on pasture and producing their own veal. They sell the meat directly from their farm, with peace of mind that the calf's life was one of freedom, grass and milk.

Saying No to Drugs

Aurora Organic Dairy, with large-scale farms in Texas and Colorado, rejects the use of any growth hormones or antibiotics in its cows, since the widespread use of antibiotics has resulted in strains of diseases that are antibiotic-resistant and reduces a cow's natural hardiness and disease resistance (see "Weird Science"). Instead, they use an Early Sick Cow Recognition program, employing staff to monitor the well-being of the cows, recognizing when a cow needs extra rest or water and providing homeopathic or probiotic remedies. As part of its organic stewardship commitment, Aurora employs 110 people, from veterinarians to maternity specialists, to prevent illness in the cows and ensure their overall well-being.

The Value of Colostrum

Just like baby humans, baby calves need the benefit of their mothers' first milk, the colostrum, to kick-start their immunity and overall health. Baby calves need 12 pints of colostrum within their first 18 hours.[5] Colostrum is more readily absorbed by a newborn calf in the presence of its mother,[6] even when hand fed, and uptake is facilitated by her grooming and licking. The initial bond benefits the mother, too: she is less apt to retain the placenta when allowed to nurse her newborn calf.[7]

88

for African Grey Parrots

Come here. I love you. I'm sorry.
I want to go back.
— Alex, the African Grey Parrot,
on being left at a veterinary
office for surgery[1]

African Grey parrots are very popular companions because of their high level of intelligence and their amazing ability to mimic human voices and other sounds. Due to their popularity in the Western world, the trade in illegally obtained parrots is big business. Wild Greys are snatched from their native forests in 23 countries across tropical Africa and shipped in small crates to unsuspecting buyers in the West, who believe they've been bred and raised in captivity. The birds frequently end up traumatized, injured and highly suspicious of humans, leading to their eventual abandonment or death.

The parrot family contains more globally threatened species than any other bird: 94 parrot species are listed as vulnerable, endangered or critically threatened. The primary cause for the population decline for nearly all of these species is capture by humans.

A Solution at Work
The real solution for African Grey parrots is to leave them in their natural surroundings. Make it illegal to import them into any country and enforce the ban; otherwise the black market will continue to thrive.

In the United States, the importation of wild birds is already prohibited, yet it still continues. In Canada common birds, including most parrots, are freely traded. The people who capture the parrots simply ship them to Canada, where they are bought cheaply, smuggled into the US and sold for a premium on the black market.[2]

In Europe there are no regulations on the importation of parrots and other wild birds, but public awareness is growing. Over 230 organizations are working together in the name of parrot conservation, and in 2004 the World Parrot Trust presented a declaration to the European Parliament calling for an end to the importing of wild birds for commercial purposes.

Why the African Grey?
What is so special about the species, and why is its place in the wild so important? African Grey parrots have remarkable intelligence. Domesticated parrots have problem-solving skills at the level of a four-year-old child. They can distinguish color, shapes and quantities, master a vocabulary of over 100 English words and demonstrate an astonishing array of emotions. Domestic parrots demonstrate problem-solving skills that outdo most dogs.[3]

Removing these wonderful beings from the wild is incredibly cruel. Observed in the wild, African Greys are extremely social birds. Their flocks stay tightly together, both for safety and emotional well-being. They have intelligence and feelings, and they do not belong in solitary

- Alex Foundation: www.alexfoundation.org
- European Union Wild Bird Declaration: www.fosterparrots.com/news/WBDecFin.pdf
- Kooky Congos — wild bird trade: www.kookycongos.ca/wptrade.htm
- Parrots International: www.parrotsinternational.org
- World Parrot Trust: www.worldparrottrust.org

captivity. They belong in the wild, with others of their kind.

The World of Alex

Alex the Grey Parrot has gained considerable recognition through the research of Dr. Irene Pepperberg, who has worked with Alex for most of his 29 years. Alex can identify and name over 50 objects, count up to 6 objects at a time, identify 7 colors and 5 shapes, and has functional use of phrases such as "I want ..." and "I wanna go ...." He is very clear about what he wants. "If he says that he wants a grape and you give him a banana, you are going to end up wearing the banana."

Despite Alex's fame, his behavior is not unlike that of other parrots, including his remarkable cognitive abilities. Alex even vocalizes his impatience. Dr. Pepperberg was engaged in conversation and not heeding Alex's request for a nut. "We're going on and on and Alex is clearly getting more and more frustrated. He finally gets very slitty-eyed, and he looks at me and states, 'Want a nut. Nnn, uh, tuh.' She adds, "There's a lot more going on inside these little walnut-sized brains than you might at first imagine."[4]

The Trade of Wild-Caught African Grey Parrots 1994-2003[5]

Key Exporters	Number of Greys
Cameroon	156,855
Democratic Republic of Congo	118,780
Congo	31,946
Cote d'Ivoire	18,903
Liberia	11,045
Sierra Leone	10,911
Guinea	6,465
Europe's share in imported wild-caught Greys	93 %
Post-capture, pre-export mortality rate	44 %

Numbers reflect legal trade only, following the United States' 1992 ban on the import of all wild-caught birds.

89

For Chickens

> I have been particularly concerned with the sufferings of chickens for many years ... when I see a row of plucked chickens hanging in a meat shop it hurts.
>
> — His Holiness, the Dalai Lama

There is no animal species subjected to more suffering than the chicken. In the United States, 95% of the nation's 300 million egg-laying hens are confined to battery cages,[1] with four or more hens pressed both against each other and against the wire sides of a 16-inch cage, unable to stretch their wings or legs. Similarly, in Canada 98% of the nation's 26 million laying hens are confined to battery cages.[2] Male chicks from the egg-laying industry have no role since they can't lay eggs and haven't been genetically bred for profitable meat production, so they are killed upon hatching. In the United States, 250 million male chicks are killed annually.[3]

Chickens raised for meat suffer just as badly. Genetically manipulated for rapid weight gain, they suffer from painful leg disorders and heart failure. During slaughter, they are shackled upside down while conscious and have their throats slit. If the blades miss their throat, they are killed by a dip into scalding water to loosen their feathers.[4] But the greatest measure of suffering for chickens is the enormity of the industry. In the United States, 9 billion chickens are killed for meat every year.[5] Worldwide, over 50 billion chickens are slaughtered yearly.[6]

Chicken Solutions for Farmers

Having been domesticated for 5,000 years, most chickens are not capable of long flights, but they do enjoy stretching out their wings while exploring their surroundings. They are gregarious birds and live as a flock, roosting together above ground for safety, taking dust baths and using many different sounds to communicate.

The solution is to use an aviary system with a large open barn, containing platforms for greater floor space, litter trays for dust bathing, perches for roosting and nest boxes to satisfy their natural nesting instincts. Allow them access to the outdoors, giving them true free range.

FARM SANCTUARY

The Egg Mobile

Joel Salatin and his third-generation farming family live in the Shenandoah Valley, Virginia, where Joel's innovative approach to farming has made him one of the most sought-after sources for sustainable agriculture in the United States. To Joel, having a stationary, free-range chicken operation makes no sense, since the impact of chickens and their high-nitrogen manure leaves the soil they live on exposed and raw. The Salatins developed a pastured poultry model of raising chickens for eggs and meat, using light range shelters which are moved daily, either by hand or by tractor. Chickens in the "Egg Mobiles" actually live on the ground, catching bugs and scratching at a new paddock every day, leaving the previous day's area free for regrowth. The Salatin's chickens follow their cows around the fields, as the cows also rotate fields daily, leaving the chickens plenty of insects to feed on, in and under their cowpies. The Egg Mobiles are protected from foxes and hawks by trained guard dogs, and the Salatins are always improving their pasturing systems to help cope with predators and weather. They have even designed special Egg Mobiles for use in the winter months, with thick composting mulch underfoot. The Salatin's 550-acre Polyface Farm is one of the most productive small farms in North America, producing $15,000 of eggs yearly and raising 8,000 chickens for meat. Joel lectures across the country every winter and has written five books on sustainable farming.

- Ban Battery Cages: www.exploreveg.org/feat/bbc
- Chicken Out: www.chickenout.ca
- Pasture Poultry model: www.westonaprice.org/farming/pasturedpoultry.html
- Polyface Farm: www.polyfacefarms.com
- United Poultry Concerns: www.upc-online.org

What You Can Do

Buy local and know where your eggs and chickens come from. Although buying eggs labeled "free-range" means the hens have access to the outdoors, there is no way of telling how much access they had. Typically free-range hens have only one to two square feet of space per bird.[7] The US regulates the use of the term "free-range" on chicken but not on eggs, and Canada doesn't regulate either.[8] When choosing eggs or chicken from a grocer, always buy certified organic products. This will benefit your health and help ensure that the chickens are being allowed to live a more natural life.

If you can't find a humane supplier for eggs and chicken, you can go a step farther and eliminate them from your diet. Flax seeds are high in essential Omega-3 fatty acids and fiber and make an excellent substitute for eggs. Sprinkle one tablespoon of ground flax seeds on a meal a day, or stir one tablespoon of ground flax into three tablespoons of warm water for two minutes to create a gel-like egg substitute for any recipe.[9]

90

For Bats

By pollinating plants, dispersing seeds and controlling insect pests, bats provide great benefits to humanity.

— Michelle Evelyn, bat conservationist

Even though they are more feared than revered by most humans, bats are one of the most integral animals on Earth and yet one of the most misunderstood. All around the world, bats play a key role in every ecosystem they inhabit, but their habitats are being threatened by pollution and their homes displaced by urban sprawl. Due to lack of understanding, bats aren't getting the attention that many other threatened species get, and in many areas of the world, their populations are in rapid decline.

Stepping up to Bat

The simplest way to help is by providing them with safe places to live. Having bat houses around tends to make people uncomfortable,

US National Park Service

Samoan Fruit Bat.

but with a little awareness, most people can realize their benefit. A single little brown bat can catch up to 1,200 mosquitoes in just one hour.[1] Whether in residential neighborhoods, industrial areas or out in the country, bats need a safe place to roost during the day. A bat house construction needs to be about two feet high and more or less square. There are lots of designs available, and they are a great project for parents and children to build together. They can be mounted on a building or a pole and, once inhabited by bats, will become a welcome part of any residential setting.

Bat Lodges

Bat lodges are designed homes for entire colonies of bats, typically installed underneath bridges, where bats enjoy roosting. With the help of Bat Conservation International (BCI), there are bat lodge projects underway in Texas, Florida and Pennsylvania, with the state transportation departments assisting on each project. A single lodge can create a safe roosting space for between 3,000 and 5,000 bats. The Congress Avenue Bridge in Austin, Texas, is home to 1.5 million bats (see Solution 26).

Mineshaft Gates

Abandoned mineshafts frequently become home to bat colonies. When mines are blasted closed for safety reasons, thousands of bats are often killed. If the mines are left unsealed, however, they provide excellent

Bat Awareness 101[2]

- Bats are warm-blooded mammals like us that give birth to babies and nurse their young.
- Bats live longer than any other mammal of their size on Earth; some as long as 30 years.
- Bats are specially adapted to hang upside down and sleep during the day in out-of-the-way places where predators can't reach them. They fly and feed during the night, using a special sonar system called echolocation, bouncing sounds off objects such as insects to navigate as they fly. If you see a bat flying during the day, it is a sign that its roosting spot was disturbed, not that the bat is dangerous.
- There are over 1,100 species of bats worldwide: they have adapted to live in nearly every ecosystem.
- The state of Arizona has 30 species of bats — Canada has 19.
- 70% of all bats in the world eat only insects. Frugivorous bats living in tropical locations exist solely on fruit.
- Carnivorous bats eat small rodents, fish, birds and frogs. They pose no threat, however, to humans.
- Vampire bats live in Latin America and do not kill their host animals. They prick an animal with their teeth and lap up a small amount of blood, while the host animal continues to sleep.
- Bats can carry rabies, but they will not swoop down and bite you. The rule of thumb when encountering a bat that appears to be sick or injured is to avoid handling it with your bare hands.

- Basically Bats: www.basicallybats.org
- Bat Conservation International: www.batcon.org
- Bat Conservation Society of Canada: www.cancaver.ca
- Bat Conservation Trust: www.bats.org.uk
- California Bat Conservation Fund: www.californiabats.com
- Organization for Bat Conservation: www.batconservation.org

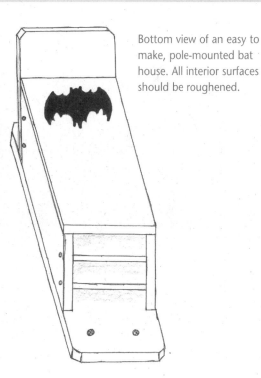

Bottom view of an easy to make, pole-mounted bat house. All interior surfaces should be roughened.

habitat for bat colonies, benefiting both bats and people. The answer is to construct a gate across the mineshaft, sealing the opening from people and larger animals but leaving it accessible to bats. A set of gates that were installed at the Magazine Mine in Illinois has created a hibernation home for upwards of 20,000 bats. This project was led by BCI, the Assisted Unimin Minerals Corporation and the Illinois Department of Natural Resources.

91

Recognize the Sentience of Animals

We need a new global vision for the future of life on Earth; one that is born through an awareness of the connection between all species, and recognizes the sentience of animals. A greater awareness like this, on a global scale, comes from two sources:

- Desire to see life on Earth continue. Because of the rapid consumption of Earth's resources, those among us who are taking the time to study the consequences of our actions are seeing a real threat to human existence.

A Landmark Conference

In 2005 London, England, hosted a first-of-its-kind conference, called "From Darwin to Dawkins: The Science and Implications of Animal Sentience," sponsored by Compassion in World Farming Trust, with a keynote speech by Dr. Jane Goodall. The conference drew 600 participants from 50 countries, making it the largest and most international event ever dedicated to animal sentience. Organizers and participants had one united purpose: to place animal sentience firmly on the global agenda. Delegates from universities, animal welfare groups, governments, the meat industry and veterinarians concluded the conference by supporting a united animal sentience mission:

This conference calls on the UN, the WTO, the World Animal Health Organization and their member governments to join us in recognizing that sentient animals are capable of suffering, and that we all have a duty to preserve the habitat of wild animals and to end cruel farming systems and other trades and practices which inflict suffering on animals.[1]

The whole climate over whether to accept sentience has changed hugely in the last 15 years. It has huge implications for all the ways we use animals. It implies all farm animals are entitled to humane lives and deaths. And millions are denied them.

— Joyce D'Silva,
Compassion in World Farming

- A place deep inside that we have become separated from. In our hearts, we know and respect our relationship with animals.

Globally, we must recognize the sentience of animals and return to a place where there is balance and respect between species.

Animals As Sentient Beings

Anyone who has shared their home with a dog or cat knows that they can feel, think and have "self." On a scale that is perfect for their particular species, animals interact with life on Earth just as we do. Some species, like primates, seem to think in a pattern somewhat similar to ours, so we're able to recognize their sentience a little easier. Some species, like cetaceans, have a highly developed sense of intelligence nothing like ours, so we're only able to guess at what's going on in their consciousness. When it comes to farm animals, the possibility of their sentience is often ignored, because the consequence of our treatment of them is just too horrible.

A Global Move Forward in Europe

In a very important and groundbreaking move, the European Union has created an annex to their Treaty of Amsterdam that recognizes animals as sentient beings. It is the first legally binding protocol of its kind ever created between a group of nations. The protocol states clearly that its member nations must recognize animals as sentient beings and that they must "pay full regard to the welfare requirements of animals."

- Animals Voice: www.animalsvoice.com
- Compassion in World Farming — animal sentience: www.animalsentience.com
- Eurogroup for Animal Welfare: www.eurogroupanimalwelfare.org
- Institute for Animals in Society: www.animalsandsociety.org
- Sentience: www.farmedanimal.net/faw/faw5-11.htm
- Treaty of Amsterdam details: www.worldanimal.net/eu-legis.html

The move toward the EU's legislation began in 1991, when Compassion in World Farming collected a million signatures, covering all EU member nations, and presented a petition to the European Parliament, calling for animals to be given new status as sentient beings. In 1994 the petition was endorsed by the Parliament, and in 1995, it called for measures making concern for animal welfare one of the fundamental principles of the EU. Then in 1997, the member nations met at the Intergovernmental Conference in Amsterdam and finalized the Treaty, which came into force in 1999.

The legislation means that the well-being of animals must be considered and includes regulations for:

- Transportation
- Slaughter
- Battery hens
- Veal calves and pigs
- Animal experimentation
- Drift netting
- Seals
- Fur trapping
- Conservation/wild birds

IAN MCALISTER/RAINCOAST.ORG

The protocol identifies that even though we may not relate to how animals are feeling, the simple fact that they are feeling is enough. The Treaty falls short in some areas, such as its exemption for "religious rites, cultural traditions and regional heritage." This leaves animal treatment in circuses, rodeos, animal fighting events and religious customs up to individual governments. Since 1999, individual European nations have used the guidelines of the Treaty of Amsterdam to revise their constitutions and create legislation to protect animals (see 20 Solutions for Governments).

92

Restore the Earth

The future well-being of humanity, and the Earth's other ten-million-plus species, is contingent on restoring the planet's ability to nurture and sustain life.

— Alan Watson Featherstone

The past 150 years has been a time of unprecedented impact by human beings upon the natural world, contributing to the recorded extinction of 120 animal species, 80 of which were birds. Now a new century is under way and our destructive behavior is continuing unchecked. The World Conservation Union estimates that 5,200 species are facing extinction, and, by the end of the century, if we continue living the way we do, two-thirds of all animal and plant species on Earth will be extinct (see Solution 64). There is a lot more awareness and understanding, yet we continue to do things the same way. We need a global solution; not only for animals but for the whole planet, because we simply can't go on this way or there won't be anything left. This is the century for a global effort to save our beautiful world.

Restoring the Earth

Restoring the Earth was established to create a new global vision for the 21st century to make the ecological restoration of the world's ecosystems the uniting mission of all nations. It was created by Alan Watson Featherstone, a member of the Findhorn Community since 1978 and founder and Executive Director of Trees for Life. Restoring the Earth is based in Scotland and endorsed by organizations and individuals around the world. The project has six primary initiatives:

- That the United Nations declares the 21st century as the Century of Restoring the Earth.
- That restoration of the world's degraded ecosystems becomes the focus of human endeavor.
- That each nation commits significant resources, either in cash or in kind, to ecological restoration work.
- That an international Earth Restoration Service be established, to engage volunteers from all over the world in essential restoration programs.
- That a Global Restoration Network be established, to coordinate and network restoration projects and programs.

The creation of the Earth Restoration Service is already underway, providing a database of ecological restoration projects around the world, linking ideas, successes and volunteers from many nations. Technical support for projects and opportunities for individuals from all over the planet can be found through the Earth Restoration Service website.

Inner Niger Delta, Mali.

LEO SWARTZ/WETLANDS INTERNATIONAL

The Millennium Ecosystem Assessment

In 2001 the United Nations launched an international work program called the Millennium Ecosystem Assessment (MA). It focuses on ecosystem services, how their changes affect people; both now and in the future, and what options are adoptable on a local, national and global scale. The MA synthesizes information gathered from the scientific community and private sectors, including those of indigenous peoples, and works all their findings through a rigorous review process before arriving at conclusions and options. Essentially, the MA is a planning and management tool that provides insight and ideas for cultivating sustainable ecosystems. MA has already worked closely with decision-makers in four international Conventions: the Convention on Biological Diversity, Convention to Combat Desertification, Convention on Wetlands (Ramsar) and Convention on Migratory Species.

- Earth Restoration Service: www.earthrestorationservice.org
- Global Partnership on Forest Landscape Restoration: www.unep-wcmc.org/forest/restoration/ globalpartnership
- Millennium Ecosystem Assessment: www.millenniumassessment.org
- Restoring the Earth: www.restore-earth.org
- Trees for Life: www.treesforlife.org
- World Conservation Union: www.iucn.org

NASA

A Restoration Partnership

In 2003 The Global Partnership on Forest Landscape Restoration was formed by the IUCN, World Wide Fund for Nature and the Forestry Commission of Great Britain, overseen by the United Nations Environment Programme, networking with governments, NGOs and communities to create a global effort for forest restoration.

The Partnership is working with farmers and villagers in Chiapas, Mexico, to restore degraded land: 1,500 acres of trees have been planted, and a trust fund has been set up as a clearinghouse for carbon credits. The restoration project improves the quality of life for villagers, providing forest goods, fruit, medicinal plants, fuelwood and saleable timber, while improving soil and preventing erosion.

In 2003 the Partnership, led by IUCN, held a workshop in Ghana, where 2.5 million acres of forest were lost to logging from 1990 to 2000. IUCN continues to work with the Forestry Research Institute of Ghana and the International Tropical Timber Organization, creating an action plan which has been embraced by a government that has committed itself to new policies of sustainable forest management, improved living standards and employment generation.

In 2006 the Partnership held a similar workshop in Argentina, aimed at creating a South American alliance for reforestation. Fifty participants from Argentina, Paraguay, Uruguay and Chile attended, analyzing case studies and establishing a forest restoration focus for each country.

93

Redefine the Role of the United Nations in Animal Welfare

For the health and future of all species, we need a global organization that governs the welfare of animals everywhere. From farm animals to endangered species, this organization would oversee a set of standards established by the global community and ensure the humane treatment and preservation of all species.

The United Nations

In 1945 following World War II, the United Nations (UN) was created to preserve peace with a mission of fostering "international cooperation and collective security." It has grown from 50 member nations in 1945 to 189 today, all of which have agreed to adopt the UN Charter as a treaty obligation while continuing their own national sovereignty.

> No such international agreement on animal welfare exists; the aim is for the United Nations to adopt an animal welfare declaration recognizing animals as sentient beings that feel pain, and should be protected from cruelty.
>
> — World Society for the Protection of Animals (WSPA)

Originally established to govern global security, the UN plays a lead role in many global issues, including peacekeeping, disarmament, social justice, equality for women and children, global health, sustainable development and environmental preservation.

Unfortunately, there is no UN body specifically concerned with animal welfare. There are some loosely specified terms in the UN's Food and Agriculture Organization that suggest animal welfare standards, but they lack any significant governance. Animals deserve much more than to be lumped together under food and agriculture. The United Nations Environmental Programme includes conservation but doesn't set standards for animal welfare or protection.

It's time for animals to be included; not hidden under the governance of an umbrella organization. Animals deserve their own charter and a governing body that sets clear guidelines and respects the sentience and basic rights of all non-human species. The new UN body would follow a set of guiding principles, such as those outlined by World Society for the Protection of Animals with its Universal Declaration for the Welfare of Animals (see Solution 100), which would:

Animals Matter to Me

At the WSPA's Biennial Symposium in London in 2006, 300 animal welfare groups gathered to launch the "Animals Matter to Me" petition, with a mission of collecting 10 million signatures worldwide to present to the United Nations in support of the WSPA's proposed Universal Declaration for the Welfare of Animals. Local and national animal welfare organizations in 142 countries are campaigning to reach the petition's goal, and five UN member nations (Costa Rica, Kenya, India, Czech Republic and the Philippines) have formed a steering group committed to taking the initiative forward to the UN.

This is the largest ever global animal welfare initiative. It is a huge milestone in our work to build a world free from cruelty and suffering for billions of animals.

— Major General Peter Davies,
Director General of WSPA

- Establish a global governmental vision for animal welfare based on an agreed set of principles.
- Demonstrate that animal welfare is recognized as an issue of importance by the United Nations family and the international community.
- Act as a catalyst for better animal welfare provisions worldwide.

- Animals Matter to Me: www.animalsmatter.org
- Food and Agriculture Organization of the United Nations: www.fao.org
- International Fund for Animal Welfare: www.ifaw.org
- Ramsar Convention on Wetlands: www.ramsar.org
- United Nations: www.un.org
- World Conservation Union: www.iucn.org

Following the Lead of Ramsar

The United Nations Convention on Wetlands of International Importance, created in Ramsar, Iran, is one of the most valuable tools the UN has to help animals. The Ramsar Convention is an international treaty that facilitates cooperation for the conservation of wetlands. Nearly 1600 sites worldwide have Ramsar status, protecting delicate wetland ecosystems for the thousands of species that live within them.

Conventions such as Ramsar create a model that directly benefits many species of animals. What is needed is a convention that benefits not just their home but also the animals themselves.

We need an international treaty that will protect the welfare of animals, whether they live in wetlands, mountains, barns, cages or our own backyards.

The first step is for the UN to draft a convention on the welfare of animals, and then arrange an international conference to establish a set of global agreements that can be applied to animal protection everywhere. The UN should also call for all member nations to introduce animal protection into their constitutions and charters (see Solution 51).

94

Restructure CITES to Ensure the Protection of Endangered Species

> Trade has been the foremost factor in the decimation of scores of species, from tigers to cod.
>
> — Richard Leakey,
> Kenya Wildlife Service

The Convention on International Trade in Endangered Species (CITES) is a global treaty that governs the trade in plants and animals; 168 nations have signed on and ratified the treaty. CITES is administered by a Secretariat based in Geneva that establishes a list of endangered and threatened species, as agreed upon by the member nations, and lays out a system of recommended trade restrictions. They also have a mandate to establish humane methods of transportation and handling, meeting every three years to discuss a variety of issues.

Created Globally, Enforced Nationally
By its voluntary nature, CITES can not police the treaty on a global level, so enforcement is left to individual nations. Each member nation creates its own CITES legislation and allocates responsibility to a government body. In the United States, CITES is implemented through the Endangered Species Act. To curb illegal trade between countries, member nations rely on

- Convention on International Trade in Endangered Species: www.cites.org
- EndangeredSpecie.com: www.endangeredspecie.com
- Government of Canada — Species at Risk: www.speciesatrisk.gc.ca
- TRAFFIC: www.traffic.org
- United States Endangered Species Act: www.fws.gov/Endangered/esa.html
- World Conservation Union: www.iucn.org

organizations such as Interpol to help enforce the treaty.

A Call for Transparency
CITES is well-intentioned in its protection of endangered species, but this is a treaty that is governed by commerce. The central purpose of the treaty is to protect endangered species to preserve them for future trade. This, unfortunately, results in a lot of less-than-transparent decisions between countries. Until recently, as few as 11 nations could demand a secret ballot to vote on proposals. However, a campaign is underway that a full third of the nations must be in agreement for a secret ballot. This would bring considerably more fairness to the table and improve standards for the animals involved.

Bringing Everyone to the Table
Non-governmental organizations (NGOs) and other interested parties are welcome to sit in on CITES meetings. Although they can't vote on proposals, their presence as observers is essential. Their knowledge and watchful eye on behalf of all species has added a very important aspect to the treaty that brings a sense of balance to the underlying theme of commerce. Despite the objections of countries who want to forbid observers from the meetings, every vote to do so has failed to gain enough support.

An Essential Alliance
CITES has been harshly criticized for its failure to truly protect endangered species involved in international trade. There have also been irate

reactions to the results of some CITES votes, such as the 2004 approval of trade in carved ivory from Namibia.

Nonetheless, we should not be too quick to condemn CITES for its inconsistencies. The organization plays a critical role, and animal welfare advocates must continue to work with member nations, not against them. The continued presence of NGOs at CITES meetings is vital, as well as the continued communication between nations. There is a pathway to a far more humane world, even one that perpetuates the international trade in animals. With greater transparency and constructive reform, CITES can serve as a global alliance based on ethics as well as commerce.

GALAPAGOS NETWORK/ECOVENTURA S.A

Watching Out for Elephants

Since 2002 CITES has been using two organizations to monitor the illegal trade of elephant products. Monitoring the Illegal Killing of Elephants (MIKE) and Elephant Trade Information System both study different aspects of the illegal trade and report their findings to CITES and the wildlife trade monitoring network, TRAFFIC. A 2004 report by MIKE showed the urgent need for greater elephant protection, reporting the annual illegal killing of 4,000 African elephants for use in both the illegal ivory and the bushmeat trades (see Solution 74).[1]

Seahorse fidelity fact — Seahorses are monogamous creatures, staying with one mate for their whole lives. If a seahorse dies (or is captured), its partner will often never mate again

CITES for Seahorses

In 2004 a new treaty came into effect under CITES to protect wild populations of seahorses. Seventy-seven countries are involved in the seahorse trade, capturing around 24 million seahorses annually. Most are sold to pet stores, while many are dried and shipped around the world for medicinal purposes (seahorses are believed to alleviate sexual dysfunction and other ailments). It's estimated that some 70 tons of dried seahorses are sold globally every year.[2] Under the new CITES protection, all 33 seahorse species will be protected from overfishing. The CITES agreement will not end the commercial trade in seahorses, but it will monitor it closely, following a conservation manual established by the World Wildlife Fund and the World Conservation Union that has been distributed to law enforcement officials in 165 countries.

95

Make Suffering in the Name of Fashion Illegal

In no other area is the suffering of animals more unnecessary than in the world of fashion. The fashion industry is responsible for a pitiful level of suffering and death among animals around the world, all in the name of vanity. A new consciousness needs to prevail, and global solutions must be found. And it is a global issue. A country can create laws to require the production of beauty products without the use of animals, but this can easily be circumvented by trade with countries that don't have such legislation. Countries must work together to create a global community that will no longer tolerate animal suffering in the name of fashion.

It's a slow process. A hundred years ago people thought that black people shouldn't have the rights of white people. And 30 years ago people thought that smoking was okay for you. It's a matter of becoming a more advanced society, and more caring individuals.

— Marc Bouwer, fashion designer who doesn't use fur or leather

A Fashionable Choice for Europe

The European Parliament has taken a huge step forward with its 2003 decision to ban the sale of virtually all animal-tested cosmetics within the European Union. This groundbreaking legislation, which will be fully in place by 2009, involves all member nations of the EU and is significant because it will also end the import of cosmetics that have been tested on animals in other countries. It is so far-reaching that it may force cosmetic companies everywhere to start using the readily available alternatives, instead of using animals in product testing.

Some critics of the new legislation in the EU say it doesn't go far enough. The legislation outlaws 11 of the 14 tests that are currently used in animal product testing, with a ten-year limit on the remaining 3 testing methods. It also allows for a two-year extension on the 3 testing methods beyond the ten-year limit. That means that it could be

US NATIONAL PARK SERVICE

- Beauty Without Cruelty: www.bwcsa.co.za
- Coalition to Abolish the Fur Trade: www.caft.org.uk
- Cows Are Cool (leather industry): www.cowsarecool.com
- European Alliance to End Animal Experiments: www.eceae.org
- European Public Health Alliance — cosmetics testing: www.epha.org/a/190
- Fur Free Alliance: www.infurmation.com

2011 before the legislation completely protects animals from being subjected to the cruel and unnecessary practice of cosmetic testing.
A whole lot of animals will suffer and die before 2011 rolls around.

Using the EU's Model
The European Parliament's precedent-setting legislation serves as a model that other legislation can be built around to make suffering in the name of fashion a thing of the past. The model could be extended to cover producers of leather, fur, wool, ivory and any other animal product that is used for fashion. No species should have to suffer or die for another species' fashion whims. We must work together to create a global UN Convention on Animal Rights, which will include the elimination of:

- Product testing on animals for the cosmetics industry.
- The use of leghold traps.
- The operation of fur farms.
- The import/export of animals killed solely for their fur, skins or other products for the fashion industry.
- The production and trade of cat and dog fur.

The legislation will also dictate that every product made from an animal source is labeled, including which species were used in its production.

Never before in history have alternatives to tradition been so readily accessible. It's time for the global community to embrace compassion and welcome fashionable alternatives. As Marc Bouwer said, "With leather, even more than fur, the technological alternative is so apparent that you can't even make an argument about it — the look and feel is there."

Global Furry Facts[1]

- Globally, 40 million animals are killed for their fur every year: 10,000 every day, 4,500 every hour.
- 30 million of these are farmed for their fur; the rest being caught in the wild.
- For those caught in the wild, many more non-target animals are dying in traps.
- 69 countries, including the entire European Union, have banned leghold traps.
- Britain banned the leghold trap over 30 years ago.
- 19 countries have banned all traps whatsoever.
- Britain and Austria have banned fur farming.
- Fox farming is illegal in Sweden and is being phased out in the Netherlands.
- 7 countries have banned the sale of cat and dog fur.

96

Unite to End Suffering in Factory Farms

Factory farms were designed to bring animals to market as quickly and cheaply as possible. Yet they invite a host of environmental, animal welfare and public health problems.
— Danielle Nierenberg, Worldwatch

The animal suffering and environmental contamination created by factory farms have become a global issue. With farm animals outnumbering humans three to one,[1] it's no longer just animal welfare groups and environmentalists campaigning for changes. Governments are funding scientists to look for solutions to the contamination and seriously depleted water reservoirs caused by factory farms, while writing legislation to govern the living conditions of farm animals (see Solution 62). Countries need to work together, writing global legislation that protects the welfare of animals and preserves the environment that factory farming is steadily eroding.

The First Step in Compassionate Farming
The European Union has become the first group of nations to make factory farming an international issue by banning the use of battery cages. This monumental legislation is another move by a region that is consistently showing leadership in animal welfare. As with most wide-ranging international decisions, the battery cage ban will take several years to take full effect, with the legislation being fully in place by 2012. While the laying hens of today won't be getting much of a break, after 2012 they'll be living in considerably more tolerable conditions.

A Coalition of Compassionate Farming
The first global conference on farm animal compassion took place in London, England, in March 2005. More than 600 delegates from 50 countries attended the Compassion in World Farming Trust (CIWF) conference which enjoyed global media coverage, drawing much attention to the cause of farm animals. The delegates heard from numerous scientists who have been studying the autonomy of farm animals, observing their social nature and the interaction between various animals. Consistently, they spoke of research showing that all farm animals feel pain, fear, pleasure and a wide range of other emotions. Their work touched the hearts of all those in attendance, as well as those observing from overseas who calling for a reform of farming practices on a global level.

CIWF was established in 1967 by dairy farmer Peter Roberts, because he

FARM SANCTUARY

and his wife, Anna, were becoming very disturbed by the intensive farming practices that were being developed in the 1960s. Roberts couldn't get the support of any government body, nor could he get leading animal welfare groups to pay any heed to the suffering of farm animals. So CIWF was born and raised from the Roberts' house and grew into an international farm animal welfare organization with offices in Ireland, France and Holland; representatives work in South Africa, Australia, New Zealand, China, Brazil, the Ukraine, Hungary, Poland, Romania, Slovakia and the Czech Republic. CIWF hosts major international conferences and initiates far-reaching campaigns to raise awareness about factory farming. The combined efforts of CIWF and international animal welfare and farming organizations are behind many of the EU's initiatives, and their conferences and campaigns have earned a great deal of respect from governments and farmers worldwide.

A Global Solution

Governments must work together to create global legislation by learning from organizations like CIWF, while working closely with farmers and listening to their concerns. Animal welfare groups need to partner with NGOs from other countries to create global solutions. From individuals and industry leaders to government policy-makers, cooperation is needed to create change. And change is what farm animals desperately need.

- Beyond Factory Farming Coalition: www.beyondfactoryfarming.org
- FactoryFarming.com: www.factoryfarming.com
- Farm Animal Reform Movement: www.farmusa.org
- Humane Farming Association: www.hfa.org

A Healthier World

A more compassionate existence for farm animals equals a healthier global community for all species. With concentrated animal feeding operations (the industry term for factory farms) producing over 40% of the world's meat, crowded and unhygienic conditions are providing the perfect incubator for diseases such as avian flu, mad cow disease and foot-and-mouth disease.[2] The connection between the growth of industrialized farming and the development of diseases is increasingly clear (see "Weird Science"). How we farm on land also affects the health of our oceans, since one-third of the total marine catch from our overfished oceans (see "The Deep Grey Sea" and "Five Solutions for Fishers") is converted to fish meal, two-thirds of which is used to fatten livestock for human consumption.[3]

97

Unite to Tackle Global Climate Change

The Age of Nations is past. The task before us now, if we would not perish, is to shake off our ancient prejudices, and build the Earth.

— Pierre Teilhard de Chardin

This book has already begun to describe what could be achieved to reduce the suffering of animals if the leaders of the world's nations sat down and worked together. Nowhere is this more true than with the daunting challenge of global climate change. The warnings are ominous in the extreme (see "The Ravages of Climate Change") and should serve to make every one of us sit up and take action. There are changes we can make as individuals, schools, cities, businesses and governments. A challenge so global in nature, however, demands that we work together as a world to craft shared solutions that can change the whole direction of our planet, away from fossil fuels, towards a more sustainable way of living that is in harmony with all creation.

- **The Kyoto Protocol on Climate Change** is a good beginning, because it commits its member countries to reduce their emissions. The US under George Bush refused to ratify the Treaty, but this may change under a new president. Whatever the skeptics say, it is a good treaty which enables the world to work together. India, China and other large developing nations need to join the Kyoto process soon and make formal commitments to reduce their emissions.

- **A Global Solar Treaty** would do wonders to spread the use of solar electricity. Solar energy works: the only drawback is the price. In 2007, if you put a 2 kilowatt system on your roof at an unsubsidized price, it would cost you $20,000. The price is determined by the scale of production. If every nation in the developed world agreed that starting in 2012, every new house would include a 2 kW solar system on its roof, the global demand would be so great that the price would fall to $2 a watt, kick-starting the widespread use of solar energy.

- **A Global Energy Efficiency Treaty** could achieve a similar result by requiring that all new fridges, cookers and washers (etc.) were built to the highest standard of energy efficiency, while driving down the price of such appliances.

- **A Global Plug-In Hybrids Treaty** could enable cities, businesses and governments around the world to make advance purchasing commitments for the remarkable Plug-In Hybrid Electric Vehicle, enabling manufacturers to ramp up to mass production and reduce the price.

- **A Global Carbon Tax** on international flights (and other carbon sources). With 2 billion people taking flights every year, contributing enormously to the problems of

Some key climate change sites:
- BBC: www.bbc.co.uk/climate
- Greenpeace: www.greenpeace.org/~climate
- New Scientist: www.newscientist.com/channel/earth/climate-change
- World Wide Fund for Nature: www.panda.org/climate

C. CLARK/NOAA/OAR/ERL/NATIONAL SEVERE STORMS LABORATORY

climate change, a carbon tax of $20 per flight would generate $40 billion a year, which could be used to help us move more rapidly into a post-carbon world.

- **A Global Sustainable Forestry Treaty**. If all nations agreed to phase in nationwide sustainable forestry practices by 2025, certified by the Forest Stewardship Council, it would enable us to stop the destruction of the world's forests, which contributes so much both to the loss of habitat for millions of plants and animals and to global climate change.

- **A Global Organic Farming Treaty**. Similarly, if all nations agreed to move to 100% organic agriculture by 2025, it would stop the destruction of biodiversity on and around farmland and help restore the health of farm animals, while reducing the major impact that farming has on global climate change.

- **A Global "F" Gas Phase-Out Treaty**. These little-known industrial gases (HFCs, HCFCs, PFC, SF6) are responsible for 10% to 12% of the climate change problem. Right now, even though they are included in the Kyoto treaty, they are being allowed to drift, both in people's minds and in the atmosphere.

As a world, we need to have far more confidence in our ability to cooperate to solve our problems. If these seem like big dreams, it is only because we have allowed our vision to grow small under the constant bickering and competition that goes on between nations.

It is especially up to people in the US to relinquish their belief that they are entitled to dominate the world, whether by trade or by military force. The US has refused to sign many international treaties, in spite of the urgent desire by many Americans to play a more constructive, cooperative role. Global climate change can *only* be solved if we all work together as one world.

The polar bears have no voice that can ask for this. Nor do the elephants, or the million other species which face extinction if we do not act. It is up to *us*.

98

Unite to Preserve our Oceans and Fisheries

We have to understand how close to extinction some of these populations really are. And we must act now, before they have reached the point of no return.
— Ransom Myers, fisheries biologist, Dalhousie University in Halifax, Nova Scotia

No issue is more in need of a global solution than the preservation of our oceans. Overfishing, habitat destruction and chronic pollution from agriculture, sewage, industry and oil spills are rapidly turning our international waters into environmental dumping grounds unfit for life for any species. Marine conservation, fisheries and ocean waste-disposal practices are in desperate need of an international overhaul and solutions that we can work on together as a global community.

A Convention That Works

Countries everywhere, both coastal and landlocked, need to work together to create effective global legislation to protect oceans and preserve their fisheries. Countries must unite behind a new United Nations Convention with meaningful guidelines for ocean conservation.

In 1994 the United Nations Convention on the Law of the Sea (LOS) was agreed to by nations around the world and heralded by the UN as "the most important international achievement since the approval of its Charter in 1945." LOS, which has been ratified by 145 countries with a jurisdiction that covers 72% of the planet's surface, has the potential to preserve life for millions of species, many of which have never been seen by human eyes. Sadly, after more than a decade in existence, LOS has failed to slow the destruction of the world's oceans, being hindered by the United States' refusal to ratify the agreement and by the conflict between member nations over conservation proposals. To be effective, LOS needs an overhaul, with all member nations agreeing to measures such as bycatch limits, a moratorium on bottom trawling and an end to offshore fish farming (see "5 Solutions for Fishers").

In 2002, at the UN's Johannesburg World Summit on Sustainable Development, 192 nations called on the global community to preserve its oceans and restore fisheries stocks. The delegates agreed to stop destructive fishing practices, establish protected marine areas and networks by 2012 and restore fish stocks, where possible, to levels that can be sustainably harvested by no later than 2015. Although the agreement is promising, critics say the use of "where possible" waters it down and may be too little, too late, with 70% of commercially important fish stocks around the globe already threatened with extinction.[1]

Sanctuary in the Mediterranean

Countries around the Mediterranean Sea have accepted the urgent need to preserve its warm waters, where hundreds of animal and plant species are being threatened with extinction by the heavy impact of tourism.

Italy, France and Monaco have agreed to work with the World Wildlife Fund (WWF) to manage a large marine sanctuary in the northwestern Mediterranean between Sardinia, the Cote d'Azur and the Italian Ligurian coast. The new reserve is large, covering 84,000 kilometers, and is home to 2,000 whales and 40,000 dolphins during the summer months. This is the first marine protected area in the northern hemisphere to include international waters and sets a precedent for other countries to work together to create global solutions.

A Global Proposal from New Zealand

In 2006 New Zealand proposed new international trade rules to stop governments paying massive subsidies to fishers to exploit the world's already overfished oceans. The proposal, part of New Zealand's ongoing campaign for greater sustainability of the world's marine resources, was presented at the World Trade Organization in Geneva to convince the world's wealthiest nations that they play a critical role in the global fisheries crisis. New Zealand's trade minister points out that industrialized nations pay out between $15 billion and $20 billion in subsidies annually,[2] allowing overfishing to continue at unsustainable levels. The proposal prohibits all forms of fishery subsidies, with some flexibility for less-developed nations.

Since 1950, with the onset of industrialized fisheries, we have rapidly reduced the resource base to less than 10%. Not just in some areas — but for entire communities of these large fish species from the tropics to the poles.

— Ransom Myers

- IUCN Global Marine Programme: www.iucn.org/themes/marine
- International Marine Mammal Association: www.imma.org
- Marine Conservation Society: www.mcsuk.org
- Mediterranean Dolphin Conservation: www.delphismdc.org
- National Coalition for Marine Conservation: www.savethefish.org
- Nature Conservancy's Global Marine Conservation Initiative: www.nature.org/initiatives/marine

SHEL NEUFELD/WILDARTPHOTOGRAPHY.COM

99

Practise Reverence for Life

It was unreasonable to me ... even before I had gone to school, that in my evening devotions I should pray only for people.

— Albert Schweitzer

Albert Schweitzer was the son of a Lutheran minister, and even as a small child in the 1880s, he felt a strong connection to all living creatures. After his mother had prayed with him and kissed him goodnight, he would secretly add his own prayer: "Dear God, guard and bless everything that breathes. Keep them from all evil and let them sleep in peace."

Schweitzer became a musical prodigy and was an accomplished pianist while still a child,

yet he followed his father's path and studied theology and philosophy, earning his Doctorate at Strasbourg University in Germany. In 1913 he established a missionary hospital in French Equatorial Africa (Gabon), which cared for 2,000 patients in its first year. It was there that Dr. Schweitzer spent most of his life and developed his ethic of Reverence for Life. Asked to lecture on the spiritual/ethical relationship of the universe, he would describe it as: "Reverence for Life gives us something more profound and mightier than the idea of humanism. It includes *all living beings* [his emphasis]. We reject the idea that man is 'Master' of other creatures, 'Lord' above all others. We must realize that all life is valuable, and that we are united to all life. By ethical conduct toward all creatures, we enter into a spiritual relationship with the Universe."[1]

Schweitzer is best known for a lifetime of ministering to people in the Lambarene hospital, receiving the Nobel Peace Prize in 1952 and from then until his death in 1965, campaigning against nuclear weapons with Albert Einstein and Bertrand Russell. In his autobiography, he wrote at length about caring for the many animals that crossed his path. The Albert Schweitzer Society is still an active force today, ministering to people in 25 countries, and is chaired by Rhena Schweitzer Miller, who carries on her father's message of practising Reverence for Life.

All God's Creatures

In 2006 God's Creatures Ministry hosted the Concern for All God's Creatures Conference at

Caldwell College in New Jersey. The event was open to people of all faiths and included animal welfare speakers, educational resources, a vegan luncheon and musical entertainment, promoting the connection between spirituality and animal advocacy.

The Christian God's Creatures Ministry has many initiatives to help animals, including fundraising hikes and a charity dinner to raise money for the Association of Veterinarians for Animal Rights volunteers who traveled to India to help animals that were stranded by the Tsunami in December 2004.

Circle of Compassion
The Worldwide Prayer Circle for Animals (PCA) is a non-denominational circle of people devoted to using action and the power of prayer to help animals on a global scale. Its vision is to create an energy field of compassion and caring for all beings of Earth, while elevating global consciousness to the awareness that all life is sacred and interconnected. PCA honors the prayer traditions of all religions and encourages participants to use whatever form of prayer or focused thought that is comfortable to them. There is no need to formally join PCA – just the participation in an intentional prayer for the animals at the same time every day: "Compassion encircles the Earth for all beings."

PCA was created by Circle of Compassion, a Kansas-based group co-founded by Judy Carman, author of *Peace to All Beings: Veggie Soup for the Chicken's Soul*, a 320-page collection of inspiring prayers for animals, people and the environment.

Prayer ... properly understood, and applied, is the most potent instrument of action.
— Mahatma Gandhi

Living in Ahimsa

Ahimsa, the principle of nonviolence, is an important doctrine in Hinduism, Jainism and Buddhism, signifying peace and reverence for all sentient beings. The term was first mentioned in Indian philosophy dating back to 800 BCE, in the Hindu Upanishads scriptures, and was brought to the West by Mahatma Gandhi, who wrote: "Ahimsa is the highest duty. Even if we cannot practise it in full, we must try to understand its spirit and refrain as far as humanly possible from violence."[2]

- Albert Schweitzer Society: www.globalhealthaction.org/aboutschweitzer.html
- All Creatures: www.all-creatures.org
- Catholic Concern for Animals: www.catholic-animals.org
- Christian Vegetarian Association: www.christianveg.com
- Jewish Veg: www.jewishveg.com
- Islamic Concern: www.islamicconcern.com
- Worldwide Prayer Circle for Animals: www.circleofcompassion.org

100

Create a Global Effort Around Animal Awareness

To my mind, the life of a lamb is no less precious than that of a human being.

— Mahatma Gandhi

We can act as individuals by the small choices we make every day and by sharing our concerns with others. We can do it in our classrooms by teaching compassion for animals. We can do it in our boardrooms by choosing animal-free products. We can do it on our farms by practising humane animal husbandry. We can do it at sea by treating marine life with respect and dignity. We can do it in our government offices by creating effective animal welfare legislation.

These are all independent solutions that work for the greater good of animals. Yet we need to take a giant step forward from there, actually working together to create something global. Then we'll all be living as a compassionate global community.

A World of Protection for Animals

There are several well-established international action groups that provide excellent models to work from in creating this global effort around

Ethan Smith

animal awareness; none more so than the World Society for the Protection of Animals (WSPA).

WSPA is the world's largest federation of animal welfare societies, with over 500 member organizations from more than 100 countries. At its conception in1953, campaigns were limited to helping animals in the UK and the United States. In the 1980s, it added field offices around the world and greatly increased the range of projects.

WSPA has introduced animal welfare programs into regions where there were none. They have successfully created humane slaughter methods for livestock in developing nations. They have helped communities to assist stray animal populations. They support the creation of new animal protection groups and have established the WSPA Member Society Network, which involves 600 animal protection organizations from 140 countries. They have brought emergency equipment, supplies and volunteers to disaster relief projects from earthquakes to oil spills. Their emergency relief methods have become so successful that they have been used as a model by many countries in dealing with disasters.

They have also created high-profile campaigns that have brought attention to many of the world's most pressing issues. In 1985 they took responsibility for the International Council against Bullfighting and have been leading a successful charge against that tradition ever since. They launched a No Fur campaign in 1988 that contributed in a huge way to consumer consciousness. They have worked to help many individual species, assisting in the creation of nature preserves. They have set the

WSPA

WSPA disaster relief team at work.

- Animal Defenders International:
  www.ad-international.org
- Global Conference on Animal Welfare:
  www.oie.int/eng/Welfare_2004/home.htm
- World Animal Net: www.worldanimal.net
- World Society for the Protection of Animals:
  www.wspa-international.org
- WSPA Universal Declaration for the Welfare of Animals:
  www.wspa-usa.org/pages/28_universal_declaration.cfm

Get Involved

To connect your group with the Member Society Network, contact WSPA's offices:

International (UK)	wspa@wspa.org.uk
Africa	enquiries@wspaafrica.org
Asia	call +66 2 513 0475
Australia	wspa@wspa.org.au
Brazil	wspabrzl@iis.com.br
Canada	wspa@wspa.ca
Columbia	wspa@wspa.org.co
Costa Rica	wspacr@racsa.co.cr
Denmark	info@wspa.dk
Germany	info@wspa.de
Netherlands	info@wspa.nl
New Zealand	wspa@wspa.org.nz
United States	wspa@wspausa.com

standard for pet care in many parts of the world, and their Pet Respect Program has raised awareness for, and assisted, stray dogs and cats in dozens of countries, including their mobile veterinary clinics throughout Latin America.

The Importance of a Global Effort

What is so significant about WSPA is that they have never acted alone. They are a vast, successful network, built up over time by cooperation with like-minded organizations. They have held the welfare of animals in their hearts and fearlessly asked for the cooperation of individuals, action groups, schools, businesses and governments to help save the lives of animals and raise awareness worldwide. And they've gotten that help. Why? Because, deep inside, we all have compassion to tap into, and it feels so good to be part of a global movement.

A New Declaration for a New Century

WSPA marked the start of the 21st century by launching its biggest campaign ever: the Universal Declaration for the Welfare of Animals, which was unveiled at the Animals

2000 World Conference and has been ratified by 270 animal welfare organizations in 78 countries. The goal of the Declaration is to secure international legal recognition for the principles of animal welfare and have the United Nations officially create a Convention on Animal Welfare. The Declaration is currently in the hands of several governments, where it is being considered for formal presentation to the United Nation's Economic and Social Council.

101

Be a Solution to Animal Suffering

Our task must be to free ourselves from this prison by widening our circle of compassion to embrace all living creatures and the whole of nature in its beauty.

— Albert Einstein

In December 2005 a research team organized by Conservation International and the Indonesian Institute of Science was trekking through northwestern New Guinea when they discovered something miraculous: deep in the Foja Mountains they found a jungle teeming with life — dozens of new species of animals and plants in a vibrant paradise, far from civilization of any kind. "It's beautiful, untouched, unpopulated forest. There's no evidence of human impact or presence up in these mountains," said Dr. Bruce Beehler, co-leader of the group. The jungle is so remote that the research team had to be dropped into the region by helicopter. Even the local indigenous people, the Kwerba and Papasenas who accompanied the research team on their journey, were astonished at the beauty and isolation of the jungle. Not

even in the stories of their ancestors was there any mention of the place. The jungle lies within a protected zone and is, Dr. Beehler believes, secure at least in the short term, supported by the stewardship of the surrounding communities.

Living in Awe

Imagine yourself in this jungle. Let your senses be tickled by the moistness, the birdsongs and the depth of life around you. Discover life for the first time. As precious as this newly discovered paradise in New Guinea is, it draws from the very same source of life that you do. The same air, the same sun, the same watery planet connecting us to one another in the complex dance of life. The same breath that sustains this tropical paradise also sustains a newborn lamb. The same breath sustains you.

Reconnecting to Life

Animal awareness begins when we see beyond the myth of separation. Animals do not exist as one entity and us as another. Rather we are all living beings, each of us perfectly unique for our own species and inexorably connected to each other through the air we breathe. Let go of separation, embrace connection wholeheartedly and you will have entered into a world of animal awareness; a world in which the suffering of any species hurts and cries out for love.

Being a Solution

How do you move beyond finding solutions to actually being a solution? The author and

ETHAN SMITH

humane educator Zoe Weil suggested: "Be a representative of a club worth joining." This means living your life guided by your principles, letting your actions reflect the "you" that you want the rest of the world to see. Hope, compassion and action can accomplish just about everything. Make your life an exciting place to visit, and people will be drawn to you and your cause.

Learn from Animals

Follow the movements of a cat for a day. Study a songbird and gaze into the big, dark eyes of a cow. To be a voice for animals, you need to know their language. You need to listen to them, even in their silence. What is it that makes your heart sing? What is it that makes your heart break? What are you willing to do to create a more compassionate world?

Closer to the Edge

Come on over and take a look into the world of compassion. Look at the people of Gaviotas, Columbia, living harmoniously and sustainably in a war-ravaged land. And there's a rescue team assisting starving alley cats. There's a grocer proudly placing cage-free labels on his organic eggs. There's a woman releasing a mouse from a humane trap into the safety of the forest. There's a politician lobbying for a progressive animal welfare bill. It's all happening, but you have to step right up to the edge to see it. Look, there's a forest, bursting with life. Would you believe its trees were once carefully harvested?

And look over there. There's a fourth-grade class cleaning up a riverbank.

We're going to leave you with this. It's time for us to move on. Thank you for coming this far, and we wish you well on your journey. From here at the edge, your voice can be heard for miles.

WSPA

Notes

Introduction

A CALL TO COMPASSIONATE ARMS

1. Gary Francione's proposal for animal rights is explored in depth in "One Right for All," *New Scientist*, Oct. 8, 2005.
2. *Five Kingdoms of Life*. Accessed Jan. 26, 2007 from waynesword.palomar.edu/trfeb98.htm.
3. *Welcome to the Rainforest*. Accessed Jan. 26, 2007 from rain-tree.com/facts.htm.

PAWS TO REFLECT

1. The chronology is a compilation of information drawn from the following primary sources, as well as others: *BBC News*. "The Evolution of Man." Accessed Jan. 26, 2007from bbc.co.uk/science/cavemen/chronology/contentpage2.shtml; International Museum of the Horse. Accessed Jan. 26, 2007 from imh.org/imh/kyhpl1a.html; Share the World. Accessed Jan. 26, 2007 from sharetheworld.com/ctcm-sheet1.html; Joanne Bower. *Treatment of Animals in Agriculture*. Renaissance Universal. Accessed Jan. 26, 2007 from ru.org/arttreat.html; Go Veg.com. *Early Human Evolution*. Accessed Jan. 26, 2007 from goveg.com/naturalhumandiet_evolution.asp; Piers Beirne. *The Law Is an Ass*. Society & Animals Forum. Accessed Jan. 26, 2007 from psyeta.org/sa/sa2.1/beirne.html.
2. Modern day animal mortality numbers are from Howard Lyman, the Mad Cowboy. Accessed Jan. 26, 2007 from madcowboy.com/01_FactsAR.000.html.
3. Vegetarian Resource Group, citing Harris Interactive poll. Accessed Jan. 26, 2007 from vrg.org/journal/vj2003issue3/vj2003issue3poll.htm.

SENTIENCE AND SENSIBILITY

1. North American Commission for Environmental Cooperation. *The State of the Environment*. Accessed Jan. 26, 2007 from cec.org/soe.
2. Dr. Jane Goodall and Steven M. Wise. "Presentation to the Senior Lawyers Division of the American Bar Association." Center for the Expansion of Fundamental Rights. Accessed Jan. 26, 2007 from cefr.org/goodall_wise_pres_frame.htm.
3. Animal Sentience. Accessed Jan. 26, 2007 from ciwf.org.uk/sentience.

SUFFERING ON OUR PLATES

1. Danielle Nierenberg. *Happier Meals: Rethinking the Global Meat Industry*. Worldwatch Institute, 2005.
2. Howard Lyman, the Mad Cowboy. Accessed Jan. 26, 2007 from madcowboy.com/01_FactsAR.000.html.
3. Ibid.
4. Meat consumption table from Solution 5, Canadian and US average.
5. Fiorella Gardella. Seminar on global sustainability. University of Southern California, Irvine, 1999. Accessed Jan. 26, 2007 from darwin.bio.uci.edu/%7Esustain/global/sensem/MeatIndustry.html.
6. The Green Life. Eat Sustainable. Accessed Jan. 27, 2007 from thegreenlife.com/eat_sustainable.html.
7. Jeremy Rifkin. "There's a Bone to Pick with Meat Eaters." *LA Times*, May 27, 2002. Accessed Jan. 27, 2007 from upc-online.org/environment/020527latimes_bone.html.
8. Timothy Jones. *Using Contemporary Archeology and Applied Anthropology to Understand Food Loss in the American Food System*. University of Arizona. 2005. Accessed Jan. 27, 2007 from community-compost.org/info/usafood.pdf.

FURY OVER FACTORIES

1. Danielle Nierenberg. *Happier Meals: Rethinking the Global Meat Industry*. Worldwatch Institute, 2005.
2. Ibid.

3. UN Food and Agriculture Association. *The Role of Transnational Corporations*. Accessed Jan. 27, 2007 from fao.org/DOCREP/005/Y4671E/y4671e0e.htm.
4. "How Foul Is Fowl?" *McDougall Wellness Center Newsletter*, Feb. 2006. Accessed Jan. 27, 2007 from drmcdougall.com/debate.html.
5. See Note 1.

DECEPTIONS OF DAIRY

1. Dawn Watch. *Animals As Food*. Accessed Jan. 27, 2007 dawn-watch.com/dairy.htm.
2. PETA. *Milk: A Cruel and Unhealthy Product*. Accessed Jan. 27, 2007 from peta.org/mc/factsheet_display.asp?ID=98.
3. No Veal.org. Accessed Jan. 27, 2007 from noveal.org.
4. American Gastroenterological Association. Guidelines for the evaluation of food allergies. Accessed Jan. 27, 2007 from guideline.gov/summary/summary.aspx?ss=15&doc_id=3059&nbr=2285.
5. "Lactose Intolerance Linked to Ancestral Environment." *Science Daily*, June 2, 2005. Accessed Jan. 27, 2007 from sci-encedaily.com/releases/2005/06/050602012109.htm.
6. Melanie Fridl Ross. *UF Researchers Cite Possible Link Between Autism, Schizophrenia and Diet*. University of Florida, 1999. Accessed Jan. 27, 2007 from napa.ufl.edu/99news/autism.htm.

WEIRD SCIENCE

1. John Stauber. "Feeding Cows to Cows." *Common Dreams Newscenter*, Dec. 17, 2004. Accessed Jan. 27, 2007 from common-dreams.org/views04/1217-27.htm.
2. Ibid.
3. Ibid.
4. People and Planet. *Avian Flu*. Accessed Jan. 27, 2007 from peopleandplanet.net/doc.php?id=2539.
5. Ibid.
6. International Forum on Globalization. *Fast Facts on the Corporate Consolidation of Industrialized Agriculture*. Accessed Jan. 27, 2007 from ifg.org/pdf/indust_ag-fas=_facts_consol.pdf.
7. Ibid.
8. See Note 1.
9. *Facts About Avian Influenza*. Accessed Jan. 27, 2007 from iwar.org.uk/news-archive/2005/03-18-4.htm.
10. *Facts about Foot and Mouth Disease*. Accessed Jan. 27, 2007 from ag.ndsu.nodak.edu/aginfo/dairy/dairyext/FAQs/faq14.htm.
11. GoVeg.com. *Pollution*. Accessed Jan. 27, 2007 from goveg.com/environment-pollution.asp.
12. Organic Consumers Association. *Virulent Bacteria Widespread in US Meat*. Accessed Jan. 27, 2007 from organicconsumers.org/toxic/virulentpoultry.cfm.
13. Janet Raloff. "Retail Meats Host Drug-Resistant Bacteria." *Science Daily*. Oct. 20, 2001. Accessed Jan. 27, 2007 from sciencenews.org/articles/20011020/fob5.asp.
14. Ibid.

MEANWHILE, BACK AT THE FAMILY FARM

1. Peter M. Rosset. "Food First." *The Multiple Functions and Benefits of Small Farm Agriculture*. Accessed Jan. 28, 2007 from food-first.org/pubs/policybs/pb4.html.
2. Third World Traveler. *Losing the Farm*. Accessed Jan. 28, 2007 from thirdworldtraveler.com/Third_World/Losing_Farm.html.
3. World Hunger Year. Food Security Learning Center. Accessed Jan. 28, 2007 from worldhungeryear.org/fslc/faqs2/ria_600.asp?section=9&click=1#2.
4. *Farm Aid*. Accessed Jan. 28, 2007 from farmaid.org; Sustainable Table. Accessed Jan. 28, 2007 from sustainabletable.org/issues/familyfarms.

A Very Fishy Tale

1. Animal Aid. *The Fish Business*. Accessed Jan. 28, 2007 from animalaid.org.uk/campaign/vegan/fish01.htm.
2. Ibid.
3. Janet Larsen. Other Fish in the Sea, But for How Long? People and Planet. Peopleandplanet.net, July 18, 2003. Accessed Jan. 28, 2007 from peopleandplanet.net/doc.php?id=2017.
4. Ibid.
5. Ibid.
6. Fred Pearce. "No More Seafood by 2050?" *New Scientist*, Nov. 02, 2006. Accessed Jan. 28, 2007 from newscientist.com/article.ns?id=dn10433&feedId=online-news_rss20
7. See Note 3.
8. Western Canada Wilderness Committee. Accessed Jan. 28, 2007 from wildernesscommittee.org/campaigns/marine/policy/fish_farms.
9. WCWC. *Global Impact of Salmon Farms*. Accessed Jan. 28, 2007 from wildernesscommittee.org/campaigns/marine/policy/fish_farms/reports/Vol24No07/facts.
10. University at Albany. Institute for Health and the Environment. Accessed Jan. 28, 2007 from albany.edu/ihe/salmonstudy/background.html, with metric tones converted to US short tons.

Hunting: Subsistence vs. Sport

1. *Outdoor Illinois*, citing 2001 statistics. Accessed Jan. 28, 2007 from lib.niu.edu/ipo/2002/oi0212tc.html.
2. Gerhard Damm. Africa Conservation Forums. Accessed Jan. 28, 2007 from africanconservation.org/dcforum/DCForumID21/44.html.
3. As of 2005. HSUS. Accessed Jan. 28, 2007 from hsus.org/wildlife/wildlife_news/pay_per_view_slaughter.html.
4. HSUS. Accessed Jan. 28, 2007 from hsus.org/wildlife/issues_facing_wildlife/wildlife_trade/bushmeat.html.

Laboratory Labyrinth

1. Physicians Committee for Responsible Medicine. Accessed Jan. 28, 2007 from pcrm.org/resch/PDFs/ae_coelem.pdf.
2. Karen Dawn. *Dawnwatch*. Accessed Jan. 28, 2007 from dawnwatch.com/animal_testing.htm.
3. Michael Budkie. *The Rising Tide of Animal Experimentation*. All Creatures. Citing information from the United States Department of Agriculture for the year 2002. Accessed Jan. 28, 2007 from all-creatures.org/wlalw/report-rt-ns.html.

The Price of Entertainment

1. Captive Wild Animal Protection Coalition. Accessed Jan. 29, 2007 from cwapc.org/news/faq.html.
2. Bill Samuels. *Exotics As Pets*. ASPCA. Accessed Jan. 29, 2007 from aspca.org/site/PageServer?pagename=edu_resources_exotics. Ebola reference is from CWAPC. Accessed Jan. 29, 2007 from cwapc.org/education/API_3_Reasons.html.
3. Ibid.
4. Brian Handwerk. "Big Cats Kept as Pets Across US Despite Risk." *National Geographic News* [online], Oct. 9, 2003. Accessed Jan. 29, 2007 from news.nationalgeographic.com/news/2002/08/0816_020816_EXPLcats.html. The exact numbers are impossible to establish as most private ownership of tigers is unreported.
5. Ownership estimates are from CWAPC. Accessed Jan. 29, 2007 from cwapc.org/education/download/cwapc_factsheets1.pdf. Monkey estimates are from *National Geographic*, Sept. 2003, subtracting CWAPC's great ape estimate from total primate estimate. Industry value figure is from Richard Farinato, *The Whims and Dangers of the Exotic Pet Market*, Humane Society of the United States. Accessed Jan. 29, 2007 from hsus.org/wildlife/issues_facing_wildlife/should_wild_animals_be_kept_as_pets/the_whims_and_dangers_of_the_exotic_pets_market.html.

From Pets to Companions

1. New Leash on Life. Accessed Jan. 29, 2007 from newleash.org/petoverpopulation.asp.
2. Lucy Middleton. "Me and My Pet." *New Scientist*, June 4, 2005.
3. Furry Friends. Accessed Jan. 29, 2007 from furryfriendsnkh.org.
4. Petroglyphs. Accessed Jan. 29, 2007 from petroglyphsnm.org.
5. See Note 2 for US, Australia and UK stats. Canadian stat is from the Farley Foundation. Accessed Jan. 29, 2007 from farleyfoundation.org. All figures are in US dollars, and cost per person is based on 2006 national populations.

A Day in the Life of a Puppy Mill

1. HSUS. *Get the Facts on Puppy Mills*. Accessed Jan. 29, 2007 from hsus.org/pets/issues_affecting_our_pets/get_the_facts_on_puppy_mills/index.html.
2. Ibid.

Beauty is Only Skin Deep

1. Fur Free Alliance. Accessed Jan. 29, 2007 from infurmation.com/facts.php.
2. Coalition to Abolish the Fur Trade. Accessed Jan. 29, 2007 from caft.org.uk/factsheets/mink-impact.html.
3. Furisdead.com. Accessed Jan. 29, 2007 from furisdead.com/indians.asp.
4. All figures are from PETA. Accessed Jan. 29, 2007 from shedyourskin.com/facts.aspx and peta.org/mc/factsheet_display.asp?ID=58; except for the kangaroo figure which comes from *Wired Magazine* [online], June 3, 2002. Accessed Jan. 29, 2007 from wired.com/wired/archive/10.06/start.html?pg=9.

Wasting Their Habitat

1. WWF. Species Loss in Wetlands. Citing 2003 data. Accessed Jan. 29, 2007 from panda.org/news_facts/newsroom/index.cfm?uNewsID=7343&uLangID=1.
2. EPA advisory. Accessed Jan. 29, 2007 from epa.gov/waterscience/fishadvice/advice.html.
3. United Nations Earthwatch. Accessed Jan. 29, 2007 from earthwatch.unep.net/emergingissues/forests/forestloss.php.
4. Janet Larsen. The Sixth Great Extinction. Earth Policy Institute, citing IUCN data. Accessed Jan. 29, 2007 from earth-policy.org/Updates/Update35.htm.
5. Environment Canada. Accessed Jan. 29, 2007 from ec.gc.ca/cleanair-airpur/Wildlife-WS945F2849-1_En.htm.
6. Mysteries of Migration. Accessed Jan. 29, 2007 from naturia.per.sg/buloh/birds/migration.htm.
7. Environment Canada. Accessed Jan. 29, 2007 from on.ec.gc.ca/wildlife/acidrain/ar-intro-e.html.
8. Richard Black. "More Species Slide to Extinction." BBC News online, May 1, 2006. Accessed Jan. 29, 2007 from news.bbc.co.uk/2/hi/science/nature/4963526.stm.
9. Richard Black. "World Needs New Wildlife Body." BBC News online, July 20, 2006. Accessed Jan. 29, 2007 from news.bbc.co.uk/2/hi/science/nature/5196008.stm. As of 2006, the experts were still lobbying for support of the panel from international governments.
10. People and Planet. Accessed Jan. 29, 2007 from peopleandplanet.net/doc.php?id=2571.

The Ravages of Climate Change

1. Roger Harriban. "Top Scientist's Fears for Climate." BBC News, Aug. 31, 2006. Accessed Jan. 29, 2007 from news.bbc.co.uk/1/hi/sci/tech/5303574.stm.
2. Michael McCarthy. "The Century of Drought" Independent (UK), Oct. 4, 2006.

3. Chris D. Thomas et al. "Extinction Risk from Climate Change." Nature, 427, pp. 145-148, Jan.8, 2004.
4. Paul Brown. "Drought Threatens Amazon Basin." Guardian, July 17, 2006.
5. Stephen Leckie. "Global Warming: The Inconvenient Truth About Diet." Accessed Jan. 29, 2007 from veg.ca/content/view/136/111.

THE DEEP GREY SEA
1. Marine Conservation Society. Accessed Jan. 29, 2007 from mcsuk.org/mcsaction/pollution/chemicals.
2. Ibid.
3. Ibid. Accessed Jan. 29, 2007 from mcsuk.org/mcsaction/pollution/nutrients.
4. Alaska Marine Conservation Council. Accessed Jan. 29, 2007 from akmarine.org/ourwork/fact-trawl.shtml.
5. Ibid.
6. Marine Conservation Society. Accessed Jan. 29, 2007 from mcsuk.org/mcsaction/pollution/litter.

CETACEANS: OUR TEACHERS, OUR ELDERS
1. "Japan Leads Whaling Nations to Symbolic Victory." Taipei Times (online), June 20, 2006. Accessed Jan. 29, 2007 from taipeitimes.com/News/world/archives/2006/06/20/2003314606.
2. Earth Island. Accessed Jan. 29, 2007 from earthis-land.org/immp/eins54_final.pdf.
3. Richard Black. Last Chance for China's Dolphin. BBC News online. Accessed Jan. 29, 2007 from news.bbc.co.uk/2/hi/science/nature/5122074.stm.
4. Cetacean Bycatch Resource Center. Accessed Jan. 29, 2007 from cetaceanbycatch.org.
5. Robert McClure. "Dead Orca Is a Red Alert." Seattle PI online, May 7, 2002. Accessed Jan. 29, 2007 from seat-tlepi.nwsource.com/local/69418_whale07.shtml.
6. Ibid.
7. IUCN Redlist, as of 2006. Accessed Jan. 29, 2007 from iucnredlist.org.

ANIMALS AND FAITH
1. "Animal Welfare Takes on Religion." BBC News online. Accessed Jan. 29, 2007 from news.bbc.co.uk/1/hi/uk/3590731.stm.
2. Piers Beirne. "The Law Is an Ass." Society & Animals Forum. Accessed Jan. 29, 2007 from psyeta.org/sa/sa2.1/beirne.html.

ANIMALS IN THE BOARDROOM
1. Richard Steiner. 1% Earth Profits Fund. University of Alaska. 2005. IUCN. Accessed Jan. 29, 2007 from iucn.org/themes/ceesp/Wkg_grp/Seaprise/Ref%205%20Earth%20Profits%20Fund.doc.
2. Monsanto's history is drawn from the following sources: Jule Klotter. A History of Monsanto. The Light Party. Accessed Jan. 29, 2007 from lightparty.com/Health/HistoryOfMonsanto.html; Monsanto Watch. Monsanto's Sordid History. From the Center for Food Safety. Accessed Jan. 29, 2007 from monsantowatch.org/index.php?page=none; Liane Casten. "Seeds of Judgement." Conscious Choice, Jan. 2004. Accessed Jan. 29, 2007 from consciouschoice.com/2004/cc1701/seedsofjudgment1701.html.
3. All numbers, and a link to the full proposal, are from the IUCN. Accessed Jan. 29, 2007 from iucn.org/themes/ceesp/seaprise.htm#origin.
4. National Cancer Institute. Accessed Jan. 29, 2007 from cancercontrol.cancer.gov/5ad_5_mess.html, dividing McDonald's annual ad budget of $1 billion by 52 weeks.

THE POWER OF BUSINESS
1. Richard McGill Murphy. "Food Safety: Why People Are Turning to Organics." Organic Consumers Association, March 1, 2004. Accessed Jan. 29, 2007 from organicconsumers.org/organic/demographics031604.cfm.

2. Government of Alberta Agriculture, Food, and Rural Development. Accessed Jan. 29, 2007 from www1.agric.gov.ab.ca/$department/deptdocs.nsf/all/apa5178?opendocument.
3. Kate Ravilious. "Food Crisis Feared As Fertile Land Runs Out." The Guardian, Dec. 6, 2005. Accessed Jan. 29, 2007 from guardian.co.uk/science/story/0,3605,1659467,00.html.
4. Elizabeth Mygatt. World's Forests Continue to Shrink. Earth Policy Institute, April 4, 2006, with figure converted from hectares. Accessed Jan. 29, 2007 from earth-policy.org/Indicators/Forest/2006.htm.

BUILDING A GLOBAL MOVEMENT
1. WWF. Accessed Jan. 29, 2007 from panda.org/index.cfm?uNewsID=80480.

SOLUTION 1
1. National Council on Pet Population Study & Policy. Accessed Jan. 29, 2007 from petpopulation.org/statsurvey.html.
2. The Dog Hause. Accessed Jan. 29, 2007 from doghause.com/spay.asp. Also the source for the prostate cancer reference.
3. PETA. Accessed Jan. 29, 2007 from peta.org/mc/factsheet_display.asp?ID=44.
4. More information can be found in James A. Peden, Vegetarian Cats & Dogs, Harbingers, 1995 or online at sites such as helpingani-mals.com/h-vegcat-meals.html.
5. Pet Synergy. Accessed Jan. 29, 2007 from petsynergy.com/overview.html.

SOLUTION 2
1. Vegan Society. Accessed Jan. 29, 2007 from vegansociety.com/html/animals/care/pest_control.php; Carolyn Herriot, A Year on the Garden Path; other sources and personal experience.

SOLUTION 3
1. PETA's Caring Consumer ingredient list. Accessed Jan. 29, 2007 from caringconsumer.com/resources_ingredients_list.asp.

SOLUTION 5
1. PCRM. Powerful Tools for Health. Accessed Jan. 29, 2007 from pcrm.org/health/veginfo/vsk/veg_foods.html.
2. A growing percentage of the medical community supports the benefits of a vegan diet. This is, as with all nutrition, dependent on an individual's commitment to eating a well-balanced diet.
3. John Robbins. May All Be Fed. Harper Collins, 1993. Best summed up in this quote by the author: "If Americans were to reduce our meat consumption by only 10 percent, it would free land and resources to grow over 12 million tons of grain annually for human consumption, more than enough to adequately feed every one of the 40 to 60 million human beings who will starve to death on the planet this year."
4. The study of grain production for a single hamburger has been made many times, and the results vary between 12 and 16 pounds of grain. Our figures, and the calculations for bread and spaghetti, were drawn from Earthsave International. Accessed Jan. 29, 2007 from boston.earthsave.org/awareness/awareness.htm.
5. Jedediah Purdy. "The New Culture of Rural America." The American Prospect, 1999. Accessed Jan. 29, 2007 from prospect.org/print/V11/3/purdy-j.html.
6. John Robbins. The Food Revolution.Conari, 2001, p. 236, citing statistics from the University of California Agricultural Extension.
7. Rainforest Action Network. Accessed Jan. 29, 2007 from ran.org/who_we_are/publications/factsheets.
8. Rain-tree.com. The Disappearing Rainforest. Accessed Jan. 29, 2007 from rain-tree.com/facts.htm. Predictions vary, but most experts agree that, at current deforestation rates, there will be little or no tropical rainforest left by 2050.
9. Based on Vegan Outreach's estimated calculation of the average American consuming 35.7 land animals per year. Accessed Jan. 29, 2007 from veganoutreach.org/enewsletter/20021014.html.

10. World Resources Institute, citing 2002 data from the UN's FAO. Accessed Jan. 29, 2007 from earthtrends.wri.org/searchable_db/index.php?theme=8&variable_ID=193&action=select_countries.

SOLUTION 6
1. Dr. McDougall quoted from Share Guide interview with Dennis Hughes. Accessed Jan. 29, 2007 from shareguide.com/McDougall.html.
2. National Institute of Diabetes and Digestive and Kidney Diseases. Accessed Jan. 29, 2007 from digestive.niddk.nih.gov/ddiseases/pubs/lactoseintolerance.
3. Selene Yeager. "Milk: A Glassful of Goodness." *Prevention Magazine* [online]. Accessed Jan. 29, 2007 from prevention.com/article/0,5778,s1-3-91-126-3955-1,00.html.
4. Drawn from the nutrition guide created by the Vegetarian Resource Group. Accessed Jan. 29, 2007 from vrg.org/nutrition/calcium.htm#table1.

SOLUTION 13
1. Jane Weaver. "Puppy Love: It's Better Than You Think." *MSNBC News* [online] from April 8, 2004. Accessed Jan. 29, 2007 from msnbc.msn.com/id/4625213. Also the source for the opening quote by Dr. Alan Beck.

SOLUTION 14
1. Shelter-starting tips drawn and condensed from the ASPCA's "Start a Shelter" guide. Accessed Jan. 29, 2007 from www.aspca.org/site/PageServer?pagename=cruelty_startashelter.
2. Animal Ark. Accessed Jan. 29, 2007 from animalarkshelter.org.

SOLUTION 20
1. David R. Wooley. *Making Online Forums Work.* Association for Community Networking. Accessed Jan. 29, 2007 from thinkofit.com/webconf/afcnart.htm.
2. The entire text of the Asilomar 2004 Accords can be viewed by visiting asilomaraccords.org. Accessed Jan. 29, 2007.

SOLUTION 22
1. The full text of the Children's Earth Summit Declaration can be read at vsa.cape.com/~roots. Accessed Jan. 29, 2007.

SOLUTION 23
1. Rethink Waste. Accessed Jan. 29, 2007 from rethinkwaste.org/newsletters/SBW-FA2004.pdf.

SOLUTION 24
1. Physicians Committee for Responsible Medicine. Accessed Jan. 29, 2007 from pcrm.org/resch/anexp/elem_sec_alternatives.html.
2. InterNICHE. *Alternatives.* Accessed Jan. 29, 2007 from interniche.org/alt.html.

SOLUTION 25
1. The Vegetarian Resource Group. Accessed Jan. 29, 2007 from vrg.org.
2. Toronto Vegetarian Association. Accessed Jan. 29, 2007 from veg.ca/living/veg-position-paper.html.
3. "Vegetarian Choices." *Everybody's Fundraising and Edutainment Guide,* 2000. Feature Accessed Jan. 29, 2007 from fundandedutain.com/veg.html.
4. *Teen Research Unlimited* accessed Jan. 29, 2007 from teenresearch.com.
5. The Vegetarian Resource Group. Accessed Jan. 29, 2007 from vrg.org
6. Accessed Jan. 29, 2007 from *Everybody's Fundraising and Edutainment Guide.* fundandedutain.com/articles.htm.

SOLUTION 26
1. A detailed explanation of the Arcata Marsh's wastewater treatment system can be found at humboldt.edu/~ere_dept/marsh. Accessed Jan. 30, 2007.

SOLUTION 27
1. Holden Frith. "Urban Farms: Oasis in the Inner City." *Conscious Choice.* Accessed Jan. 30, 2007 from consciouschoice.com/2003/cc1610/urbanfarms1610. This article was also the source of Ken Dunn's quotes, as well as other information about urban farming.
2. Ibid.

SOLUTION 28
1. "Barcelona Votes to End Bullfights." *BBC News* [online]. Accessed Jan. 30, 2007 from news.bbc.co.uk/1/hi/world/europe/3605225.stm.
2. Coalition for No Whales in Captivity. Accessed Jan. 30, 2007 from whaleprotection.org/vancouveraquarium.

SOLUTION 29
1. Equine Advocates. Accessed Jan. 30, 2007 from equineadvocates.com/carriage.html.
2. International Fund for Horses. Accessed Jan. 30, 2007 from fund4horses.org/info.php?id=769.
3. Animal Aid. Accessed Jan. 30, 2007 from animalaid.org.uk/campaign/sport/omnibus.htm#no19.

SOLUTION 30
1. Paul Brubaker. "Dawn's Early (Laer) Light." *Montclair Times,* March 10, 2005. Accessed Jan. 30, 2007 from montclairtimes.com/page.php?page=9318.
2. Toronto Environmental Alliance. Accessed Jan. 30, 2007 from torontoenvironment.org.
3. Ibid.
4. Ibid.
5. Pesticide Action Network North America. Accessed Jan. 30, 2007 from panna.org/campaigns/pesticideFreeLawns.html.
6. Ibid.
7. National Tap Water Quality Database. Accessed Jan. 30, 2007 from ewg.org/tapwater/findings.php.

SOLUTION 31
1. National Agriculture Statistics Service. Accessed Jan. 30, 2007 from nass.usda.gov/Census_of_Agriculture/index.asp.
2. Farm Aid. *Why Family Farms Need Help.* Accessed Jan. 30, 2007 from farmaid.org/site/PageServer?pagename=info_facts_help.
3. Ibid.
4. Environmental Protection Agency. *Land Use Overview.* Accessed Jan. 30, 2007 from epa.gov/agriculture/ag101/landuse.html.
5. Care 2 Make a Difference. Accessed Jan. 30, 2007 from care2.com/channels/solutions/guides/449.

SOLUTION 33
1. "Organic Connection." Accessed Jan. 30, 2007 from organicconnection.net; *E-Medicine Consumer Health.* Accessed Jan. 30, 2007 from emedicinehealth.com/articles/40435-1.asp.
2. Joel Salatin. *Pastured Poultry.* The Weston Price Foundation. Accessed Jan. 30, 2007 from westonaprice.org/farming/pasturedpoultry.html.
3. *Blueprint.* "Organic Farming Benefits Wildlife." Oct. 6, 2005. Accessed Jan. 30, 2007 from ox.ac.uk/blueprint/2005-06/0610/21.shtml.
4. Guy Dauncey. "10 Reasons Why Organic Food Is Better." *Earthfuture.* Accessed Jan. 30, 2007 from earthfuture.com/earth/cg-tenreasonsorganic.asp.
5. Ibid.
6. Adapted from Jane Goodall, *Harvest for Hope.* Warner, 2006, p. 59. "Animals and GMOs."
7. As of 2006, statistics from the Organic Trade Association. Accessed Jan. 30, 2007 from ota.com/pics/documents/2004_Survey_Overview.pdf.
8. Ibid.

9. Frédéric Forge. *Organic Farming in Canada*. Government of Canada. Accessed Jan. 30, 2007 from dsp-psd.communication.gc.ca/Collection-R/LoPBdP/BP/prb0029-e.htm.
10. Organic Trade Association. Accessed Jan. 30, 2007 from ota.com/organic/mt/export_executivesummary.html.

SOLUTION 35
1. Juliet Gellatley. "Food for a Future." *VIVA Livewire Guide*. Accessed Jan. 30, 2007 from viva.org.uk/books/goingveggie/ch09.html.
2. Ibid.
3. World Resources Institute, citing 2002 data from the Food and Agriculture Organization of the United Nations. Accessed Jan. 30, 2007 from earthtrends.wri.org/searchable_db/index.php?theme=8&variable_ID=193&action=select_countries.
4. Juliet Gellatley. "Food for a Future.' *VIVA Livewire Guide*. Accessed Jan. 30, 2007 from viva.org.uk/books/goingveggie/ch09.html.
5. *Science Daily*. Accessed Jan. 30, 2007 from sciencedaily.com/releases/1997/08/970812003512.htm. Numbers on this vary widely. Viva Livewire Guide estimates it at 1.9 billion people, while Science Daily reports 800 million. Since most scientists estimate between these numbers, 1 billion is a conservative guess.
6. Tim Appenzeller. "The End of Cheap Oil." *National Geographic*, June 2004.
7. Based on 20 lbs. of CO_2 being produced for every gallon of gasoline burned: 283 gallons x 20 = 5660 lbs or 2.8 tons.
8. Donald E. Johnson. "Emissions of Nitrous Oxide from Livestock Operations." American Dairy Science Association. Accessed Jan. 30, 2007 from adsa.org/discover/intersummaries/Johnson.doc.
9. US Environmental Protection Agency. Accessed Jan. 30, 2007 from epa.gov/rlep/faq.html.
10. (a) Oil. 283 gallons over a 5-year lifetime – 56.6 gallons a year. A gallon produces 19.5 lbs CO_2 = 1103 lbs. of CO_2 per year. (b) Methane: 285 lbs. per year x 23 = 6555 lbs. of CO_2e (CO_2 equivalent) a year. (c) Nitrous Oxide: 20 lbs. of N_2O per year x 296 = 5920 lbs. of CO_2e. Total 1103 + 6555 + 5920 = 13578 lbs. = 6.8 tons.
11. A cow produces 570 lbs. of beef. An average North America meat eater consumes 69 lbs. of beef a year, so the cow feeds 8 people. Since the cow produced 6.2 tonnes a year for 5 years before it was slaughtered, those 8 meat-eaters are collectively eating beef that produced 5 x 6.2 tonnes = 31 tonnes of CO_2e. Divide by 8, and the meat-eating habit produces 3.9 tonnes (3.8 tons) of CO_2 per person per year.
12. Agriculture and Agrifood Canada. Accessed Jan. 30, 2007 from agr.gc.ca/pfra/nesa/nesa7.htm.
13. Steve Boyan. *How Our Food Choices Can Help Save the Environment*. Earthsave. Accessed Jan. 30, 2007 from earthsave.org/environment/foodchoices.htm.
14. Ibid.

SOLUTION 36
1. David Adam. "Time Running out to Curb Effects of Deep Sea Pollution, Warns UN." *The Guardian*, June 17, 2006. Accessed Jan. 30, 2007 from guardian.co.uk/science/story/0,,1799817,00.html?gusrc=rss.
2. Ibid.
3. United Nations Environment Programme. Accessed Jan. 30, 2007 from unep.org/Documents.Multilingual/Default.asp?DocumentID=480&ArticleID=5300&l=en.
4. Marine Work Group. Accessed Jan. 30, 2007 from mwg.utvinternet.com/fisheries_overfishing.html.
5. "Action Urged to Protect Deep Seas." *BBC News* [online], June 16, 2006. Accessed Jan. 30, 2007 from news.bbc.co.uk/2/hi/science/nature/5086506.stm.
6. UNEP. See Note 3.
7. Ibid.
8. Ibid.

9. Drawn from the UN's FAO Statistics division. Metric totals have been converted to imperial tons (1 = 1.1) and rounded to the nearest whole figure. Accessed Jan. 30, 2007 from fao.org/statistics.

SOLUTION 37
1. Sea Turtle Restoration Project. Accessed Jan. 30, 2007 from seaturtles.org/pdf/ExecSummary.blue.final.pdf.
2. Caribbean Conservation Corporation. Accessed Jan. 30, 2007 from cccturtle.org/alerts/a_UN-leatherback-letter.htm.
3. Sea Turtle Restoration Project. Accessed Jan. 30, 2007 from seaturtles.org/pdf/ExecSummary.blue.final.pdf.
4. Ibid.
5. "McArthur Gives Albatross Support." *BBC News*, April 27, 2005. Accessed Jan. 30, 2007 from news.bbc.co.uk/1/hi/sci/tech/4486939.stm.
6. Environment News Service, March 9, 2005. Accessed Jan. 30, 2007 from ens-newswire.com/ens/mar2005/2005-03-09-02.asp.
7. National Marine Fisheries Service. Accessed Jan. 30, 2007 from swr.nmfs.noaa.gov/pir/feis/Chapter%202.pdf.

SOLUTION 38
1. Caribbean Conservation Corporation. Accessed Jan. 30, 2007 from cccturtle.org/threats.htm.
2. Deep Seas Conservation Coalition. Accessed Jan. 30, 2007 from savethehighseas.org/sixreasons.cfm.
3. Ibid. Accessed Jan. 30, 2007 from savethehighseas.org/trawling.cfm.
4. Alaska Marine Conservation Council. Accessed Jan. 30, 2007 from akmarine.org/ourwork/fact-trawl.shtml. Figure converted from metric 40 tons to imperial 44 tons.
5. Ibid.
6. World Wildlife Fund. Accessed Jan. 30, 2007 from wwf.org.nz/news/2004/04-10-6-Trawling.cfm.
7. Ian Herbert. "Deep Sea Fish Plundered to Extinction by Bottom Trawling." *Independent News* [online]. June 20, 2006. Accessed Jan. 30, 2007 from news.independent.co.uk/environment/article548921.ece.

SOLUTION 39
1. *Fishing 101*. Accessed Jan. 30, 2007 from fishinghurts.com/fishing101.asp.
2. Ibid. Accessed Jan. 30, 2007 from fishinghurts.com/FishFeelPain.asp.
3. *PETA's Animal Times*. Accessed Jan. 30, 2007 from peta.org/Living/AT-Summer1999/fish.html.
4. Juliet Eilperin. "Ban on Finning Offers Hope for Survival of Atlantic Sharks." *Washington Post*, Nov. 22, 2004. Accessed Jan. 30, 2007 from washingtonpost.com/wp-dyn/articles/A5626-2004Nov22.html.
5. Ibid.
6. *Fishing Hurts*. Accessed Jan. 30, 2007 from fishinghurts.com/feat-fishNorway.asp?int=weekly_enews.

SOLUTION 40
1. Terry McArthy. "Is Fish Farming Safe?" *Time.com*, Nov. 17, 2002. Accessed Jan. 30, 2007 from time.com/time/globalbusiness/article/0,9171,1101021125-391523,00.html.
2. Ibid.
3. Alexandra Morton, Raincoast Research Society. Accessed Jan. 30, 2007 from raincoastresearch.org.
4. Compassion in World Farming. Accessed Jan. 30, 2007 from ciwf.org.uk/publications/reports/in_too_deep_summary_2001.pdf.
5. *Fishing Hurts*. Accessed Jan. 30, 2007 from fishinghurts.com/fishFarms1.asp.
6. Friends of Clayoquot Sound. Accessed Jan. 30, 2007 from focs.ca/fishfarming/index.asp.
7. James Owen. "Salmon Farm Escapees Threaten Wild Fish Stocks." *National Geographic News*. June 16, 2003. Accessed Jan. 30, 2007 from

news.nationalgeographic.com/news/2003/06/0616_030616_
farmsalmon_2.html.
8. Ibid.
9. Friends of Clayoquot Sound. Accessed Jan. 30, 2007 from
focs.ca/fishfarming/index.asp.
10. See Note 7.
11. See Note 9
12. David Suzuki Foundation. Accessed Jan. 30, 2007 from david-
suzuki.org/Campaigns_and_Programs/Salmon_Aquaculture/News_
Releases/newsaquaculture03290501.asp.
13. Ibid.
14. Ibid.

SOLUTION 41
1. Michael McGraw. *PETA Ends Campaign Against Company*. Accessed Jan.
31, 2007 from peta.org/mc/NewsItem.asp?id=5861.
2. PETA. *Leather: No Friend of the Earth*. Accessed Jan. 31, 2007 from
cowsarecool.com/environment.asp.
3. Tom's of Maine's website. Accessed Jan. 31, 2007 from tomsof-
maine.com/about/press/2006_02_08_WindEnergy.asp.

SOLUTION 42
1. Sue Ellis. "Australian Wool in Animal Rights Row." *BBC News* [online].
July 20, 2005. Accessed Jan. 31, 2007 from
news.bbc.co.uk/1/hi/programmes/crossing_continents/4699931.stm.

SOLUTION 43
1. Adapted from Zoe Weil, *The Power and Promise of Humane Education*. New
Society Publishers, 2004, p. 19, "The Four Elements of Humane Education."

SOLUTION 44
1. PETA Media Center on product testing. Accessed Jan. 31, 2007 from
peta.org/mc/factsheet_display.asp?ID=91.
2. For a list of companies that use alternatives to animal testing, see
allforanimals.com/cruelfree1.htm. Accessed Jan. 31, 2007.
3. Ian Blessing. PETA Media Center. Accessed Jan. 31, 2007 from
peta.org/mc/NewsItem.asp?id=8397.
4. Ibid.

SOLUTION 45
1. Progressive Animal Welfare Society. *Omak Suicide Race*. Accessed Jan.
31, 2007 from paws.org/outreach/campaigns/omak.php.
2. Animal Defenders International. *Success in Portugal*. Accessed Jan. 31, 2007
from ad-international.org/animals_in_entertainment/go.php?id=476&ssi=10.
3. People for the Ethical Treatment of Animals. *The 'Ihurtadog' Race*.
Accessed Jan. 31, 2007 from peta.org/feat/iditarod.

SOLUTION 46
1. PETA. "Ralph Lauren Goes Fur-Free." Accessed Jan. 31, 2007 from
furisdead.com/feat-RalphLaurenVictory.asp.
2. Ibid. "Fur FAQ." Accessed Jan. 31, 2007 from furisdead.com/FAQ.asp.

SOLUTION 47}
1. Katherine Kim. National Restaurant Association. Accessed Jan. 31,
2007 from restaurant.org/pressroom/pressrelease.cfm?ID=484.

SOLUTION 49
1. Rainforest Action Network. Accessed Jan. 31, 2007 from
ran.org/who_we_are/publications/factsheets.

SOLUTION 50
1. *Common Dreams News Wire*. March 3, 2005. Accessed Jan. 31, 2007
from commondreams.org/news2005/0303-16.htm.
2. Guy Dauncey. *Econews*, June 2006. Accessed Jan. 31, 2007 from
earthfuture.com/econews/back_issues/06-06.asp.

3. IKEA. *Business and Sustainable Development: Global Guide*. Accessed Jan.
31, 2007 from bsdglobal.com/viewcasestudy.asp?id=119.

SOLUTION 51
1. Details of the German Government's Animal Welfare Law from Animal
Legal and Historical Center. Accessed Jan. 31, 2007 from ani-
mallaw.info/nonus/statutes/stdeawa1998.htm.
2. More details in Guy Dauncey, *Econews*, Dec. 2003. Accessed Jan. 31,
2007 from earthfuture.com/econews/back_issues/03-12.asp.

SOLUTION 52
1. Owens Foundation for Wildlife Conservation. Accessed Jan. 31, 2007
from owens-foundation.org/docs/sponsor2.htm.
2. Duc Nguyen. *Poaching of Black Bears in Canada*. University of
California. Accessed Jan. 31, 2007 from
dbc.uci.edu/~sustain/global/sensem/nguyen97.htm.
3. See Note 1.
4. Ibid.
5. Indian Tiger Society. Accessed Jan. 31, 2007 from
indiantiger.org/wild-cats/cougar.html.
6. International Fund for Animal Welfare. *Ontario Bans Penned Hunts*. Accessed
Jan. 31, 2007 from ifaw.org/ifaw/general/default.aspx?oid=123732.
7. As of 2006. Data is from the Humane Society of the United States.
Accessed Jan. 31, 2007 from
hsus.org/wildlife/issues_facing_wildlife/hunting/trophy_hunting.
8. HSUS. *Learn the Facts About Hunting*. Accessed Jan. 31, 2007 from
hsus.org/wildlife/issues_facing_wildlife/hunting/learn_the_facts_about_
hunting.html.
9. US Fish and Wildlife Service. *Hunting Statistics and Economics*. Accessed
Jan. 31, 2007 from fws.gov/hunting/huntstat.html.
10. HSUS. Accessed Jan. 31, 2007 from hsus.org/wildlife/issues_facing_
wildlife/hunting/learn_the_facts_about_hunting.html.
11. Ibid.
12. Animal Protection Institute. Accessed Jan. 31, 2007 from
bancrueltraps.com/facts?p=63&more=1.

SOLUTION 53
1. In Defense of Animals. *Bullfighting*. Accessed Jan. 31, 2007 from
idausa.org/facts/fighting.html; World Society for the Protection of Animals.
Accessed Jan. 31, 2007 from wspa.org.uk/index.php?page=645.

SOLUTION 54
1. Canadian law does not protect whales captured elsewhere and
imported in the country. Captive Animals Protection Society. Accessed
Jan. 31, 2007 from captiveanimals.org/aquarium/orca.htm.
2. Ibid.
3. Orca Network. *Bring Lolita Home*. Accessed Jan. 31, 2007 from
orcanetwork.org/captivity/captivity.html.

SOLUTION 55
1. Linda Bren. *Keeping Pets (and People) Healthy*. USDA. Accessed Jan. 31,
2007 from fda.gov/FDAC/features/2004/104_pets.html.
2. Council of Europe. Details of the Convention for the Protection of Pet
Animals. Accessed Jan. 31, 2007 from conven-
tions.coe.int/Treaty/en/Treaties/Html/125.htm.

SOLUTION 56
1. IFAW Canada. Accessed Jan. 31, 2007 from
ifaw.org/ifaw/general/default.aspx?oid=89449.
2. DeViney, Dickert, & Lockwood study, from Potter League. Accessed
Jan. 31, 2007 from potterleague.org/advocacy_violence.html.
3. Maryland's Peoples Law Library. Accessed Jan. 31, 2007 from
peoples-law.org/domviol/pets/protect_pet.html.

SOLUTION 57

1. International Fund for Animal Welfare. Accessed Jan. 31, 2007 from ifaw.org/ifaw/dfiles/file_480.pdf.
2. Ibid.
3. *About:* "Exotic Pets." Accessed Jan. 31, 2007 from exoticpets.about.com.
4. Humane Society of the United States. *Live Reptile Trade.* Accessed Jan. 31, 2007 from hsus.org.

SOLUTION 58

1. Get Bear Smart Society. Accessed Jan. 31, 2007 from bears-mart.com/bearsBackyard.

SOLUTION 59

1. Nedim C. Buyukmihci, V.M.D. "Serious Moral Concern Is Not Species-Limited (And Other Thoughts)." *Animal Place.* Accessed Jan. 31, 2007 from animalplace.org/serious.html.
2. National Anti-Vivisection Society. *Alternatives Save Money.* Accessed Jan. 31, 2007 from navs.org/site/DocServer/Alternatives_Save_Money.pdf?docID=501.

SOLUTION 60

1. American Anti-Vivisection Society. *Testing Alternatives.* Accessed Jan. 31, 2007 from aavs.org/testing03.html.
2. USDA info-sheet on CAT scans and cancer risk. *Whole Body Scanning.* Accessed Jan. 31, 2007 from fda.gov/cdrh/ct.
3. See Note 1.
4. Council of Europe. Accessed Jan. 31, 2007 from conven-tions.coe.int/Treaty/en/Treaties/Html/123.htm.

SOLUTION 61

1. Organic Trade Association. Accessed Jan. 31, 2007 from ota.com/organic/benefits/species.html.
2. World Resources Institute. Accessed Jan. 31, 2007 from earth-trends.wri.org/pdf_library/data_tables/fg5n_2000.PDF.
3. See Note 1.
4. Marya Skrypiczajko. "BC the Organic Way." *Common Ground,* June 2005.
5. Organic Europe. Accessed Jan. 31, 2007 from organic-europe.net/europe_eu/default.asp#action.
6. Organic Transitions program. Accessed Jan. 31, 2007 from csrees.usda.gov/fo/fundview.cfm?fonum=114.
7. Seedquest. Accessed Jan. 31, 2007 from seedquest.com/News/releases/2006/may/15877.htm.
8. All figures from The World of Organic Agriculture. Accessed Jan. 31, 2007 from orgprints.org/5161/01/yussefi-2006-overview.pdf. It must be noted that much of Australia's organic farmland is used for low-inten-sity grazing, so a hectare of land is not comparable in productivity to a hectare in most European countries.
9. Ibid.
10. Guy Dauncey: *Econews,* May 2006. Accessed Jan. 31, 2007 from earthfuture.com/econews/back_issues/06-05.asp.
11. See Note 8.

SOLUTION 62

1. Peter Singer. *Common Dreams News Centre.* Aug. 20, 2005. Accessed Jan. 31, 2007 from commondreams.org/views05/0820-28.htm.
2. Ibid.

SOLUTION 63

1. California Climate Change Portal. Accessed Jan. 31, 2007 from climat-echange.ca.gov.
2. "Sweden Aims for Oil-free Economy." *BBC News,* Feb. 8, 2006. Accessed Jan. 31, 2007 from news.bbc.co.uk/1/hi/sci/tech/4694152.stm.

SOLUTION 64

1. David Boyd. *The Race to Save the World's Forests.* Sierra Legal Defense Fund. Accessed Jan. 31, 2007 from fanweb.org/patrick-moore/dboyd.html. (1 hectare = 2.471 acres)
2. As of 2004, the Sierra Club. Accessed Jan. 31, 2007 from sierra-club.org/wildlands/anniversary2.asp.
3. Redpath Museum. Quebec Biodiversity. Accessed Jan. 31, 2007 from redpath-museum.mcgill.ca/Qbp/3.Conservation/sppvsland.htm.
4. World Resources Institute. Accessed Jan. 31, 2007 from earth-trends.wri.org/pdf_library/country_profiles/bio_cou_124.pdf.
5. *For the Record.* National Resources Canada. Accessed Jan. 31, 2007 from nrcan-rncan.gc.ca/cfs-scf/national/what-quoi/sof/sof05/for_the_record_e.html.
6. As of 2004, World Wildlife Fund. Accessed Jan. 31, 2007 from worldwildlife.org/wildplaces/kla/pubs/padshort2.pdf.
7. As of 2005, EcoBC. Accessed Jan. 31, 2007 from ecobc.org/Action_Alert/2005/11/ActionAlert1565/index.cfm.
8. As of 2003, World Resources Institute. Accessed Jan. 31, 2007 from earthtrends.org/pdf_library/country_profiles/bio_cou_554.pdf.

SOLUTION 65

1. United Nations Development Programme. *What is Biodiversity?* Accessed Jan. 31, 2007 from www.undp.org/biodiversity/about_us.html.
2. Endangered Species Coalition. Accessed Jan. 31, 2007 from stopextinction.org/site/c.epIQKXOBJsG/b.704799/k.CCB4/Home.htm.
3. World Wildlife Fund. Accessed Jan. 31, 2007 from world-wildlife.org/wildplaces/ngp/index.cfm.
4. Full details of the Species at Risk Act. Accessed Jan. 31, 2007 from speciesatrisk.gc.ca.
5. More information on SARA – Western Canada Wilderness Committee wildernesscommittee.org/campaigns/species/sara.
6. Forest Ethics. Accessed Jan. 31, 2007 from forestethics.org/article.php?id=1453.
7. David Suzuki. "Ambrose Delivers Death Sentence to Owls." *CNEWS,* Aug. 23, 2006. Accessed Jan. 31, 2007 from cnews.canoe.ca/CNEWS/Science/Suzuki/2006/08/23/1771595-ca.html.

SOLUTION 66

1. Amy Wagener. *Endangered Species: Traded to Death.* World Resources Institute. Accessed Jan. 31, 2007 from earth-trends.wri.org/features/view_feature.php?theme=7&fid=25.
2. American University, Washington, DC. Accessed Jan. 31, 2007 from american.edu/TED/elephant.htm.
3. Ibid.
4. *Action Plan Launched to Save Endangered Parrots.* World Wildlife Fund. Accessed Jan. 31, 2007 from wwf.org.uk/news/n_0000000308.asp.
5. See Note 1.
6. Jamie Bowman. *NACEC Newsletter.* Accessed Jan. 31, 2007 from cec.org/trio/stories/index.cfm?varlan=english&ed=6&ID=83.

SOLUTION 67

1. Kevin Hansen. *Predator Conservation.* Accessed Jan. 31, 2007 from predatorconservation.org/predator_info/forest_predators/Mountainlion.html.
2. Tina Adler. "Tracking the Rocky Mountain Carnivores." *Science News Online.* Accessed Jan. 31, 2007 from science-news.org/pages/sn_arch/11_30_96/bob1.htm.
3. *Predator Conservation: The Truth about Predators.* Accessed Jan. 31, 2007 from predatorconservation.org/predator_info/predatorinfo.html.

SOLUTION 68

1. Gibbons, also referred to as lesser apes, belong to a different family, hylobatidae, and resemble monkeys. They are apes, however, and are closely related to hominids.

SOLUTION 69

1. Oceana. Accessed Jan. 31, 2007 from oceana.org/index.php?id=93; Charles Clover. *The End of the Line: How Over-fishing Is Changing the World and What We Eat*. New Press, 2006. This also gives an in-depth case for ending government subsidies for fisheries.
2. Janet Larsen. *World Fish Catch Hits Limits*. Earth Policy Institute. Accessed Jan. 31, 2007 from earth-policy.org/Indicators/Fish/2005.htm.
3. Oceana. Accessed Jan. 31, 2007 from oceana.org/index.php?id=93.
4. *Environmental Science and Technology Online*. Accessed Jan. 31, 2007 from pubs.acs.org/subscribe/journals/esthag-w/2003/jun/policy/jp_oil.html.
5. Juliet Eilperin. "Fish Farming's Bounty Isn't Without Barbs." *Washington Post*. Accessed Jan. 24, 2007 from washingtonpost.com/wp-dyn/articles/A31159-2005Jan23.html.
6. Ibid.
7. European Commission — Fisheries and Maritime Affairs. Accessed Jan. 31, 2007 from ec.europa.eu/comm/fisheries/news_corner/doss_inf/info34_en.htm.

SOLUTION 70

1. Public Works Canada. Accessed Jan. 31, 2007 from pwgsc.gc.ca/comm/min/text/speeches/2004-11-02-00-e.html.
2. McGuire Woods LLP. Accessed Jan. 31, 2007 from mcguirewoods.com/departments/corporate_services/government_contracts.asp.
3. Josh Harkinson and Jim Motavalli. "Buying Green." *E Magazine*, Sept./ Oct., 2002. Accessed Jan. 31, 2007 from emagazine.com/view/?1100.
4. Ibid.

SOLUTION 71

1. *Tourism Tomorrow*. World Travel and Tourism Council, 2005. Accessed Feb. 1, 2007 from wttc.org/news115.htm.
2. International Emissions Trading Association. Accessed Feb. 1, 2007 from ieta.org/ieta/www/pages/index.php?IdSitePage=1072.

SOLUTION 72

1. Mongabay, citing UN statistics from 2005. Accessed Feb. 1, 2007 from news.mongabay.com/2005/1115-forests.html.
2. Daniel Kamman. *Cookstoves for the Developing World*. Accessed Feb. 1, 2007 from socrates.berkeley.edu/~kammen/cookstoves.html.

SOLUTION 73

1. Conservation International. Accessed Feb. 1, 2007 from conservation.org/xp/CIWEB/regions/priorityareas/hotspots.xml.

SOLUTION 74

1. *Controlling Bushmeat Trade*. Jane Goodall Institute. Accessed Feb. 1, 2007 fromjanegoodall.org/africa-programs/objectives/controlling-bushmeat-trade.asp.
2. Ibid. Accessed Feb. 1, 2007 fromjanegoodall.org/africa-programs/objectives/bushmeat-fact-sheet.asp.
3. Bushmeat Crises Task Force. Accessed Feb. 1, 2007 from bushmeat.org/cd/bushmeat_Webquest/ecoecon3.html.
4. Justin S. Brashares. "Bushmeat Hunting, Wildlife Declines and Fish Supply in West Africa." *Science Magazine*. Nov. 12, 2005
5. Ibid.

SOLUTION 75

1. Save the Whales Again. Accessed Feb. 1, 2007 from savethewhalesagain.com/isabel_lucas_shoot.html.
2. *Greenpeace News*. June 13, 2006. Accessed Feb. 1, 2007 from greenpeace.org/international/news/2006-whale-meeting.
3. *CDNN News Online*. June 20, 2006. Accessed Feb. 1, 2007 from cdnn.info/news/eco/e060620.html.

4. José Truda Palazzo, Jr. "Whose Whales? Developing Countries and the Right to Use Whales by Non-lethal Means." *Journal of International Wildlife Law & Policy*, 1999. Accessed Feb. 1, 2007 from jiwlp.com/contents/palazzo.pdf.

SOLUTION 76

1. "Poaching Curbed." *New Scientist*, April 9, 2005. Accessed Feb. 1, 2007 from newscientist.com/article/mg18624944.000.html.
2. Rael Loon. "Shooting with Rifle or Camera." *Mail & Guardian Online*, July 29 2005. Accessed Feb. 1, 2007 from mg.co.za/articlePage.aspx?articleid=246713&area=/earthyear/earth_features.
3. Ibid. Accessed 02 01 07 from mg.co.za/articlePage.aspx?articleid=254903&area=/breaking_news/breaking_news_national.
4. Ibid. As of mid-2006, South Africa was still committed to new legislation, but had not finalized dates or details; Bonnie Tsui. "Trophies in a Barrel." *New York Times*, April 9, 2006.

SOLUTION 78

1. WSPA. Accessed Feb. 1, 2007 from wspa.ca/news.asp?newsID=18.
2. World Resources Institute. Accessed Feb. 1, 2007 from earth-trends.wri.org/text/agriculture-food/feature-24.html.
3. Ibid.
4. See Note 1.
5. "India in Effort to Save Vultures." *BBC News*, March 22, 2005. Accessed Feb. 1, 2007 from news.bbc.co.uk/2/hi/south_asia/4372783.stm.
6. Birdlife International. Accessed Feb. 1, 2007 from birdlife.org/news/news/2006/08/vulture.html.
7. Agro Link. Accessed Feb. 1, 2007 from agrolink.moa.my/jph/dvs/nipah/oie990808.html.
8. Union of Concerned Scientists. *Nepal Drug Boost for Vultures*. Accessed Feb. 1, 2007 from ucsusa.org/food_and_environment/antibiotics_and_food/european-union-ban.html.

SOLUTION 79

1. Vandana Shiva, in *Ecoworld Interview*, March 6, 2004. Accessed Feb. 1, 2007 from ecoworld.com/home/articles2.cfm?tid=346.
2. Ibid.
3. United Nations FAO. Accessed Feb. 1, 2007 from fao.org/docrep/W5830E/w5830e0b.htm.

SOLUTION 81

1. Forests. Accessed Feb. 1, 2007 from forests.org/archive/brazil/amazon.htm.
2. Ibid.
3. Rhett Butler. *Mongabay*. March 22, 2006. Accessed Feb. 1, 2007 from news.mongabay.com/2006/0322-amazon.html.
4. Guy Dauncey. "Crisis in the Amazon." *Econews*, Sept. 2006. Accessed Feb. 1, 2007 from earthfuture.com/econews/back_issues/06-09.asp.
5. See Note 3.
6. Greenpeace. Accessed Feb. 1, 2007 from greenpeace.org/international/campaigns/forests/amazon.
7. Rhett Butler. *Mongabay*, Dec. 5, 2005. Accessed Feb. 1, 2007 from news.mongabay.com/2005/1205-amazon.html.

SOLUTION 82

1. "Birds vs. Towers." *Science Daily*, Sept. 23, 1999. Accessed Feb. 1, 2007 from sciencedaily.com/releases/1999/09/990923071729.htm.

SOLUTION 83

1. "Tiger Killings Must Stop." *BBC News Online*. Jan. 27, 1998. Accessed Feb. 1, 2007 from news.bbc.co.uk/2/hi/special_report/1998/chinese_new_year/50218.stm. As of 2006, the Chinese policy is under threat, as

the government has suggested the possible use of products from farmed tigers: Accessed Feb. 1, 2007 from planetark.com/dailynewsstory.cfm/newsid/32676/story.htm.
2. All figures drawn from WWF. Accessed Feb. 1, 2007 from panda.org/about_wwf/what_we_do/species/publications/index.cfm?uNewsID=62980.
3. Ibid.
4. Ibid. Accessed Feb. 1, 2007 from worldwildlife.org/tigers.
5. WWF India. Accessed Feb. 1, 2007 from wwfindia.org/about_wwf/what_we_do/tiger_wildlife/our_work/tiger_conservation/sunderbans/index.cfm.
6. WWF. Accessed Feb. 1, 2007 from worldwildlife.org/trade/tcm_successes.cfm.

SOLUTION 84
1. Seal Hunt.ca. Accessed Feb. 1, 2007 from sealhunt.ca/Resources/letter_writing.html.
2. HSUS. Accessed Feb. 1, 2007 from hsus.org/marine_mammals/protect_seals/the_truth.html.
3. Ibid. Accessed Feb. 1, 2007 from hsus.org/marine_mammals/protect_seals/facts_about_the_canadian_seal_hunt.html.
4. Council of Europe. Accessed Feb. 1, 2007 from assembly.coe.int/Main.asp?link=/Documents/WorkingDocs/Doc06/EDOC11008.htm.
5. ARC Halifax, citing 2005 Environics Research poll. Accessed Feb. 1, 2007 from archalifax.com/resources/Seal%20MythsandTruths%20final.doc.
6. HSUS. Accessed Feb. 1, 2007 from hsus.org/press_and_publications/press_releases/canadian_seafood_boycott_impending.htm

SOLUTION 85
1. UNEP-IUCN. Accessed Feb. 1, 2007 from globio.info/download.cfm?File=region/africa/GRASP_5.pdf%20.
2. All Africa. Accessed Feb. 1, 2007 from allafrica.com/stories/200607070004.html (subscribers).
3. Orangutan Conservancy. Accessed Feb. 1, 2007 from orangutan.com/threats/threatstoorangutans.htm.

SOLUTION 86
1. Claire Doole. Killing Killer Whales with Toxics. WWF. Accessed Feb. 1, 2007 from panda.org/news_facts/newsroom/features/index.cfm?uNewsID=53540.
2. North Gulf Oceanic Society. Accessed Feb. 1, 2007 from whalesalaska.org.
3. Seaflow. Accessed Feb. 1, 2007 from seaflow.org/downloads/seaflow_factsheet.pdf.
4. Jay Lindsay. "Oceans Getting Louder." Associated Press/Environmental News Network. Accessed Feb. 1, 2007 from enn.com/today.html?id=7554.
5. Eric Hoyt. Whale Watching 2001. IFAW/Oceana. Accessed Feb. 1, 2007 from oceania.org.au/soundnet/features/hoytifaw.html.
6. Orca Relief Citizen's Alliance. Accessed Feb. 1, 2007 from orcarelief.org/pressreleases.php.
7. Ibid. ORCA details the studies by Dr. Birgit Kriete, Dr. David Bain, and Glenn VanBlaricom with Carlos Alvarez-Flores.
8. Ibid.

SOLUTION 87
1. Compassion in World Farming Trust. Accessed Feb. 1, 2007 from ciwf.org.uk/publications/reports/Industrial_Animal_Farming_bklt.pdf.
2. Richard Lacey. How Now Mad Cow? Accessed Feb. 1, 2007 from mad-cow.org/lacey.html.
3. Joseph M. Stookey. Accessed Feb. 1, 2007 from usask.ca/wcvm/herdmed/applied-ethology/articles/dairysem.html.
4. Animal Welfare Institute. Accessed Feb. 1, 2007 from awionline.org/pubs/Quarterly/03-52-4/524p12.htm.
5. Humane Society of the United States. Accessed Feb. 1, 2007 from eap.mcgill.ca/LPAW_1.htm.
6. See Note 3.

7. Ibid.

SOLUTION 88
1. Drawn from Steven M. Wise, Drawing the Line, Perseus, 2002, p. 106.
2. BC SPCA. Accessed Feb. 1, 2007 from spca.bc.ca/animalissues/parrot.asp.
3. Wise, p.129.
4. A Talk with Irene Pepperberg. Edge.org. Accessed Feb. 1, 2007 from edge.org/3rd_culture/pepperberg03/pepperberg_index.html.
5. CITES. Accessed Feb. 1, 2007 from cites.org/eng/com/AC/22/E22-10-2-A1.pdf.

SOLUTION 89
1. HSUS. Accessed Feb. 1, 2007 from hsus.org/farm/resources/research/practices/mortality_eggs.html.
2. Toronto Vegetarian Association. Accessed Feb. 1, 2007 from veg.ca/issues/egg-campaign.html.
3. United Poultry Concerns. Accessed Feb. 1, 2007 from upc-online.org/chickens/chickensbro.html.
4. HSUS. hsus.org/farm/news/ournews/national_chicken_month_2006.html.
5. Ibid.
6. See Note 3. Accessed Feb. 1, 2007 from
7. See Note 2.
8. Ibid.
9. Flax Council of Canada. Accessed Feb. 1, 2007 from flaxcouncil.ca/english/index.php?p=g1&mp=nutrition.

SOLUTION 90
1. Jena Ball. "For Love of Bats." Environmental Magazine. Accessed Feb. 1, 2007 from emagazine.com/view/?2471.
2. Many of these facts were drawn from Bat Conservation International. Accessed Feb. 1, 2007 from batcon.org.

SOLUTION 91
1. Compassion in World Farming. Accessed Feb. 1, 2007 from ciwf.org.uk/education/international.html.

SOLUTION 94
1. CITES. Accessed Feb. 1, 2007 from cites.org/eng/cop/13/doc/E13-15.pdf.
2. All-Creatures. Accessed Feb. 1, 2007 from all-creatures.org/articles/ar-seahorses.html.

SOLUTION 95
1. All statistics gathered from Beauty Without Cruelty. Accessed Feb. 1, 2007 from bwcsa.co.za/fur_trade/fur.html.

SOLUTION 96
1. Friends of Animals. Accessed Feb. 1, 2007 from friendsofanimals.org/actionline/summer-2005/whole-foods-market.html.
2. People and Planet. Accessed Feb. 1, 2007 from peopleandplanet.net/doc.php?id=2539.
3. Worldwatch Institute. Accessed Feb. 1, 2007 from worldwatch.org/node/1826.

SOLUTION 98
1. National Resources Defense Council. Accessed Feb. 1, 2007 from nrdc.org/international/summit/summit.asp.
2. Underwater Times. Accessed Feb. 1, 2007 from underwatertimes.com/news.php?article_id=51428031076.

SOLUTION 99
1. Humane Religion. Accessed Feb. 1, 2007 from all-creatures.org/hr/hraschweitzer.htm.
2. Claudette Vaughan. Ahimsa, Animal Rights and Spirituality. Toronto Vegetarian Association. Accessed Feb. 1, 2007 from veg.ca/lifelines/mayjun/ahimsa.htm.

Index

About the Authors

Ethan Smith is a writer, father and animal welfare advocate living in British Columbia's southern Gulf Islands. He was raised on a family farm in a remote valley in the West Kootenays, unencumbered by the modern distractions of electricity, television or public school, and much of his education came from his natural surroundings. At the age of 11, he helped raise an orphan fawn, an experience that left him with an enduring connection to animals and the environment.

In 2002 Ethan contacted 200 people from across North America who had inspired him with their commitment to a more sustainable society, and published 30 of their essays along with his own story, in the anthology *Softly on This Earth: Joining Those Who Are Healing Our Planet*.

Guy Dauncey is an author, speaker and organizer who works to develop a positive vision of a sustainable future, and to translate that vision into action. He is author of *Stormy Weather: 101 Solutions to Global Climate Change* (New Society Publishers, 2001) and other titles, and publisher of *EcoNews*, a monthly newsletter serving the vision of a sustainable Vancouver Island. He is President of the BC Sustainable Energy Association and Co-Chair of Prevent Cancer Now. He lives in Victoria, British Columbia. His website is www.earthfuture.com.

If you have enjoyed *Building an Ark: 101 Solutions to Animal Suffering*
you might also enjoy other

BOOKS TO BUILD A NEW SOCIETY

Our books provide positive solutions for people who want to
make a difference. We specialize in:

**Sustainable Living • Green Building • Peak Oil • Renewable Energy
Environment & Economy • Natural Building & Appropriate Technology
Progressive Leadership • Resistance and Community
Educational and Parenting Resources**

For a full list of NSP's titles, please call **1-800-567-6772** *or check out our website at:*

www.newsociety.com

NEW SOCIETY PUBLISHERS